Legal Aspects of Brexit

Implications of the United Kingdom's Decision
to Withdraw from the European Union

Jennifer A. Hillman and Gary Horlick,

Editors

Legal Aspects of Brexit

Implications of the United Kingdom's Decision to Withdraw from the European Union

Jennifer A. Hillman and Gary Horlick,

Editors

Published by the Institute of International Economic Law
Georgetown Law
Washington, DC

The Institute of International Economic Law

The Institute of International Economic Law (IIEL) is the focal point for the study of international economic law at Georgetown University and one of the leading centers for international economic law and policy in the world. Founded in 1999 by the late University Professor John H. Jackson, the IIEL's objective is to facilitate thoughtful and scholarly research and teaching, convene stakeholder meetings and conferences bringing together public and private sector leaders, and offer Executive Education on a broad range of subjects that concern the law of international economic activity. Originally focused on trade, the Institute's portfolio has grown to include leading capabilities and international renown in a range of areas including investment and arbitration, financial regulation, tax, business and monetary law. The Institute actively approaches these fields as interrelated and at times overlapping policy spheres that impact how law is devised, practiced and enforced.

IIEL hosts fora for policy debate and research with a wide range of international organizations, firms, NGOs and government agencies, and welcomes new partnerships. The Institute also contributes to the analysis of today's most pressing global economic law and policy issues, via its Issue Brief Series, among other mechanisms.

Institute of International Economic Law
Georgetown Law
600 New Jersey Avenue, NW
Washington, DC 20001
lawiiel@georgetown.edu
http://iielaw.org

The Roadmap to Legal Aspects of Brexit included as Part IV of this book is also available as a PDF document at http://www.iiel.org.

Names: I. Hillman, Jennifer A., Editor
          II. Horlick, Gary, Editor
Title: Legal Aspects of Brexit: The Implications of the United Kingdom's Decision to Withdraw from the European Union
Subjects: Law -- European Union, international trade, World Trade Organization, commercial policy

ISBN-13: 978-0692866030 (Institute of International Economic Law)

Table of Contents

PART III: CROSS-CUTTING AND EU ISSUES

PART IV

PREFACE

Less than two weeks after the shocking results of the June 23, 2016 British referendum in favor of leaving the European Union (EU), my colleague and long-time Georgetown Law adjunct professor Gary Horlick called me suggesting that we should—indeed must—put together a seminar on the legal aspects of Brexit to be taught at Georgetown in the fall of 2016. Given that classes were set to begin in less than eight weeks, I had significant concerns about our ability to pull together a meaningful syllabus that could appropriately structure the inquiry that we would be asking the students to conduct, to find appropriate reading materials, to line up experts that could supplement our own knowledge and experience, to obtain the requisite approvals from the administrators at the Georgetown University Law Center, and most importantly, to attract a group of engaged and interested students. Yet I knew, as Gary did, that Brexit has the potential to be the most significant international economic law event of our lifetimes and that we simply could not sit on the sidelines.

And so a seminar on Brexit and the Law was launched in August of 2016 at Georgetown Law school—to our knowledge the first course [by one day—Harold Koh offered a Brexit course at Yale] in the United States focused solely on the depth and breadth of issues that arise and will need to be addressed in the course of the United Kingdom (UK)'s journey to remove itself from the treaties and institutions that make up the European Union.

We conceived of the course as beginning with an examination of the European Union, its treaties and institutions, in order to frame the examination of just what the UK was giving up and what it might be getting in leaving the EU, always with a primary focus on trade and investment implications. It then moved on to examining in sequential order the legal relationships that would need to be reformulated post-Brexit, starting with the UK's relationship with the EU, moving on to the UK's status in the World Trade Organization (WTO), before focusing on relationships between the UK and its many other trading partners. The course then turned to focus on a number of cross-cutting issues, including Brexit's effect on the four pillars of the EU single market—the free movement of goods, services, capital and people and on the acquired rights of UK nationals living in the EU and EU nationals living and working in the UK. Added in were examinations of the economic implications of Brexit for the UK, the EU and the rest of the world, and a closer look at the particular effects on financial services, competition law, data privacy and human rights.

Midway through the semester, the High Court of England and Wales handed down its decision that UK Prime Minister Theresa May lacks the legal authority to begin the withdrawal process provided for in Article 50 of the Treaty on the European Union. The High Court determined that because withdrawal from the EU would have a profound effect on the rights of UK citizens under a number of existing laws, authorization of Parliament was required before the withdrawal process and the invocation of rights under Article 50 could begin. The class was therefore presented with a perfect opportunity to examine UK domestic law and institutions surrounding the Brexit procedures and to debate the legal merits of the High Court's decision.

The seminar called upon each student to use what they had learned in the course to write a paper addressing a particular Brexit-related issue. The architecture of the papers was to start with an examination of the EU law on the topic that was the subject of the paper, to then determine how that particular law was transposed into the UK—whether through the enactment of free-standing UK law or through direct effect, and finally to determine what, if any, of the EU law would remain as binding law in the post-Brexit UK. The papers go on to address what the UK can or should do to fill any holes created in their legal framework as result of Brexit and what new or different obligations might be placed on the EU or its institutions in a post-Brexit world. We were extremely pleased with the variety and breadth of subjects that the students chose to address in their papers—ranging from the implications for the border between Ireland and Northern Ireland, to the potential for investor-state disputes, to the status of EU trade agreements with Canada, Korea and the East African Community to the effect on everything from human rights, to data privacy, to geographical indications, to financial services, to the English Premier League soccer player and more. Each of the papers is presented in their entirety in this book, broadly grouped into those addressing the UK's trade relationships in Part I, internal UK issues in Part II and cross-cutting issues in Part III.

Our path to making this course a reality was substantially aided by the enthusiasm and tireless work of our research assistant, Aymar Claret de Fleurieu, who immediately set to work tracking down sources and materials, carefully culling and cataloguing them as to which of the many legal aspects of Brexit they addressed. Mr. Claret de Fleurieu continued to add materials to our initial collection, ultimately organizing them into a roadmap to guide anyone interested in examining any Brexit issue to the most relevant sources of information on each particular topic. We proudly present that roadmap as the final chapter (Part IV) of this book. We believe it is an extremely useful compilation of all things Brexit.

Jennifer Hillman and Gary Horlick
Washington DC
March 2017

ACKNOWLEDGMENTS

The authors gratefully acknowledge the contributions and support from our smart and diligent research assistants, Aymar Claret de Fleurieu and Jin Woo (Jay) Kim, without whom this book and its roadmap to the many sources of information and analyses of Brexit would not have been possible; our guest lecturers, Mark Kent, the Head of the Trade and Agricultural Team at the UK's embassy in Washington, DC who shared some early insights into the process facing the UK in its effort to craft agreements shaping the UK's trade relationship with the EU and others; Damien Levie, the Head of the Trade and Agriculture Section of the European Union delegation to the United States, who outlined the variety of agreements that could be fashioned under EU law and procedures to respond to and carry out the UK's withdrawal intentions; Lord Anthony P. Lester of Horne Hill QC, who thoughtfully shaped our understanding of the implications of Brexit on human rights law in the UK and the EU and on a number of British domestic law matters related to the legal power and role of the Prime Minister and the British Parliament in the Brexit process; Chad Bown, Senior Fellow at the Peterson Institute of International Economics, who enlightened us on the economic implications of Brexit for the UK, the EU and the rest of the world; and John Cooke, Chairman, Liberalization of Trade in Services Committee, TheCityUK, who greatly aided our understanding of Brexit's implications for the financial services industry and for those reliant on the right to "passport" their services from the UK to continental Europe; to scholars in the UK and the EU whose writing formed the core of the readings for the seminar, with particular thanks to Dr. Lorand Bartels, Reader in International Law at the University of Cambridge, UK for sharing early drafts of his writing on the UK's status in the World Trade Organization (WTO); Professor Christopher Brummer and Christine Washington at Georgetown Law's Institute of International Economic Law (IIEL) for their enthusiastic support for this project and their inclusion of the seminar students in IIEL's ambassadors forum on Brexit; the deans at Georgetown Law for their swift approval and support for the Brexit seminar; Alina Schmidt, Anna

Selden, Betsy Kuhn, Ines Hilde, Jin Woo (Jay) Kim and Christine Washington for their tireless work in formatting and designing this book; and last, but certainly not least, to those students brave enough to take this brand-new class, with its ever changing focus and last-minute reading assignments, Alexis A. Baker, Francie N. Berger, Evelyn Ederveen, Nour M. El-Kebbi, Isabel Fressynet, Pavan Krishnamurthy, Shawn Greene, Raphaelle Johnston, April Kent, Cody M. Kermanian, Sohil Khurana, Jin Woo (Jay) Kim, Joseph Lumley, Shannon Togawa Mercer, Aakanksha Mishra, Matthew Moore, Anna Weinberger, Susan Yin, and Christine Zhao, who enlivened the debate and crystallized our thinking and learning about the varied and complex legal aspects of Brexit.

Jennifer A. Hillman

Gary Horlick

CHAPTER 1: INTRODUCTION

On June 23, 2016, British voters went to the polls in an advisory referendum to answer a simple question: should the United Kingdom (UK) remain a member of the European Union (EU) or should it leave the EU? The answer—a vote of 52% in favor of leaving the EU—surprised many in the UK and around the world. And that vote for the UK to formally withdraw from the EU launched what may be the largest legal project of this century, given how deeply and intricately EU law is embedded in the UK.

Article 50 of the Treaty on the European Union

The legal work necessarily begins with a focus on the provision of the Treaty on the European Union (TEU) establishing both a right and a process for a member state such as the UK to withdraw from the EU. Just 261 words in length and never before interpreted or applied, Article 50 raises a number of legal conundrums. In its first paragraph, it provides that "[a]ny Member State may decide to withdraw . . . in accordance with its own constitutional requirements," thereby immediately raising the question of just what the UK's constitutional requirements are, given the absence of any formal constitution in the UK. Initially, the UK's new post-referendum Prime Minister, Theresa May, contended that the Crown—acting through the executive in the form of the Secretary of State for Exiting the EU—is entitled to use its prerogative powers to give notice under Article 50 of the UK's intention to withdraw from the EU. Two UK citizens reacted to that contention by filing a claim asserting that the government could not lawfully trigger the Article 50 withdrawal process without an authorization from the UK Parliament. On November 3, 2016, the British High Court ruled in favor of the claimants, finding that the UK government must have the Parliament's approval to trigger Article 50 TEU. The Court reasoned that legislation, including the 1972 European Communities Act under which the UK both joined the then-European Community (now the European Union) and established the process by which European Community law would be incorporated into the domestic law of UK, had been enacted by both Houses of Parliament, thereby becoming the supreme law of the UK. As such, the legislation could not be displaced by the government alone through the exercise of the Crown's prerogative powers. Although the government appealed, the UK's Supreme Court upheld, on an eight to three vote, the High Court's decision.

A number of consequences flow from the courts' rulings. First, the courts' decisions opened the door to a potential delay or even deferral of the decision to invoke Article 50. Following the Supreme Court's ruling, the government introduced legislation authorizing it to invoke Article 50 in the UK's lower house of Parliament, the House of Commons. On February 8, 2017, the bill to allow the May government to invoke Article 50 passed by a vote of 494 to 122. However, the bill ran into trouble in the Parliament's upper chamber, its House of Lords, which voted on March 1, 2017 (by a vote of 358 to 256) to amend the bill to include a provision guaranteeing the right of the nearly three-million EU citizens living in the UK to remain after Brexit. The Lords vote prompted a high-stakes game of chicken, as the House of Commons, with the strong urging of the Prime Minister, passed a bill rejecting the Lords amendments. In the end, on March 14, the Lords backed down, voting not to insist on their original amendments. Therefore the May Government ultimately received the Parliamentary approval it needed to invoke Article 50 and the Government is expected to do so before the end of March 2017.

Second, in the proceedings before both the High Court and the Supreme Court, two important stipulations were made and accepted: 1) that Article 50 is irrevocable, such that once it is invoked, the request to start the withdrawal process cannot be taken back, and 2) that the invocation of Article 50 cannot be made conditional, so the ultimate withdrawal from the EU does not depend on a subsequent approval by the UK Parliament of the terms of the withdrawal agreement worked out between the UK and the EU. These stipulations mean that once the UK invokes Article 50, the withdrawal from the EU would occur either under conditions and terms agreed to in a negotiated withdrawal agreement or unilaterally two years after the date of invocation of Article 50, unless an extension of time for the withdrawal negotiations is unanimously agreed upon by the European Council.[1] While scholars might dispute the irrevocability of a withdrawal request, particularly in light of Article 68 of the Vienna Convention on the Law of Treaties which provides that a notification of intention to withdraw from a treaty "may be revoked at any time before it takes effect," the fact that all parties and both the High Court and the Supreme Court accepted the

---

[1] As the Supreme Court stated: "It follows from this [the 'common ground' that the invocation of Article 50 is irrevocable and not conditional] that once the United Kingdom gives Notice, it will inevitably cease at a later date to be a member of the European Union and a party to the EU Treaties." Paragraph 26, Supreme Court Judgement: R (on the application of Miller and another) (Respondents) v Secretary of State for Exiting the European Union (Appellant), Hilary Term, 2017, UKSC 5 On appeals from: 2016, EWHC 2768 (Admin) and 2016, NIQB 85.

irrevocability of the withdrawal request makes it unlikely that the UK can easily reverse course if it has a change of heart mid-way through the negotiation process.

Third, the text of Article 50 spells out two important timing elements. It presumes that a withdrawal agreement will be worked out between the withdrawing state and the EU and provides that "The Treaties on the European Union shall cease to apply to the State in question from the *date of entry into force* of the withdrawal agreement..." (emphasis added).[2] The reference to the date of entry into force suggests that the UK and the EU could agree upon terms for the UK's exit within two years, while establishing a date of entry into force that is farther down the road, thereby giving both sides a much longer transition period in which to begin implementing their Brexit-related commitments. Second, Article 50 provides that, in the absence of a withdrawal agreement, the treaties of the EU shall cease to apply to the UK "two years after the notification [of the intent to withdraw] . . . unless the European Council, in agreement with the Member State concerned, unanimously decides to extend this period."[3] This provision both mandates a "unilateral divorce" in the absence of an agreement, but also provides important flexibility to extend the negotiating time frame beyond two years if both sides determine that additional time to work out the withdrawal agreement is needed. It remains to be seen how accommodating the EU member states are prepared to be in granting extensions of time as they work toward a mutually agreeable withdrawal agreement.

What Law and Institutions Remain Post-Brexit?

A second major legal issue embedded within the Brexit process is sorting out what law remains in place in the UK post-Brexit. As a general matter and as a result of obligations under Article 288 of the Treaty on the Functioning of the European Union, the UK is required to "transpose" EU law that is adopted at the level of a directive into UK law through the passage of domestic law that achieves the result set forth in the EU directive. However, EU law other than directives, particularly regulations and decisions, take direct effect in the UK and do not necessarily require the adoption or amendment of any UK law or regulation in order to become binding law in the UK. As such, that portion of EU law that was enacted in the form of directive is likely to

---

[2] Article 50, Paragraph 3, Treaty on the European Union.
[3] Id.

remain in effect in the post-Brexit UK unless and until the UK Parliament decides to amend or repeal it. However, the vast majority of EU law has come into the UK through the direct effect of regulations, which means that absent some further action, that EU law would disappear after Brexit, leaving huge gaps in UK law. Prime Minister May has stated that the Government intends to introduce The Great Repeal Bill in 2017 to repeal the 1972 European Communities Act under which the UK joined the EU and which established the process by which EU law is transposed into UK law. The Prime Minister has indicated that as part of that Great Repeal Bill, the *acquis* of EU law will be "grandfathered" so as to remain in place until decisions can be made about which portions of the many EU regulations will be maintained and which will be amended or repealed.[4]

The concept of leaving in place the *acquis* of EU law raises numerous questions. While it may be possible to grandfather the substance of EU regulations, it is not possible to grandfather access to the EU institutions that are responsible for implementing and updating those regulations. As such, even as the UK takes the time it needs to determine exactly what its legal and regulatory standards will be and which portions of the *acquis* of EU law it wishes to keep, it will need some institutions to implement and maintain those rules in the interim period. For example, if the UK wishes to impose anti-dumping measures on imports that are injuring its domestic producers, who will investigate a claim for duties by UK producers given that the UK will no longer have access to the Commission's Directorate-General for Trade (and British exporters will not have DG Trade's help when charged with dumping in third countries)? Similarly, crucial EU regulatory functions requiring deep technical expertise, such as the approval of new pharmaceuticals or the regulation of hazardous chemicals, will have to be performed by new UK-only agencies. And it is not just the main institutions of the European Commission, the Council of Ministers, the European Parliament and the Court of Justice of the European Union that the UK will lose access to. The UK will also be giving up its connection to everything from the European Investment Bank to the European Data Protection Supervisor, Europol, the European Centre for Disease

---

[4] See "The United Kingdom's exit from and new partnership with the European Union," Presentation to Parliament by the Prime Minister on Command of Her Majesty, February 2017 (White Paper), noting that "[t]he Government's general approach to preserve EU law is to ensure that all EU laws which are directly applicable in the UK (such as EU regulations) and all laws which have been made in the UK, in order to implement our obligations as a member of the EU, remain part of domestic law on the day we leave the EU. . . . [t]he Government also believes that the preserved law should continue to be interpreted in the same way as it is at the moment." (p. 10).

Prevention and Control, the European Aviation Safety Agency, the European Fisheries Control Agency and so much more.[5] The number and reach of institutions that would somehow need to be replicated in the UK is wide and deep, making the Brexit transition a large and likely expensive endeavor to recruit, hire and train those with the requisite expertise to perform the implementation and regulatory functions of those EU agencies that the UK would no longer have access to. While it is true that there are a number of critical bodies in which the UK would remain a member—including NATO, the Council of Europe, the Organization for Security and Co-operation in Europe, the European Bank for Reconstruction and Development, the European Space Agency, and the European Organization for Nuclear Research (CERN)—the agencies most involved in crafting and implementing domestic regulations and standards on everything from food to chemicals to energy will be off-limits to the post-Brexit UK.

Future Trade Relationships—A "Hard" Brexit?

Currently, the UK enjoys complete and free access to the other 27 member states of the EU as a result of the EU's status as a customs union and a single market. As a customs union, no tariffs are applied to any goods traded between and among the 28 member states of the EU, while all EU members impose a common external tariff on goods imported from outside the EU.[6] As a single market, the EU provides for the free movement of goods, services, capital and people in and among its member states. How much of that access the UK will continue to enjoy remains to be seen. The initial speculation was that the UK might try to retain some form of membership in the single market (a so-called "soft Brexit") by possibly following the approach taken by Norway or Switzerland. However, in unveiling her plans for Brexit in mid-January

---

[5] See, for example, "A Brexit Act in 19 ¾ Pages," for a list of main EU agencies and bodies that the UK would cease to be a member of or eligible for benefits from. Allen & Overy, LLP, August 30, 2016.

[6] The member states of the EU are: Austria (1995), Belgium (1958), Bulgaria (2007), Croatia (2013), Cyprus (2004), Czech Republic (2004), Denmark (1973), Estonia (2004), Finland (1995), France (1958), Germany (1958), Greece (1981), Hungary (2004), Ireland (1973), Italy (1958), Latvia (2004), Lithuania (2004), Luxembourg (1958), Malta (2004), Netherlands (1958), Poland (2004), Portugal (1986), Romania (2007), Slovakia (2004), Slovenia (2004), Spain (1986), Sweden (1995), and United Kingdom (1973). In 2014, 45% of the UK's exports were to the other members of the EU and 53% of UK's imports came from the EU.

2017, the Prime Minister effectively ruled out that soft-Brexit option.[7] Instead, the Government indicated that it aims to establish a comprehensive Free Trade Agreement (FTA) with the EU, without a customs union, with this FTA to be worked out as part of the two-year withdrawal agreement negotiations to be conducted pursuant to Article 50.[8] In the event that such an FTA cannot be achieved, the UK will default to trading with the EU under the World Trade Organization (WTO) rules and tariffs (a so-called "hard Brexit"). Given that the EU has insisted that countries such as Norway that want free access to the EU market accept a number of the features of the single market, including free movement of persons and payment into the budget of the EU, it is far from clear whether an FTA between the EU and the UK can be worked out, particularly in the short two-year time frame in which many issues in addition to trade must also be negotiated.

Also vexing for the UK will be the need to establish or re-establish its trading relationship with the many countries with whom the EU has negotiated various forms of trade agreements, whether Free Trade Agreements (such as those with Korea and Canada) or Economic Partnership Agreements (including those with the Caribbean or East African countries) or others. Among the difficulties for the UK is the timing and sequencing of such negotiations, as the UK does not have the legal authority to negotiate trade agreements on its own until its withdrawal from the EU has come into effect—presumably sometime after March of 2019. Until then, all trade negotiations must be done by the European Commission on behalf of the EU. And beyond trade agreements, the UK as a member state is covered by more than 1000 other agreements with third parties, such as agreements on the exchange of passenger data necessary for airplane traffic, or the UK-France-Ireland agreement on the cross-border travel of race horses (which requires an EU veterinary certificate). In the absence of any agreements being worked out or transition periods agreed to, trade with these countries would likely also revert to WTO rules and tariffs.

The UK could simply let its trade relationships with its former free-trade or preferential trade agreements partners be governed by WTO rules, but that seems highly unlikely in a world of rapidly increasing numbers of regional trade agreements (RTAs). Indeed, some claim that the UK is now in a position to negotiate optimal trade agreements, since all the prior EU agreements were, inevitably, compromises among the

---

[7] "The Government's negotiating objectives for exiting the EU: PM speech," Prime Minister's Office, January 17, 2017.
[8] HM Government, *The United Kingdom's exit from and new partnership with the European Union*, (White Paper) CM 9417, February 2017.

various EU member states, and likely suboptimal for each individual EU member. Already there are claims that the United Kingdom will become a low tariff, light regulation, low tax country which will thrive for those very reasons. In practice it is possible that it may be difficult to negotiate FTA's with other countries until the UK-WTO negotiations have been completed with those very same countries, as well as other trading partners. How much leverage the UK has left after completing its WTO-related negotiations also remains to be seen.

Finally, all of this occurs against a background of opposition to new trade agreements, symbolized in part by the Brexit vote (and the US election of Donald Trump) itself. That said, despite claims by some very respected thinkers that "the era of new trade agreements is over," which even if true for some US and EU politicians, will certainly not be true for the current Conservative government of the UK which, as a result of Brexit, must negotiate—and fairly quickly—with a large number of trading partners. Nor is the "no new trade agreements" sentiment taking hold in the Asian countries busy negotiating FTA's among themselves without regard to what US and European observers might assume, and without regard to implications of Brexit.

WTO Schedules—Not as Easy as it Looks?

The WTO, which grew out of the General Agreement on Tariffs and Trade (GATT), is founded on an agreed set of rules governing trade in goods and services, with additional rules on intellectual property, standards, regulatory barriers, dispute settlement and more. While it is the EU that formally speaks for the UK at the WTO, the UK is and will continue to be a member of the WTO in its own right.[9] However, what remains to be settled are the terms of the UK's membership in the WTO, in particular its schedules indicating its commitments with respect to tariffs and services. The UK Government has indicated that it intends to effectively "cut and paste" the current EU schedules into its own. As UK Secretary for International Trade Liam Fox put it, "In order to minimize the disruption to global trade as we leave the EU . . . the Government will prepare the necessary draft schedules which replicate as far as

---

[9] The UK was one of the original members of the GATT in 1947, giving it membership in the WTO under Article XI: of the WTO Agreement. The WTO's current Director General, Roberto Azevedo, confirmed the UK's continuing membership in his October 2016 statement: "The UK is a member of the WTO today, it will continue to be a member tomorrow."

possible our current obligations."[10] While that appears at first blush to be a relatively easy exercise, in fact it likely raises a number of legal and economic issues.

First, simply replicating the EU's tariff schedule (which itself has not yet been fully 'certified' within the WTO) assumes that all the tariffs in the EU's WTO tariff schedules are *ad valorem*, i.e., charged as a percentage of the import value. That is not the case; many of the EU's tariff are expressed in specific terms, charging a certain number of Euros per kilogram or per ton (for example, oranges, tariff item numbers 0851.016 to 1066, varying 6 times a year based on both an *ad valorem* rate plus a specific duty expressed in Euros per ton).[11] It is not clear that the UK would want to continue to charge duties on the basis of Euros per metric unit of measure. If not, it raises the question of what conversion rate from Euros to pounds sterling is the correct conversion rate to maintain the balance of the negotiations that originally set the tariff—the rate in 1994 when the tariff was negotiated, which was pre-Euro? The rate when the Euro-denominated scheduled was notified? The rate on the date when the UK submits its own schedule? Similarly, the EU has tariff-rate quotas on imports of numerous products, which includes a specific quantitative amount permitted to be imported at a certain rate of duty. How will those TRQ's be split up between the EU and the UK? It was quite possible that there are TRQ's where the original TRQ negotiated by the EU was intended mainly to be consumed in the UK, or in the alternative, to be consumed entirely in the EU. Dividing up those TRQs requires quite a negotiation both for the UK and for the EU with other WTO members, and possibly each other (if trade between the UK and EU will have such TRQs). Within the agriculture sphere, additional questions arise regarding the negotiated limits on permissible EU agricultural subsidies, including how the limits are split up and which exchange rate maintains the appropriate balance. And those questions do not even begin to scratch the surface of the complexity of converting the European Union's commitments on services under GATS into separate sets of commitments for the UK and the EU, and possibly between each other.

---

[10] "UK's Commitments at the World Trade Organization," Written Ministerial Statement, December 5, 2016, HCWS316, Secretary of State for International Trade, Rt. Hon Dr Liam Fox MP.

[11] The EU tariff commitments for sweet oranges are: April — 10.4% (of the price) + €71 per ton, first half of May—4.8% + €71 per ton, second half of May—3.2% + €71 per ton, June to mid-October—3.2%, mid-October to end of November—16%, December to March—16% + €71 per ton.

Economic Consequences from Loss of Single Market

Equally difficult to predict are the economic consequences of Brexit for the UK, the EU and the rest of the world. Most indications point to significant negative consequences for all, with the exact amount hard to quantify until the trading relationship between the UK and the EU and the UK and all of its other main trading partners is sorted out. The Peterson Institute of International Economics' Chad Bown presented an early analysis showing that the UK is likely to suffer both short and long term declines in its median income for households due to: 1) UK exports to the EU becoming more costly in the absence of the zero tariffs and reductions in non-tariff barriers the UK currently enjoys as part of the single market, 2) the UK being left out of further and ongoing intra-EU trade cost reductions, and 3) the UK could be left out of trade cost reductions being negotiated with the rest of the world. On the investment side, Bown noted additional likely declines. The UK could be less attractive as an export platform because UK exports to the EU could now face new EU tariff and non-tariff barriers while potential barriers on movement of people could make the UK less attractive as an investment destination for EU supply chains. A study done by the London School of Economics pointed to short term losses in the income of UK households of 1.3% to 2.6%, with more significant losses (-6.3% to - 9.5% of GDP) over the longer term.[12] The remaining EU-27 is also predicted to experience significant losses as a result of Brexit, which will make for an interesting negotiation between the two.

A more recent study by the Peterson Institute focusing solely on the impact on financial services and the City of London finds that if the "hard Brexit" result of WTO rules came to pass, new restrictions could be placed on the EU-related business that can be transacted by London-based financial firms.[13] The study suggests that up to 50 percent of EU-related activity (approximately £18 billion in revenue and £10.5 billion in value added) and as many as 30,000 jobs could be at risk.

---

[12] "The consequences of Brexit for UK trade and living standards," Swati Dhingra, Gianmarco Ottaviano, Thomas Sampson and John VanReenen, Centre for Economic Performance (CEP) at the London School of Economics, http://eprints.lse.ac.uk/66144/1/_lse.ac.uk_storage_LIBRARY_Secondary_libfile_shared_repository_Content_LSE%20BrexitVote%20blog_brexit02.pdf.

[13] The City of London after Brexit, Simeon Djankov, Peterson Institute for International Economics, February 2017.

Range of Legal Issues Explored in Student Papers

A number of these legal issues were explored in the papers researched and written by the students of our Brexit seminar. With respect to the issue of the UK's status and schedules in the WTO, Aakanksha Mishra's paper, "A Post Brexit UK in the WTO: The UK's New GATT Tariff Schedule," explores in detail many of the issues involved in the "cutting and pasting" exercise noted above. Three of the papers delve into the details of the legal status of the post-Brexit UK's trading relationship with three different trading partners:, Korea (with an already completed and in-force Free Trade Agreement), Canada (with whom the EU has just recently completed a Free-Trade Agreement that is still in the process of being formally ratified), and the East African Customs Union of Burundi, Kenya, Rwanda, South Sudan, Tanzania, and Uganda (with which the EU negotiated an Economic Partnership Agreement that has not yet been ratified by all members nor come into force).[14] Finally, one paper, "The Legal Basis For the UK to Adopt the Norway Model: Reducing Potential Negative-Impacts of Brexit" by Sohil Khurana makes the case for the UK working to maintain some form of membership in the European single market in a manner close to what Norway has done, rather than relying solely on WTO rules and tariffs or a potentially unrealistic hope for a Free Trade Agreement between the EU and the UK.

Additional WTO or trade issues outside of the tariff or trade-agreement context were addressed in papers relating to the WTO disciplines on *geographical indications* ("The Fate of Scotch Whisky Post Brexit—Implications for Geographical Indications" by Christine Zhao), *government procurement* ("The United Kingdom's Public Procurement Regime in a Post-Brexit Landscape" by Joseph Lumley), and *financial services* ("Envisaging a Post-Brexit Financial Services Sector under the GATS Framework—a Case Study of Euro Clearing" by Susan Yin), while one paper focused on the likely WTO obligations and potential negotiations in store for the EU-27 in clarifying its tariff and other relations with WTO members ("The European Union's WTO Rights and Obligations Post-Brexit: Negotiation and Enforcement" by Pavan Krishnamurthy).

Two papers examine the implications of Brexit for the tens of thousands of foreign investors whose investments are protected by one or more of the more than 90 *Bilateral Investment Treaties* (BITs) that the

---

[14] See Chapter 4: "Is the United Kingdom still a Party to the EU - Korea FTA after Brexit?" By Jin Woo (Jay) Kim; Chapter 6: "The Legal Impact of Brexit on the Comprehensive Economic Trade Agreement (CETA) between the European Union and Canada" by Isabel Fressynet; and Chapter 5: "Brexit and the East African Community (EAC)-European Union Economic Partnership Agreement (EPA)" by April Kent.

UK has agreed to, along with the provisions of the Lisbon Treaty that now include foreign investment as part of the EU's Common Commercial Policy subject to exclusive competence by the EU. One paper examines the overall investment disciplines in the UK under both BITs and the Treaty on the Functioning of the EU (TFEU), with a particular emphasis on the doctrine of legitimate expectations ("Brexit and Legitimate Expectations: A Case for Foreign Investors?" by Aymar Claret de Fleurieu). A second paper explores the issue of whether the potential imposition of tariffs on UK exports of automobiles to the EU could be viewed as violating the UK's commitment under investment treaty law ("A Violation of the Fair and Equitable Treatment Standard under Bilateral Investment Treaties as a Result of Brexit: The Example of Tata Motors" by Raphaelle Johnston).

Many of the difficult, complex legal issues that touch on a number of the so-called "trade and" issues that the EU and others tried to bring within the ambit of the WTO are addressed in the papers on *competition policy* ("UK Competition Law after Brexit: The Prospect of Divergence from the EU Legal Regime" by Matthew Moore) and *data privacy* ("Exploring the Potential for Coalescence and Divergence in U.K-EU Data Policy After Brexit" by Shannon Togawa Mercer).

An additional area of study was whether Brexit would result in the addition or diminution of rights currently enjoyed by EU citizens living and working in the UK, looking at the issue from the broad perspective of *human rights* ("Brexit and Human Rights: Implications for the Laws and People of the United Kingdom" by Francie N. Berger) to the general *rights of residency* for EU nationals currently living in the UK ("The Right of Residency of EU Citizens in the UK after Brexit" by Evelyn Ederveen) to the more specific (and potentially more essential for many Brits) *rights of EU soccer stars* to continue playing for Premier League teams ("Brexit and the English Premier League: Implications for Players and Broadcasting Rights" by Cody M. Kermanian).

Finally, Brexit's potential to upset a number of current UK policies and practices was also examined. For example, one paper explored whether the EU law requiring a hard border (with customs and immigration inspection) would require Ireland, even against its will, to erect a true border between Ireland and Northern Ireland, despite the fact that the border has been open and free for decades ("The Common Travel Area between Ireland and the United Kingdom after Brexit" by Alexis A. Baker). Another examined the implications of Brexit on the devolved power to Scotland and what the process for acting on the "leave" vote means for the power of the Scottish Parliament ("Scot-In Even

Through Brexit? Scotland's Legal Options in the Wake of the UK Referendum to Leave the EU" by Nour M. El-Kebbi). Finally, in light of the EU Commission decision to order Ireland to collect €13 billion from Apple for uncollected taxes that were deemed by the Commission to be illegal "state aid," one paper examines whether one of the benefits of Brexit for the UK is to get out from under EU state aid restrictions ("State Aid Regulations after Brexit: A Good Deal for the UK?" by Anna Weinberger). Collectively these papers touch on a broad and deep set of legal issues facing both the UK and the EU (and the UK's other trading partners) as a result of the UK's far-reaching decision to leave the European Union.

PART I:

UK Trade Relationships

CHAPTER 2: A POST BREXIT UK IN THE WTO: THE UK'S NEW GATT TARIFF SCHEDULE

AAKANKSHA MISHRA[1]

I. INTRODUCTION

Following the United Kingdom's ("the UK") vote to leave the European Union ("the EU"), most people have assumed that negotiating Brexit with the EU's 27 member states will be Theresa May's biggest task as Prime Minister, but the real challenge will be dealing with the World Trade Organization ("the WTO"). When the UK leaves the EU, it's been widely taken for granted that it will be freeing itself to set its own trade policy. However, this freedom is limited by the WTO's complicated architecture, which the UK will still have to conform to.[2] The UK's membership of the WTO will have to be revisited and renegotiated. Though the UK is a founding member of the multilateral trading system, its WTO commitments are tied to that of the EU and will cease once it withdraws from the EU. Such a situation is unique in the WTO history and there exists no precedent, no clear rules for an existing member to implement an entirely new set of trading terms. A key question is how easy will it be for the UK to extract its own WTO commitments currently bundled with that of the EU's. Can the UK simply transpose the EU commitments or will it have to negotiate all commitments afresh? There are certain ways by which the UK could establish itself as a WTO member in its own right. However, each approach is fraught with a set of complexities. Brexit supporters want to turn the UK into a global trading powerhouse. How quickly the UK is able to trade on WTO terms in its own right will depend significantly on the political will of its leadership. However, until the country has sorted out its legal standing, it risks merely sitting on the sidelines. Daniel Guéguen, Head of Strategy and Lobbying at PACT European Affairs has aptly described Brexit when he says, "The fifth-largest economic power in the world leaving the European Union is no small matter. The stakes are so large and the problems so interwoven with each other that the issue, while vital,

---

[1] LLM Candidate 2017, Georgetown University Law Center, am3565@georgetown.edu.
[2] Indra Warnes, *Forget EU trade deals…Britain needs to crack WTO post-Brexit, say experts*, Express, October 7, 2016, http://www.express.co.uk/news/world/718908/Forget-EU-trade-deals-Britain-needs-to-crack-WTO-post-Brexit-say-experts.

becomes virtual— almost theoretical. It is like not knowing how to find the end of a ball of wool."[3]

The following paper just touches the tip of the iceberg when it comes to the UK's post-Brexit WTO strategy. Part II lays down the background of the UK's founding member status at WTO and why it won't have to accede to the WTO as a new member. Part III discusses whether the UK can inherit its WTO rights and obligations from the EU in accordance with the public international law concept of 'succession of states.' Part IV proceeds to discuss the UK's commitments under the General Agreement on Tariffs and Trade ("GATT"). The key questions, addressed here, concern the identification of the UK's rights to access the country-specific EU tariff rate quotas bound by other WTO Members under the GATT 1994 and the identification of the UK's scheduled commitments in relation to the current EU tariff rate quota commitments and agricultural subsidies under the GATT 1994. It is pertinent to point out now that this paper deals only with the UK's schedule of tariff commitments under Article II of GATT post-Brexit and does not address any other issue that might arise from the GATT or the covered agreements. Part V highlights some other roadblocks, like negotiations based on an uncertified EU-28 schedule of commitments, exchange rate agreements for converting specific duties from euro to pound sterling and whether the UK's presentation of a new tariff schedule amounts to modification or rectification of its commitments. Part VI suggests that the best way for the UK to proceed with its WTO negotiations post a formal Brexit would be to seek a waiver of WTO obligations. Part VII concludes that diplomacy and goodwill will be the key to making Brexit work.

II. UK'S MEMBERSHIP AT WTO POST BREXIT

In a public intervention in the Brexit debate on 25 May 2016, the WTO Director General, Roberto Azevêdo, warned that the UK would face "tortuous negotiations" with the WTO members. This was interpreted by some to mean that the UK would have to undergo the WTO accession process on leaving the EU based on the reasoning that the UK is currently "a member of the WTO via the EU."[4] However, the UK is already a full member of the WTO in its own right. Article XI:1 of the WTO Agreement states:

---

[3] Daniel Guéguen, *Brexit: A WTO issue first and foremost*, September 28, 2016, https://danielgueguen.blogactiv.eu/2016/09/28/brexit-a-wto-issue-first-and-foremost/.

[4] Richard North, *Brexit Monograph 8: WTO schedules and concessions*, August 21, 2016, http://www.eureferendum.com/documents/BrexitMonograph008.pdf.

"The contracting parties to GATT 1947 as of the date of entry into force of this Agreement, and the European Communities, which accept this Agreement and the Multilateral Trade Agreements and for which Schedules of Concessions and Commitments are annexed to GATT 1994 and for which Schedules of Specific Commitments are annexed to GATS shall become original Members of the WTO."

This applies to the UK in a straightforward way. The UK was a contracting party to the GATT 1947 and it 'accepted' the WTO Agreement and the multilateral trade agreements, in accordance with Article XIV:1 of the WTO Agreement, by ratification on 30 December 1994.[5]

The EU, invoking its own legal personality, is also a member in its own right. But the EU treaty database records the Agreement Establishing the WTO as a "mixed agreement," with the EU Member States separately identified as contracting parties, including the UK.[6]

Separately, the WTO database records the UK as a full member (alongside the EU) and a linked web-page notes that, "The 28 member States of the EU are also WTO members on their own right."[7] There can, therefore, be absolutely no doubt that, after withdrawal from the EU, the UK will remain a full member of the WTO. This was confirmed by Azevêdo himself on 7 June, 2016 during a speech in London, when he stated that the UK, as an individual country, "would of course remain a WTO member."[8] But, he added, it would not have defined terms in the WTO for its trade in goods and services. It only had these commitments as an EU member. And thus, it would need to re-establish its terms of trade with the WTO members.[9]

---

[5]Note 1 to the Marrakesh Agreement Establishing the World Trade Organization (1995) 1867 UNTS 155.

[6]*Summary of Treaty: Agreement Establishing the WTO*, EUROPA, (December 22, 2016), http://ec.europa.eu/world/agreements/prepareCreateTreatiesWorkspace/treatiesGeneralData.do? step=0&redirect=true&treatyId=565

[7]*Member Information: The European union and the WTO*, World Trade Organization, (December 22, 2016), https://www.wto.org/english/thewto_e/countries_e/european_communities_e.htm.

[8]*Azevêdo addresses World Trade Symposium in London on the state of global trade*, World Trade Organization News, (December 22, 2016), https://www.wto.org/english/news_e/spra_e/spra126_e.htm.

[9]*Azevêdo addresses World Trade Symposium in London on the state of global trade*, World Trade Organization News, (December 22, 2016), https://www.wto.org/english/news_e/spra_e/spra126_e.htm.

III. CAN THE UK SIMPLY INHERIT ITS WTO RIGHTS AND OBLIGATIONS FROM THE EU?

Within the EU, trade is an exclusive competence of the EU, which left the European Commission to negotiate the schedules of concessions 'en bloc' for the entire membership at the time. States acceding to the EU after 1994 have been required to withdraw their GATT tariff schedules and adopt the EU's (which themselves have required adjustment as a result). Once the UK leaves the EU, however, it will emerge without its own, country specific schedules, whence it is expected that it will have to start afresh to create its own schedules, covering both goods and services. The UK Government's White Paper on the process of leaving the EU also highlighted this concern as it said:

> … we would need to update the terms of our WTO membership where the commitments taken have previously applied to the EU as a whole. This would not be a straightforward process as, if we leave the EU, then we would need all other WTO Members to agree how the UK will take on the rights and obligations which we have formerly taken as a part of the EU. This would mean negotiating and agreeing updated UK schedules of commitments with all 161 WTO members. And until our schedule of commitments was updated, there could be questions surrounding our rights to access WTO members' markets, and our ability to enforce those rights.[10]

The UN International Law Commission negotiated and adopted the Convention on Succession of States in respect of Treaties in 1978. A particular application of the rule of state succession to treaties is the succession of states in international organizations. The convention establishes the first definition of succession under international law, according to which, "succession of States means the replacement of one State by another in the responsibility for the international relations of territory."[11] This definition considers the territorial aspect of state succession, the constituent nature of international organizations making membership a personal right of each state.

---

[10] *The process for withdrawing from the European Union*, Presented to Parliament by the Secretary of State for Foreign and Commonwealth Affairs by Command of Her Majesty, February   2016, https://www.gov.uk/government/uploads/system/uploads/attachment_data/file/504 216/The_process_for_withdrawing_from_the_EU_print_ready.pdf, p.15.
[11] Article 2 (1)(b), Vienna Convention on the Succession of States in Respect of Treaties of 1978, 1946 UNTS 3.

To get to know if a successor state has the right to participate in the international organization to which the predecessor state was a party, we should first understand the process of acquiring membership in an international organization. There are international organizations such as the WTO which provide a two-step procedure for admission of new members, that requires at the first instance, a formal request followed by an approval obtained from a qualified majority of the member states in the organization (two-thirds of member states in case of the WTO).[12] The successor state in order to gain membership in the organization to which the predecessor state was a member, must therefore express its desire to become part in the organization's founding treaty and then follow the procedures for admission of any new member.

Therefore, we can assert that in case of succession to international organizations, the general rule is that the successor state is not the continuator of the predecessor state in terms of membership in the international organization, and must satisfy by its own account the necessary conditions to become in turn a member in that organization.[13] A successor state must show willingness to be a member in the international organization concerned and also, must go through the new member's admission procedures; the state cannot be automatically considered as continuator of the predecessor state and, moreover, a party in the organization. If the EU were a state, it would be uncontroversial that the rules of succession would apply to the UK. However, the European Union is not a sovereign state under international law at the first place. The explicit right to withdraw from the European Union may well be regarded as evidence that the European Union is not a state and that the member states have not lost their sovereignty. This is also supported by the German Federal Constitutional Court's decision of 30 June, 2009 which entered a lengthy discussion as to whether with the entry into force of the Lisbon Treaty the European Union were to become a State.[14] Hence it is unlikely that the principles of state succession will permit the UK to inherit its WTO rights and obligations from that of the EU's.

---

[12] Nasty Marian Vladoiu, *State Succession to International Intergovernmental Organizations under the International Public Law*, 1 International Journal of Law and Jurisprudence 2015, p. 13-21, http://internationallawreview.eu/fisiere/pdf/3_4.pdf.

[13] Nasty Marian Vladoiu, *State Succession to International Intergovernmental Organizations under the International Public Law*, 1 International Journal of Law and Jurisprudence 2015, p. 13-21, http://internationallawreview.eu/fisiere/pdf/3_4.pdf.

[14] BVerfG, Judgment of the Second Senate of 30 June 2009 - 2 BvE 2/08, The Federal Constitutional Court of Germany, http://www.bverfg.de/e/es20090630_2bve000208en.html.

However, there are also several precedents for the succession of states to treaties binding on predecessors that are unions or federations with legal personality. For example, in 1953 the Federation of Rhodesia and Nyasaland was formed, and succeeded to the rights and obligations of Southern Rhodesia. In 1963 the Federation dissolved, and Southern Rhodesia succeeded to the rights and obligations of that Federation. Both times, GATT contracting parties accepted the claim to succession by the formerly autonomous entity.[15] Another notable example is the case of the Czech Republic and Slovakia (officially the Slovak Republic). These two countries were part of the former Czechoslovakia, which was one of the 23 founding members of the GATT that entered into force in January 1948. The GATT Contracting Parties, at their Forty-Eighth Session held on 2-3 December 1992, agreed that the Czech Republic and the Slovak Republic could accede to the General Agreement under the same terms applied by the former Czechoslovakia, without carrying out any negotiations. The required number of affirmative votes, two-thirds of the contracting parties, was reached and the two countries' accession took effect on 15 April 1993.[16] This precedent is interesting because while both the Czech Republic and the Slovak Republic had to make fresh applications to join the WTO (i.e. rule of state succession did not apply to membership in the WTO), their rights and obligations at the WTO remained the same as those before their disintegration. This was possible only because all the GATT Contracting parties agreed or assented to it.

Given that the UK remains a member of a common European market until it formally exits the EU, it is unlikely that all WTO members today would be agreeable to permit the UK to simply inherit the EU's rights and obligations post Brexit without negotiating and rebalancing its trading relations with individual members of the WTO. Yet some commentators argue that, in accordance with customary international law on state succession, the UK has a right to succeed to the EU's rights and obligations in respect of its territory.[17] Lorand Bartels, Faculty of Law, University of Cambridge, argues that the UK has a right to inherit the EU's rights and obligations with respect to the WTO based on the

---

[15] Lorand Bartels, *Understanding the UK's position in the WTO after Brexit (Part II – The consequences)*, International Centre for Trade and Sustainable Development, September 26, 2016, http://www.ictsd.org/opinion/understanding-the-uk-0.

[16] *Czech Republic and Slovak Republic accede to the GATT*, GATT/1573, April 16, 1993, https://www.wto.org/gatt_docs/English/SULPDF/91690160.pdf.

[17] Lorand Bartels, *Understanding the UK's position in the WTO after Brexit (Part I – The UK's status and its schedules)*, International Centre for Trade and Sustainable Development, September 26, 2016, http://www.ictsd.org/opinion/understanding-the-uk.

principle of customary international law reflected in Article 34 of the 1978 Convention on Succession of States in respect of Treaties, and on past practice under the GATT 1947.[18]

Assuming that law of state succession doesn't apply to the UK post Brexit, is there any other way the UK could transpose the EU's schedule of commitments into its own schedule without having to enter into protracted negotiations with individual WTO member countries?

Lorand Bartel argues that Article XI:1 of the WTO Agreement is an unusual provision, although not unique, insofar as it allows for the possibility that original WTO Members will lack autonomy in all matters covered by the WTO agreements. Specifically, this provision was designed for the EU and its Member States, each of which lacked full autonomy in areas covered by the WTO agreements. But Article XI:1 has no effect on the "rights and obligations" of the EU and its Member States, which remain those of ordinary WTO Members. There is no suggestion anywhere in the WTO Agreement, or in any relevant instruments, that the WTO rights and obligations of the EU Member States, or of the EU, are in any way limited to their areas of autonomy. The conclusion that the EU Member States have full WTO rights and responsibilities has also been endorsed in WTO jurisprudence. In *EC and certain member States—Large Civil Aircraft*, the Panel rejected an EU request to remove five EU Member States as respondent, which would have left the EU as the sole remaining respondent. It said that each of these five is, in its own right, a Member of the WTO, with all the rights and obligations pertaining to such membership, including the obligation to respond to claims made against it by another WTO Member. The Panel added that "whatever responsibility the European Communities bears for the actions of its member States does not diminish their rights and obligations as WTO Members, but is rather an internal matter concerning the relations between the European Communities and its member States."[19]

If the UK already possesses all of the rights and obligations of an original WTO Member, it will continue to possess all of these rights and obligations once it leaves the EU. What will change is the EU's role in exercising these rights and assuming responsibility for performing these

---

[18] Lorand Bartels, *Understanding the UK's position in the WTO after Brexit (Part II–The consequences)*, International Centre for Trade and Sustainable Development, September 26, 2016, http://www.ictsd.org/opinion/understanding-the-uk-0.

[19] WTO Panel Report, *EC and certain member States – Large Civil Aircraft*, WT/DS316/R, June 1, 2011, paras 7.174-7.175.

obligations, a role which henceforth will be exercised by the UK.[20] What remains is to identify and apportion the rights and obligations between the EU and the UK.

IV. NEGOTIATING UK'S GATT SCHEDULE OF TARIFF COMMITMENTS

The UK is already a WTO member, but its membership terms are bundled with that of the EU's. Re-establishing the UK's WTO status in its own right means both the UK and the EU would have to negotiate simultaneously with the rest of the WTO members to extract their separate membership terms. Agreement on the UK's terms is unlikely before those of the EU. The UK would have to negotiate on the one hand with the EU itself, and on the other hand with the US, China, Russia, India, Brazil, and any trading nation or group of nations that request negotiations, large or small, rich or poor. A singular objection by any WTO member is sufficient to hold up the talks because the WTO operates by consensus.[21] Will countries bend over backwards to make life easy for the UK in the WTO? The assumption is that they will consider trade with Britain to be too important to disrupt. Some such as Australia might take this view. But each of them will still have specific interests, for example, visas for professionals—a priority for India—and so on.[22] Others might be less accommodating. An official Japanese government task force on Brexit has produced a 15-page list titled 'Japan's message to the UK and the EU,' detailing expectations for Brexit negotiations.[23] The report highlights that several Japanese businesses, invited by the Government in some cases, have invested actively in the UK, which was seen to be a gateway to Europe, and have established value-chains across Europe. It enjoined the UK government to consider this fact seriously and respond in a responsible manner to minimize any harmful effects on these businesses. The report states that the UK leaving the EU would damage exports from Britain to third countries because of trade privileges within the EU single market around so-called

---

[20] Lorand Bartels, *The UK's status in the WTO after Brexit*, Peace Palace Library, September 23, 2016, https://www.peacepalacelibrary.nl/ebooks/files/407396411.pdf.

[21]Peter Ungphakorn, *Nothing simple about UK regaining WTO status post-Brexit*, International Centre for Trade and Sustainable Development, June 27, 2016, http://www.ictsd.org/opinion/nothing-simple-about-uk-regaining-wto-status-post-brexit.

[22] Peter Ungphakorn, *Second bite — how simple is the UK-WTO relationship post-Brexit?*, Trade β Blog, August 20, 2016, https://tradebetablog.wordpress.com/2016/08/17/2nd-bite-how-simple-uk-eu-wto/.

[23] Japan's Message to the United Kingdom and the European Union, Ministry of Foreign Affairs of Japan, (December 22, 2016), http://www.mofa.go.jp/files/000185466.pdf.

rules of origin. The report concludes, "Brexit would make such products unable to meet the rules of origin as EU products, which means that Japanese companies operating in the EU would not be able to enjoy the benefit of the Free Trade Areas concluded by the EU. Japanese businesses with their European headquarters in the UK may decide to transfer their head-office function to Continental Europe if the EU laws cease to be applicable in the UK after its withdrawal." [24]

Despite the best will in the world, the negotiations could eventually become complicated as the UK and the EU struggle to balance conflicting interests amongst their trading partners. To achieve consensus among all 164 WTO members will be an arduous task. A way to avoid such complicated negotiations would be for the UK to unilaterally become a free trader, somewhat like Singapore. This would undeniably simplify the UK's WTO negotiations because a new set of low-tariff, low subsidy commitments would face little opposition from the WTO membership. However, this option is not feasible. Trade negotiations tend to follow three simple principles. First, in any bargain, the alternative to the deal on the table is to walk away from it. The better the alternative of "no deal," the stronger the negotiating position. It follows that market size equals bargaining strength, because the bigger partner needs the smaller partner less than vice versa. Second, patience is a virtue: if one side can hold out a bit longer than the other, it will get the better deal. Lastly, even though we would all be better off in a world without trade barriers, countries need to hold on to theirs so that they can offer to reduce them in exchange for access to the other party's market.[25] Unilateral liberalization would mean that the UK is yielding bargaining leverage in a system which works on the principle of reciprocity. If UK government adopts a free trader route it would have to balance conflicting interests domestically as well. A free trader route will not be politically viable as vulnerable domestic industries such as steel will continue to seek protection.[26]

EU runs a common commercial policy on behalf of its member states. It has negotiated on trade matters for its member states in the

---

[24] Faisal Islam, *Japan's Unprecedented Warning to UK Over Brexit*, Sky News, September 7, 2016, http://news.sky.com/story/japans-unprecedented-warning-to-uk-over-brexit-10564585.

[25] Mark Manger, *David Davis has demonstrated a decidedly muddled understanding of trade policy*, The London School of Economics and Political Science EUROPP Blog, http://blogs.lse.ac.uk/europpblog/2016/07/18/david-davis-brexit-trade-agreements.

[26] Peter Ungphakorn, *Second bite — how simple is the UK-WTO relationship post-Brexit?*, Trade β Blog, August 20, 2016, https://tradebetablog.wordpress.com/2016/08/17/2nd-bite-how-simple-uk-eu-wto/.

WTO and taken on collective commitments. The UK by virtue of being a EU member state is bound by these commitments that are undertaken by the EU at the WTO. Once the UK has exited the EU, it will no longer be covered by the collective commitments, and will therefore have to establish its own Schedule. As discussed previously, it is doubtful whether the law of succession of states will apply to the EU as it doesn't qualify as a state in the strictest sense of the term. Moreover, even if the UK were to inherit its schedule of commitments from that of the EU's, there will be questions about allocating shares of the EU's tariff-rate quotas and subsidy entitlements to the UK.

A. ALLOCATING THE TARIFF RATE QUOTAS BETWEEN UK AND EU

An import quota, a direct restriction on the quantity of some goods that may be imported, is a quantitative restriction generally prohibited by WTO law. A tariff rate quota ("TRQ"), by contrast, does not limit the quantity of imports per se; it allows (in theory at least) enhanced access to a market for a limited quantity of goods by virtue of a low in-quota tariff. Once this quota is filled, subsequent imports are still permitted, but must pay the full tariff.[27] In other words, TRQs are where quantities within the quota are either duty-free or are charged a low tariff (in-quota tariff), while the duties on quantities outside the quota (out-quota tariffs) can be so high and prohibitive that they can make importing impossible. The EU has almost one hundred TRQs, out of which 86 are for agricultural products.[28] The largest number of TRQs (one third) are meat-related, followed by cereals, dairy products, fruits and vegetables.[29] These TRQs have been increased, as required under GATT Article XXIV, with each round of EU enlargement, where the adoption of the EU external tariffs for newly joined members has represented a reduction in market access for WTO partners. The TRQs vary considerably in both size and form, some providing a zero duty in-quota tariff rate, others with tariffs below the WTO bound rate; some remain open to all WTO members,[30] but others are allocated to specific

---

[27] Chris Downes, *The Post-Brexit Management of EU Agricultural Tariff Rate Quotas*, November 21, 2016, https://ssrn.com/abstract=2874371.

[28] Peter Ungphakorn, *The Hilton beef quota: a taste of what post-Brexit UK faces in the WTO*, Trade β Blog, August 10, 2016, https://tradebetablog.wordpress.com/2016/08/10/hilton-beef-quota/.

[29] Certification of Modifications of Notifications to Schedule CXL – European Communities, WLI/100, March 19, 2010.

[30] Commission Regulation (EC) No 973/2006 of 29 June 2006, O.J. L 330/323.

countries and often further restricted by elaborate conditions.[31] The TRQs are therefore a complex mix of bilateral obligations between the EU and specific countries and collective obligations towards all WTO partners.[32]

1. UK's share of tariff rate quotas offered by other WTO Members

UK has a right to access another WTO Member's tariff rate quota when it has a substantial interest in those exports. It also has a right to access a quota, on a non-discriminatory basis, when that WTO Member has allocated part of that quota to any WTO Member without a substantial interest or to non-WTO Members. Furthermore, it is up to the importing WTO Member to ensure that it allocates its tariff rate quotas in accordance with Article XIII of the GATT 1994. However, the problem here could be that, unbundled from the EU's exports as a whole, the UK's exports may be sufficiently low so that the UK will not have a substantial interest guaranteeing it a share of the quota. But that is a commercial, not a legal problem. [33]

2. UK's share of import tariff rate quotas offered by EU-28

In a post Brexit scenario, the UK and the EU will have to agree upon a mechanism to divide the import tariff rate quotas presently imposed by the EU-28. One approach would be to establish a UK-EU ratio to be applied across quotas, "for example, the UK pledging to set a quota that is 10% of the original, leaving the EU with 90%."[34] Another approach in line with the established GATT Article XIII practice,[35] would be to extrapolate quota share from a representative period (typically three

---

[31] Consider, for example, the conditions that have to be met by New Zealand to qualify for the EU's high-quality the quota: 'Selected beef cuts derived from exclusively pasture grazed steers or heifers, the carcasses of which have a dressed weight of not more than 370 kilograms. The carcasses shall be classified as A, L, P, T or F, be trimmed to a fat depth of P or lower and have a muscling classification of 1 or 2 according to the carcass classification system administered by the New Zealand Meat Board'. Council Decision 2011/767/EU of 27 October 2011, O.J. L 317/2.

[32] Joost Pauwelyn, *A Typology of Multilateral Treaty Obligations: Are WTO Obligations Bilateral or Collective in Nature?*, 14 European Journal of International Law 907 (2003).

[33] Lorand Bartels, *The UK's status in the WTO after Brexit*, Peace Palace Library, September 23, 2016, https://www.peacepalacelibrary.nl/ebooks/files/407396411.pdf.

[34] Peter Ungphakorn, *The Hilton beef quota: a taste of what post-Brexit UK faces in the WTO*, Trade β Blog, August 10, 2016, https://tradebetablog.wordpress.com/2016/08/10/hilton-beef-quota/ (predicting that agricultural quotas would have to be negotiated, and it would be particularly tough, but not impossible, because quotas are so political and complex).

[35] GATT Panel Report, *EEC Restrictions on Imports of Apples from Chile*, L/5047–27S/98, November 10, 1980, paras. 4.8 and 4.16.

years) of import data.[36] Some EU import TRQs such as butter from New
Zealand are particularly important for the UK because a significant share
of in-quota imports are destined for the UK market. Whether the EU
would want to share these quotas would be a matter to be negotiated in
the withdrawal negotiations. One could envisage that a more
protectionist EU might be only too delighted to offload a larger than
pro-rata share of its TRQs to the UK. However, getting the other WTO
Members to agree to the reduction of TRQs in the EU schedule and the
introduction of the TRQs in the new UK schedule would be more
difficult. This is because different countries have different dependencies
on the UK versus the EU-27 markets. No matter what allocation key is
used, some third countries are bound to be aggrieved and will feel that
their exports either to the UK or to the EU-27 markets would now face
greater market access difficulties than before. If no agreement is
forthcoming at the WTO, this could lead to a formal dispute over claims
for compensation.[37]

The key aspects of TRQ which will have to be considered are:

a. How should the present EU TRQs be split to create separate
    TRQs for the UK and the EU–27?
b. How should the shares for specific exporting countries be
    handled keeping in mind that their proportionate interests in the
    UK and the EU markets may vary?
c. Should the trade between the UK and EU post Brexit be added
    to the existing TRQs?
d. How should the sum of the EU–27 and the UK TRQs be
    expanded and can these adjustments still fall under the scope of
    'rectification' of schedules rather than "modification" which is a
    lengthier process with more specific requirements for
    negotiations?

In short, the task of extracting UK TRQs from the EU's will require
potentially contentious decisions on both technical and political matters
with real commercial interests involved.[38]

---

[36] Lorand Bartels, *Understanding the UK's position in the WTO after Brexit (Part II – The consequences)*, International Centre for Trade and Sustainable Development, September 26, 2016, http://www.ictsd.org/opinion/understanding-the-uk-0.

[37] Alan Matthews, *WTO Dimensions of a UK 'Brexit' and Agricultural Trade*, CAP Reform EU, January 5, 2016, http://capreform.eu/wto-dimensions-of-a-uk-brexit-and-agricultural-trade/.

[38] Peter Ungphakorn, *Six things I've learnt since the Brexit referendum: seeing both the wood and the trees*, Trade β Blog, January 9, 2017, https://tradebetablog.wordpress.com/category/tariff-rate-quotas/.

While splitting the EU quotas may appear to be providing comparable trading volumes, third countries may well argue that the value of the EU's commitment lies not only in the quantity, but in its geographical reach and flexibility in terms of accessing different country markets, including the UK. The liberalization to which the EU committed is premised on the fact that the imported goods can roam freely in the EU and are treated as EU goods once customs have been cleared.[39] A simple division of quotas may fail to take into account that a TRQ dividing into binding limits in two markets is less valuable than the same TRQ with the flexibility to switch exports between two markets.[40] There is therefore no guarantee that the EU-27 TRQs and the UK TRQs combined, will quantitatively replicate the current EU-28 concessions and necessarily adhere to the 'no less favorable treatment' provisions of Article II:1.[41]

Peter Ungphakorn, former Senior Information Officer, World Trade Organization Secretariat has provided the example of Hilton Beef Quota of EU to explain the complex nature of apportioning tariff rate quotas between EU and UK.[42] The Hilton Beef Quota is one of the EU TRQs consisting of a quota of 58,100 tonnes of high-quality fresh, chilled and frozen beef. The Hilton Quota beef enjoys a duty preference vis-à-vis the EU Most Favored Nation import regime. Technically, as well as politically, TRQs are complex because many of them are also divided up among exporting countries.[43] For the Hilton beef quota, the countries immediately concerned would be at the very least Argentina, Australia, Brazil, Canada, New Zealand, Paraguay, Uruguay, the US—and the EU itself. The WTO members would be negotiating two sets of revised TRQ commitments simultaneously—the EU's as well as the UK's; it is difficult

---

[39] Markus W. Gehring, *Brexit and EU UK Trade Relations with Third States*, EU Law Analysis, March 6, 2016, http://eulawanalysis.blogspot.be/2016/03/brexit-and-eu-uk-trade-relations-with.html.

[40] Alan Matthews, *WTO Dimensions of a UK 'Brexit' and Agricultural Trade*, CAP Reform EU, January 5, 2016, http://capreform.eu/wto-dimensions-of-a-uk-brexit-and-agricultural-trade/.

[41] Chris Downes, The Post-Brexit Management of EU Agricultural Tariff Rate Quotas, November 21, 2016, https://ssrn.com/abstract=2874371.

[42] Peter Ungphakorn, *The Hilton beef quota: a taste of what post-Brexit UK faces in the WTO*, Trade β Blog, August 10, 2016, https://tradebetablog.wordpress.com/2016/08/10/hilton-beef-quota/.

[43] Peter Ungphakorn, *Written evidence to the inquiry of the UK House of Lords' EU External Affairs Sub-Committee on Brexit: future trade between the UK and the EU*, Trade β Blog, https://tradebetablog.files.wordpress.com/2016/10/replies-to-questions-for-blog-22-10-16.pdf.

to envision one being agreed to before the other. [44] Hence the negotiations between the UK-EU, between UK-WTO members and EU-WTO members will have to be contemporaneous. Each of the supplying countries (Argentina, Australia, Brazil and so on for Hilton beef) would also wrangle over the shares allocated to them individually for their exports, out of the EU's and UK's respective tariff quotas. For this particular product, one of the supplying countries might be more interested in the UK market, while another country might be more interested in the rest of the EU-27 market.

Moreover, in the latest available EU schedule the duty-free lamb TRQ is shared out among Argentina, Australia, Chile, New Zealand, Uruguay and nine other countries (several now EU members) with only 200 tonnes out of 283,825 left for "other" countries. If the UK and the EU do not conclude a free trade agreement, and the UK wants to continue exporting lamb to the EU through the EU's TRQ, it will have to fight for a share of the 200 tonnes left for 'other' countries. But in 2015, the UK shipped almost 75,000 tonnes duty-free to the EU, much over the 200 tonnes left for other countries to share. [45] Since UK-EU trade would also come under the two quotas—unless covered by a bilateral UK-EU free trade agreement, some quantities might also have to be added to the total of the UK and EU TRQs to ensure that third countries are not put at a detriment as a part of quota initially allocated to them is being diverted to the UK post Brexit.[46]

Another possibility is to ignore the question of the UK's legal obligations, and focus rather on the reasonable expectations of the traditional importers under a tariff rate quota. This can be done by means of a non-violation complaint against the UK under Article XXIII:1(b) of the GATT 1994, based on a claim that the UK has nullified or impaired benefits accruing to that complainant under the GATT 1994 by a measure, regardless of whether or not it violated a WTO rule, that was not reasonably expected at the time that the tariff rate quota was negotiated. Such a claim would have to satisfy several conditions. It

---

[44] Peter Ungphakorn, *The Hilton beef quota: a taste of what post-Brexit UK faces in the WTO*, Trade β Blog, August 10, 2016, https://tradebetablog.wordpress.com/2016/08/10/hilton-beef-quota/.

[45] *Written evidence by Peter Ungphakorn*, The Select Committee on the European Union, House of Lords, http://data.parliament.uk/writtenevidence/committeeevidence.svc/evidencedocument/eu-external-affairs-subcommittee/brexit-future-trade-between-the-uk-and-the-eu/written/39818.html.

[46] Peter Ungphakorn, *The Hilton beef quota: a taste of what post-Brexit UK faces in the WTO*, Trade β Blog, August 10,2016, https://tradebetablog.wordpress.com/2016/08/10/hilton-beef-quota/.

would need to be established that the UK's leaving the EU, and its consequent new schedule, nullified benefits accruing to that WTO Member under Article XIII of the GATT 1994. As quota shares under Article XIII:2 are subject to fluctuation, a disaffected WTO Member could not have any reasonable expectation of exporting any given quantity under the tariff rate quota. However, it is plausible that it was not expected at the time the tariff rate quota were agreed that non-UK EU imports would be allocated shares of that quota.[47] Second, the measure at issue must have been reasonably unexpected at the time the tariff rate quota was agreed. This would be the case for any tariff rate quota agreed at least between 6 August 1974, the date of circulation of the first EU schedule including the UK,[48] and the date when that WTO Member can be said to have been aware of the possibility that the UK might leave the EU. Any such expectations would also have to be limited to imports into the UK from EU Member States at the time the relevant tariff rate quota was agreed. If these conditions are made out, then a complaining WTO Member would be entitled to a mutually satisfactory adjustment, which may include compensation.[49] If successful, that complainant would then be entitled to a 'mutually satisfactory adjustment' from the UK, which would most likely be achieved by an increase in the UK tariff rate quota to include imports from the EU-27 imports (or, perhaps, only from those EU Members who were Members at the time that the tariff rate quota was agreed).

Another radical alternative would be for the UK to scrap all TRQs, and to instead adopt the in-quota tariff rates as the only tariff to unlimited quantities of imports on those lines or products where the EU-28 has TRQs.[50] However, in case the UK adopts this approach in respect of the TRQs, it faces the risk that the EU will push back on other sectors, further complicating negotiations between the UK and the EU-27 post Brexit.

---

[47] WTO Panel Report, *EC – Poultry*, WT/DS69/R, March 12, 1998, para 293, noting that Brazil had not made such a claim, suggesting implicitly that it might have made such a claim.

[48] WTO Panel Report, *Japan – Film*, WT/DS44/R, April 22, 1998, paras 10.64-10.70.

[49] Article 26(1)(b), Article 26(1)(d), Understanding on Rules and Procedures Governing the Settlement of Disputes, 1869 UNTS 401.

[50] Clemens Boonekamp, *Alternative thinking: Out of the box for Brexit—and radically*, February 12, 2017, https://tradebetablog.wordpress.com/category/tariff-rate-quotas.

B. ALLOCATING AGRICULTURAL SUBSIDIES BETWEEN THE UK AND THE EU

1. UK's share of export subsidy entitlements

The apportionment of export subsidy entitlements will not be an issue. Following the Nairobi Ministerial Council meeting of the WTO in December last year, the EU and all other developed country members agreed to eliminate remaining scheduled export subsidy entitlements with immediate effect (with some limited exceptions which will expire in 2020). As the negotiations leading to a withdrawal agreement are very unlikely to be completed by then, subsidies on agricultural exports will be prohibited by the time that this happens.[51]

2. UK's share of the EU's Bound Total Aggregate Measurement of Support commitments

The UK will also want a share of the EU's Bound Total Aggregate Measurement of Support commitments which, together with its de minimis limits of product-related and non-product-related distorting support, represent the limit on the amount of trade-distorting support it can provide.[52] The amount of Bound Total AMS that would be apportioned between the UK and the EU27 is huge and vastly exceeds recent AMS support in the EU. At the moment, the EU28 does not make full use of its Bound Total AMS, and its Current Total AMS is well below its bound ceiling. EU's actual domestic subsidies are only 7% of its scheduled amount.[53] The relevance for the EU of keeping a large Bound Total AMS as space for future AMS support is much reduced if the EU stays the course on shifting away from trade-distorting support.[54] The apportionment of the AMS is unlikely to prove contentious as the UK is not likely to want to increase its use of trade-distorting support after Brexit.[55]

---

[51] Alan Matthews, *WTO Dimensions of a UK 'Brexit' and Agricultural Trade*, CAP Reform EU, January 5, 2016, http://capreform.eu/wto-dimensions-of-a-uk-brexit-and-agricultural-trade/.

[52] Alan Matthews, *WTO Dimensions of a UK 'Brexit' and Agricultural Trade*, CAP Reform EU, January 5, 2016, http://capreform.eu/wto-dimensions-of-a-uk-brexit-and-agricultural-trade/.

[53] In the marketing year 2012/13, domestic support was €5.9bn of a possible €72.3bn: WTO Committee on Agriculture, Notification–European Union, WT/G/AG/N/EU/26, November 2, 2015.

[54] Lars Brink, *UK Brexit and WTO farm support limits*, July 13, 2016, http://capreform.eu/uk-brexit-and-wto- farm-support-limits/.

[55] Alan Matthews, *WTO Dimensions of a UK 'Brexit' and Agricultural Trade*, CAP Reform EU, January 5, 2016, http://capreform.eu/wto-dimensions-of-a-uk-brexit-and-agricultural-trade/.

WTO law supplies no direct rules or principles for determining the UK's share of a shared liberty to subsidize agricultural production. The origins of the UK's and EU's respective subsidy commitments might be a suitable basis for this calculation. As with tariff rate quotas, this might be relevant with respect to a non-violation complaint. Given the reduction in commitments over time, however, it is unlikely that any WTO Member would make such a claim. A more realistic option would be based on the UK's existing shares of the EU's subsidization policy, either in terms of its higher contributions or its lower receipts.[56] Given that the purpose of the commitments is to reduce distortions in the domestic marketplace, it is suggested that the stronger basis for determining the UK's right to subsidize would be the UK's receipts from the EU's Common Agricultural Policy, rather than its contributions to that policy, which are based on the UK's share of EU gross national income.[57] The relative shares in the value of gross agricultural output can also be a factor to be used for apportionment and would not meet with objection at the WTO.[58]

C. TARIFF NOMENCLATURE

Post Brexit UK would recover the ability to adopt its own rules in respect of its tariff schedule, including its own tariff nomenclature. This could be an opportunity for the UK to get rid of some extremely complicated tariff schemes which have been adopted by the EU. For example, in its WTO commitment, the EU classifies bakery and confectionary products, food preparations and more as "composite agri-goods." They are not just defined as "biscuits" or "chocolate" but have additional definitions based on the percentages of their ingredients. This allows an extra set of import duties to be charged depending on how much of four agricultural ingredients are used to make the product: milk fat, milk proteins, starch or glucose, or various forms of sugar. The result used to be 27,720 categories of composite agri-goods for the purposes of charging import duties. That's 54 products each having a possible 504 recipes using different combinations of those ingredients. The figure has now been trimmed to 27 products, still with 504 recipes, in the EU's current WTO commitment, leaving 13,608 categories of biscuits, bread,

---

[56] Lars Brink, *UK Brexit and WTO farm support limits*, July 13, 2016, http://capreform.eu/uk-brexit-and-wto-farm-support-limits/.

[57] Lorand Bartels, *The UK's status in the WTO after Brexit*, Peace Palace Library, September 23, 2016, https://www.peacepalacelibrary.nl/ebooks/files/407396411.pdf.

[58] Alan Matthews, *WTO Dimensions of a UK 'Brexit' and Agricultural Trade*, CAP Reform.EU, January 5, 2016, http://capreform.eu/wto-dimensions-of-a-uk-brexit-and-agricultural-trade/.

chocolate, etc., each potentially charged a different import duty. The EU has promised to strip it back to "less than 300" categories as part of the WTO's Doha Round negotiations, but the talks are moribund. All of this is designed to protect European farmers as well as biscuit makers.

As the UK heads out of the EU, it could use this opportunity to simplify this extremely complicated tariff which it inherits from the EU. Such a simplification would reduce uncertainty, avoid potential rebuffs and free the UK to pursue trade relations with third parties on simpler terms.[59] As the UK renegotiates its WTO commitments, it should unilaterally declare that it will not use such a complicated scheme to set its own tariffs.

D. RULES OF ORIGIN

Rules of origin are used to determine whether a product originated in a free trade area and is eligible to enter a market duty-free. Because the EU, as a customs union, operates with a common external tariff, goods entering from outside can travel freely within the Union once that tariff has been paid (e.g. a mobile phone imported into the UK from China can be re-exported to the rest of the EU tariff free). Determining where a good originated, and hence whether it should attract tariffs, is done through the EU's Rules of Origin. Given the complexity of some global supply chains and the range of preferential trading relationships the EU operates, this can be a difficult, time-consuming and often a subjective process.[60]

With the UK as a customs union member within the European Union, UK firms were saved the compliance and administrative costs linked to proving the origin of products shipped in the European market. With Brexit, the UK will be taking direct control over its external trade policies and operating outside the customs union. Hence rules of origin would become necessary to identify qualifying UK goods under any prospective free trade agreement with the EU customs union or other UK FTA partners. Demonstrating origin can be onerous and the costs involved have been known to deter importers from seeking zero tariff.[61]

---

[59] Clemens Boonekamp, *Alternative thinking: Out of the box for Brexit — and radically*, February 12, 2017, https://tradebetablog.wordpress.com/category/tariff-rate-quotas.

[60] *Brexit: impact across policy areas*, Briefing Paper Number 07213, House of Commons Library, August 26, 2016, http://www.transatlanticbusiness.org/wp-content/uploads/2016/07/Brexit-Impact-Across-Policy-Areas-House-of-Commons-Library-Report.pdf.

[61] *Trade and Investment Balance of Competence Review*, Centre for Economic Policy Research, London, November 2013, https://www.gov.uk/government/uploads/system/uploads/attachment_data/file/271

The additional costs and time delays associated with Rules of Origin would reduce the benefits of the free trade agreement and might disrupt time-sensitive supply chains, in particular.[62]

This means UK firms would be exposed to a combination of administrative and compliance costs linked to rules or origin, ranging from 4 percent to perhaps 15 percent of the cost of goods sold. For low tariff products, it is therefore likely that firms would instead simply opt to pay the common external tariff of the EU, and so avoid costs linked to rules of origin. This means that, for low tariff products, there would be very little difference between no trade agreement, and one involving free trade combined with rules of origin.[63]

V. OTHER COMPLICATIONS IN TARIFF NEGOTIATION

A. *SHOULD POST-BREXIT UK SUBMIT ITS NEW SCHEDULE OF COMMITMENTS AS 'RECTIFICATION' OR 'MODIFICATION'?*

The current procedure for making changes to a GATT 1994 schedule is set out in the 1980 Decision on Procedures for Modification and Rectification of Schedules of Tariff Concessions,[64] which is binding as part of the GATT 1994. This Decision distinguishes between modifications, on the one hand, and 'other changes,' on the other. Paragraph 1 describes 'modifications' as follows:

Changes in the authentic texts of Schedules annexed to the General Agreement which reflect modifications resulting from action under Article II, Article XVIII, Article XXIV, Article XXVII or Article XXVIII shall be certified by means of Certifications.

784/bis-14-512-trade-and-investment-balance-of-competence-review-project-report.pdf, p.15.

[62] *Trade and Investment Balance of Competence Review*, Centre for Economic Policy Research, London,   November   2013, https://www.gov.uk/government/uploads/system/uploads/attachment_data/file/271784/bis-14-512-trade-and-investment-balance-of-competence-review-project-report.pdf, p.36.

[63] *Trade and Investment Balance of Competence Review*, Centre for Economic Policy Research, London,   November   2013, https://www.gov.uk/government/uploads/system/uploads/attachment_data/file/271784/bis-14-512-trade-and-investment-balance-of-competence-review-project-report.pdf, p.58.

[64] GATT Contracting Parties, Procedures for Modification and Rectification of Schedules of Tariff Concessions, Decision of 26 March 1980, L/4962.

It is notable that each of the provisions listed in this paragraph is concerned with negotiations following a desire of a WTO Member to increase duties or other barriers to trade.

By contrast, paragraph 2 of the 1980 Decision describes 'other changes' as follows:

> Changes in the authentic texts of Schedules shall be made when amendments or rearrangements which do not alter the scope of a concession are introduced in national customs tariffs in respect of bound items. Such changes and other rectifications of a purely formal character shall be made by means of Certifications.

Since the UK is already a WTO member in its own right, the process of the UK having its own GATT schedule can happen in two ways: 'rectification' or 'modification'. The former is relatively simple, and only requires that no WTO Member state raises any objections to be approved or 'certified'. This could happen in a matter of months rather than years. A full modification process however requires rounds of negotiations over the tariffs and TRQs and could become bogged down for years. Rectification is possible for "rearrangements which do not alter the scope of a concession and other rectifications of a purely formal character." Modification of schedules implies a substantive change of a concession. The dividing line between rectification and modification is thus determined by ascertaining whether the changes made will put another WTO member in a position worse off under the new rules.[65]

Mr. Richard Eglin, Senior Trade Policy Adviser, White and Case LLP, explained that if the Government amended the UK's schedules by means of a rectification of the EU's schedules, the process could be completed in "three months in the case of the goods schedule and forty-five days in the case of the services schedule." He added, "there is nothing in the WTO rules that says you cannot adopt somebody else's schedule."[66] Lord Price agreed that "one of the first things to do would be to "go through the technical process of adopting our own schedules." He continued, "the advice we have is that what we intend to do is

---

[65] Raoul Ruparel, *Priorities for the new Department for International Trade post-Brexit*, Open Europe, July 27, 2016, http://openeurope.org.uk/today/blog/priorities-for-the-new-department-for-international-trade-post-brexit/.

[66] *Corrected oral evidence: Brexit: future trade between the UK and the EU*, The Select Committee on the European Union, House of Lords, October 13,2016, http://data.parliament.uk/writtenevidence/committeeevidence.svc/evidencedocument/eu-external-affairs-subcommittee/brexit-future-trade-between-the-uk-and-the-eu/oral/41317.html.

predominantly technical, moving from an EU schedule to a UK schedule."[67] To summarize the position taken by the above-mentioned experts, the suggestion is that so long as the UK maintains the same tariff schedule as that of the EU, there would not be any great difficulty in classifying UK's new schedule as 'a rectification of the schedule.' However, these experts also recognize that a lot of negotiations will be involved in more contentious issues like dividing the TRQs and agricultural subsidies between UK and EU. If that is true, one would assume that the new TRQs or agricultural subsidies imply a substantive change of concessions and therefore are modifications to the schedule instead of rectification.

Bearing these factors in mind, some believe that the UK adopting the EU's schedules goes beyond the simple 'rectification' and instead are a 'modification' of the EU's schedules. Mr. Luis González García told the House of Lords that the UK's negotiation will alter the EU's schedules and therefore cannot be considered a rectification.[68] Mr. Peter Ungphakorn agreed that other countries might see separating out the UK's TRQs as a modification of the EU's schedules. He opined, "For regular most favored nation (MFN) tariffs, many of the EU's scheduled tariffs can be adopted by the UK with little difficulty and this would probably come under simpler WTO rules on 'rectifying' schedules. However, some MFN tariffs may still face negotiations if other countries (such as South Africa) question the UK's need to continue with the EU's complex tariffs protecting certain producers (such as Mediterranean orange producers). UK retailers and consumers might also want lower tariffs and cheaper products. This could lead to a debate within the UK itself, along with a triangle of external negotiations between the UK, EU (on behalf of Spain et al) and non-EU exporting countries."[69]

---

[67] *Corrected oral evidence: Brexit: future trade between the UK and the EU*, The Select Committee on the European Union, House of Lords, October 13,2016, http://data.parliament.uk/writtenevidence/committeeevidence.svc/evidencedocument /eu-external-affairs-subcommittee/brexit-future-trade-between-the-uk-and-the-eu/oral/41317.html.

[68] *Written evidence by Luis Gonzalez Garcia,* The Select Committee on the European Union, House of Lords, http://data.parliament.uk/writtenevidence/committeeevidence.svc/evidencedocument /eu-external-affairs-subcommittee/brexit-future-trade-between-the-uk-and-the-eu/written/39823.html.

[69] *Written evidence by Peter Ungphakorn,* The Select Committee on the European Union, House of Lords, http://data.parliament.uk/writtenevidence/committeeevidence.svc/evidencedocument /eu-external-affairs-subcommittee/brexit-future-trade-between-the-uk-and-the-eu/written/39818.html.

Then there is a third view espoused by Lorand Bartels, who argues that the UK's departure from the EU is the same as the situation described by Article XXVI:5(c) of the GATT 1947, insofar as both concern the acquisition by a customs territory of full autonomy in matters covered by the GATT 1947, or WTO. Article XXVI:5(c) of the GATT 1947 permitted newly autonomous customs territories, which in practice was mainly decolonized independent states, to which the GATT 1947 had been made applicable, to succeed to GATT contracting party status, upon request and with the sponsorship of the responsible (or formerly responsible) GATT contracting party. Upon succession, the newly autonomous territory inherited all of the rights and obligations that were previously applicable to its territory, including scheduled commitments (and qualifications) which the formerly responsible contracting party had made effective in respect of its territory. Sometimes, this meant that succeeding contracting parties preferred not to inherit these rights and obligations, and rather accede to the GATT 1947 as a new contracting party.[70] Importantly, and relevantly to the present situation, the submission of new GATT 1947 schedules in this context were treated as 'other changes,' except when the schedule required an increase in duties beyond the bound rate.[71]

It is true that the purpose of Article XXVI:5(c) was to establish a right of succession to contracting party status, whereas the UK is already a full WTO Member. However, both the UK and such new independent states share the same need to adopt, in their own name, the schedule of concessions that formerly applied to their territories by virtue of a GATT contracting party (or WTO Member) with autonomy and responsibility in matters covered by the GATT 1947 and WTO respectively. For this reason, practice under Article XXVI:5(c) of the GATT 1947 should 'guide' the WTO in the adoption of a post-Brexit UK tariff schedule, even though technically the practice only applies to cases falling under Article XXVI:5(c), which is no longer operative. Mr. Bartel argues that this is another reason why the UK is entitled to submit a new schedule to the GATT 1994 as a 'change not amounting to a modification,' so as

---

[70] An example was Cambodia, which preferred not to commit to the high scheduled commitments that had been applied to its territory (as part of the Indo-China customs union) under France's schedule of concessions. See GATT Contracting Parties, Accession of Cambodia: Statement by Cambodia, GATT Doc L/900, November 1, 1958.

[71] For example, Cameroon accepted that it would have been required to renegotiate its schedule under Article XXIV:6 of the GATT 1947 if it had to increase its tariff bindings due to its membership of a customs union. See GATT, Accession by Newly-Independent African States to the GATT, INT(62)142, November 3, 1962, para 18.

to enable the UK to avoid having to go through the lengthy and complicated procedures for modification.[72]

B. AT WHAT EXCHANGE RATE WILL SPECIFIC DUTIES IN THE EU SCHEDULE BE CONVERTED WHEN TRANSPOSED INTO THE UK SCHEDULE?

Tariffs can be expressed in different ways. An 'ad valorem' tariff is a duty paid as a percentage of the import price when the good crosses the border. So, if a certain type of cheese has an ad valorem tariff of 10 %, and an importer imported € 100 worth, the importer would have to pay a € 10 import tax on it. "Specific" duties on the other hand are a fixed amount paid per physical unit i.e. kilos, litres, % of alcohol content, etc. EU's tariff structure is extremely complex. In addition to simple ad valorem tariffs (e.g. 10%) there are ad valorem tariffs with a minimum and/or maximum entry price (e.g. 18.4% min 22 €/100 kg max 24 €/100 kg), compound duties (5% + 24 €/100 kg), specific duties with a minimum/maximum ad valorem equivalent (0.5 €/p/st min 2.7% max 4.6%) and specific duties only (0.9 €/%vol/hl).[73]

While EU's specific duties are designated in Euros, a post Brexit UK is likely to designate the specific duties in pound sterling and not Euro. The most contentious issue will be at what exchange rate should the duties denominated in Euros be converted into pound sterling.

Article II para 3 of GATT stipulates that no contracting party shall alter its method of converting currencies to impair the value of any of the concessions provided for in the appropriate Schedule annexed to this Agreement. Under long-standing GATT practice, even purely formal changes in the tariff schedule of a contracting party, which may not affect the GATT rights of other countries, such as the conversion of a specific to an ad valorem duty without an increase in the protective effect of the tariff rate in question, have been considered to require renegotiations.[74] Therefore, the UK cannot unilaterally adopt an exchange rate to convert the specific duties designated in Euro to pound sterling neither can it convert the specific duties into ad valorem equivalents without negotiating with other members.

---

[72] Lorand Bartels, *The UK's status in the WTO after Brexit*, Peace Palace Library, September 23, 2016, https://www.peacepalacelibrary.nl/ebooks/files/407396411.pdf.

[73] Christopher Stevens, Jane Kennan, *Trade Implications of Brexit for Commonwealth Developing Countries*, Issue 133, The Commonwealth Trade Hot Topics, 2016, http://thecommonwealth.org/sites/default/files/news-items/documents/TradeImplicationsBrexit_0.pdf.

[74] Panel Report, *European Communities—Regime for Importation, Sale and Distribution of Bananas*, WT/DS27/R/ECU, May 22, 1997.

Lars Brink, an expert on domestic support issues in the WTO Agreement on Agriculture has rightly pointed out that if the UK wished to take its Bound Total AMS in its local currency (pound sterling), agreement would be needed on the exchange rate. Depending on how apportioning was carried out, details for discussion could include an average exchange rate for a period of time e.g. based on historical shares from the 1986–94 Uruguay Round negotiations, when the EU's schedule was originally established or the exchange rate at an instant in time, e.g., the moment of withdrawal from the EU.[75] There is even the option to dodge exchange rates completely and keep the UK's commitments in euros although it is not something that Brexiteers will want politically.[76]

Before the Euro was adopted, the European currency unit (ECU), a basket of currencies of the European Community member states, was used as the unit of account of the European Community and the European Community's specific duties were designated in ECU. One would think that knowing how the specific duty was converted from ECU to EU would provide useful guidance to convert EU into pound sterling, but this is not the case. One unit of ECU was equivalent to one unit of Euro, and hence there was no problem of simply designating ECU specific duties in Euro terms.

The Report of the Working Party on Specific Duties[77] concluded that the right to adjust specific duties in the monetary situation present at that time (referring to 1978 situation) could not be called into question. The report discussed the question of how depreciation in currency is to be calculated, what period of exchange rate movement should be examined for the purpose of measurement. The Working Party further analyzed the case of contracting parties members of a customs union with common specific duties but no common currency that define their specific duties in terms of a unit of account composed of the currencies of the member States. It noted that the European Community defines the specific elements in its common customs tariff in terms of European Unit of account. The Working Party recognized that the common unit of account served in such cases as a substitute for a common currency and it therefore concluded that the depreciation to be taken into account should in these cases be the depreciation of the value of the unit of

---

[75] Lars Brink, *UK Brexit and WTO farm support limits*, July 13, 2016, http://capreform.eu/uk-brexit-and-wto-farm-support-limits/.

[76] Peter Ungphakorn, *Brexit, Agriculture, the WTO and uncertainty*, Tradeβ Blog, October 17, 2016, https://tradebetablog.wordpress.com/category/tariffs/.

[77] Report of the Working Party on Specific Duties, General Agreement on Tariffs and Trade, L/4858, November 2,1979, https://www.wto.org/gatt_docs/English/SULPDF/90970011.pdf.

account in terms of third currencies each weighted by its share in the total imports of the common market.[78] In light of this report, some might argue that UK can convert the duties designated in Euros to pound sterling without the fear such adjustment being challenged and that the Working Party report on specific duties could provide useful guidance in determining the appropriate exchange rate. However, one must remember that the report of the working party was made in the context of a changing international monetary order marked by a shift from a par value system to a floating exchange rate system. Besides, in the context of Brexit it is not a question of adjustment of the specific duty in terms of the same currency but conversion of duty into another currency altogether. Moreover, UK has not been a part of the Eurozone ever. Hence the logic underpinning the findings of the working party report may not be applicable in this situation.

C. ARE TARIFF NEGOTIATIONS FURTHER COMPLICATED DUE TO EU'S FAILURE TO GET ITS SCHEDULE OF COMMITMENTS CERTIFIED?

According to a March 1980 decision adopted by the council setting out procedures for modification and rectification of schedules of tariff concessions, it was to be done through the means of certification. A 1987 Secretariat Note on "Harmonized System Negotiations under Article XXVIII" highlighted the legal effect of certification noting that:

> Although the uncertified loose-leaf schedules represent important sources of information and bases for negotiations, they have no legal status. It follows that past protocols and other legal instruments continue to keep their legal status until the time of certification of the respective loose-leaf schedules or their entry into force by means of a protocol.[79]

As the EU membership has enlarged over time, it has allowed in larger quantities of imports than the quotas it had previously agreed to under its TRQ commitments without these being formally recorded through certification. Until recently, the last certified EU Schedule was at the time

---

[78] Report of the Working Party on Specific Duties, General Agreement on Tariffs and Trade, L/4858, November 2, 1979, https://www.wto.org/gatt_docs/English/SULPDF/90970011.pdf.

[79] Harmonized System negotiations under Article XXVIII, Note by the Secretariat, Committee on Tariff Concessions, General agreement on Tariffs and Trade, TAR/W/65/Rev.1, January 14, 1987, https://www.wto.org/gatt_docs/English/SULPDF/91260122.pdf.

of EU-15.[80] Only on 14 December, 2016 the WTO circulated the EU's "schedules" of commitments on goods (not services) to reflect its 2004 expansion from 15 to 25 members.[81] They are also the UK's current official WTO commitments. However, this updated schedule still doesn't account for Bulgaria and Romania, which joined in 2007, to become EU–27, and then Croatia which joined in 2013 to make it EU-28.

If the UK is negotiating its share of TRQs from the EU-28 schedule, it will be negotiating shares of officially unknown tariff quotas because it lacks an official EU-28 schedule of commitments on goods. If a third country were to challenge the apportionment of TRQ, the legal basis for them would be benefits impaired with respect to the last certified EU schedule which is the EU-25 schedule in case of goods. Therefore, the House of Lords sought expert opinion on whether the fact that the EU's current WTO quotas have not yet been certified complicate the process of the UK renegotiating its WTO schedules.

Richard Eglin, Senior Trade Policy Adviser, White and Case LLP, opined to the House of Lords that it would not matter or create any particular difficulty as the WTO is a commercial contract that everyone has an interest in seeing work effectively, and that no WTO Member is remotely likely to allow such a narrow legal issue to stand in the way of its overall trade relationship with the UK.[82] Peter Ungphakorn, Former Senior Information Officer, World Trade Organization Secretariat, also expressed his view that if all the countries concerned are willing to accept the schedules that the EU is applying in practice, then negotiations can proceed on them. But if other countries wanted to be difficult, they might insist on knowing the schedules for EU-28 and negotiating from official versions.[83] Luis González García, Associate Member, Matrix Chambers said that getting an agreement on TRQs with the WTO members will potentially become a problematic exercise if such allocation is based on

---

[80] *Brexit Brief: 10 things to know about the World Trade Organization*, Institute for Government, October 31, 2016, https://www.instituteforgovernment.org.uk/brexit/brexit-brief-10-things-know-about-world-trade-organization-wto.

[81] Peter Ungphakorn, *12 years on, EU's certified WTO goods commitments now up to date to 2004*, Tradeβ Blog, February 4, 2017, https://tradebetablog.wordpress.com/2017/02/04/after-12-years-eu-25-goods-commitments/#eu25.

[82] *Evidence Volume, Brexit: the options for trade*, External Affairs Sub-Committee and Internal Market Sub-Committee, European Union Committee, House of Lords, https://www.parliament.uk/documents/lords-committees/eu-sub-com-b/Evidence%20volume-Brexit-options%20for%20trade.pdf, p.61.

[83] *Evidence Volume, Brexit: the options for trade*, External Affairs Sub-Committee and Internal Market Sub-Committee, European Union Committee, House of Lords, https://www.parliament.uk/documents/lords-committees/eu-sub-com-b/Evidence%20volume-Brexit-options%20for%20trade.pdf, p.148.

the certified EU-15 (now certified EU-25) schedule because these are outdated schedules. It may be less complicated for the UK if the schedule is based on the proposed EU-28 schedule. However, the EU-28 schedule has not been agreed on and it is managed by the EU Commission on a bilateral basis in a non-transparent manner. This, he thinks, is likely to trigger further discussions between the WTO members and the EU which will have an impact in the UK's WTO renegotiation.[84]

VI. UK CAN SEEK A WAIVER FROM WTO OBLIGATIONS

WTO members anticipating a breach of WTO obligations can avail themselves of a remedy within the WTO system known as the 'waiver of obligations,' exempting them from specific obligations. Waivers may be requested by application citing the reasons which prevent the WTO member from achieving policy objectives. The waivers last for two years unless extended, which they can be, without limit.[85] Specifically, the function of a waiver is to relieve a WTO Member, for a specified period of time, from a particular obligation and is exceptional in nature, subject to strict disciplines. Waiver may be used to 'flexibilise' international law and thus address the tensions between domestic needs and international requirements, defusing potential conflict by suspending the law before the tensions escalate to the point where nations may be forced to choose between one or the other.[86]

For the UK seeking to manage the Brexit process, there could be no doubt about the exceptional nature of the situation. A waiver would be of possible value in two respects. Firstly, it could be used to cover any time gap between leaving the EU and regularizing its schedules, allowing it to continue trading under current arrangements. Alternatively, it could be used to neutralize the effect of any political blockage arising from one of more members lodging reservations to any proposed schedule, buying time for further mediation and eventual resolution.[87] WTO members might allow both parties, UK as well as EU, transitional periods or temporary waivers to allow the EU-UK negotiations to continue after the day of formal Brexit without pressure from Geneva. Of course, that

---

[84] *Evidence Volume, Brexit: the options for trade*, External Affairs Sub-Committee and Internal Market Sub-Committee, European Union Committee, House of Lords, https://www.parliament.uk/documents/lords-committees/eu-sub-com-b/Evidence%20volume-Brexit-options%20for%20trade.pdf, p.77.

[85] Article IX, Marrakesh Agreement Establishing the World Trade Organization, Apr. 15, 1994, 1867 U.N.T.S. 154.

[86] Richard North, *Brexit: Waivers and Safeguards*, August 24, 2016, http://eureferendum.com/blogview.aspx?blogno=86191.

[87] Richard North, *Brexit Monograph 8: WTO schedules and concessions*, August 21, 2016, http://www.eureferendum.com/documents/BrexitMonograph008.pdf.

does assume goodwill on all sides which should not be taken for granted.[88]

CONCLUSION

To summarize, on the basis of the analysis offered here, the UK is a founding member of WTO and will not have to re-apply for membership of WTO through the accession route post a formal Brexit. The UK by virtue of being a WTO member in its own right will possess full WTO rights and obligations. Some tariff commitments could be easily transposed from the EU schedule into post-Brexit UK's new schedule through the rectification process. However, complications will arise where the UK's rights correspond to part of a right or obligation, determined on a quantified basis, which is currently set out in the EU's schedules. Such rights include the share of EU-28 import TRQs and agricultural subsidies that a post Brexit UK will be entitled to. Any apportionment of TRQs and agricultural subsidies will entail discussions not only between the UK and the EU, but also necessarily involve other interested WTO members as their right to a common European market is affected. A new tariff schedule on WTO terms would require consensus of 160 members including the 27 countries that are also EU members. Many countries will first examine any EU-UK deal and determine if the UK remains an attractive base for European operations. Since the issues are intertwined and have effect on the entire multilateral trading community, UK's WTO negotiations may have to be conducted simultaneously alongside UK- EU27 negotiations. Negotiations may further be impeded by lack of an updated and certified EU-28 schedule on goods and services, disagreements on exchange rate for conversion of duties from Euro to pound sterling and differences over the scope of concessions that undergo alteration.

The success of post Brexit UK at the WTO hinges on its relationship with the EU-27 once it formally exits the EU. Negotiations with WTO members will depend primarily on how successful it is in retaining access to EU markets. Prime Minister Theresa May has made it clear that the UK will not be a part of the EU Common Market. While it is undoubtedly regrettable that the UK is leaving, the truth is that free trade with the EU does not necessarily have to be accompanied by free movement of people. The best alternative would be a free trade agreement (FTA) between a post Brexit UK and the EU-27 in order for

---

[88] *The World Trade Organization: A Safety Net for A Post-Brexit UK Trade Policy?*, Briefing Paper 1, UK Trade Policy Observatory, University of Sussex, July 2016, https://www.sussex.ac.uk/webteam/gateway/file.php?name=briefing-paper-1.pdf&site=18.

the UK to retain tariff-free goods trade with the EU and hence simplify negotiations with WTO members. If no deal is reached between the UK and EU-27, the costs to the UK will be even larger.

Anything in WTO is total consensus. Brexit is a unique and unprecedented situation. Diplomacy will be an important tool in approaching this novel situation. [89] The head of the World Trade Organization has vowed to ensure that the UK will not face a trade "vacuum or a disruption," however tough its exit from the European Union may be.[90] All that is certain is that if the UK is to make a success of Brexit, it will need to draw on vast reserves of global goodwill. [91] Hopefully, the three leading Brexiteer ministers—David Davis, Liam Fox and Boris Johnson—will understand the significance of diplomacy and goodwill. If they resort to thumping the table and threatening other governments, they are likely to delay the very deals which the UK needs. The longer the UK government takes to complete these negotiations, the worse would be the uncertainty for the UK economy.[92]

---

[89] Simon Nixon, *Brexit Success Hinges on Global Goodwill*, The Wall Street Journal, August 17, 2016, http://yaleglobal.yale.edu/content/brexit-success-hinges-global-goodwill.

[90] Ed Conway, *Brexit will not cause UK trade 'disruption' - WTO boss*, Sky News, October 26, 2016, http://news.sky.com/story/brexit-will-not-cause-uk-trade-disruption-wto-boss-10632803.

[91] Simon Nixon, *Brexit Success Hinges on Global Goodwill*, The Wall Street Journal, August 17, 2016, http://yaleglobal.yale.edu/content/brexit-success-hinges-global-goodwill.B.

[92]Charles Grant, *The Brexit negotiations: the UK government will have incentives to compromise*, The London School of Economics and Political Science Blog, August 4, 2016, http://blogs.lse.ac.uk/brexit/2016/08/04/the-brexit-negotiations-the-uk-government-will-have-incentives-to-compromise/.

CHAPTER 3: THE LEGAL BASIS FOR THE UK TO ADOPT THE NORWAY MODEL: REDUCING POTENTIAL NEGATIVE-IMPACTS OF BREXIT

SOHIL KHURANA

During the 2016 campaign over the Brexit referendum, then-Mayor of London Boris Johnson passionately advocated for the "Leave" campaign, arguing that the United Kingdom (UK) needed a breakaway from the constraints of the European Union, including the single market as well as jurisdiction of various European Union institutions. However, after the success of the "Leave" campaign in the referendum and his ultimate appointment as Foreign Secretary, Johnson indicated a shift in his rhetoric, arguing, "…there will still be intense and intensifying European cooperation and partnership in a huge number of fields…. EU citizens living in this country will have their rights fully protected, and the same goes for British citizens living in the EU…. British people will still be able to go and work in the EU; to live; to travel; to study; to buy homes and to settle down…and *there will continue to be free trade, and access to the single market*." [emphasis added][1] The priorities and goals mentioned in this shift are more than just rhetorical; indeed, they represent a substantial shift in referring to what type of model the UK will seek to implement after it invokes Article 50 of the Lisbon Treaty.

This paper will examine the legal basis for the effectiveness of the UK emulating the Norway Model post-Brexit, with the goal of as Secretary Johnson noted in his remarks, balancing the competing interests between the "leave" campaign and the economic interests of those who favor retaining access to the single market and four freedoms, as required under the Norway Model. Specifically, this paper will analyze 1) the legal process for how the UK can join the European Economic Area (EEA) and implement the Norway Model, 2) the effect of EEA law in the UK in relation to EU Institutions and domestic law, 3) substantive impacts of implementing the Norway Model in key policy areas namely immigration, trade, and financial passporting rights, as well as 4) how the UK can seek exceptions similar to that of Norway in order to make implementation of the Norway Model politically and economically

---

[1] Katie Forster, Boris Johnson says Brexit vote does not mean leaving Europe 'in any sense', *The Independent*, http://www.independent.co.uk/news/uk/politics/boris-johnson-brexit-vote-does-not-mean-leaving-europe-in-any-sense-eu-referendum-reshuffle-a7137056.html (July 14 2016).

feasible, thus allowing for the establishment of a limited bespoke agreement between the UK and the EU member states.

BRIEF SUMMARY & HISTORICAL OVERVIEW OF THE NORWAY MODEL

Before analyzing specific effects of the implementation of the Norway Model for the UK post-Brexit, it is important to first provide the historical overview and summary of what features constitute the Norway Model. As such, the Norway Model refers to the relationship between Norway and the European Union (EU) member states. In 1994, Norway had a popular referendum on whether to become a EU member state, in which the majority of the country voted to remain separate and not join the EU.[2] Concerned about possible negative economic effects of the referendum result, then Norwegian Prime Minister Gro Harlem Brundtland and her ruling Labor Party decided to implement a distinctive relationship with the EU member states that would allow Norway to retain formal independence, while gaining access to the EU's single market in exchange for agreeing to the EU's four freedoms. This relationship includes quasi-sovereignty and jurisdiction of the Court of Justice of the European Union (CJEU) and other EU legislation over Norway's domestic laws.[3] As such, Norway was able to benefit from gaining access to the EU single market, which refers to the notion of the EU as one territory without internal borders or regulatory obstacles to the free movement of goods and services, and in return had to apply the four freedoms which constitute the free movement of goods, free movement of services (and freedom of establishment), free movement of persons, and free movement of capital.[4] Additionally, the Norway judicial system would be bound to follow case law of the ECJ, and the Norwegian parliament and other legislative entities would be bound to incorporate legislation passed by the EU parliament into domestic law.

The legal mechanism for enabling Norway to develop this unique relationship with the EU member states was the European Economic Area Agreement (EEA), established in 1994. The EEA Agreement is an international treaty that establishes a free trade area known as the European Economic Area, enabling access to the EU's single market between the EU member states and the states of Lichtenstein, Iceland, and Norway, all of whom (in addition to Switzerland) constitute the

---

[2] Jon Stone, Norway's prime minister warns that leaving the EU wouldn't work for Britain, *The Independent,* http://www.independent.co.uk/news/uk/politics/norway-s-prime-minister-warns-that-leaving-the-eu-wouldnt-work-for-britain-a6853476.html (February 4, 2016).

[3] Carl Baudenbacher, *The Handbook of EEA Law,* 7-9 (2016).

[4] *Id.*

European Free Trade Association (EFTA).[5] The EFTA refers to the free trade area between the four aforementioned states, and allows access to the single market through the EEA Agreement. The EEA Agreement also established the EFTA Surveillance Authority and EFTA Court that monitors compliance with the EEA Agreement, and adjudicates subsequent disputes respectively.[6] Moreover, since the EEA is not a joint customs area, EFTA member states have the ability to manage their own bilateral trade agreements with third parties as well as establish joint trade agreements between the EFTA as a whole and third party states.[7] Lastly, while the EEA Agreement requires compliance with EU directives and regulations related to the single market in return for access to the single market, it does not cover and thus allows EFTA states to enact their own policies on a wide array of subjects, including common agriculture and fisheries, trade policy, foreign and security policy, justice and home affairs, as well as direct and indirect taxation.[8] Since the EEA Agreement is between the EU member states and the EFTA member states, it is within this framework that the UK must accede to in order to start the process of implementing the Norway Model.

I. THE LEGAL PROCESS FOR HOW THE UK CAN JOIN THE EUROPEAN ECONOMIC AREA (EEA) AND IMPLEMENT THE NORWAY MODEL

Article 128 of the EEA Agreement states that only members of the European Union or member states of the EFTA may apply for membership within the EEA.[9] Based on this, the main legal question that governs how the UK should initiate this process is: in invoking Article 50 of the Lisbon Treaty, has the UK left the EEA Agreement, and thus is it required to re-apply in order to re-join the EEA, or does the UK remain a party to the EEA Agreement notwithstanding Brexit and its future status as a non-member of the EU?[10] To answer this question, there are two differing interpretations that would have vast implications on the UK as it ultimately negotiates its withdrawal from the EU after invoking Article 50.

First, under a plain reading of Article 128, it is clear that the provision requires membership within the EEA to be limited to either EU

---

[5] *See id.*
[6] *Id.*
[7] *Id. at 14-15.*
[8]   Fladgate   LLP,   *Brexit-Where*   *Next,* https://www.fladgate.com/assets/uploads/2016/06/Post-Brexit-briefing-June-2016.pdf (last visited Dec. 11, 2016).
[9] Thomas Donegan, *Brexit: Options for and Impact of the Possible Alternatives to EU Membership,* Shearman & Sterling (March. 2016).
[10] *See id.* at 7.

members or EFTA member states.[11] Moreover, Article 50(3) states, "The Treaties shall cease to apply to the State in question from the date of entry into force of the withdrawal agreement or, failing that, two years after the notification referred to in paragraph 2."[12] Thus, under a plain reading of Article 128 and Article 50 respectively, once the UK has invoked Article 50 and a withdrawal agreement is in force, it is no longer a EU member and any EU treaties or Protocols no longer apply to the UK. Once a withdrawal agreement is in force or the treaty period of two years has elapsed, the UK will have lost its EU membership and with that its membership within the EEA agreement. Consequently, under this interpretation of Article 128 of the EEA Agreement, the UK would have to first seek membership within the EFTA, and then seek membership through the EEA Agreement, since it would no longer be a EU member and the EEA Agreement is limited to either EU states or EFTA states.

In order to join the EFTA, the UK will have to accede to the EFTA Convention, which is the legal treaty between the four states (Liechtenstein, Norway, Iceland, and Switzerland) that constitute the EFTA.[13] The main requirements for accession to the EFTA Convention are listed in Article 56, in which EFTA states are required to accept the four freedoms, namely freedom of goods, services/establishment, persons, and capital. Thus, as an EFTA state, the UK would not be allowed to have customs duties on imports or exports from other EFTA states.[14] In regards to trade, Article 56 could provide the UK some leeway in that the UK can apply to join any of the 37 free trade agreements the EFTA has negotiated with third parties; however, the four EFTA states and the third party country must agree to the UK's entry into the agreement.[15] Thus, if the UK does not get approval from the third party within the trade agreement, the UK retains the right to negotiate its own free trade agreement with that or any other country. Of course there will be domestic political opposition to the UK accepting an obligation to implement the four freedoms, particularly free movement of persons; however, analysis of such concerns and how Britain can overcome them will be analyzed in a later section within this paper. In order to accede to the EFTA Convention, the British

---

[11] *See Id.*

[12] Treaty of Lisbon, article 50(3), *opened for signature* Dec. 13, 2007, *adopted* Dec. 1, 2009.

[13] Donegan, *Brexit: Options for and Impact of the Possible Alternatives to EU Membership*, Shearman & Sterling, 7.

[14] *See id.* at 5

[15] Fladgate LLP, *Brexit-Where Next*, https://www.fladgate.com/assets/uploads/2016/06/Post-Brexit-briefing-June-2016.pdf (last visited Dec. 11, 2016).

Parliament would have to pass an agreement ratifying the Convention, after a minimum of 21 days for parliamentary debate. This would be consistent with the Constitutional Reform and Governance Act of 2010 that mandated that international treaties be ratified by Parliament before entering into force.[16] Lastly, all four EFTA states would have to approve of the UK joining the EFTA before its accession would be complete.[17] While a few EFTA states, namely Norway and Iceland, have offered tepid support to the UK joining the EFTA, as they are concerned their influence might wane if a country as economically dominant as the UK joins, it seems likely that they would ultimately approve the UK's entry as they would get a chance to form their own free trade agreement with the UK as well as use the UK's dominant economic position in Europe to provide gravitas and influence to the EFTA as a whole, particularly when the EFTA negotiates with the EU.[18]

The second interpretation of Article 128 of the EEA Agreement is that the UK could remain an EEA member nothwithstanding Brexit. The Preamble of the EEA Agreement explicitly refers to the UK as a "contracting party" as it does to the other EU and EFTA states, while Article 127 of the EEA Agreement provides a specific withdrawal process for any "contracting party" in that they must provide at least 12 months written notice before withdrawing.[19] As such, the UK could assert that because it is explicitly labeled within the agreement as a "contracting party," even if it is no longer a EU member, its withdrawal from the EEA is governed under Article 127, and thus it has not withdrawn from the EEA Agreement unless it has fulfilled the requirements of written consent under Article 127. Consequently, the UK would argue under this interpretation that because it has not given written consent to withdraw under Article 127, it does not need to accede to the EFTA Convention and then re-apply to join the EEA in order to retain access to the EU's single market.

With two seemingly opposite interpretations present for Article 128, it is important to note that international law under the Vienna Convention of the Law of Treaties provides tools for accurately interpreting both the letter and spirit of the law.[20] The UK is a party to the convention so the convention is binding upon it, and even if it was not, much of the Treaty constitutes customary international law and thus is binding upon the UK. Under Article 31 of the Treaty, Treaties are

---

[16] Ciaran Burke, Olafur Isberg Hanneson & Kristin Bangsund, *Life on the Edge: EFTA and the EEA as a Future for the UK in Europe,* European Public Law, 77-78.

[17] *Id.*

[18] *See id.*

[19] Donegan, Shearman & Sterling, at 7.

[20] Vienna Convention on the Law of Treaties art. 31, *opened for signature May 23,* 1969.

interpreted in good faith according to the ordinary meaning of their terms and in light of their context, while Article 26 contains the principle of *pacta sunt servada* meaning that the object and purpose of every treaty in force is binding upon the parties to it and must be performed by them in good faith.[21] Applying these principles, it is evident that the second interpretation of Article 128 does not suffice as the UK likely does not meet the standard of good faith and looking at the treaty's context as prescribed under Articles 26 and 31.

For instance, the context and overall justification for the EEA Agreement was to develop an economic understanding between the EU member states and the EFTA states, in which the scope of the agreement was limited to territories where EU treaties and protocols apply as well as specifically Norway, Liechtenstein, and Iceland, since Switzerland has its own approach and economic relationship with the EU. This is evidenced by the fact that Article 126 of the EEA Agreement clearly states, "The Agreement shall apply to the territories to which the Treaty establishing the European Economic Community is applied…and to the territories of Iceland, the Principality of Liechtenstein, and the Kingdom of Norway…."[22] Thus, if the UK invoked article 50 and was no longer a EU member, and simultaneously refused to join the EFTA but still presented itself as a party to the EEA Agreement, then the scope of the agreement would be expanded to include a country that was not part of the original scope, justification, and context for the Agreement. Consequently, it seems likely that the first interpretation of the UK having to re-apply to join the EEA Agreement is more valid.

After passing a legal agreement ratifying the EFTA Convention, the UK would then be allowed to gain access to the EU Single Market by applying for EEA Membership under Article 128. Joining the EEA Agreement would require the UK to negotiate with the contracting parties, in which the UK would have to agree to the four freedoms, accept jurisdiction of the EFTA Court and EFTA Surveillance Authority, and allow EU law to be enacted in the UK even though the UK would have no formal role in EU institutions including the EU Parliament, EU Commission, and the European Court of Justice.[23] Lastly, the UK would need approval from all of the EU member states as well as Norway, Liechtenstein and Iceland, in order to join the EEA.[24] While countries such as France have spoken out against a specialized

---

[21] Vienna Convention on the Law of Treaties art. 26, *opened for signature May 23*, 1969.

[22]   Fladgate   LLP,   *Brexit-Where*   *Next*, https://www.fladgate.com/assets/uploads/2016/06/Post-Brexit-briefing-June-2016.pdf (last visited Dec. 11, 2016).

[23] Burke, Hanneson & Bangsund, at 77-78.

[24] *Id.*

bespoke agreement between the UK and the EU, there are numerous alternative options the UK can utilize to negotiate access to the Single Market through EEA membership, retain some political goals of the "leave campaign," and convince the other EU countries that they would benefit from such a deal. Such options include negotiating over financial passporting rights, trade agreements, and the UK agreeing to pay higher fees and payments to the EU. Further analysis of the legal basis for the UK's ability to negotiate such an agreement with the EU member states will be specified later in this paper, after analysis of key features of substantive law within the EEA Agreement.

II. THE EFFECT OF EEA LAW AND CONCERNS OVER UK SOVEREIGNTY

Politicians ranging from David Cameron to Boris Johnson have criticized the Norway Model as an option for the UK post-Brexit primarily because on the face of it it seems that the UK would lose a great deal of sovereignty.[25] Specifically, as a party to the EEA Agreement via status as an EFTA member state, the UK would still have to provide financial contributions to the EU; however, it would not have any seats in the EU parliament, no power to appoint judges to the ECJ, and no representation in the EU Commission.[26] Moreover, Article 106 of the EEA Agreement dictates that law relevant to the single market passed by the EU Parliament is then incorporated into the EEA Agreement via the EEA Joint Committee, and thus incorporated into the respective domestic law of the EFTA states.[27] While, on the face of it, it seems that the UK stands to lose sovereignty, as it would have no representation but would still have to contribute financial payments and abide by EU law, this criticism ignores the multitude of legal provisions built into the EEA Agreement that limit such loss of sovereignty and provide the UK opportunities to exercise its influence within the EU legislative process.

First of all, the EEA Agreement explicitly calls for the EFTA states to have a role in the decision-making process of various EU institutions, including the EU Parliament and the EU Commission. Specifically, Articles 99-101 require that as soon as EFTA relevant legislation is being considered, the EU Commission shall call on experts from EFTA states, just as it would from EU states, to consult the Commission.[28] Furthermore, any EFTA state can demand a preliminary exchange of views within the EFTA Joint Committee to make its views heard, and EFTA states also have access to and the right to participate in various

---

[25] Allen & Overy, *Brexit Law-EEA membership: what does it mean*, (July 2016), 6-7.
[26] European Economic Area Agreement, article 105-06, *adopted* Jan. 1, 1994.
[27] *Id.*
[28] *Id.* at Article 99

program committees, referred to as comitology, as established by the EU Commission to analyze specific issues or policy fields.[29] At first glance, it may seem that these options provided to EFTA states are minor concessions, and that without any formal representation in EU institutions, the EFTA states in reality do not have influence on legislation or regulations promulgated by the EU Commission and EU Parliament. However, there is significant evidence indicating that Norway and Liechtenstein have been able to make their legislative preferences known, and ultimately use their lobbying opportunities within the EEA Agreement to achieve policy goals. For example, the Norwegian EEA Review Committee's 2012 report *Utenfor og innenfor-Norges avtaler med eu 193-194* provides several instances where the Norwegian Government was able to use its role in the EU's decision making process to cause favorable changes to EU regulations involving consumer protection, while non-governmental organizations representing Norwegian interests were able to lobby for changes to EU reforms in a wide array of policy fields, namely requiring blood alcohol levels to be below 0.5 in member states, adopting an emissions trading scheme in line with Norway's domestic carbon level targets, obtaining a 6 month testing period for low sulphur fuel ports, and abandoning anti-dumping measures against Norwegian domestically farmed trout and salmon.[30] With the UK being a much more dominant economy than that of Norway, it seems reasonable to assert that the UK would have even more influence in utilizing the opportunities provided to the EFTA states within the EEA Agreement to have a role during consideration of new EU regulations and directives.

Even after the decision-making process, the EEA Agreement provides EFTA states other opportunities as well to preserve their sovereignty. EU relevant law is not itself binding on EFTA states until the EEA Joint Committee has incorporated the legislation into the EEA Agreement.[31] However, the Joint Committee consists of members appointed by both the EFTA states as well as the EU, and there have been historical instances where various EFTA states have been able to negotiate with the EU states to permit exceptions or changes to the EU law, and include such exceptions within the Joint Committee Decision that is then incorporated into the EEA Agreement.[32] For example, Liechtenstein received an exception from the Joint Committee for an EU directive regarding veterinary regulations, while in 2007 Iceland was able to negotiate an exception to the EU bans and limitations on fishmeal to

---

[29] *Id.* at Article 81.
[30] Burke, Hanneson & Bangsund, at 84, FN 63-64.
[31] European Economic Area Agreement, article 102, *adopted* Jan. 1, 1994.
[32] Burke, Hanneson & Bangsund, at 84.

ruminants and the feed ban regarding Transmissible Spongiform Encephalopathies.[33]

One last option for preserving domestic sovereignty under the EEA Agreement is for an EFTA state to seek a reservation to a specific EU regulation or directive that the country opposes.[34] Under Article 102, if a state seeks a reservation, then all parties are obligated to work in good faith towards reaching an agreement; however, if they fail, then the matter is referred to the Joint Committee.[35] If within six months the matter is not resolved, then the relevant portion of the EEA Agreement that relates to the disputed EU regulation is suspended, which would likely cause the EFTA state to be locked out of the Single Market for the policy areas or products affected by the regulation.[36] As such, because the consequence of losing access to the single market is so significant, the use of the reservation option has never been exercised by any EFTA state; however, it can be argued that if the UK were to invoke the Article 102(5) reservation option, it might have a better chance of reaching an amenable agreement with the Joint Committee because of its leverage as one of Europe's dominant political and economic states. Unlike Norway, Iceland or the other EFTA states, the UK would come to any negotiation with the Joint Committee with far more influence due to its economy and political stature and thus might be able to use the right of reservation as a way of amending any EU regulation to meets its policy objectives. Since only EU law that is related to the EEA (i.e., related to the single market, four freedoms, merger control, state aid, etc.) is incorporated through the Joint Committee, the UK can use the opportunities afforded to it through the decision-making process and under Article 102(5) to achieve its interests regarding such policy issues, and at the same time be free to enact its own domestic policies on a wide array of subjects not regulated under the EEA Agreement such as common agriculture, justice and home affairs, taxation, etc.

In regards to jurisprudence, opponents of the Norway model argue that because the UK would be unable to appoint judges on the ECJ, the UK would be bound to ECJ case law without any representation, as the EFTA Court is bound to follow ECJ precedent via homogeneity rules under the EEA Agreement.[37] While this may be the case, there are

---

[33] *Id.* at FN 65.

[34] European Economic Area Agreement, article 102(5), *adopted* Jan. 1, 1994.

[35] Bergasel, Annie, *Norway's Planned Reservation of the Third European Postal Directive and the Future of the European Economic Agreement*, Stanford—Vienna Transatlantic Technology Law Forum, 2012, 7-8.

[36] *Id.*

[37] Carl Baudenbacher, *After Brexit: Is the EEA an option for the United Kingdom*, Speech at King's College-London, https://1exagu1grkmq3k572418odoooym-wpengine.netdna-

important caveats that indicate that the UK would be able to preserve its sovereignty under the jurisdiction of the EFTA Court. For example, if the EFTA Court finds one of the EFTA states in noncompliance with the EEA, the Court cannot demand a penalty payment from the state. Most importantly, Article 34 of the Surveillance and Court Agreement, the legal agreement that founded the EFTA Surveillance Authority and EFTA Court, only gives the EFTA Court the right to issue non-binding advisory opinions, rather than binding legal opinions as the ECJ is provided.[38] Hence, there is no formal obligation of domestic courts of the EFTA states to refer to and be bound by EFTA Court case law.[39] Lastly, the EFTA Court has been found to make rulings on a variety of legal issues before the ECJ did so; consequently, in such cases the EFTA Court is not bound by ECJ case law, and more importantly the ECJ has made over 150 references to 250 EFTA Court opinions. Thus, it is evident that the UK can use its appointment powers for EFTA judges to help craft opinions on legal issues that are then referenced to and ultimately utilized by ECJ judges on new and emerging legal issues.[40] All in all, this indicates that in regards to jurisprudence, were the UK to implement the Norway Model, the sovereignty of the UK's domestic judicial system would likely be preserved under the jurisdiction of the EFTA Court as prescribed under the EEA Agreement.

III. SUBSTANTIVE IMPACTS OF IMPLEMENTING THE NORWAY MODEL IN KEY POLICY AREAS

A. IMMIGRATION

After concerns over sovereignty, the second major issue with the Norway Model is the fact that implementing the model would require the UK to accept the four freedoms, which include the free movement of persons. Data shows that a third of individuals voted in favor of Brexit because of their concerns over immigration; thus, it is argued that the acceptance of the free movement of persons as required under Article 1 of the EEA would be politically unfeasible.[41] However, there is precedent for an EFTA state to negotiate and obtain a narrow bespoke agreement that limits the state's acceptance of the free movement of

---

ssl.com/wp-content/uploads/2016/11/Baudenbacher-Kings-College-13-10-16.pdf, Oct. 13, 2016, 11-12.

[38] *See id.*

[39] *Id.*

[40] *Id.*

[41] Kim Hjelmgaard and Gregg Zoroya, *Exploding UK immigration helped drive 'Brexit' vote*, USA Today, http://www.usatoday.com/story/news/world/2016/06/28/exploding-uk-immigration-helped-drive-brexit-vote/86424670/, June 28, 2016.

persons. For example, in 1998, Liechtenstein and the EEA Joint Committee negotiated an agreement that enabled Liechtenstein to restrict the number of residence permits it could issue to Norwegian, Icelandic and EU nationals.[42] Specifically, under Protocol 15 of the EEA Agreement, Liechtenstein was required to restrict new resident permits with a minimum floor of 1.75% of the total number of Icelandic, Norwegian and EU nationals present in the country. More importantly, Liechtenstein could restrict issuing residence permits to only those individuals who had "prior authorization entry, residence, and employment," in which the agreement is reviewed every five years.[43] Protocol 15 provided special status to Liechtenstein in regards to immigration primarily because of Liechteinstein's unique circumstances, specifically a small population of 37,000 and territory of only 160 square kilometers.[44]

While it is not fully clear if the UK could obtain a limited bespoke agreement analogous to that of Liechtenstein regarding the immigration restriction, the UK could certainly seek legal justification for it, mainly through EFTA and EEA member status and then by beginning to negotiate with the EFTA Joint Committee, which is represented by both EFTA and EEA members. The UK could argue that the main justification for Liechtenstein's special status through Protocol 15 is not really unique as Liechtenstein's population density is 266.4/km² similar to that of the UK, which is 232.8/km².[45] Moreover, the most important basis for Liechtenstein's special agreement is that the agreement is reviewed on a rolling five-year basis so the UK could also argue for a transitional agreement, with the goal of letting the political polarization over immigration subside by the time the agreement comes up for review. Consequently, Protocol 15 demonstrates that there is clear legal precedent for the UK to seek and negotiate over limited exceptions to the free movement of persons.

---

[42] Stephen Booth, *As the UK searches for a post-Brexit plan, is the EEA a viable option,* Open Europe, http://openeurope.org.uk/intelligence/britain-and-the-eu/as-the-uk-searches-for-a-post-brexit-plan-is-the-eea-a-viable-option/, (Aug. 4, 2016).

[43] Peter Spence & Szu Ping Chan, *Safe Harbour: why the Norway option could take the risk out of Brexit,* The Telegraph, http://www.telegraph.co.uk/business/2016/06/18/safe-harbour-why-the-norway-option-could-take-the-risk-out-of-br/, (June 28, 2016).

[44] *See id.*

[45] Booth, http://openeurope.org.uk/intelligence/britain-and-the-eu/as-the-uk-searches-for-a-post-brexit-plan-is-the-eea-a-viable-option/, (Aug. 4, 2016).

B. FINANCIAL PASSPORTING RIGHTS

A significant impact of Brexit on the financial services industry is regarding passporting rights. Passporting rights refer to EU regulations and directives that allow EEA banks, brokers, fund managers, and other financial services entities that are regulated in the UK the right to establish branches or subsidiaries and conduct cross-border activity into other EEA member states without further regulatory approval.[46] The legal basis for Passporting rights is based on the EU freedom of establishment and free movement of services grounded in Articles 34, and 36-39 of the EEA Agreement, as well as various EU directives.[47] Under the Norway model, access to the single market would continue, and thus financial entities based in the UK, particularly the City of London, would continue their financial Passporting rights when dealing with branch offices or other cross-border activity.

In contrast, the negative economic effects of a loss of Passporting rights in a "hard" Brexit would be significant. In the absence of passporting rights, financial entitites looking to conduct cross-border activity in the UK would be governed under the EU third-party regulatory regime.[48] Specifically, under this regime, for financial industry entities of the various EU states to access markets in the UK, the entities would have to not only meet their own country's regulatory requirements, but also meet an equivalency standard test, in which the UK's regulatory regime regarding co-operation arrangements, the European Securities & Markets Authority as well as anti-money laundering and tax arrangements, must be deemed equivalent to that of the EU.[49] Thus, under a "hard Brexit," the UK would have to negotiate over any policy areas where the UK parliament refused to incorporate already existing EU law.[50] Realistically speaking, such "equivalence determination" negotiations are not guaranteed and can take a long time, thus negatively impacting UK financial entities as well as any financial sector participants of the EU who have branches or cross-border activity based in London. With the financial sector playing a large part in the UK's economy, namely 3% of jobs, 8% of income, and 11% of total British tax revenue, the delay and no guarantee of achieving passporting rights in a "hard" Brexit would undoubtedly pressure various UK and EU financial service entities to move their branches out of London, rather than go through the administrative and technical costs of meeting

---

[46] Donegan, Shearman & Sterling (March. 2016), 6-7.
[47] *Id.*
[48] *See id.*
[49] *Id.* at 7.
[50] *Id.*

new regulatory requirements in the UK.[51] Thus, the Norway Model approach would safeguard passporting rights for the financial industry, and allow London to maintain its status as the financial hub of Europe.

C. TRADE

Since the EEA is a free trade area, not a customs union such as the EU, third country imports crossing EU internal borders constitute duty free trade; however, imports crossing the EU and EEA border do not have duty free trade.[52] Thus, the EFTA states have the option of negotiating free trade agreements as a bloc as they have with 37 countries, or individual countries can negotiate unilateral free trade agreements.[53] In doing so, it would seem on the face of it that the Norway Model would provide a greater degree of flexibility in enabling the UK to selectively negotiate unilateral free trade agreements with third party countries, while at the same time benefitting from multi-lateral free trade agreements negotiated through the EFTA bloc as a whole. However, this understanding is not complete, as access to the single market serves as a key imitation on such flexibility regarding trade.[54] Specifically, free trade agreements contain several provisions dealing with non-tariff barriers such as food security and technical standards that are already determined under EU regulations, and thus incorporated into EEA law as per the Joint Committee.[55] Thus, even if the UK has the flexibility to initiate and negotiate over new trade agreements with other countries on a unilateral basis, it would likely be bound by EU law on such portions of a free trade agreement that are relevant to the single market. Nonetheless, on any issues not relevant to the single market and thus bound by EU law, the UK would have the independence to negotiate unilaterally with any country to achieve its interests.

This is within the context that there are very limited options for the UK in regards to establishing a tariff schedule with the World Trade Organization (WTO), if all else fails and the UK fails to emulate the Norway Model or a bespoke agreement. As a current EU member-state, the UK follows the EU's custom union tariff schedule that applies a common external tariff across all the EU member states.[56] Consequently,

---

[51] Richard Baldwin, *Brexit Beckons: Thinking ahead by leading economists*, Center for Economic & Policy Research, (Aug. 1, 2016), 9.

[52] Peter Holmes, *Roos and Rules: Why the EEA is not the same as membership of the single market*, UK Trade Policy Observatory, (Oct. 5, 2016), 1-2.

[53] Id.

[54] Booth, http://openeurope.org.uk/intelligence/britain-and-the-eu/as-the-uk-searches-for-a-post-brexit-plan-is-the-eea-a-viable-option/, (Aug. 4, 2016).

[55] *Id.*

[56] Simon Nixon, *Brexit Success Hinges on Global Goodwill*, Yale Global Online, (Aug. 7, 2016), 1-2.

the UK does not have its own WTO tariff schedule, and if it wanted to adopt its own schedule, WTO rules require that the UK obtain the unanimous consent of all 160 WTO members.[57] Thus, the easiest option for the UK would be to adopt the EU tariff schedule with the WTO, which would require that the UK negotiate with the EU on import quotas for various economic sectors such as agriculture, as well as obtain the unanimous consent of the 28 EU member-states.[58]

Additionally, there would be great complexity in regards to rules of origin principles that have the potential of negatively impacting small and medium sized businesses. Since the EFTA states are not a customs union, there is duty free access for goods originating in the EEA member states; however, any EFTA state can unilaterally impose its own tariffs on goods originating from third-party countries. The legal basis for this is found in Articles 8 and 48-50 of the EEA Agreement, which codifies the free movement of goods throughout the EFTA states. Usually, a product must contain 60% local value in order to receive duty free import status from the EFTA to the EU.[59] Under UK domestic law, the burden of proof on showing the 60% local value is on the exporter, in that "all materials are considered to be non originating unless you hold evidence to prove that they originate."[60] Consequently, implementing the Norway model would make it harder and more costly for exporters to meet such rules of origin requirements; since the UK would no longer be a part of the EU's tariff schedules, there would have to be some form of customs checks for any products travelling between the EU and the UK.[61] Such customs checks would be costly not only because prior to Brexit, exporters would not have faced such custom checks and thus have to adapt to them, but more importantly, exporters would likely face repercussions involving disrupted supply chains.[62] For instance, if an exporter produced a good in the EU, but used parts originating from the UK, then under the Norway Model, the exports might lose preferential status with third countries that have free trade agreements with the EU as the export would not necessarily be a EU locally produced product.[63] This is just one example of how enforcing new rules of origin between the UK as an EFTA member that does not have the tariff schedule of the EU would lead to increased costs for exports engaged in cross-border trade between the EU, the UK, and third-party countries. Nonetheless,

---

[57] *Id.*

[58] *Id.*

[59] Holmes, UK Trade Policy Observatory, (Oct. 5, 2016), 2.

[60] *Id.* at FN 8

[61] *Id.* at 2.

[62] *Id.*

[63] *Id.*

even if there is greater complexity and potential costs regarding rules of origin enforcement, the effect of trade within the Norway Model is part of a balancing test between the benefits of access to the single market, sustained financial passporting rights, and individual ability to negotiate unilateral free trade agreements against the drawbacks of higher costs ranging from rules of origin enforcement. Ultimately, the importance of the financial sector to the British economy, and economic benefits of the continued access to the single market are greater than the drawbacks to potential costs due to rules of origin enforcement. Thus, while the Norway Model would enable the UK to reap significant economic benefits, it is clear that there would be some potential disadvantages ranging from the enforcement of rules of origin.

IV. HOW THE UK CAN SEEK EXCEPTIONS SIMILAR TO THAT OF NORWAY IN ORDER TO MAKE IMPLEMENTATION OF THE NORWAY MODEL POLITICALLY AND ECONOMICALLY FEASIBLE

Ultimately, in order to seek a limited bespoke agreement with the EU, the UK will have to build upon precedent set by Norway and Liechtenstein. In 1998, during its negotiation process to join the EFTA and ultimately become a part to the EEA Agreement, the Norwegian government under Article 128 of the Agreement, negotiated with the EU specific exemptions for its agriculture and fisheries products. [64] Specifically, since Norway was focused on protecting its domestic fishing quotas and agricultural products, it wanted to insulate those industries from the free circulation of such products allowed under the EU. Thus, the EEA Agreement did not cover agriculture or fisheries. Instead, under Article 19, the Agreement calls for Norway and the other contracting parties to negotiate a transitional agreement that is reviewable every two years, in which Norway would be permitted to impose duties on agricultural products and not be subject to EU common fishing quotas within its waters.[65]

Similarly, the legal basis for Liechtenstein to negotiate an exception to the EU's mandated free movement of persons was through Article 128 of the EEA Agreement, allowing it to apply for EEA membership, and then negotiate through the EEA Joint Committee.[66] Specifically, Liechtenstein negotiated Protocol 15 to the EEA Agreement where Liechtenstein was permitted to limit the number of residence permits it issued annually to those individuals who had "prior authorization entry,

---

[64] Burke, Hanneson & Bangsund, at 87-88.
[65] *Id.*
[66] Spence & Chan, http://www.telegraph.co.uk/business/2016/06/18/safe-harbour-why-the-norway-option-could-take-the-risk-out-of-br/, (June 28, 2016).

residence, and employment."[67] During this negotiation, one key aspect of Protocol 15 that made its establishment more amenable to the EU representatives was that the agreement is reviewable every five years, and grants the EU the option to limit the exception based on changing economic or political circumstances.[68]

On the basis of these aforementioned exceptions granted to two of the four EFTA states, the UK could similarly apply for membership to become an EEA party under Article 128, and then negotiate a protocol analogous to Protocol 15, that would permit the UK to seek a limitation on the free movement of persons. Since immigration was such a potent reason for the success of the Leave campaign, the British government will have to most likely find a way to limit immigration in order to assuage such concerns. However, it is also evident that many EU states, particularly France, are weary of permitting a bespoke agreement for the UK, for fear that other states would then leave the EU and seek bespoke agreements as well. Pursuant to this, EEA membership of the UK and the consequent establishment of any protocol limiting immigration would need the unanimous approval of all the EU member states, which would be difficult in the face of the EU member states' concerns.[69]

Nonetheless, there are aspects of Article 19 and Protocol 15 that indicate the UK may have an adequate chance of achieving a limited bespoke agreement. First of all, the main component of both Article 19 and Protocol 15 is that both provisions are transitional and explicitly reviewable every certain number of years.[70] Incorporating a required time period for review and re-negotiation would likely assuage EU states' concerns, while at the same time allow UK politicians to publically boast that they were able to meet their constituents' goal of limiting immigration. Moreover, as the mandated review every certain number of years is done by the EFTA Joint Committee, the UK would be able to indicate its assertions and play an influential role in such deliberations since, as an EFTA member, it would be able to appoint individuals to the EFTA Court and Joint Committee. Additionally, the UK could offer to target its limitations on immigration, as Liechtenstein did in regards to residence permit quotas. As the location for several of Europe's greatest universities and academic institutions, the UK could allow for free movement of international students, and faculty whose immigration status is in flux right now as the UK government decides its steps post-Brexit. For example, it is estimated that 15% or more of all UK academic faculty and/or staff would be forced to leave their posts if the UK

---

[67] *See id.*
[68] *See id.*
[69] *See id.*
[70] Burke, Hanneson & Bangsund, at 88.

withdrew from the free movement of persons.[71] Thus, focusing on international university students and faculty would almost certainly be seen as a show of good faith across the EU, while also serving to sustain the British economy and prevent any threat of a brain drain. Additionally, just as Liechtenstein was able to negotiate a minimum floor of 1.75% residence permits per the total number of Icelandic, Norwegian and EU nationals present in the country, the UK could similarly push for limitations on the issuance of residence permits, which would assuage the British people's fears about permanent immigration, while at the same time be seen as compatible by the other EU states since there is precedent for such an agreement under Protocol 15.

Most importantly, the UK could also agree to pay a greater financial contribution than the other EFTA states do as part of the Norway Model. For example, under Article 82 of the EEA Agreement, EFTA states do not pay the required financial contributions to the EU budget that the EU member states do; instead, the amounts they pay are based on a proportionality test balancing out several factors including their GDP, participation in EU/EEA trans-boundary projects, and other factors.[72] Since, the UK would be seeking a limited bespoke agreement that enables them to restrict free movement of persons, the UK could agree to increase their financial contribution to that as if they were a regular EU member, or pay the smaller EFTA state contribution, but then make a legally binding obligation to participate and provide resources to the various EU and EFTA sponsored programs such as Horizon 2020, Justice Cosme, Erasmus or the European Regional Development Fund, in addition to others. Lastly, the UK could agree to provide its military forces to support and participate in a EU Army, as supported by a number of other EU states. Currently, under the EEA Agreement, there is no mention of any EU standing army, and for the past decade, the UK has been a consistent opponent to any EU standing army proposals primarily because it sees a EU standing army as unnecessary due to the presence of NATO.[73] However, with the election of Donald Trump as President of the United States, who as a candidate repeatedly vowed to limit the United States' role in NATO, as well as a politically resurgent Vladamir Putin of Russia, it is likely that the UK's

---

[71] Jon Henley, Stephanie Kirchgaessner and Philip Oltermann, *Brexit fears may see 15% of UK university staff leave, group warns*, The Guardian, https://www.theguardian.com/education/2016/sep/25/brexit-may-force-15-of-staff-at-uk-universities-to-leave-warns-group, (Sept. 25, 2016).

[72] European Economic Area Agreement, article 82, *adopted* Jan. 1, 1994.

[73] Jonathan Marcus, *Brexit vote revives dream of EU army*, The British Broadcasting Corporation (BBC) News, http://www.bbc.com/news/world-europe-37317765, (Sept. 9, 2016).

reversal on now supporting a EU standing army would lend credence to any negotiation with the EU member states to obtain a limited bespoke agreement, and would be seen as a sign of good faith during the negotiations.

Ultimately, the UK has a legal basis in seeking these exceptions, mainly through the Article 128 negotiation process of applying for EEA membership, and the continued use of Protocol 15 and Article 19 as precedent for exceptions given to Norway and Liechtenstein. However, in order to ensure that other EU states would not have their own "Brexit" in the hopes of seeking bespoke agreements, the UK government would likely have to limit their negotiated agreement to immigration or other targeted policy areas such as Protocol 15. In return for the exceptions, the UK would have to offer a wide array of concessions ranging from increased financial contributions to supporting a standing EU army.

CONCLUSION

The main justification for preserving the UK's access to the single market and the subsequent benefits of a continued relationship with the EU is borne from the fact that today almost half of the UK's total imports and exports come from the EU, as compared to only 14% in 1959.[74] Consequently, with the UK deciding on which model to base its post-Brexit relationship with the EU, it is imperative that the UK implement an approach that preserves the UK's international trade with the EU, mainly through the single market. Fortunately, the Norway Model provides an effective legal basis for the UK to maintain the benefits of having a continued relationship with the EU, mainly access to the single market and preserved financial passporting rights while at the same time allowing for the UK to have greater autonomy over a wide array of subject areas such as foreign affairs, and taxation. Although there are drawbacks, such as the complexities involving rules of origin enforcement, acceptance of free movement of persons, and loss of some influence in formulating EU policies and legislation, ultimately the Norway Model allows for the UK government to minimize negative economic impacts from Brexit while at the same time achieving specific goals of the "leave" campaign. The EEA Agreement contains multiple provisions, mainly Article 128, as well as Article 19 and Protocol 15 that provide a legal basis for the UK to negotiate with the EEA Joint Committee, and allay concerns regarding immigration and influence with EU institutions that proponents of a "hard" Brexit might have. Although many British political leaders have ruled out the Norway Model over

---

[74] Burke, Hanneson & Bangsund, at 95.

such aforementioned concerns, this paper demonstrates that the British government would indeed benefit from the Norway Model, as well as have an effective legal basis to negotiate over potential concerns under the EEA Agreement.

CHAPTER 4: IS THE UNITED KINGDOM STILL A PARTY TO THE EU–KOREA FTA AFTER BREXIT?

JIN WOO (JAY) KIM

INTRODUCTION

On June 23, 2016, Britons voted in a referendum on Britain's membership in the European Union ("EU") to leave the union, which is referred to as Brexit. The new prime minister of the United Kingdom ("UK"), Theresa May, is preparing for Brexit negotiations and declared that the country will invoke Article 50 of the Treaty on European Union ("TEU")[1] before the end of March 2017.[2] This means that the UK may leave the EU as early as March 2019.[3] As no one really knows how Brexit negotiations will proceed and what the relationship between the EU and the UK will look like, the British decision to exit the EU poses a serious threat to the global economy. Especially, it brings significant uncertainty to international trade, posing questions for the EU-UK trade relationship and UK's membership status in the World Trade Organization ("WTO"). It is also unclear how the post-Brexit trade relationship between the UK and non–EU countries will change. Currently, the UK's external trade with third-party countries is governed by 53 trade agreements that the EU had concluded on behalf of its Member States. The UK, as a Member State of the EU, is a party to these trade deals and enjoys the benefits of these agreements.

The Free Trade Agreement between the EU and the Republic of Korea ("Korea") ("EU-Korea FTA") provides a good example.[4] After the EU and Korea signed the trade deal on October 6, 2010, the EU-Korea FTA provisionally entered into force as of July 1, 2011 with the

---

[1] Consolidated Version of the Treaty on European Union art. 50, Jun. 7, 2016, 2016 O.J. (C 202/01) 43 [hereinafter TEU].

[2] Jessica Elgot, *Theresa May to trigger article 50 by end of March 2017*, The Guardian, Oct. 2, 2016, https://www.theguardian.com/politics/2016/oct/01/theresa-may-to-propose-great-repeal-bill-to-unwind-eu-laws.

[3] TEU art. 50(3). The provision sets out a two-year deadline for concluding an withdrawal agreement. In principle, this time limit can be extended if all 27 other EU Member States agree to do so.

[4] Free Trade Agreement between the European Union and its Member States on the one part, and the Republic of Korea, on the other part, May 14, 2011, 2011 O.J. (L 127) 6 [hereinafter EU–Korea FTA].

exception of provisions relating to the criminal enforcement of intellectual property rights[5] and certain provisions of the Protocol on Cultural Co-Operation.[6] The agreement, which is the EU's first trade agreement with an Asian country, is characterized by its far-reaching and comprehensive nature.[7] The trade pact eliminates custom duties on nearly all products and provides for progressive liberalization of trade in services covering all modes of supply.[8] In addition, the trade agreement covers a broad range of issues that go beyond traditional aspects of trade liberalization.[9] It includes strict regulations on sensitive trade-related areas such as government procurement (Chapter 9), intellectual property rights (Chapter 10), competition policy (Chapter 11), transparency (Chapter 12), sustainable development (Chapter 13), and even cultural cooperation (Protocol 3).

However, in the aftermath of Brexit, the question arises whether the UK still remains a party to the EU-Korea FTA. There are two contradictory viewpoints. If the UK stays as a party to the FTA, the UK will be able to avoid painful trade negotiations with Korea and continue to enjoy benefits from the free-trade pact without any substantial change.[10] On the other hand, if the UK ceases to be a party to the agreement, it must negotiate a new trade deal and will lose all the benefits if it fails to do so in a timely manner.[11] The answer to this question is

---

[5] EU–Korea FTA arts. 10.54 to 10.61.

[6] EU–Korea FTA, Protocol on Cultural Co-operation arts. 4(3), 5(2), 6(1), 6(2), 6(4), 6(5), 8, 9, and 10.

[7] *Report From the Commission to the European Parliament and the Council: Annual Report on the Implementation of the EU-Korea Free Trade Agreement*, at 2, COM (2015) 139 final (Mar. 26, 2015), available at: http://trade.ec.europa.eu/doclib/docs/2015/march/tradoc_153271.pdf.

[8] European Commission, *The EU-Korea Free Trade Agreement in Practice* 3 (2011), available at: http://trade.ec.europa.eu/doclib/docs/2011/october/tradoc_148303.pdf.

[9] *Id.*

[10] Lorand Bartels, *The UK's Status in the WTO Post-Brexit* 5-6 (Sept. 20, 2016) (unpublished manuscript); No scholars specifically argue that the UK would remain a party to the EU –Korea FTA in the post-Brexit era. However, in the context of the UK's membership status in the WTO after Brexit, Bartels contends that the UK has separate rights and obligations of an original WTO Member and will continue to possess all of these rights and obligations once it leaves the EU. He reasons that the UK was a contracting party to the General Agreement on Tariffs and Trade ("GATT") 1947 before its accession to the EU and accepted the WTO Agreement and other multilateral trade agreements by ratification. Although this argument cannot be simply exported to justify the application of the EU–Korea FTA to the UK after Brexit, these two issues touch upon the key question of what it means to be a party to international agreements.

[11] James Robinson, James Lindop, Elizabeth Coleman & Monica Zejden-Erdmann, *Brexit and Trade law: The Implications of a Vote to Leave the EU*, Lexology (Jul. 28, 2016), http://www.lexology.com/library/detail.aspx?g=8abc5130-6a3e-4387-aee8-a148c0d6395d.

momentous as it will have profound implications. This matters not only to the post-Brexit trade relationship between the UK and Korea but also with other non-EU countries. Broadly speaking, this analysis would be applicable to EU international agreements dealing with policy areas other than trade where the UK participated as a Member State of the EU.

This paper aims to analyze the applicability of the EU-Korea FTA to the UK after Brexit and its ramifications on the post-Brexit UK trade relationship with Korea and other non-EU countries. For clarification, post-Brexit refers to a period starting from the date of entry into force of a withdrawal agreement between the EU and the UK.[12] This paper contends that the UK ceases to be a party to the EU-Korea FTA in the post-Brexit era and should negotiate a new trade deal with Korea in order to acquire preferential market access. This article proceeds in three parts. Section I examines the language of Article 1.2 of the EU-Korea FTA where it defines "the Parties" to this agreement and then identifies a correct rule of interpretation, namely the Vienna Convention on the Law of Treaties ("Vienna Convention").[13] Section II provides a legal interpretation of Article 1.2 of the EU-Korea FTA in accordance with the guidance under Article 31 of the Vienna Convention and refutes counterarguments that the UK alone can be a party to the trade agreement after Brexit. Finally, Section III analyzes implications of this interpretation on the post-Brexit UK trade relationship with Korea and other non-EU countries as well as its relationship with the rest of the world outside the scope of trade.

I.   ARTICLE 1.2 OF THE EU-KOREA FTA: ITS LANGUAGE AND RULE OF INTERPRETATION

Article 1.2 of the EU-Korea FTA defines the parties to the agreement. It is a key provision that determines whether the UK remains a party to the EU-Korea FTA after Brexit. Article 1.2 provides the definition of "EU Party" as follows:

[T]he Parties mean, on the one hand, the European Union or its Member States or the European Union and its Member States within their respective areas of competence as derived from the Treaty on European Union and the Treaty on the Functioning

---

[12] TEU art. 50(3).
[13] Vienna Convention on the Law of Treaties, May 23, 1969, 1155 U.N.T.S. 331 [hereinafter Vienna Convention].

of the European Union (hereinafter referred to as the "EU Party"), and on the other hand, Korea.[14]

A. THE LANGUAGE OF ARTICLE 1.2 OF THE EU-KOREA FTA

Due to the ambiguous nature of the provision, it is not clear at first sight who precisely is the EU Party to the EU-Korea FTA. Article 1.2 begins by dividing the EU Party into three different categories by using the conjunction "or." The provision suggests three possible options of the EU Party: (i) the EU alone; (ii) Member States alone; or (iii) the EU and its Member States together. If we stop the reading of Article 1.2 here, it may be argued that the UK alone can be a party to the EU-Korea FTA in its own right and remains a party to the agreement even after Brexit. However, the provision then continues by stating "respective areas of competence as derived from the Treaty on European Union and the Treaty on the Functioning of the European Union." The TEU and the Treaty on the Functioning of the European Union ("TFEU")[15] are two of the three fundamental EU Treaties that form the basis of EU law.[16] The TEU provides for overarching aims of the EU, means to achieve these objectives, institutional framework and general principles on the EU's external action. The TFEU sets out details with specific provisions on internal market, four free movements (i.e. goods, persons, services and capital), and fields of EU action and policies. That is, the latter part of Article 1.2 provides further guidance on the interpretation of three sub-categories of the EU Party by making reference to the TEU and the TFEU.

To sum up, Article 1.2 can be disentangled into two sections: the former where it divides the EU Party into three sub-categories and the latter where it mentions "respective areas of competence" with reference to the EU Treaties. In order to ensure a concrete interpretation of Article 1.2 of the EU-Korea FTA, it is crucial to give equal importance to both the former and latter part of the provision.

---

[14] EU–Korea FTA art. 1.2.

[15] Consolidated Version of the Treaty on the Functioning of the European Union, Jun. 7, 2016, 2016 O.J.   (C 202/01) 47 [hereinafter TFEU].

[16] TEU art. 1(3) provides that:

> "The Union shall be founded on the present Treaty and on the Treaty on the Functioning of the European Union (hereinafter referred to as 'the Treaties'). Those two Treaties shall have the same legal value . . . ."

B. RULE OF INTERPRETATION: ARTICLE 31 OF THE VIENNA CONVENTION

Article 14.16 of the EU-Korea FTA provides general principles of interpreting the trade agreement, which reads as follows:

> Any arbitration panel shall interpret the provisions referred to in Article 14.2 in accordance with customary rules of interpretation of public international law, including those codified in *the Vienna Convention on the Law of Treaties* . . . . (emphasis added).[17]

Consequently, the correct interpretation of provisions of the EU-Korea FTA, including Article 1.2, should be in accordance with the general rule of treaty interpretation under the Vienna Convention. Particularly, Article 31 of the Vienna Convention states:

> 1. A treaty shall be interpreted in good faith in accordance with *the ordinary meaning to be given to the terms of the treaty* in their *context* and in the light of *its object and purpose.*
> 2. *The context* for the purpose of the interpretation of a treaty *shall comprise, in addition to the text, including its preamble and annexes*: . . . . (emphasis added).[18]

Article 31(1) of the Vienna Convention articulates three main elements of the general rule of interpretation: *text, context* and *object and purpose.* The first element requires giving an ordinary meaning to the "terms of the treaty." In order to establish the ordinary meaning of the term, international judicial bodies often turn to dictionaries and start with the dictionary meaning of that term.[19] Then, the terms of the treaty have to be interpreted "in their context." This is because the ordinary meaning of the words can only be determined when considered in the context in which they are used.[20] Article 31(2) of the Vienna Convention clarifies that the entire text of the treaty has to be taken into account as context which includes title, preamble and annexes and any protocol to it. Lastly, Article 31 requires a treaty interpreter to consider the terms "in the light of the object and purpose" of the treaty. To determine the object and purpose of a treaty, interpreters can have

---

[17] EU – Korea FTA art. 14.16.
[18] Vienna Convention art. 31.
[19] Oliver Dörr, *Article 31: General Rule of Interpretation, in* Vienna Convention on the Law of Treaties: A Commentary 542 (Oliver Dörr & Kirsten Schmalenbach eds., 2012).
[20] *Id.*, at 543.

recourse to the title or the preamble of the agreement.[21] Generally, a reading of all its substantive provisions will be required to establish the object and purpose.[22] It is important to note that the general rule of interpretation under the Vienna Convention does not create a sequence of separate tests to be applied in a hierarchical order.[23] Rather, it requires treaty interpreters to take into account all the three factors simultaneously for one holistic interpretation.[24]

Therefore, an appropriate interpretation of Article 1.2 of the EU-Korea FTA relies on considering all the three elements of treaty interpretation and reading the provision as a whole.

II. INTERPRETATION OF ARTICLE 1.2 OF THE EU-KOREA FTA

This section interprets Article 1.2 of the EU-Korea FTA pursuant to the general rule of treaty interpretation under Article 31 of the Vienna Convention. Concerning the former part of the provision where it differentiates the EU Party into three sub-categories, the paper focuses on the term "Member State" and then interprets this term in its context by examining the Preamble, the Title and another provision in the EU-Korea FTA. The emphasis should be put on the conjunction "and" expressed in the Preamble and the Title. Then, with regard to the latter part of Article 1.2, the paper analyzes the meaning of "competence" in connection with two EU Treaties and views the provision as a whole by linking this to the term "Member State."

A.   THE FORMER PART OF ARTICLE 1.2: "MEMBER STATES OF THE EUROPEAN UNION"

In order to answer whether the UK still remains a party to the EU-Korea FTA in the post-Brexit period, we must start with interpreting the term "Member States" in the former part of Article 1.2. We begin with the ordinary meaning of "Member States" by looking at the dictionary. The relevant dictionary definition of "member" is "each of the individuals, countries, etc., belonging to or forming a society or assembly." [25] The pertinent definition of "state" is "a nation; a

---

[21] *Id.*, at 546.

[22] *Id.*

[23] *Id.*, at 541; *See* also Panel Report, *United States—Sections 301–310 of the Trade Act 1974*, ¶ 7.22, WT/DS152/R (Dec. 22, 1999).

[24] Appellate Body Report, *China—Measures Affecting Trading Rights and Distribution Services for Certain Publications and Audiovisual Entertainment Products*, ¶ 176, WT/DS363/AB/R (Dec. 21, 2009); *See* also Peter Van Den Bossche & Werner Zdouc, The Law And Policy of the World Trade Organization 187-188 (3rd ed. 2013).

[25] 1 New Shorter Oxford English Dictionary on Historical Principles ("Dictionary vol. 1") 1748 (6th ed. 2007).

commonwealth; a community of people occupying a defined area and organized under one government."[26] When read together, the ordinary meaning of "member states" would be "nations that form or belong to an association or an organization." Here, however, we need to pay heed to the fact that the term "Member States" in Article of the 1.2 EU-Korea FTA is a proper noun with capital letters. This indicates that the term is used to designate unique entities with particular definition.

This brings us to consider the entire text of the agreement as "context," which includes preamble and title, as stated in Article 31 of the Vienna Convention. Preamble to the EU-Korea FTA lists the then 27 Member States[27] of the EU and defines "Member States of the European Union" as follows:

> Contracting Parties to the Treaty on European Union and the Treaty on the Functioning of the European Union, hereinafter referred to as the "Member States of the European Union."[28]

According to this definition, Member States of the EU in the context of the EU-Korea FTA are "Contracting Parties to the TEU and TFEU." In other words, if a current Member State is no longer a contracting party to the EU Treaties, the country ceases to be a party to the EU-Korea FTA. This is exactly what will happen to the UK when it terminates its membership from the EU. From the date when the withdrawal agreement enters into force, the TEU and TFEU do not apply to the UK[29] and the exiting country loses its status as the "Member State of the European Union." Consequently, the UK is not a party to the EU-Korea FTA after Brexit.

As a counterargument, the British government might contend that the UK still remains a party to the trade agreement regardless of Brexit and reason that the UK is listed in the Preamble as parties to the agreement along with the then other 26 Member States of the EU.[30]

---

[26] 2 New Shorter Oxford English Dictionary on Historical Principles ("Dictionary vol. 2") 3005 (6th ed. 2007).

[27] When the EU–Korea FTA was concluded on October 6, 2010, Croatia was not a Member State of the EU. Croatia became the 28th member of the EU on July 1, 2013. The trade agreement was amended in 2014 to allow Croatia to benefit from the same preferences as the other 27 EU Member States. Articles 1 and 2 of the Additional Protocol to the EU–Korea FTA to Take Account of the Accession of Croatia to the European Union provides that Croatia becomes a Party to the Agreement and that Croatia shall be added to the list of Parties to the EU–Korea FTA.

[28] EU–Korea FTA preamble.

[29] TEU art. 50(3).

[30] The relevant part of the Preamble to the EU–Korea FTA reads as follows:

However, this argument should fail because it overlooks the definition of "Member States of the European Union." Although the UK is enumerated in the list of the Member States of the EU in the Preamble to the EU-Korea FTA, it is listed there only as a Member State. Again, once the withdrawal agreement takes effect, the UK is no longer a Member State of the EU. Thus, the fact that the UK is listed in the Preamble would lose its legal meaning and its name should be eliminated from the list in a potential subsequent amendment of the trade agreement between the EU and Korea. In other words, the list alone cannot save the UK from being kicked out from the EU-Korea FTA.

Moreover, Article 15.15(1) of the EU-Korea FTA, which governs the territorial application of the agreement, confirms that the UK ceases to be a party to the trade agreement in the post-Brexit period. The provision reads as follows:

> This Agreement shall apply, on the one hand, to the territories in which the Treaty on European Union and the Treaty on the Functioning of the European Union are applied and under the conditions laid down in those Treaties, and, on the other hand, to the territory of Korea. References to "territory" in this Agreement shall be understood in this sense, unless explicitly stated otherwise.[31]

The EU-Korea FTA only applies to the territories where the EU Treaties take effect and those of Korea. Upon the UK's divorce with the EU, the TEU and the TFEU are no longer applicable to the territories of the UK. Thus, the trade agreement ceases to apply to the UK after Brexit. If we ignore the definition of the "Member State of the European Union" and interpret that the UK remains a party to the EU-Korea FTA in the post-Brexit era, this would render Article 15.15(1) void and cause inconsistent interpretation among different provisions in the trade agreement. Since any interpretation that would render parts of

---

"The Kingdom of Belgium, the Republic of Bulgaria, the Czech Republic, the Kingdom of Denmark, the Federal Republic of Germany, the Republic of Estonia, Ireland, the Hellenic Republic, the Kingdom of Spain, the French Republic, the Italian Republic, the Republic of Cyprus, the Republic of Latvia, the Republic of Lithuania, the Grand Duchy of Luxembourg, the Republic of Hungary, Malta, the Kingdom of the Netherlands, the Republic of Austria, the Republic of Poland, the Portuguese Republic, Romania, the Republic of Slovenia, the Slovak Republic, the Republic of Finland, the Kingdom of Sweden and the United Kingdom of Great Britain and Northern Ireland."

[31] EU–Korea FTA art. 15.15(1).

the treaty superfluous or diminish their practical effect is to be avoided,[32] a potential counterargument from the British argument cannot be accepted.

B. THE PREAMBLE AND THE TITLE: THE CONJUNCTION "AND"

As mentioned above, it is unclear who exactly is the EU Party under Article 1.2 of the EU-Korea FTA because the provision divides the EU Party into three different categories by using the conjunction "or": (i) the EU alone; (ii) Member States alone; or (iii) the EU and its Member States together. However, when reading Article 1.2 along with the Title and the Preamble to the EU-Korea FTA, it becomes self-evident that the only possible interpretation is that the EU and its Member States collectively are parties to the agreement. This is because both the Title and the Preamble connects the EU and its Member States by employing the conjunction "and." The Title of the EU-Korea FTA reads as follows:

> Free Trade Agreement between the European Union *and* its Member States, of the one part, and the Republic of Korea, of the other part (emphasis added).[33]

Likewise, the Preamble follows the structure of the Title. After enumerating the then 27 Member States of the EU and providing the definition of "Member States," the Preamble uses the conjunction "and" to make a link between Member States and the EU. The relevant part of the Preamble states as follows:

> Contracting Parties to the Treaty on European Union and the Treaty on the Functioning of the European Union, hereinafter referred to as the "Member States of the European Union", *and* the European Union (emphasis added).[34]

The related dictionary definition of "and" is "coordinating, introducing a word, phrase, clause, or sentence which is to be taken side by side with, along with, or in addition to, that which precedes."[35] This shows that the EU and its Member States are interlinked for the purpose of defining the EU Party to the EU-Korea FTA. In other words, both the EU and its Member States collectively are parties to the trade agreement. If drafters intended that either the EU alone or a Member

---

[32] Dörr, *supra* note 19, at 545.
[33] EU–Korea FTA title.
[34] EU–Korea FTA preamble.
[35] Dictionary vol. 1, *supra* note 25, at 79.

State alone can be a party to the trade agreement, they would have instead used the conjunction "or" in the Title and the Preamble.

Yet, as another counterargument, the British government may assert that the UK alone can be a party of the EU-Korea FTA by putting an emphasis on the conjunction "or" used in the main text of Article 1.2. The UK may put this argument forward emphasizing the dictionary definition of "or," which is "introducing the second of two, or all but the first or only the last of several, alternatives." [36] However, this argument is not persuasive since it focuses only on one part of Article 1.2, namely the conjunction "or." This reasoning fails to examine the provision as a whole by ignoring not only the rest of the provisions but also its context such as the title and the preamble. This approach goes against the general rule of treaty interpretation under Article 31 of the Vienna Convention. While this paper disregards the possible counterargument from the UK, it nevertheless does not provide satisfactory explanation on why Article 1.2 of the EU-Korea FTA uses the conjunction "or" and does not follow the same framework as the Title and the Preamble. In order to answer this, we now turn to the latter part of the provision.

C. THE LATTER PART OF ARTICLE 1.2: "RESPECTIVE AREAS OF COMPETENCE"

The latter part of the Article 1.2 of the EU-Korea FTA, where it mentions "respective areas of competence" with reference to the TEU and the TFEU, provides further guidance to interpreting the former part of the provision. Here, the keyword is "competence." While the relevant dictionary meaning of "competence" is "power, ability, capacity, to do, for a task etc.," [37] this term must be understood with reference to the TEU and the TFEU as stated in Article 1.2. The term "competence" is a term in EU law that is used to describe the division of competence between the EU and its Member States. [38] Since the EU is a supranational organization consisting of its Member States, the EU has only the competences conferred on it through the TEU and the TFEU. [39] This is so-called the principle of conferral. Under this principle, the EU may act only within the limits of the competences conferred upon by its Member States via the EU Treaties. [40] Article 2 of the TFEU establishes three categories of EU competence: (i) exclusive competence of the

---

[36] Dictionary vol. 2, *supra* note 26, at 2016.
[37] Dictionary vol. 1, *supra* note 25, at 470.
[38] Paul Craig & Gráinne De Búrca, EU Law: Text, Cases and Materials 73 (6th ed. 2015).
[39] TEU arts. 3(6) and 5(1).
[40] TEU art. 5(2).

Union;[41] (ii) shared competence between the Union and the Member States;[42] and (iii) competence only to support, coordinate or supplement actions of the Member States ("supportive competence"). [43] Then, Articles 3, 4 and 6 of the TFEU respectively specify the relevant policy areas that fall under each competence. First, the EU has the exclusive competence, for example, over customs union and common commercial policy. [44] Second, the EU exercises the shared competence with its Member States on environment and area of freedom, security and justice.[45] Lastly, the EU enjoys the supportive competence in the field of culture, tourism and education.[46] Competences not conferred upon the EU through the TEU and the TFEU remain with its Member States.[47]

In accordance with the division of competence between the EU and its Member States, different parts of the EU-Korea FTA would be placed in different categories of EU competence.[48] The vast majority of the EU-Korea FTA would fall under the scope of the EU exclusive

---

[41] TFEU art. 2(1). When the EU has exclusive competence, only the EU can legislate and adopt binding acts.

[42] TFEU art. 2(2). When competences are shared between the EU and its Member States, both the EU and its Member States can legislate and adopt binding acts. However, under shared competence, insofar as policy areas are occupied by EU law, the Member States lose their competence. Thus, EU action supersedes Member State competence.

[43] TFEU art. 2(5). When the EU has competence to support, coordinate or supplement the actions of the Member States ("supportive competence"), both the EU and its Member States can act. This looks similar to shared competence, but there is a huge difference. Under supportive competence, the EU may not adopt legally binding acts that require the Member States to harmonize their laws and regulations. In other words, EU action cannot supersede Member State competence.

[44] TFEU art. 3(1).

[45] TFEU art. 4(2).

[46] TFEU art. 6.

[47] *Id.*

[48] For the precise analysis to decide which parts of the EU – Korea FTA fall within the EU exclusive competence and which remain within the remit of the Member States, we would have to go through every single provision of the agreement. However, for the purpose of this paper, analysis has been made simply on the ground of titles of chapters and protocols. The precise examination may result in different categorization. The exact same question in the context of the EU–Singapore FTA ("EUSFTA") is pending before the European Court of Justice ("ECJ"). *See* Opinion 2/15, Request for an opinion submitted by the European Commission pursuant to Article 218(11) TFEU. Before submitting a proposal to the Council for the signature and conclusion of the envisaged FTA with Singapore, the European Commission requested an Opinion from the ECJ on whether the EU has the necessary competence to sign and conclude alone the EUSFTA. The case has been filed on July 10, 2015 and Eleanor Sharpston, an Advocate-General ("AG") of the ECJ, issued an Advisory Opinion on December 21, 2016. AG Sharpston considered that, as a mixed agreement, the EUSFTA could only be concluded by the EU and the Member States acting jointly. Sharpston's opinion does not bind the ECJ, but the Luxembourg-based court generally follows the views of AG in a majority of cases.

competence because its subject matters mainly deal with the common commercial policy.[49] Under EU law, the common commercial policy includes the conclusion of tariff and trade agreements relating to trade in goods and services, and the commercial aspects of intellectual property, foreign direct investment, the achievement of uniformity in measures of liberalization, export policy and measures to protect trade such as those to be taken in the event of dumping or subsidies.[50] The EU-Korea FTA covers elimination of custom duties (Annex 2-A), liberalization of trade in services (Chapter 7), intellectual property rights (Chapter 10), trade remedies (Chapter 3), technical barriers to trade (Chapter 4) and sanitary and phytosanitary measures (Chapter 5).

On the other hand, small parts of the EU-Korea FTA would fall within the scope of either shared competence or supportive competence because the agreement goes well beyond a mere reduction of tariffs. The trade pact includes provisions that ensure the respect of social, environmental, developmental and cultural standards in order to foster trade. The EU would have to share its competence with the Member States with regard to Chapter 13 (Trade and Sustainable Development) of the EU-Korea FTA since the chapter partly deals with matters that are environmental in nature. [51] Provisions relating to the criminal enforcement of intellectual property rights in Chapter 10 (Intellectual Property Rights) [52] would also fall within the sphere of the shared competence since they touch upon area of freedom, security and justice.[53] In addition, the EU would have supportive competence when it comes to Protocol 3 on Cultural Cooperation of the EU-Korea FTA. The Protocol 3 sets a framework to engage in policy dialogue on culture and audiovisual issues, and cooperate in facilitating exchanges regarding cultural activities.[54]

While the EU-Korea FTA does not govern policy areas where competence remains exclusively with the Member States (i.e. national security),[55] the effective enforcement of the trade pact heavily depends on the cooperation, and if necessary the compliance, of Member States.[56] Pursuant to the principle of sincere cooperation, the EU and Member States are required to closely cooperate, in full and mutual

---

[49] TFEU art. 3(1)(e).

[50] TFEU art. 207(1).

[51] TFEU art. 4(2)(e). The EU has shared competence in the policy area of environment.

[52] EU–Korea FTA arts. 10.54 to 10.61.

[53] TFEU art. 4(2)(j). The EU enjoys shared competence in the policy area of freedom, security and justice.

[54] TFEU art. 5(c). The EU exercises supportive competence in the policy area of culture.

[55] TEU art. 4(2).

[56] Craig, *supra* note 38, at 377.

respect,[57] both in the process of negotiation and conclusion and in the fulfillment of the commitments entered into.[58] While this duty of sincere cooperation applies regardless of whether the EU-Korea FTA governs the sphere of the common commercial policy where the EU enjoys the exclusive competence or subject matters where both the EU and its Member States have competence, this is particularly essential in the case of the latter category.

D. THE HOLISTIC INTERPRETATION OF ARTICLE 1.2 OF THE EU-KOREA FTA

With this background on how the EU and its Member States divide their competence under EU law as well as how different parts of the EU -Korea FTA would be categorized into respective EU competence, the whole structure of Article 1.2 of the EU-Korea FTA finally becomes clear. The former part of the provision where it divides the EU Party into three different categories by using the conjunction "or" reflects how competence could be distributed between the EU and its Member States in the context of the EU-Korea FTA. The first category "the European Union" in Article 1.2 indicates that the EU enjoys the exclusive competence in the sphere of the common commercial policy under which the vast majority of the trade agreement is covered. The second classification "its Member States" suggests that Member States play a crucial role for the strong enforcement of the trade pact. The last group "the European Union and its Member States" demonstrates that both the EU and its Member States exercise competence to act in policy areas that fall within either shared or supportive competence of the EU.

Drafters could have stated only "the European Union and its Member States" in Article 1.2 as they have done in the Title and the Preamble. It appears that they took extra efforts to spell it out in the main provision to clarify what this phrase exactly means. At the same time, drafters were wise to state only "the European Union and its Member States" in the Title and the Preamble since this captures all the three possible options when it comes to the division of competence under EU law. This also prevented the language of the Title and the Preamble from being overly complicated.

In fact, the wording "the European Union and its Member States" points out the key feature of the EU-Korea FTA as a "mixed agreement." Under EU law, mixed agreements are agreements to which both the EU

---

[57] TEU art. 4(3).
[58] Opinion 1/94, Competence of the Community to Conclude International Agreements Concerning Services and the Protection of Intellectual Property, 1994 E.C.R. I-5267, ¶ 107.

and the Member States are contracting parties because not all matters in the agreement fall exclusively within EU competence or exclusively within Member State competence.[59] A mixed agreement will also be used in a case where competence over the subject matter of the agreement is shared between the EU and the Member States.[60] As mentioned above, the EU-Korea FTA covers the subject matters that belong to the EU exclusive, shared and supportive competence. From the procedural perspective, the trade deal between the EU and Korea as a mixed agreement had to be ratified by all the Member States each according to their own constitutional requirements,[61] alongside the consent by the European Parliament.[62] It took more than four years for all the Member States to ratify the EU-Korea FTA. Italy was the last Member State to ratify the trade pact on September 14, 2015. Upon ratification from all the Member States, the Council adopted a decision concluding the EU-Korea FTA on October 1, 2015[63] and the agreement fully entered into force as of December 13, 2015.[64]

Taking into account all these factors, the correct interpretation of Article 1.2 of the EU-Korea FTA is that the EU and its Member States collectively are parties to the trade pact. While the EU and its Member States would exercise their competences, either exclusively or jointly depending on different subject matters covered by the agreement in accordance with the TEU and the TFEU, this does not change the fact that the EU and its Member States as a whole are the parties. In other words, neither the EU nor a Member State alone is a party to the EU-Korea FTA. Allowing this would make the whole agreement inutile since it simply disregards the division the competence under EU law and thus impedes the enforcement of the EU-Korea FTA. Therefore, the UK ceases to be a party to the EU-Korea FTA from the date when the withdrawal agreement enters into force.

---

[59] Craig, *supra* note 38, at 352.

[60] *Id.*

[61] The Directorate General for Trade of the European Commission ("DG Trade"), *Trade Negotiations Step by Step* 6 (2013), available at: http://trade.ec.europa.eu/doclib/docs/2012/june/tradoc_149616.pdf.

[62] TFEU art. 218(6)(a)(v).

[63] Press Release, Council of the EU, EU-South Korea Free Trade Agreement Concluded, 691/15 (Oct. 1, 2015), available at: http://www.consilium.europa.eu/en/press/press-releases/2015/10/01-korea-free-trade/.

[64] The free trade agreement is provisionally applied in the EU until all EU Member States ratify it. While waiting for the completion of the ratification, the EU–Korea FTA provisionally entered into force as of July 1, 2011.

III. The Implication on the Post-Brexit UK Trade Relationship and Far-reaching Impact Beyond the Realm of Trade

This interpretation of Article 1.2 of the EU-Korea FTA has significant implications on the UK's future trading relationship not only with Korea, but also with other non-EU countries. More importantly, from a broad perspective, this approach has profound implications on the British relationship with the rest of the world that goes beyond trade.

A. UK TRADE RELATIONSHIP WITH KOREA AFTER BREXIT

The interpretation of Article 1.2 of the EU-Korea FTA is a huge blow to the post-Brexit trade relationship between the UK and Korea. In accordance with solid legal interpretation, the UK is no longer a party to the EU-Korea FTA after Brexit. The exiting country must negotiate a new trade deal with Korea if it wants to enjoy the similar market access it had enjoyed under the EU-Korea FTA. However, this can be a lengthy and complicated task. To start with, bilateral trade negotiation should only start after the UK officially terminates its membership of the EU, which would be March 2019 at the earliest. Since the EU has exclusive competence over common commercial policy, only the EU has the power to negotiate and enter into trade agreements with non-EU countries. Even after the UK triggers Article 50 of the TEU, the country still remains as a Member State of the EU and is bound by the EU law until the withdrawal agreement takes effect. Therefore, the UK is prohibited from entering into trade negotiation at least for the upcoming two years.[65]

Even if the UK were allowed to embark on any negotiation, Korea would not be interested in hammering out a new trade deal with the UK in a hurry. The Asian trading partner will first want to know what trade arrangement the UK has with the EU and whether the UK keeps its access to the EU single market.[66] In other words, Korea will not wish to grandfather any concessions into a bilateral agreement with the UK

---

[65] It remains ambiguous what would happen if the UK ignores the EU exclusive competence and embarks on trade negotiations, especially informal talks, with non-EU countries.

[66] For non-EU countries, it is important that the UK maintains its access to the EU single market, because it eliminates not just tariffs but also non-tariff barriers. For instance, in September 2016, the Japanese government published a paper urging the UK to negotiate a post-Brexit deal that safeguards UK's current rights in single market. George Parker, *Japan calls for 'soft' Brexit—or companies could leave UK*, Sept. 4, 2016, https://www.ft.com/content/98dd4eb4-729f-11e6-bf48-b372cdb1043a; The memo on Japan's Brexit demands is posted on its ministry of foreign affairs website, available at: http://www.mofa.go.jp/files/000185466.pdf.

alone.[67] Once negotiation initiates, more obstacles are expected. It will be extremely difficult for the UK to include as favorable terms as those that the EU currently has with Korea, given the UK's smaller market and significantly reduced bargaining power.[68] The UK would end up with signing a less comprehensive trade agreement with Korea compared to the EU-Korea FTA.

If no arrangement were reached, the post-Brexit trade relationship between the UK and Korea would have to fall back under WTO rules. This would be hurtful for both parties. Under WTO commitments, the UK and Korea would be permitted to increase tariffs that are currently zero under the EU-Korea FTA to an average of 13.3 percent for British exports to Korea and an average of 5.3 percent for Korean exports to the UK.[69] Given these negative influences, some British lawyers and legislators suggest that both the UK and Korea make a reciprocal statement that the two trading partners intend to continue to operate terms of the EU-Korea FTA on a mutual basis until further notice.[70] They point out that this would provide for the smooth and continued flow of trade between the UK and Korea after Brexit while not requiring any additional negotiation. [71] However, while this temporary policy might be helpful to maintain the status quo, it is certainly not based on, if not against, the definite legal interpretation Article 1.2 of the EU-Korea FTA. Since the agreement simply does not allow the UK to be a party to the trade deal after Brexit, application of the EU-Korea FTA to the exiting country takes the risk of rendering the whole agreement inutile and void. In addition, we need to consider the EU's position concerning this issue since the EU concluded the agreement on behalf of its Member States. It is unlikely that the EU would agree with this compromise because this would open a path for the UK to cherry-pick.

---

[67] *The Tories and Brexit: Mind Your Step*, The Economist, Oct. 8, 2016, at 53.

[68] Robinson, *supra* note 11.

[69] WTO & International Trade Centre (ITC) & United Nations Conference on Trade and Development (UNCTAD), *World Tariff Profiles 2015*, 75 and 98 (2015), available at: https://www.wto.org/english/res_e/booksp_e/tariff_profiles15_e.pdf; These figures represents the simple average of applied most-favored nation ("MFN") tariffs. The UK's tariff schedule is subject to change after Brexit depending on how it sets out its own tariff schedules. The current figure of 5.3 percent only demonstrates the EU's tariffs as its Member States are prohibited from having its own tariff schedule.

[70] *Brexit and International Trade*, Lawyers for Britain, http://www.lawyersforbritain.org/int-trade.shtml (last visited Feb. 24, 2017); Iain Mansfield, *The IEA Brexit Prize: A Blueprint for Britain–Openness not Isolation*, Institute of Economic Affairs (Apr. 9, 2014), https://iea.org.uk/publications/research/the-iea-brexit-prize-a-blueprint-for-britain-openness-not-isolation.

[71] Mansfield, *supra* note 70, at 14.

B. POST-BREXIT UK TRADE RELATIONSHIP WITH OTHER NON-EU COUNTRIES

This interpretation of Article 1.2 of the EU-Korea FTA that the UK ceases to be a party to the trade agreement after Brexit is applicable to other trade agreements concluded by the EU on behalf of its Member States. Most of the recent EU trade agreements were signed as mixed agreements where both the EU and the Member States are contracting parties. Consequently, these agreements contain a provision similar to, if not the same as, Article 1.2 of the EU-Korea FTA. For instance, Article 6(1) of the Trade Agreement between the EU and Colombia and Peru ("EU-Columbia/Peru Trade Agreement") contains the exact same language as Article 1.2 of the EU-Korea FTA, which reads as follows:

> "[P]arty" means the European Union or its Member States or the European Union and its Member States within their respective areas of competence as derived from the Treaty on European Union and the Treaty on the Functioning of the European Union (hereinafter referred to as the 'EU Party'), or each of the signatory Andean Countries . . . .[72]

Similar provisions are found in the EU trade agreement with Mexico[73] and association agreements[74] with Algeria, Egypt and Chile.[75]

---

[72] Trade Agreement between the European Union and its Member States, of the one part, and Colombia and Peru, of the other part art. 6(1), Dec. 21, 2012, 2012 O.J. (L 354) 6.

[73] Economic Partemership, Political Coordination and Cooperation Agreement between the European Community and its Member States, of the one part, and the United Mexican States, of the other part art. 55, Oct. 28, 2000, 2000 O.J. (L 276) 54.

[74] Bart Van Vooren & Ramses A. Wessel, EU External Relations Law: Text, Cases and Materials 63-64 (2014); Pursuant to Article 217 TFEU, the EU has concluded numerous *association agreements* with non-EU countries or international organizations in order to establish "an association involving reciprocal rights and obligations, common action and special procedure". An association agreement is the EU's main instrument to bring third-party countries closer to EU standards and norms. In fact, association agreements were often used as a first step towards accession and many of the current members first enjoyed an association status. In other cases, they were the follow-ups of so-called cooperation agreements which may be concluded on the basis of Article 212 TFEU. Association agreements comprises four general chapters: Common Foreign and Security Policy; Justice and Home Affairs; the Deep and Comprehensive Free Trade Area; and a fourth chapter covering a range of issues including the environment, science, transportation, and education. Free trade agreement is a core component of many association agreements.

[75] Euro-Mediterranean Agreement establishing an Association between the European Community and its Member States, of the one part, and the People's Democratic Republic of Algeria, of the other part ("EU– lgeria Association Agreement") art.106, Oct. 10, 2005, 2005 O.J. (L 265) 2; Euro-Mediterranean Agreement establishing an

This means that the UK and non-EU trading partners who already had concluded trade pacts with the EU will face the same problem described above. The UK is no longer a party to these trade agreements from the moment the withdrawal agreement takes effect. The UK and other non-EU countries must negotiate a new trade deal if they want to avoid higher tariffs relying on WTO rules. These negotiations could be slow, complex and cantankerous. As mentioned, negotiations with non-EU trading partners will be able to begin only after the UK withdraws from the EU and settles its trade relationship with the EU. In the immediate aftermath of the Brexit referendum in June 2016, there was discussion about the possibility for the UK to quickly negotiate trade agreements with existing trading partners (i.e. Korea, Mexico) and new ones with India, China and Brazil.[76] However, third-party countries have so far shown scant interest in negotiating new trade deals with the UK.[77] Only a few countries, such as Australia, New Zealand and the United States, expressed interest in striking trade deals with the UK.[78] Moreover, it is dubious whether the UK would have the capacity to conduct a plethora of negotiations simultaneously. As a result, Brexit will cause a huge gaping hole in its international trade regime and the long-term damage to the British and global economy will be grave.

C. POST-BREXIT UK RELATIONSHIP WITH REST OF THE WORLD BEYOND THE REALM OF TRADE

Unfortunately, the worst news has yet to come for the UK. The interpretation of Article 1.2 of the EU-Korea FTA has far-reaching, and somewhat terrifying, implications, which go beyond the post-Brexit UK trade relationship with non-EU countries. This is because, from a broad viewpoint, this interpretation concerns what it means to be a party to EU international agreements that were concluded as mixed agreements. The EU has concluded 1,149 bilateral and multilateral agreements with non-EU countries or international organizations, which cover a range of policy areas such as development, aviation, agriculture, fisheries, energy,

---

Association between the European Communities and their Member States, of the one part, and the Arab Republic of Egypt, of the other part art. 88, Sept. 9, 2004, 2004 O.J. (L 304) 39; Agreement establishing an association between the European Community and its Member States, of the one part, and the Republic of Chile, of the other part art.197, Dec. 30, 2002, 2002 O.J. (L 352) 62.

[76] Chad Bown, *Brexit: An Impossibly Complex Task for the UK's New Trade Negotiators?*, Peterson Institute for International Economics (Sept. 7, 2016), https://piie.com/commentary/op-eds/brexit-impossibly-complex-task-uks-new-trade-negotiators.

[77] *India and Britain: A Cooler Climate*, The Economist, Nov. 12, 2016, at 55.

[78] *Negotiating Post-Brexit Deals: Trading Places*, The Economist, Feb. 4, 2017, at 48.

visa and human rights.[79] Among these EU international agreements, more than 100 agreements are signed as mixed agreements where both the EU and the Member States are contracting parties. The following agreements are a few examples:

- Euro-Mediterranean Aviation Agreement between the European Union and its Member States, of the one part, and the Hashemite Kingdom of Jordan, of the other part ("EU-Jordan Aviation Agreement");[80]
- Agreement establishing the General Fisheries Commission for the Mediterranean (GFCM);[81] and
- Convention on Early Notification of a Nuclear Accident (with International Atomic Energy Agency).[82]

These agreements, as mixed agreements, include the provision that defines parties to the treaties as "the European Union or its Member States, or the European Union and its Member States," which is the same as Article 1.2 of the EU-Korea FTA. For example, Article 1(7) of the EU-Jordan Aviation Agreement defines contracting parties as follows:

Contracting Parties shall mean, on the one hand, the European Union or its Member States, or the European Union and its Member States, in accordance with their respective powers, and, on the other hand, Jordan.[83]

Applying the solid interpretation of Article 1.2 of the EU-Korea FTA to the relevant provision of these EU international agreements, means that the UK ceases to be a party to these hundreds of international agreements after Brexit. Unless there is an alternative way to interpret the provision as the UK still remains a party to these treaties in the post-Brexit era, the only way to recapture all these agreements is to negotiate new ones. However, it will be almost impossible for the UK to swiftly negotiate and conclude a vast number of new agreements, either with non-EU countries or international organizations, that govern different

---

[79] *Treaties Office Database*, European External Action Service (EEAS), http://ec.europa.eu/world/agreements/SimpleSearch.do (last visited Feb. 24, 2017).

[80] Euro-Mediterranean Aviation Agreement between the European Union and its Member States, of the one part, and the Hashemite Kingdom of Jordan, of the other part, Dec. 6, 2012, 2012 O.J. (L334) 3.

[81] Agreement establishing the General Fisheries Commission for the Mediterranean (GFCM), Jul. 4, 1998, 1998 O.J. (L.190) 37.

[82] Convention on Early Notification of a Nuclear Accident, Nov. 30, 2005, 2005 O.J. (L314) 22.

[83] EU – Jordan Aviation Agreement art. 1(7).

policy areas beyond the realm of trade.[84] This is worrisome as it will bring about tremendous chaos, not only for the UK, but for the rest of the world. Britons certainly didn't expect this butterfly effect when they voted to leave the EU.

CONCLUSION

On the basis of the thorough analysis of Article 1.2 of the EU-Korea FTA, the UK ceases to be a party to the trade agreement as soon as the withdrawal agreement between the EU and the UK takes effect. Article 1.2 can be divided into the two parts: the former where it divides the EU Party into three sub-categories, namely (i) the EU; (ii) Member States; and (iii) the EU and its Member States, and the latter where it mentions "respective areas of competence" with reference to the TEU and the TFEU. For the solid interpretation of Article 1.2, we must abide by the general rule of treaty interpretation under Article 31 of the Vienna Convention, as mandated by Article 14.16 of the EU-Korea FTA.

To start with, in the aftermath of Brexit, the UK fails to meet the definition of "Member States" under Article 1.2, which is defined as "Contracting Parties to the TEU and the TFEU" in the Preamble. From the date when the withdrawal agreement enters into force, the TEU and TFEU do not apply to the UK and the exiting country loses its status as the "Member State of the European Union." Furthermore, when reading Article 1.2 in connection with the Title and the Preamble to the EU-Korea FTA, it becomes clear that the EU and its Member States collectively are parties to the agreement. It is because both the Title and the Preamble connect the EU and its Member States by employing the conjunction "and." However, this does not provide adequate explanation as to why Article 1.2 still uses the conjunction "or," along with "and," in the main text, not following the same framework as the Title and the Preamble which use only the conjunction "and."

The latter part of the Article 1.2 of the EU-Korea FTA, where it mentions "respective areas of competence" with reference to the TEU and the TFEU, provides further guidance to interpret the former part of the provision. The term "competence" is a term in EU law that is used to describe the division of competence between the EU and its Member States. The EU only enjoys three types of competences conferred on it via the TEU and TFEU: (i) exclusive competence; (ii) shared competence; and (iii) supportive competence. Competences not conferred upon the

---

[84] Guillaume Van der Loo & Steven Blockmans, *The Impact of Brexit on the EU's International Agreements*, Centre for European Policy Studies (Jul. 15, 2016), https://www.ceps.eu/publications/impact-brexit-eu%E2%80%99s-international-agreements#_ftn2.

EU through the TEU and the TFEU remain with its Member States. The usage of conjunction "or" in the former part of Article 1.2 reflects how competence could be distributed between the EU and its Member States in the context of the EU-Korea FTA. In accordance with the division of competence between the EU and its Member States, different parts of the EU-Korea FTA would be placed in different categories of EU competence. The fact that both the EU and its Member States exercise their respective competence in the EU-Korea FTA demonstrates its key feature as a "mixed agreement" where the EU and the Member States are contracting parties. Given all these elements together, the correct interpretation of Article 1.2 of the EU-Korea FTA is that the EU and its Member States collectively are parties to the trade pact. To sum up, the UK alone cannot be a party to the trade agreement with Korea after Brexit.

This interpretation of Article 1.2 of the EU-Korea FTA has widespread and worrisome implications on the UK's future trading relationship with Korea and other non-EU countries. As the UK is no longer a party to the EU-Korea FTA and other trade agreements concluded by the EU on behalf of its Member States, the departing country must negotiate new trade deals with its non-EU trading partners. These negotiations will be slow, complicated and unprecedented. First and foremost, the UK and its non-EU counterparts will be able to embark on trade negotiations legally only after the UK withdraws from the EU, which will be March 2019 at earliest. In addition, other countries will not rush to conclude new trade deals with the UK until they figure out what trade arrangement the UK has with the EU and whether the UK keeps its access to the EU single market. Considering the UK's smaller market and reduced bargaining power, the UK will end up with signing less comprehensive trade agreements.

To make things worse, the implication of this interpretation goes far beyond the trade in the post-Brexit era. It is because, from a broad viewpoint, this interpretation concerns what it means to be a party to EU international agreements that were concluded as mixed agreements. The UK is a party to more than 100 EU international agreements signed as mixed agreements. These agreements cover a wide range of policy fields such as development, aviation, agriculture, fisheries, energy, visa and human rights. Like other trade agreements concluded by the EU on behalf of its Member States, the UK ceases to be a party to these international agreements after Brexit and must re-negotiate new treaties.

It is evident from this that Brexit will be a process, not a single event, involving hundreds of difficult choices. Divorce is seldom happy and countless more puzzles await. Although everything is uncertain about

Brexit at the moment, one thing is clear. The UK will certainly need more manpower in their negotiation team.

■   Appendix 1: The EU – Korea FTA and EU Competence

The Division of Competence Between the EU and its Member States under EU Law			
Types of competence	EU Exclusive competence	Shared competence	Supportive competence	Member States competence
Actors	EU only	EU and Member States	EU and Member States	Member States only
Relevant fields	Customs union; Competition rules necessary for the functioning of the internal market; [...] Common commercial policy	Internal market; [...] Environment; [...] Areas of freedom, security and justice [...]	[...] Industry; Culture; Tourism; Education, vocational training, youth and sport [...]	Competences not conferred upon the EU through the TEU and the TFEU (i.e. national security)
EU Treaties	TFEU arts. 2(1) and 3(1)	TFEU arts. 2(2) and 4(2)	TFEU arts. 2(5) and 6	TEU art. 4(2)
Chapters and Protocols in the EU – Korea FTA			
Chapters and Protocols	Elimination of custom duties (Annex 2-A); Liberalization of trade in services (Chapter 7); Intellectual property rights (Chapter 10); Trade remedies (Chapter 3); Technical barriers to trade (Chapter 4); and Sanitary and phytosanitary measure (Chapter 5).	Trade and Sustainable Development (Chapter 13); and Provisions relating to the criminal enforcement of intellectual property rights in Chapter 10	Protocol 3 on Cultural Cooperation	Enforcement on the basis of the principle of sincere cooperation

"EU Party" to the EU–Korea FTA					
Article 1.2	EU	or	EU and its Member States	or	Member States
Title; Preamble	EU and its Member States				

■ **Appendix 2: The Language of "EU Party" in Other Agreements**

EU International Agreements as "Mixed Agreements"

	Trade Agreements			Agreement Beyond the Realm of Trade
	EU – Korea FTA	EU – Columbia/Peru Trade Agreement	EU – Algeria Association Agreement	EU – Jordan Aviation Agreement
Title	Free Trade Agreement between the European Union and its Member States, of the one part, and the Republic of Korea, of the other part	Trade Agreement between the European Union and its Member States, of the one part, and Colombia and Peru, of the other part	Euro-Mediterranean establishing an Association between the European Community and its Member States, of the one part, and the People's Democratic Republic of Algeria, of the other part	EURO-MEDITERRANEAN AVIATION AGREEMENT between the European Union and its Member States, of the one part, and the Hashemite Kingdom of Jordan, of the other part
Preamble	(List of the Member States) *Contracting Parties to the Treaty on European Union and the Treaty on the Functioning of the European Union,* hereinafter referred to as the 'Member States of the European Union', *and* THE EUROPEAN UNION.	(List of the Member States) *Contracting Parties to the Treaty on European Union and the Treaty on the Functioning of the European Union,* hereinafter referred to as the 'Member States of the European Union', *and* THE EUROPEAN UNION.	(List of the Member States) *Parties to the Treaty establishing the European Community;* hereinafter referred to as 'Member States', *and* THE EUROPEAN COMMUNITY, hereinafter referred to as the 'Community', of the one part, and	(List of the Member States) *Contracting Parties to the Treaty on the European Union and the Treaty on the Functioning of the European Union,* hereinafter referred to as the 'Member States', *and* THE EUROPEAN UNION, of the one part, and THE HASHEMITE KINGDOM OF JORDAN, hereinafter referred to as 'Jordan'.

	of the one part, and THE REPUBLIC OF KOREA, hereinafter referred to as 'Korea', of the other part	of the one part, and THE REPUBLIC OF COLOMBIA (hereinafter referred to as "Colombia") and THE REPUBLIC OF PERU (hereinafter referred to as "Peru") Hereinafter referred to as the "signatory Andean Countries" of the other part	THE PEOPLE'S DEMOCRATIC REPUBLIC OF ALGERIA hereinafter referred to as , hereinafter referred to as 'Algeria', of the other part	of the other part,
Definition of Parties	Article 1.2 General Definitions Throughout this Agreement, references to: the Parties mean, on the one hand, the European Union or its Member States or the European Union and its Member States within their	ARTICLE 6 Definition of the Parties 1. For the purposes of this Agreement: "Party" means the European Union or its Member States or the European Union and its Member States within their Member States within their	Article 106 For the purposes of this Agreement, 'Parties' shall mean, on the one hand, the Community or the Member States, or the Community and its Member States, in accordance with their respective powers, and, on the other hand, Algeria.	Article 1(7) Definitions 'Contracting Parties' shall mean, on the one hand, the European Union or its Member States, or the European Union and its Member States, in accordance with their respective powers, and, on the other hand,

respective areas of competence as derived from the Treaty on European Union and the Treaty on the Functioning of the European Union (hereinafter referred to as the 'EU Party'), and on the other hand, Korea;	respective areas of competence as derived from the Treaty on European Union and the Treaty on the Functioning of the European Union (hereinafter referred to as the "EU Party"), or each of the signatory Andean Countries; "Parties" means, on the one hand, the EU Party and, on the other hand, each signatory Andean Country.	Jordan;

CHAPTER 5: BREXIT AND THE EAST AFRICAN COMMUNITY (EAC)—EUROPEAN UNION ECONOMIC PARTNERSHIP AGREEMENT (EPA)

APRIL KENT

I. INTRODUCTION

What is the legal effect of the UK's withdrawal from the European Union on the status of the East African Community-European Union Economic Partnership Agreement, and what options are open to the East African Community[1] once this occurs? Most recently, the EAC Heads of State Summit that had been scheduled for January 2017 was pushed to February after ministers failed to agree on the issues to be ratified.[2] This comes as the most recent development in a contentious struggle dating back to the beginning of the Economic Partnership Agreement negotiations nearly ten years ago. In the wake of this newest setback, this paper considers the avenues open to the East African Community with regard to the Economic Partnership Agreement, now that the UK has announced its intention to Brexit. Section II provides context for this issue by giving a brief history of the Agreement. Sections III and IV explore the legal effect of the UK withdrawal from the EU on the EPA as a mixed agreement. Lastly, Section V explains political and regional factors that are likely to affect any final decision of the East African Community.

II. BACKGROUND

Since the First Lomé Convention in 1975, the EU had granted non-reciprocal trade preferences to the African, Caribbean and Pacific (ACP) States.[3] This arrangement was successfully challenged under the General

---

[1] The EAC consists of Burundi, Kenya, Rwanda, Tanzania, Uganda, and most recently South Sudan (which formally acceded to the community in September of 2016). Note that South Sudan would not need to sign the EPA until it completes a two-year bloc membership assentation period.

[2] Mwita Weitere, *EAC Meet Delayed as EU Trae Deal Standoff Bites*, THE KENYA STAR (Jan. 5, 2017, 12:00 AM), http://www.the-star.co.ke/news/2017/01/05/eac-meet-delayed-as-eu-trade-deal-standoff-bites_c1481975.

[3] The ACP is composed of 79 African, Caribbean and Pacific states: Angola, Antigua and Barbuda, Belize, Cape Verde, Comoros, Bahamas, Barbados, Benin, Botswana, Burkina Faso, Burundi, Cameroon, Central African Republic, Chad, Congo (Brazzaville), Congo (Kinshasa), Cook Islands, Cote d'Ivoire, Cuba, Djibouti, Dominica, Dominican Republic, Eritrea, Ethiopia, Fiji, Gabon, Gambia, Ghana, Grenada, Republic of Guinea,

Agreement on Trade Tariff (GATT), forcing the European Union to reevaluate its trade relationships with the ACP and bring them into conformity with WTO rules. The Cotonou Partnership Agreement signed in 2000 replaced the Lome Agreement and allowed countries to enter into trade partnerships consistent with certain principles. In late 2002, the EU and ACP States began the process of negotiating new reciprocal trade agreements (EPAs), marking a "radical shift in EU trade policy."[4]

On November 27, 2007, the member states of the EAC and the European Commission (EC) jointly initialed the text of an Agreement Establishing a Framework for an Economic Partnership Agreement jointly.[5] The EAC and EC met for two weeks in June 2010 for further discussion but were unable to agree on several outstanding issues.[6] Negotiations between the EAC and the EU were finalized on October 16, 2014.[7]

On June 20, 2016, the Council of the European Union authorized the signature and provisional application of the EPA on behalf of the EU.[8] The European Commission's website claims that "All EU Member States and the EU have also signed the Agreement."[9] Kenya and Rwanda signed the Agreement on September 1, 2016.[10] However, the remaining

---

Guinea-Bissau, Equatorial Guinea, Guyana, Haiti, Jamaica, Kenya, Kiribati, Lesotho, Liberia, Madagascar, Malawi, Mali, Marshall Islands, Mauritania, Mauritius, Micronesia, Mozambique, Namibia, Nauru, Niger, Nigeria, Niue, Palau, Papua New Guinea, Rwanda, St. Kitts and Nevis, St. Lucia, St. Vincent and the Grenadines, Solomon Islands, Samoa, Sao Tome and Principe, Senegal, Seychelles, Sierra Leone, Somalia, South Africa, Sudan, Suriname, Swaziland, Tanzania, Timor Leste, Togo, Tonga, Trinidad and Tobago, Tuvalu, Uganda, Vanuatu, Zambia, and Zimbabwe.

[4] Kasirye Samuel, *The Geopolitics of EU Trade Policy and Implications for East Africa*, ROSA LUXEMBURG FOUNDATION 4 (2015), http://www.oefse.at/fileadmin/content/Downloads/tradeconference/Kasirye_The_g eopolitics_of_EU_trade_policy_and_implications_for_East_Africa_1.pdf.

[5] *EAC Legal Texts and Policy Documents*, TRALAC TRADE LAW CTR. (last visited Jan. 15, 2017), https://www.tralac.org/resources/by-region/eac.html.

[6] *Joint EAC-EC Communique on the Framework for an Economic Partnership Agreement (FEPA) and Negotiations for the Comprehensive EPA* (June 9, 2010), https://www.tralac.org/wp-content/blogs.dir/12/files/2011/uploads/Joint_EAC-EC_Communique_on_EPA_9_June_2010_Dar_es_Salaam.pdf.

[7] *Economic Partnership Agreement Between the EU and the Eastern African Community (EAC)*, EUR. COMM., 1 (Oct. 2015), http://trade.ec.europa.eu/doclib/docs/2009/january/tradoc_142194.pdf.

[8] Council of the European Union Press Release, East African Community: EU to Sign Economic Partnership Agreement with Burundi, Kenya, Rwanda, Tanzania and Uganda (June 20, 2016, 10:25), http://www.consilium.europa.eu/en/press/press-releases/2016/06/20-eac-eac-epa/.

[9] *Overview of Economic Partnership Agreements*, EUR. COMM. 2 (Oct. 2016), http://trade.ec.europa.eu/doclib/docs/2009/september/tradoc_144912.pdf.

[10] *Id.*

members of the East African Community—Tanzania, Burundi, Uganda, and South Sudan—have not yet done so.[11] In fact, at the end of 2016, Tanzania lodged a civil suit in the East African Court of Justice, seeking orders to stay the signing of the deal by the remaining East African countries.[12]

Brexit adds an interesting dimension to an already debated regional controversy: if the UK withdraws from the European Union, what is the legal status of as-yet-unsigned EPA between it and the East African Community? The first part of the answer to this question turns on the "mixed" nature of the European Union's economic partnership agreements.

III. THE PROBLEM OF THE MIXED AGREEMENT: AUTOMATIC TERMINATION?

Some have argued that, as a matter of law, mixed treaties such as the EU-EAC EPA would not continue to apply to the UK following Brexit and would have to be automatically terminated.[13] Given the text of the agreement itself, EU law, and common state practice outlined below, this is the correct legal approach.

A. THE MIXED COMPETENCE CLAUSE

Article 4 of the Treaty on the Functioning of the European Union defines areas in which competences are shared between the EU and its

---

[11] Tanzania has twice refused to sign the EPA, once in 2014 and more recently this past year. Weitere, *supra* note 1.

[12] George Omondi, *Tanzanian Sues to Stop Kenya from Concluding Trade Deal with Europe*, BUS. DAILY AFR. (Nov. 16, 2016, 9:36 AM), http://www.businessdailyafrica.com/539546-3453910-l6m8ur/index.html.

[13] *See, e.g.*, Panos Koutrakos, *Brexit and International Trade Treaties: A Complex, Long, and Expensive Process*, LAWYERS – IN FOR BRITAIN (last visited Nov. 28, 2016), http://lawyers-inforbritain.uk/briefings/brexit-and-international-trade-treaties-a-complex-long-and-expensive-process/; Markus W. Gehring, *'Trade Relations Will Remain Unchanged' Post-Brexit, Claims Lord Lawson. Hardly*, LONDON SCHOOL OF ECONOMICS (Apr. 12, 2016), http://blogs.lse.ac.uk/brexit/2016/04/12/trade-relations-will-remain-unchanged-post-brexit-claims-lord-lawson-hardly/ ("it can be argued that mixed agreements concluded by the EU and its Member States could be subject to automatic termination as far as the UK is concerned."); Katrin Fernekeß, Solveiga Palevičienė and Manu Thadikkaran, *The Future of the United Kingdom in Europe: Exit Scenarios and Their Implications On Trade Relations*, GRADUATE INST. OF INT'L AND DEV. STUDIES (Jan. 7, 2014), http://graduateinstitute.ch/files/live/sites/iheid/files/sites/ctei/shared/CTEI/Law%20Clinic/Memoranda%202013/Group%20A_The%20Future%20of%20the%20United%20Kingdom%20in%20Europe.pdf ("The provisions of these agreements indicate that they would be automatically terminated for the UK upon its withdrawal from the EU. In any case, the third countries with whom the agreements are concluded have the right to terminate the agreement with the UK.").

member states.[14] When an international agreement covers elements of both exclusively EU and member state competence, each of the twenty-eight member states must ratify the agreement alongside the EU, each according to their own constitutional ratification procedures. Because of this, the agreement is concluded between a third party and between both the EU and each of its individual member states.[15]

A mixed competence clause appears in Article 132(1) of the EU-EAC Agreement in its definition of the parties:

> Contracting Parties of this Agreement are the Contracting Parties to The Treaty establishing the East African Community, herein referred to as the 'EAC Partner States', on the one part, and the European Union *or* its Member States or the European Union *and* its Member States, within their respective areas of competence as derived from the Treaty on European Union and the Treaty on the Functioning of the European Union, herein referred to as the 'EU', of the other part.[16]

This language raises the question of whether the EPA is a single agreement between the East African Community and the EU, or whether it in fact constitutes twenty-eight different agreements between the East African Community, and the EU, and each of the EU member states. If there are multiple separate agreements, the argument goes, the Agreement between the UK and the EAC could survive the UK's withdrawal from the European Union. However, there are several legal arguments that point away from this line of thinking.

B. TEXT OF THE AGREEMENT: TERRITORIAL APPLICATION

First, there is the language of the Economic Partnership Agreement itself, which contains a territorial application clause in Article 141:

> This Agreement shall apply, on the one hand, to the territories in which the Treaty on the European Union and the Treaty on

---

[14] Consolidated Version of the Treaty on the Functioning of the European Union art. 4, May 9, 2008, 2008 O.J. (C 115) 47 [hereinafter TFEU]. Section 1 states "The Union shall share competence with the Member States where the Treaties confer on it a competence which does not relate to the areas referred to in Articles 3 and 6." *Id.* Section 2 lays out principal areas of shared competence, while sections 3 and 4 define areas of EU competence that nevertheless do not prevent Member States from exercising theirs. *Id.*
[15] *International Agreements and the EU's External Competences*, EUR-LEX (last updated Aug. 8, 2016), http://eur-lex.europa.eu/legal-content/EN/TXT/?uri=URISERV%3Aai0034
[16] *EU EAC EPA Consolidated Text*, EUR. COMM. art. 132 (Oct. 2015), http://trade.ec.europa.eu/doclib/docs/2015/october/tradoc_153845.compressed.pdf (emphasis added).

the Functioning of the European Union are applied and on the other hand, to the territories of the EAC Partner States. References to 'territory' in this Agreement shall be understood in this sense.[17]

This phrasing demonstrates the intent of the parties to apply the agreement only to those countries governed by the EU Treaties. When the UK ceases to be a member of the EU, these treaties will no longer cover the territory of the UK, and consequently, the Economic Partnership Agreement will no longer be applicable to the territory of the UK.[18]

C. EU LAW: BILATERAL NATURE OF MIXED AGREEMENTS

Second, European Union law itself points to the bilateral nature of mixed agreements. TFEU Article 216(2) states that agreements concluded by the Union are only "binding upon the institutions of the Union and on its Member States."[19] As a result, once the UK ceases to be a Member State of the EU, these agreements are no longer applicable to the UK because it is not bound by EU-only international agreements.[20] The intention of the parties was to grant the benefits of the trade agreement to the EU as a whole, not separately. As one commentator elaborates:

> The only rationale for the UK to have signed the agreement separately is due to the division of competences within the EU system, whereby the sovereignty of the individual Member States require them to give specific consent to the Agreements. However, this consent is not an indication that the EU Member State individually entered into an agreement with the third country. As regards the third country party, it is entering into an agreement with only the EU Member States. The status of an

---

[17] *EU EAC EPA Consolidated Text, supra* note 14, art. 141.

[18] Katrin Fernekeß, Solveiga Palevičienė and Manu Thadikkaran, *The Future of The United Kingdom In Europe: Exit Scenarios And Their Implications On Trade Relations*, INST. INT'L AND DEV. STUDIES 6 (Jan. 7, 2014), http://graduateinstitute.ch/files/live/sites/iheid/files/sites/ctei/shared/CTEI/workin g_papers/CTEI_2013-01_LawClinic_FutureUKinEurope.pdf; Guillaume Van der Loo & Steven Blockmans, *The Impact of Brexit on the EU's International Agreements*, CENTRE FOR EUROPEAN POL'Y STUDIES (July 15, 2016), https://www.ceps.eu/publications/impact-brexit-eu%E2%80%99s-international-agreements.

[19] TFEU, art. 216(2).

[20] Fernekeß et al., *supra* note 16; Van der Loo & Blockmans, *supra* note 16.

EU Member State, therefore, is essential for the UK to continue with these agreements.[21]

This interpretation of the treaty is bolstered by the language used in mixed agreements under EU law, which, again, are concluded "on the one part" by the EU and its Member States and "of the other part" by a third party—the East African Community in this case.[22] The EPA refers to the UK only in its capacity as a Member State of the EU. Once the UK withdraws from the EU, it will no longer be considered a member state and thus will also cease to be a party to the Agreement.[23]

The Court of Justice of the European Union has affirmed the idea that mixed agreements are of an essentially bilateral nature. In *European Parliament v. Council of the European Union*, the Court held that the Fourth ACP-EEC Lomé Convention "[c]oncluded by the Community and its Member States of the one part and the ACP States of the other part . . . established an essentially bilateral ACP-EEC cooperation." [24] Consequently, "[w]hilst the UK is a party to such agreements, the rights which it has enjoyed under their provisions, as well as the obligations it has assumed, would not continue to apply automatically."[25]

D. STATE PRACTICE: PROVISIONAL APPLICATION

Finally, the EU practice of provisional application suggests that the UK is included in the application of the EPA only by virtue of its membership in the European Union. The current EU-EAC EPA has had provisional application since June 2016 under Article 139(4), which states: "Pending entry into force of the Agreement, the EAC Partner States and the EU may provisionally apply the provisions of this Agreement which fall within their respective competences." [26] As can be seen from the language, the EU provisionally applies the Agreement as distinct from its member states.[27] One scholar explains:

---

[21] Fernekeß et al., *supra* note 16.

[22] *EU EAC EPA Consolidated Text*, *supra* note 14, art. 141.

[23] Koutrakos, *supra* note 11.

[24] Case C-316/91, European Parliament v. Council of the European Union, ¶ 29, 1994 E.C.R. I-00625.

[25] Koutrakos, *supra* note 11.

[26] *EU EAC EPA Consolidated Text*, *supra* note 14, art. 139(4).

[27] In fact, there appears to be a frequent concern over "competence creep" in such situations if provisional application is not "limited to matters of exclusive EU competence or for which the EU has clearly been authorised to exercise shared competence." Vaughne Miller, *EU External Agreements: EU and UK Procedures*, Commons Briefing Papers No. CBP-7192 (Mar. 29, 2016), http://researchbriefings.parliament.uk/ResearchBriefing/Summary/CBP-7192.

[W]hile the UK already derives trade benefits from those agreements by virtue of its EU membership, the UK is not even a party to them yet until all EU Member States have ratified them. Since it is not yet a party to those agreements, it obviously could not remain a party to them after Brexit.[28]

The fact that the EPA is currently being applied without the UK being a party lends more support for the view that there was never any intent for the EPA to be interpreted as containing a separate agreement between the UK and the EAC.

At the very least, the above arguments make a strong case for treating the EPA as a single agreement that, upon withdrawal of the UK from the EU, is subject to automatic termination with regard to application to the UK. Taken to an extreme, this line of reasoning could be used to show that the entire EPA must be automatically terminated upon withdrawal of the UK from the EU. However, this still leaves open the question of whether the Agreement must be automatically renegotiated.

IV. THE PROBLEM OF THE PRINCIPLE OF CONTINUITY: AUTOMATIC RENEGOTIATION?

Even if Brexit is not found to require termination of the current EPA, the parties to the Economic Partnership Agreement are permitted to renegotiate and amend the agreement consistent with Article 143.[29] This presents another question: whether the Agreement must automatically be re-negotiated, whether provisions may be salvaged to some extent, and even whether they can be left as they are.

A. THE PRINCIPLE OF CONTINUITY

Some commentators argue that the general presumption of continuity in the Vienna Convention on Succession of States in Respect of Treaties precludes automatic renegotiation.[30] This approach would

---

[28] Koutrakos, *supra* note 11.

[29] *EU EAC EPA Consolidated Text*, *supra* note 14, art. 143.

[30] *See, e.g.*, *Brexit and International Trade*, LAWYERS FOR BRITAIN (last visited Nov. 29, 2016), http://www.lawyersforbritain.org/int-trade.shtml ("The UK could simply continue to apply the substantive terms of these agreements on a reciprocal basis after exit unless the counterparty State were actively to object . . . . There will be no need for complicated renegotiation of these existing agreements as was misleadingly claimed by pro-Remain propaganda."); Richard North, *EU Referendum: Those Trade Deals*, (Mar. 5, 2016), EUREFERENDUM.COM, http://www.eureferendum.com/blogview.aspx?blogno=85960 ("Once alternative arrangements are in place, an exit agreement with the EU would hold no terrors. As we dropped out of the EU treaties, we would simply invoke the procedures leading to treaty continuity. Conveniently, there is also a template which the UK could

avoid a loophole that might allow states to withdraw from treaty obligations with a third state simply by leaving an international organization, and without the consent of the third state, which would be "problematic in terms of legal certainty and stability in the UK's treaty relationships."[31]

Although Brexit is not legally a case of state succession, the practical issues are analogous, and the principle could be applied to this situation. The Vienna Convention Article 34 states that:

> When a part or parts of the territory of a State separate to form one or more States, whether or not the predecessor State continues to exist: (a) any treaty in force at the date of the succession of States in respect of the entire territory of the predecessor State continues in force in respect of each successor State so formed; (b) any treaty in force at the date of the succession of States in respect only of that part of the territory of the predecessor State which has become a successor State continues in force in respect of that successor State alone.[32]

Instead of renegotiating substantive provisions of the Economic Partnership Agreement, the UK could simply agree to "roll over" elements of the existing Agreement. The UK would no longer be bound by the "EU-only" elements of the EPA, but could remain bound by its "mixed" elements. In theory, all that is required in this scenario are statements by the UK and the EAC that they intend to continue operating under the terms of the EPA after Brexit.[33]

There is legal precedent for "rolling over" of treaty obligations in international law in cases where an existing State splits and the resulting new states wish to continue their treaty relationships with other States. The state of Czechoslovakia dissolved in 1992 and was succeeded by two states, the Czech Republic and Slovakia. Both new states declared themselves successors to Czechoslovakia and each committed to fulfilling multilateral treaty obligations to which it had been a party.[34] The European Court of Justice found that the European Community could

---

use, in the Vienna Convention on Succession of States in respect of Treaties, even though it is not a party to it.").

[31] Jed Odermatt, *Brexit and International Law*, BLOG OF THE EUR. J. INT'L L. (July 4, 2016), http://www.ejiltalk.org/brexit-and-international-law/.

[32] Vienna Convention on Succession of States in Respect of Treaties art. 34(1), *opened for signature* Aug. 23, 1978, 1946 U.N.T.S. 3.

[33] *Brexit and International Trade*, LAWYERS FOR BRITAIN, *supra* note 28.

[34] ANTHONY AUST, MODERN TREATY LAW AND PRACTICE 317-18 (2000).

be the successor to its Member States in respect of the GATT; [35] however, it is not clear that obligations could flow in the opposite direction.

B. COMPLICATIONS OF ROLLING OVER

While it would seem to provide a simple alternative to complicated renegotiations, there are significant problems with the "roll over" approach.

First, the real-world ramifications of Brexit alone are likely to necessitate, to a certain extent, renegotiation between the EU, its twenty-seven remaining member states, and the East African Community: "the UK's extraction from a mixed agreement will have practical, economic and/or financial consequences that will need to be cushioned and secured by transitional periods and legal straps." [36] Any such amendments would require the consent of all parties involved under Article 143. More importantly, once the UK has left the Single Market, it is by no means certain that it will be capable of fulfilling its obligations under the EPA, and so automatic continuity cannot be assumed.[37]

Second, mixed agreements do not specify which elements are "mixed" in nature. This gives rise to legal uncertainty, because the Commission may claim the EU has exclusive competence, and "neither the agreement nor the EU Decisions on ratification or accession make clear which party (the EU or the Member States in their own right) is exercising competence over what part of the agreement."[38] The only way for the UK to extricate itself from the Agreement in this case is likely automatic termination as discussed above. One author speculates:

> [I]n order to extract itself from a mixed agreement, the UK will need to repeal its approval act that ratified the agreement and terminate or denounce the agreement as foreseen in the agreement's termination or suspension clause . . . . In addition, the EU will need to notify the respective third parties that the UK will cease to be a member of the Union and that the EU-only elements of the agreement will thus cease to apply to the UK's territories.[39]

---

[35] Judgment in International Fruit Company and Others v. Produktschap voor Groenten en Fruit, Joined Cases 21 to 25/72, EU:C:1972:115, para. 7.

[36] Van der Loo & Blockmans, *supra* note 16.

[37] Koutrakos, *supra* note 11.

[38] Miller, *supra* note 25.

[39] Van der Loo & Blockmans, *supra* note 16.

C. VOLUNTARY TERMINATION

As a last resort, the East African Community may voluntarily terminate the agreement in accordance with the denunciation clause of Article 140. [40] This would allow the EAC to denounce the entire agreement with the EU if they are unable to agree on a legal solution to the Brexit problem. Note that if the EPA did not contain such a termination clause, it would forgo recourse under customary international law. Because the UK had made known its intention to Brexit before any of the EAC countries signed the EPA, the East African Community could not argue that this is a fundamental change of circumstances under the Vienna Convention on the Law of Treaties that entitles it to terminate the agreement.[41]

Note, however, that this solution may lead to another complicated problem. Since the UK would not be considered a contracting party to the EPA, there is a question of whether this clause applies to termination of the UK's application of the Agreement.[42]

V. PRACTICAL CONSIDERATIONS: COMPETING INTERESTS

The decision about which of these avenues to pursue will depend on competing considerations both external to the East African Community and internal concerns unique to the region and the status of its member states as developing countries. First, there are long-standing concerns that the EPA does not take into account the unequal levels of development between the East African Community and the European Union. Second, there are regional dynamics that must be taken into consideration and which have seriously impacted the EPA negotiations.

A. UNEQUAL POWER DYNAMICS

Ostensibly, the EPA would give the East African Community quota-free and duty-free market access to the EU. The European Union's diplomatic service contends that the Agreement is "intended to enhance regional integration and economic development" in the region by providing the East African Community better access to the EU market, emphasizing "unprecedented market opportunities for agricultural and fisheries products."[43] However, since the beginning of negotiations more

---

[40] "1. A Party to this Agreement may give written notice to the other of its intention to denounce this Agreement. 2. Denunciation shall take effect one year after notification." *EU EAC EPA Consolidated Text, supra* note 14, art. 140.

[41] The Convention does not permit invoking a fundamental change of circumstances unless it "was not foreseen by the parties." Vienna Convention on the Law of Treaties art. 62(1), *opened for signature* May 23, 1969, 1155 U.N.T.S. 331.

[42] Van der Loo & Blockmans, *supra* note 16.

[43] *Economic Partnership Agreements between the European Union and the East African Community*, EUROPEAN UNION EXTERNAL ACTION SERVICE (July 13, 2016),

than a decade ago, there has been widespread criticism by East African smallholder farmers, civil society organizations, government officers, media, and religious groups on the design and structure of the Agreement.[44]

Many of these concerns center around the failure of the EPA to address differing levels of development between the EU and East African countries. Two Nigerian scholars note:

> [S]igning a reciprocal trade agreement with the EU [will] have adverse effects on African economy resulting in loss of government fiscal revenues, disruption of regional integration among African countries and extinction of infant industries which are likely to die off as a result of harsh competition from relatively cheaper and better quality products from the EU.[45]

The country director of the Southern and Eastern Africa Trade Information and Negotiations Institute (SEATINI)-Uganda stated "it is civil society's view that a careful reading of the agreement arrived at and which the EAC is being pressed to sign and ratify falls short of securing the region's overall development interests."[46] The Kenyan Institute of Economic Affairs noted the pervasive subsidization allowed by the EU's agricultural policy, negative impact of trade liberalization especially with regard to manufacturing industries in the EAC, and a possible chilling effect on EU foreign direct investment in East African countries.[47]

The EAC may face additional pressures from the EU to sign the EPA. During a regional trade meeting in Nairobi, Secretary General of the African Caribbean and Pacific Group of states (ACP) Patrick Gomes

---

https://eeas.europa.eu/headquarters/headquarters-homepage/6656/economic-partnership-agreements-between-european-union-and-east-african-community_en.

[44] *The ABC of EAC-EU Economic Partnership Agreements (EPA)*, KENYA HUMAN RIGHTS COMM., 6 (Dec. 1, 2014), http://www.khrc.or.ke/mobile-publications/economic-rights-and-social-protection-er-sp/59-the-abc-of-eac-eu-economic-partnership-agreements-epa.html.

[45] Kelechi C. Nnamdi & Kingsley C. Iheakaram, *Impact of Economic Partnership Agreements (EPA) On African Economy: A Legal Perspective*, CTR. FOR EFFECTIVE GLOBAL ACTION 1 (2014), http://cega.berkeley.edu/assets/miscellaneous_files/6-ABCA-Nnamdi-Impact_of_EPA_on_AFR_economy.pdf.

[46] Jane Nalunga, *Why EU-EAC EPA Falls Short of EAC's Development Interests*, NEW VISION (Sept. 1, 2016, 11:43 AM), http://www.newvision.co.ug/new_vision/news/1434239/eu-eac-epa-falls-short-eac-development.

[47] *See, e.g.*, Leon Ong'onge, *Trade Notes: The EAC-EU Economic Partnership Agreement: Context, Content, and Consequences*, INST. ECON. AFF.-KENYA, 6 (Aug. 2015), http://www.ieakenya.or.ke/publications/notes/eac-eu-economic-partnership-agreement-context-content-and-consequences.

warned "We need to understand that EPAs come not only with trade opportunities with Europe, but development aid as well. As it is, Tanzania, Uganda and Burundi, which have been dragging their feet in signing the trade pact, could end up losing important development aid from the EU."[48]

B. REGIONAL DIFFERENCES IN DEVELOPMENT STRATEGY

Chatter on social media and opinion pieces in regional news sites about how the EAC-EU EPA controversy points to a dissolution of cooperation among members of the East African Community.[49] The disagreement reflects different approaches to development that member states have chosen to follow. Tanzania, as well as Uganda and Burundi to some extent, has focused on local industrialization efforts, emphasizing domestic production and consumption. Kenya has instead chosen to increase free trade and foreign direct investment. Rwanda has pursued an agricultural push, taking into account its status as a landlocked country with a small population.[50]

The EPA was drafted over ten years ago, when there were no indications the UK would leave the European Union. However, Brexit is simply the newest setback in a series of longstanding internal disagreements over trade strategy. Although Tanzania has referred to the uncertainty around Brexit as one of its reasons for not wanting to sign the EPA now,[51] government statements have made clear that its opposition to the Economic Partnership Agreement is primarily motivated by longstanding concerns with the negative impact the deal would have on East African countries' development and economies.[52]

---

[48] Allan Olingo, *Tanzania, Burundi Risk Losing European Union Aid Over EPAs*, THE EAST AFRICAN (Dec. 28, 2016), http://allafrica.com/stories/201612280513.html.

[49] *See, e.g.*, Desmond Boi, *The East African Community: Another Diplomatic Headache for Kenya?*, CITIZEN DIGITAL (Jan. 6, 2017), https://citizentv.co.ke/news/the-east-african-community-another-diplomatic-headache-for-kenya-153950/ ("The jeopardy insinuated by Tanzania's decision to put aside the EPA is just one among a series of other actions taken by the current government to kill the foundation of the EAC.").

[50] Jeremy Luedi, *Under the Radar: EAC Infighting Highlights Divisions, Threatens EU Trade Deal*, GLOBAL RISK INSIGHTS (Sept. 9, 2016), http://globalriskinsights.com/2016/09/under-the-radar-eac-infighting/.

[51] The Daily News of Tanzania has quoted Magufuli as saying: "There are a number of questions to be looked upon, why are we signing the agreement while the EU has imposed sanctions on Burundi? Why are we signing while UK has pulled out of the EU?" George Mhango, *East African States Delay Signing of EU Trade Deal*, DEUTSCHE WELLE (Sept. 9, 2016), http://www.dw.com/en/east-african-states-delay-signing-of-eu-trade-deal/a-19537689.

[52] *Tanzania's Refusal to Sign EU Trade Pact Gives East Africa Time to Rethink*, THE CONVERSATION (July 21, 2016, 1:34 PM), http://theconversation.com/tanzanias-refusal-to-sign-eu-trade-pact-gives-east-africa-time-to-rethink-62707 (government

Since the initialing of the Framework Agreement, the East African Community has since nearly doubled in size and the members differ over the correct approach to take now. The EAC countries access the UK market on preferential terms through the Everything But Arms Initiative brokered with the European Commission. When Brexit occurs, this agreement will no longer apply, which could lead to trade disruption for the East African Community.[53] Out of the six EAC countries, Kenya stands to lose the most if the deal is not signed. The other member states, including Tanzania, Burundi, and Uganda, would still be eligible for preferential access under the EU's Everything But Arms initiative, given their status as Least Developed Countries.[54] Kenya, on the other hand, has no good alternative.

In 2015, the UK received about 28 percent of all Kenya's exports, including the bulk of its major exports to Europe. If the UK is no longer a party to the EPA, the balance of liberalization commitments in the Agreement will be upset.[55] An obvious source of anxiety is the impact of Brexit on Kenya's floriculture industry in exports to the EU, and to the UK in particular. Since 1990, Kenya's cut flower export volume has recorded the highest growth in volume and value every year. According to the Kenya Flower Council, the country is a lead supplier to the EU, with 38 percent of all cut flower imports into the EU coming from Kenya. Kenya's share of exports to the UK has recently increased considerably, in response to a "growing market especially on mixed bouquets, and more direct sales as compared to the auction system."[56] If the EPA is not signed, there are concerns Kenya will face substantial tariffs on these products.[57] On the other hand, UK withdrawal means

---

statement that they could not sign the EPA due to a need "to protect the economic interests of our countries by empowering the manufacturing industries").

[53] Emily Jones, *Brexit: Opportunity or Peril for Trade With Small and Poor Developing Economies?*, GLOBAL ECON. GOV. PROGRAMME (last visited Nov. 29, 2016), http://www.globaleconomicgovernance.org/brexit-opportunity-or-peril-trade-small-and-poor-developing-economies.

[54] *Trade*, E. AFR. COMMUNITY, http://www.eac.int/sectors/trade (last visited Oct. 6, 2016).

[55] Mohammad Razzaque and Brendan Vickers, *Post-Brexit UK-ACP Trading Arrangements: Some Reflections*, 137 TRADE HOT TOPICS 6 (2016), http://thecommonwealth.org/sites/default/files/news-items/documents/5jln9q109bmr-en.pdf.

[56] *Industry Statistics*, KENYA FLOWER COUNCIL (last visited Jan. 16, 2017), http://kenyaflowercouncil.org/?page_id=94.

[57] John Aglionby, *Kenya Feels Brexit Effect as UK Vote Threatens Africa Trade Deal*, FIN. TIMES (July 28, 2016), https://www.ft.com/content/01beeb54-5347-11e6-9664-e0bdc13c3bef.

that a significant portion of the flower market is no longer covered by the Agreement, a loss that will also certainly take its toll on Kenya.[58]

CONCLUSION

Brexit leaves the East African Community with multiple options. The EAC could amend the EPA to include the UK as a separate party, allowing tariffs and other benefits in the agreement to remain unchanged. Although it is arguably acceptable from a legal standpoint for the EAC to have the provisions of the EPA "roll over," there are better arguments for termination and renegotiation. Given the strong indications that the Economic Partnership Agreement is a bad deal for the East African Community and the internal disagreements within the EAC, it would appear that practical considerations support this legal outcome. These factors could tip the balance in favor of renegotiation, rather than rolling over the now-ten-year-old provisions of the current Agreement. The current situation provides the EAC with an opportunity to restructure and improve their trade relations because new trade agreements will be needed regardless. Brexit thus provides both a new chance to develop deeper ties with the UK and the prospect of securing a better arrangement with the European Union.

---

[58] Mumbi Kinyua, *Brexit to Impact Negatively on Kenya's Exports, Warns Kenya Flower Association,* STANDARD MEDIA (June 22, 2016), https://www.standardmedia.co.ke/business/article/2000206127/brexit-to-impact-negatively-on-kenya-s-exports-warns-kenya-flower-association.

Chapter 6: The Legal Impact of Brexit on the Comprehensive Economic Trade Agreement (CETA) Between the European Union and Canada

Isabel Fressynet

Introduction

The Comprehensive Economic and Trade Agreement (CETA) is one of the most important Free-Trade Agreements of the twenty-first century. Overcoming some of the difficulties leading to the breakdown in the negotiations for the Transatlantic Trade and Investment Partnership (TTIP), CETA managed to gain broader acceptance as a new and innovative model for international trade agreements. This agreement is known to be one of the most "comprehensive" agreements, aiming to "boost trade, strengthen economic relations and create jobs" between the European Union ["the EU"] and Canada. [1] Nonetheless, the agreement is not without controversy. While some considered CETA to be "a milestone in European Trade policy" and "the most ambitious trade agreement that the EU has ever concluded,"[2] others contest the power given to foreign investors and businesses under the investment chapter and perceive CETA as "an attack on democracy, workers and the environment." [3]

The agreement's negotiations ended in 2014 and, according to European procedure,[4] the agreement was proposed for signature by the European Commission to the Council of the European Union ["the Council"] in July 2016. Following the Walloon's Parliament opposition, the Council succeeded to sign the agreement on October 30, 2016. In order to become fully binding, the agreement has to be ratified by all member States and the EU Parliament. The latter requirement occurred

---

[1] European Commission, In focus; the Comprehensive Economic and Trade Agreement (CETA) chapter by chapter, European Commission website - http://ec.europa.eu/trade/policy/in-focus/ceta/ceta-chapter-by-chapter/.

[2] European Commission Press Release, European Commission proposes signature and conclusion of EU-Canada trade deal (July 5, 2016) - http://europa.eu/rapid/press-release_IP-16-2371_en.htm.

[3] International Trade, The Great CETA swindle, Corporate Europe Observatory (November 16, 2016) - https://corporateeurope.org/international-trade/2016/11/great-ceta-swindle.

[4] TFEU art. 218.

on February 15 2017,[5] by 408 votes to 254 which is a big success.[6] As Canada's Prime Minister Justin Trudeau already signed the agreement in October 2016,[7] the agreement is now ready to be provisionally applied awaiting the full ratification by member States. Council has already scheduled the provisional application to start in the second quarter of 2017.

After years of negotiations and the creation of a unique FTA, the success and promptness of the ratification is crucial for the European Union. However, the Brexit vote in June 2016 could bring important modifications to the European legal landscape and, consequently, affect CETA. This paper aims to provide a roadmap of legal consequences arising from Brexit on the agreement's ratification process. Following European Law, (I) the agreement has to be ratified by both the EU and its member States. Therefore, (II) the UK will have a role to play in the ratification, and (III) the provisional application process. This situation could bring some important legal issues concerning (IV) the rights of the UK as a party—or not—to the agreement after Brexit.

I.   THE LEGAL FRAMEWORK: QUICK OVERVIEW OF EUROPEAN LAW

CETA is an international agreement between the EU and a non-EU country. European Law defines the scope of jurisdiction of the EU and its member States through two important treaties that are the Treaty on the Functioning of the European Union ["TFEU"] and the Treaty on the European Union ["TEU"]. In order to cease the potential legal issues Brexit could bring relative to CETA, it is essential to understand (A) the competence of the EU as an independent entity, and (B) the distribution of competence between the States and the EU.

---

[5] European Parliament Committee, International Trade (EP INTRA), text adopted [provisional edition], 2014-2019 (February 15, 2017).

[6] James Kanter, EU Parliament votes to ratify Canada Trade Deal and send Trump a Message, NY Times (February 15, 2017) - https://www.nytimes.com/2017/02/15/business/canada-eu-trade-ceta.html?_r=0.

[7] Paul Walde, Trudeau signs CETA but final ratification still required by European Union, The global and mail (October 30, 2016) - http://www.theglobeandmail.com/news/national/prime-minister-trudeau-signs-canada-eu-trade-deal-in-brussels/article32586423/.

A. THE EUROPEAN UNION AS AN INDEPENDENT ENTITY WITH LARGE EXTERNAL COMPETENCE

Article 47 of the TEU provides that "the Union shall have legal personality." With those words, the treaty explicitly creates an independent entity in its own right and a subject of international law.[8] This conferral gives the EU legitimacy to conclude and negotiate international agreements, become a member of an international organization or join an international convention on its own behalf.[9] It is the foundation of the European Union itself and the legal ground allowing it to take binding decisions for all its member States.

The external competence of the EU is defined in article 216 of the TFEU. This article allows the EU to conclude international agreements in cases provided for by the founding treaties or legally binding act; where the conclusion of an agreement is necessary to achieve one of the objectives of the EU and where the agreement may affect common rules adopted in internal EU law. In addition, article 207 of the TFEU deals with the EU's trade policy giving to the European Parliament and the Council, acting by means of **REGULATIONS**, the power to adopt "the measures defining the framework for implementing the common commercial policy." Those two provisions are the legal basis allowing the EU to negotiate and conclude trade agreements, such as CETA.

B. THE DISTRIBUTION OF COMPETENCE BETWEEN THE EUROPEAN UNION AND ITS MEMBER STATES

The EU functions on two separate levels. On one level, the EU has been granted authority to legislate and complete deals directly binding for its member States without requiring their approval or ratification. In such circumstances, the EU has exclusive competence. In another level, member States retained their sovereignty, thus requiring the EU to seek approval for its actions. In these latter cases, there is a shared competence between the EU and the individual member State. Therefore, the EU cannot act on its own without overstepping its jurisdiction. The EU may only act with the consent of each individual member State or leave to the States the discretionary power to make decisions.

At the first level, article 3 of the TFEU provides a list of areas in which the EU has exclusive competence. This entails that the EU can negotiate an agreement on its own that would be automatically binding for all member States. It is a delegation of power given by the States to

---

[8] EUR-LEX, Glossary of summaries: Legal personality of the Union, EU law and publication, http://eur-lex.europa.eu/summary/glossary/union_legal_personality.html.
[9] Id.

the European Union. These powers have broadened over time and concern the following: customs union; establishing competition rules necessary for the functioning of the international market; monetary policy; conservation of marine biological resources; common commercial policy and concluding international agreements when their conclusion is required by a legislative act of the EU, when their conclusion is necessary to enable the EU to exercise its international competence and in so far as their conclusion may affect common rules or alter their scope.[10]

At the second level, article 4 of the TFEU provides a list of areas in which the EU's authority is beholden to the member States. Those areas of shared competence are the following: internal market; social policy; economic, social and territorial cohesion; agriculture and fisheries; environment; consumer protection; transport; trans-European network; energy, area of freedom, security and justice; common safety concerns in public health; research, technological development and space; development cooperation and humanitarian aid. When the EU acts within an area in which it shares competence with its member States, the resulting agreement is said to be a "mixed-agreement" as it is ratified both by the European Union and the member States. When the competence is shared between the EU and the member States, the competence can be exercised by either. Nevertheless, "it is the (UK) Government's stated policy that shared competence should be exercised by the Member States."[11]

II. BREXIT AND THE RATIFICATION PROCESS OF CETA

The distribution of competence between member States and the EU has a great impact on the ratification process. (A) As a mixed-agreement, (B) CETA will have to be ratified by all member States including the UK.

A. APPLICATION OF THE EU LAW TO CETA: A MIXED-AGREEMENT

Concerning CETA, the European Commission considers it to be a "EU-only" agreement. This means that, for the European Commission, all the provisions in the agreement fall under the exclusive competence of the European Union [article 3 TFEU]. Therefore, CETA was

---

[10] The European Citizens' initiative, FAQ on the European Competences and the European Commission powers (December 13, 2016) - http://ec.europa.eu/citizens-initiative/public/competences/faq?lg=en.
[11] House of Commons, European Scrutiny Committee, Comprehensive Economic Trade Agreement (CETA) between the EU and Canada, Eighteen Report Session 2016-17 (November 22, 2016).

supposed to be an agreement concluded only between the EU and Canada and ratified only by the Council with consent of the European Parliament following the procedure laid down in article 218-6 of the TFEU. Yet, in light of the existing contestations from some member States, the European Commission decided to classify the agreement as a mixed-agreement.[12] The trade commissioner Cecilia Malmström stated that "from a strict legal standpoint, the Commission considers this agreement to fall under exclusive EU competence. However, the political situation in the Council is clear, and we understand the need for proposing it as a mixed-agreement, in order to allow for speedy signature."[13]

Therefore, CETA is officially treated as a mixed-agreement, meaning the agreement will have to be ratified by all member States before being fully binding. This procedure is lengthy compared to the EU-only ratification and, with Brexit happening contemporaneously, the ratification process is certain to bring about previously unforeseen legal and political issues.

It is worth noting that the European Commission already had to deal with a similar issue. In October 2015, the Commission asked the European Court of Justice for a legal opinion concerning the FTA Singapore-EU. The question submitted was exactly the same as the one concerning CETA, knowingly, "does the EU have the requisite competence to sign and conclude alone the FTA with Singapore?" For the Commission, the EU-Singapore FTA should be considered a EU-only agreement. Considering that both FTAs are alike, the Court's opinion was much expected to bring valid answers concerning CETA's legal regime and be helpful for future negotiations too.[14]

On December 21 2016, the Advocate General Eleanor Sharpston concluded that "not all parts of the agreement fall within the EU's exclusive competence and therefore the agreement cannot be concluded without the participation of all of the member States."[15] The European Court of Justice's opinion brings about two comments. First, the likelihood is that CETA is in fact a mixed-agreement. Second, it could be harder now for the UK to negotiate a similar agreement with the EU inasmuch as all member States would have to ratify the agreement.

---

[12] House of Commons Library, CETA: the EU-Canada Free Trade Agreement, Briefing Paper n° 7492 (Novembre 9, 2016).

[13] Id.

[14] Eighteenth Report, see sources cited *supra* note 11.

[15] European Court of Justice Press Release No 147/16, General's Opinion in Opinion procedure 2/15 (Luxembourg, December 21, 2016).

Therefore, the EU-UK negotiations could be blocked by the member States' veto.[16]

B. THE RATIFICATION PROCESS IN THE UK

As explained above, as a mixed-agreement CETA must also be ratified by each member State according to its own national procedures.[17] The agreement has already been negotiated by the European Union and is now ready for ratification. Thus, national Parliaments have no discretionary power and must either accept the agreement as it is or object to it, but it cannot be amended without reopening the negotiations and restarting the entire process.[18] The ratification by all member States is mandatory as the agreement is a mixture of EU and member States competence. The ratification covers the entire agreement, even if there are provisions resorting to EU's exclusive jurisdiction.

Concerning the UK, the UK Parliament has to ratify the treaty according to the Constitutional Reform and Governance Act 2010.[19] Following national proceeding, the agreement and the memorandum are laid before Parliament for twenty-one sitting days. Then, if either the House of Commons or the House of Lords passes a resolution objecting to the ratification, the UK's government must give reasons why it still wants it to be ratified.

The Commons have then twenty-one days to reconsider the government's reasons for ratification and can, once more, object. The process repeats indefinitely until the House of Commons decides to pass the agreement or the UK's government decides to abandon it. Therefore, this process gives to the House of Commons the power to block ratification.[20]

As a member of the European Union until complete exit, the UK has the duty to ratify the agreement in order for it to become fully binding to all member States, meaning that if the House of Commons decides to object to it, the UK could potentially block CETA from coming into force. This situation would be really problematic as the UK, in the long run, will leave the European Union and, consequently, the agreement. Therefore, this presents the unique situation in which a

---

[16] Dr. Andrés Delgado Casteleiro, *Opinion 2/15 on the scope of EU external trade policy : some background information before next week's hearing*, EU Law Analysis (September 6, 2016), – http://eulawanalysis.blogspot.com/2016/09/opinion-215-on-scope-of-eu-external.html.

[17] CETA, art. 30.7 (1).

[18] Eighteenth report, see sources cited *supra* notes 11

[19]   2010   c.   25,   Part   2,   section   20-25   – http://www.legislation.gov.uk/ukpga/2010/25/part/2.

[20] Eighteenth report, see sources cited *supra* notes 11.

country, who will not be a party to the agreement, can block its ratification for all other countries. More so, this could turn out to be a good leverage for the UK over the European Union for the purpose of future negotiations.

In addition to the ratification process, the UK Parliament is preparing for Brexit and its legal consequences. This justifies why the House of Commons European Scrutiny Committee asked for a debate on the floor of the House concerning CETA. The Committee aims to hear from the Government on critical issues and scrutinize the agreement to help Parliament in the ratification process. The scrutiny mainly concerns policy and legal issues arising from the UK's withdrawal, such as competence distribution, provisional application and implications of Brexit.[21]

III. BREXIT AND THE PROVISIONAL APPLICATION OF THE AGREEMENT

While waiting for the agreement to be fully binding, both CETA and European Law provide for the agreement's provisional application. However, the provisional application brings two major legal issues, still pending. First, (A) the agreement did not define clearly who could trigger the provisional application and to which extent. Second, (B) the discussion concentrated on one of the agreement's major controversies, namely the investment chapter.

A. THE TRIGGERING AND SCOPE OF PROVISIONAL APPLICATION

According to article 30.7 3-a) of the agreement the "parties" may provisionally apply the agreement but a "party" can decide not to. Under European Law and article 218 TEU, the Council may adopt a decision of provisional measures and, if it wishes, may ask for the consent of the European Parliament.[22] Therefore, it has already been announced that CETA will be provisionally applied.

However, the UK Parliament asked the Minister to clarify "whether the power to trigger and terminate provisional application of CETA rests with the EU, the Member States, or a combination of the two."[23] According to the title of the agreement parties are Canada, the EU and its member States. The question is whether member States are

---

[21] Id.

[22] Id.

[23] House of Commons, European Scrutiny Committee, Comprehensive Economic Trade Agreement (CETA) between the EU and Canada, Eighteen Report Session 2016-17 (November 22, 2016).

considered as "parties" under article 30.7 3, therefore allowing them to be a part of the provisional application process. This difficulty refers to the German Constitutional Court statement according to which the German Government would "only lend approval in the Council to provisional application of those parts of CETA that lie beyond doubt within the competences attributed to the European Union under primary law. According to the German Government's submission, it will not approve the provisional application for areas that remain subject to the competence of the Federal Republic of Germany."[24]

The issue at stake relates to the fact that the boundaries of EU-only competence, State-only competence and shared competence were never clearly defined and the decision to provisionally apply the agreement did "not specify how competence is to be respected" in the areas "where member States claim to share competence with the EU."[25]

CETA is politically a mixed-agreement, but legally it is considered to be almost wholly composed of EU's exclusive competence subject-matter. Given that only the areas falling within EU competence can be provisionally applied, provisional application would entail the application of nearly the entire agreement.[26] Therefore, provisional application will utterly diminish and outweigh the UK's Parliament ratification as the agreement would be applicable with or without its approval. Here lies one of the main concerns of the UK Parliament, and the House of Commons European Scrutiny Committee inquired the Minister to hold a debate in front of the House in order to discuss the issue.[27]

B. DEBATE OVER THE INVESTMENT CHAPTER

Because the UK is still currently a member State, it would have to apply the provisional measures, with all the rights and obligations it would entail.[28]

The major concern regarding provisional application relates to the investment provisions of Chapter 8. Following article 30.9 (2) of the agreement "in the event that this agreement is terminated, the provision of chapter eight shall continue to be effective for a period of 20 years after the date of termination of this agreement in respect of investments made before that date."

---

[24] Id.

[25] Id.

[26] Eighteenth report, see sources cited *supra* in notes 11.

[27] See sources cited *supra* in notes 12.

[28] President Juncker on behalf of the Commission, Response to Parliamant question of June 28, 2016, (September 2, 2016).

The issue here was whether the UK could be bound by this provision after Brexit for investments made during the provisional application period.[29]

To answer this question, the first thing was to decide if the investment chapter fell under the EU's exclusive competence—and therefore could be provisionally applied—or if it was a shared competence not applicable before full ratification. According to article 207 TFEU foreign direct investment (FDI) is a part of the Common Commercial Policy, which is a EU exclusive competence under article 3 TFEU. However, the article is silent concerning other forms of investments. While for the member States, the fact that other forms of investments are not covered by article 207 make them a matter of shared competence, the European Commission considers them to be impliedly given to the EU as a EU-only competence.[30]

The most important concern for the UK was the provisional application of the Investment Court System included in chapter 8. Concerning the ICS, "the UK has been clear with the Commission that the investment court system of arbitration (ICS) should not be provisionally applied, as it is an area of mixed competence."[31] The European Commission answered this request and, following "robust and constructive discussions, the European Commission has conceded that a number of provisions within CETA do not fall within its exclusive competence and will not be provisionally applied before ratification by national and regional parliaments. This included the investment court system of arbitration (ICS)."[32] In order to avoid a deadlock, it has been decided that most parts of chapter 8 would not be provisionally applied. This was officially confirmed at the informal Trade Council held in Bratislava on September 23, 2016.

However, the question remains of what will happen if the agreement is fully ratified before the UK leaves the EU. Given the time needed for a full ratification, "it is possible that the UK will have left the EU by the time the CETA comes fully into force."[33] However, if this is not the case

---

[29] Wilhelm Schoellmann, International Agreements in Progress: Comprehensive Economic and Trade Agreement (CETA) with Canada, European Parliament Think Tank (October 26, 2016) - http://www.europarl.europa.eu/thinktank/en/document.html?reference=EPRS_BRI(2016)593491.

[30] Id.

[31] House of Commons, European Scrutiny Committee, Comprehensive Economic Trade Agreement (CETA) between the EU and Canada, Thirteenth Report Session 2016-17, Annex 2: Letter from Rt Hon Dr Liam to the Chairman, p. 18-19 (October 18, 2016).

[32] Id.

[33] See sources cited *supra* notes 12.

and CETA is ratified before Brexit, then the UK will be bound by all the provisions, including the ones that were not provisionally applied such as the investment chapter. Therefore, after full ratification, the UK could be bound by the investment provision for twenty years.[34] This issue is still unresolved and raises another fundamental legal issue as to whether or not the UK will remain a party to the agreement after Brexit.

IV. Brexit Implication for the UK as a Party to the Agreement

In considering the legal consequences of Brexit on the UK as a party to CETA, reference shall be made to the text of the agreement itself. According to article thirty-one of the Vienna Convention on the Law of Treaty, a "treaty shall be interpreted in good faith in accordance with the ordinary meaning to be given to the terms of the treaty in their context and in light of its object and purpose."

The Preamble of the agreement states that this is a "Comprehensive economic and trade agreement (CETA) between Canada, of the one part, *and* the European Union (*and* its member States) of the other part, hereafter jointly referred to as the "Parties" [emphasis added]." In order to determine the impact of Brexit on the UK as a party to CETA, (A) we have to analyze the meaning of "and its member States," and (B) conclude on the fact that this question is still pending (B).

A. *CETA: an Agreement between Canada and the European Union and its Member States*

1. Hypothesis as to the future of the UK as a party to the agreement

The agreement lists under "parties" all the member States, including the United Kingdom of Great Britain and Northern Ireland. By comparison, the EU-Vietnam FTA does not mention the member States at all and, most importantly, the EU-Korea FTA lists the member States only in the body of the text. Therefore, the listing of all member States in the agreement's Preamble is not insignificant. By appearing in full in the title of the agreement, the UK has a hook in CETA and, consequently, the question is to determine which legal consequences Brexit could have on the agreement's equilibrium and the UK as a party.

The House of Commons European Scrutiny Committee, on its thirteenth Report of Session, noted that "while the government highlights the potential benefits of CETA to the UK economy, and

---

[34] Id.

consider CETA ready for signature, important policy and legal issues remain unclear" among which "the Minister should clarify the Government's approach to assessing whether it would be desirable and or possible for the UK to continue to benefit from CETA after it formally withdraws from the EU."[35]

The first option would be to consider that the parties are Canada, the EU and each member State in its own right. The legal basis for it would be that States are listed in the agreement *in extenso*. Thus, each State would be a full-fledged party to the agreement.

Consequently, under this hypothesis, even after Brexit the UK would still be considered as a party. If the agreement is fully ratified before Brexit, then the UK would have ratified it as a "member State." If, by ratifying "as a member State" the given State becomes a party on its own, then Brexit will not deprive the UK from benefiting from CETA.

Nevertheless, this is an unlikely solution because the list appears under "member States" meaning the membership to the European Union is a mandatory prerequisite to be, and to remain, a party to the agreement. With this second analysis, the United Kingdom would most probably naturally lose the benefits of trade agreements concluded by the European Union, including CETA, when it leaves the EU. This analysis can be emphasized by referring to two provisions from the agreement itself.

Firstly, article 1.3 (b) of Chapter 1 "geographical scope of application" mentions that the agreement applies "for the European Union, to the territories in which the treaty on European Union and the Treaty on the Functioning of the European Union are applied […]. As regards the provisions concerning the tariff treatment of goods, this Agreement shall also apply to the area of the European Union customs territory not covered by the first sentence […]." Once it leaves the EU, the UK will not be governed by the European treaties anymore. Consequently, the UK will not fall under CETA's geographical scope. Therefore, the UK should not remain a party to the agreement after Brexit. However, if the door is closed the window is open as the tariff treatment of goods is applicable to the European Union customs territory. Thus, if the UK negotiates a deal with the EU regarding customs privileges, it might be able to benefit from CETA regarding treatment of goods. This provision could also be the basis for a special negotiation between the UK and Canada or the UK and the EU.

Secondly, the final provisions of CETA dealing with the termination of the agreement are also relevant. According to article 30.9 of the final

---

[35] Thirteenth Report, see *supra* note 29.

provisions "a Party may denounce this agreement by giving written notice of termination to the General Secretariat of the Council of the European Union and the Department of Foreign Affairs, Trade and Development Canada." Under the consideration that States are parties in their own right, this would mean that a member State could decide to terminate the agreement by giving notice to the EU and Canada's representatives, while still remaining in the European Union. This hypothesis goes against fundamental principles of the European Union where either all States are bound by the agreement with slightly different treatment, or none of them are bound, but it is not a "pick-and-choose" system.

Nonetheless, that brings us back to the issue of competences' distribution between the EU and the member States. When ratifying the agreement, the UK will do so in areas which are shared with the EU but in which the EU decided not to act, and in areas which are exclusive to member States (investment chapter, illegal camcording, administrative proceedings and appeals.)[36] Therefore, the question is whether the UK could still be bound by those specific areas not concerning the European Union. If the consideration is that the UK ratified CETA in its own right, then the UK should still be bound by the parts of the agreement that were under its own jurisdiction and released only from the provisions relating to EU-only competence. However, if the consideration is that the ratification was done only as a member State, then the UK should be released from the entire agreement after Brexit.

2. Consequences of Brexit on the European Union and Canada as parties to the agreement

The problem can also be addressed the other way around. CETA is concluded between Canada, the EU and its member States. Therefore, if the EU loses one of its member States, the question could be whether the EU still remains a fully-fledged party, and if so, what could be the legal consequences for Canada.

The EU negotiated the agreement for, and with, twenty-eight member States. Those member States are listed in the introduction of the agreement, acknowledging them as an essential part of the agreement. Therefore, the question is whether, if by losing one State, the EU still remains a party to the agreement or if Brexit could deprive the EU from staying in the agreement.

It is this paper's contention that the EU will remain a party to the agreement once the UK exits. Even though all States are listed as member States, the mere fact for the EU to lose one member should not

---

[36] Eighteenth Report, see *supra* note 11.

affect the legally binding force of the agreement for all other member States. This situation could however open new questions relative to Canada's right to renegotiate the agreement, taking into account the absence of the UK. Indeed, Brexit could impair Canada's rights and may give to Canada a reason to terminate the agreement. Knowing the fact that the UK was one of Canada's biggest markets in CETA, Brexit will definitively bring some changes in the equilibrium of the agreement. It is however relevant to mention that the agreement did not foresee Brexit, despite its currentness. Following the chronology of the events, the proposal for signature occurred after Brexit. Therefore, parties could have re-opened the negotiations following Brexit, something they decided not to do. In the same vein, article 30.10 of the agreement deals with the accession of new member States to the European Union but no provision deals with the secession of a member from the EU.

It is important to do some comparative law to understand CETA's place in the European legal landscape. This paper contends that, if the States are all listed in the Preamble of the agreement, it is because CETA is a full mixed-agreement. In the FTA with Korea, the agreement distinguishes clearly the part where it is EU-only competence, where the member States have exclusive competence and where there is a shared competence. This explains why the agreement uses the terms "Korea *and* the EU *or* its member States *or* the EU *and* its member States" [emphasis added]. Similarly, CETA is also composed of mixed competence, exclusive competence and State-only competence. However, CETA does not use the terms "or" and "and" but instead puts Canada, the EU and the member States on an equal footing. By listing the member States, CETA probably sought for transparency as to the member States' acceptance of the entire agreement. However, there is no answer as to why and for which legal reasons the member States are listed in full on the Preamble of the agreement.

B. AN UNCERTAIN FUTURE FOR THE UK: QUESTIONS CONCERNING THE LONG-TERM IMPACT OF BREXIT

Conclusively, the question of whether or not the UK is a party and will remain a party is unresolved. It may seem unrealistic to consider it, but it has not been clearly pushed aside by politics as a far-fetched proposition.

Reference can be made here to the UK Treasury Committee which said that "were the UK to leave the EU, it is very uncertain whether it would be able to continue to participate in these agreements *[i.e. the agreements between the EU and others countries]*. The extent to which the UK would have to enter into negotiations to ensure its continued participation would probably depend on the attitude of the contracting parties, about which little is known [*emphasis added.*]"[37] Emphases have been made by the European Scrutiny Committee which stated that "the Government's analysis is that on leaving the EU, the UK will lose access to the trade preferences set out in CETA 'unless arrangement to do are put in place as part of (its) negotiations with the EU.'"[38] The law firm Clifford Chance also wrote that "there are some grounds to suggest that the UK may remain bound by certain aspects of these agreements but this is very uncertain and without legal precedent."[39]

On Canada's side, the Trade Minister Chrystia Freeland announced that the country will try to build on the EU deals within the UK once Brexit occurs, rather than strike for a bilateral agreement.[40] From these statements, the conclusion is that there are no real decisions yet on what is going to happen to UK's membership on EU's trade deals. Not being a party does not necessarily mean the UK is going to lose all of the benefits of the trade agreements. As Brexit is without legal precedent little is known about what is going to happen and some unexpected legal solutions may be created by the parties involved.

CONCLUSION

Overall, Brexit is about to bring innumerous unforeseen legal and political developments that need to be resolved. This paper raised some of them without entering into the substantive provisions of the Free Trade Agreement. The UK was one of the principal countries to push for a speedy conclusion of CETA as the agreement was supposed to benefit UK's firms by 1.3 billion pounds per year.[41] Concurrently, UK was Canada's biggest trading partner in the EU.[42] It is unclear what would be the strategy adopted by the EU, Canada and the UK but the question of whether or not the UK could still benefit from the agreement is still pending. In the long run, other subsequent questions will arise such as if CETA could serve as a model for a UK-EU or UK-Canada

---

[37] See sources supra note 11, § 226 (quoting The UK Treasury Committee, *The economic and financial costs and benefits of the UK's EU membership*, HC 122, (May 27, 2016)).

[38] Thirteenth Report, see *supra* note 31.

[39] Eighteenth Report, see supra note 11.

[40] Josh Wingrove, Canada-EU Trade Deal Could Survive Brexit in UK, Bloomberg (December 30, 2016) – https://www.bloomberg.com/news/articles/2016-12-30/canada-eu-trade-deal-could-survive-brexit-in-u-k-freeland-says (« the job at that point would be to build on it and make sure nothing happens to undermine it »).

[41] UK Trade and Investment Press release, UK Trade Minister calls for speedy conclusion to £1.3 billion Canada Trade Agreement, Lord Livington and UK Export Finance (March 26, 2014).

[42] See sources cited *supra* note 40.

trade agreement. Outside the EU it will be easier for the UK to negotiate trade deals satisfying its own interests. However, this could be "counterbalanced by the fact that, being one-sixth of the size of the EU, the potential benefits to other countries of concluding a deal with the UK are smaller." [43] Concerning this issue, former President Obama already said that the UK would be "at the back of the queue" concerning the on-going negotiations for Free-Trade Agreements between the EU and the United States and between the EU and India. [44]

Yet, with the new US administration, free-trade agreement policies could change tremendously. Theresa May already said the UK "is open for business" as she announced the plan to pursue a clean cut with the EU. President Trump and the UK's Prime Minister met in Washington, DC in late January 2017 to discuss the future trading relationship between the two countries. Contrary to Obama's views, Trump believes the UK will be in front of the queue in the trading agenda.[45] Therefore, what would happen after Brexit is still unclear and depends largely on politics.

---

[43] Eighteenth Report, see sources cited *supra* note 11.

[44] Id.

[45] Jennifer Jacobs and Margaret Talev, Trump Team in Talk with U.K on Post Brexit Trade Deal, Blommberg (January 21, 2017) - https://www.bloomberg.com/politics/articles/2017-01-21/britain-s-may-mexico-s-pena-nieto-to-meet-with-trump-this-month.

PART II:

Internal UK Issues

Chapter 7: UK Competition Law after Brexit: The Prospect of Divergence from the EU Legal Regime

Matthew S. Moore

I. Introduction

Competition law and policy is a highly visible feature of the legal landscape of both the European Union and the United Kingdom. Currently, competition law in the UK is closely aligned with EU law through the Competition Act 1998[1] ("the 1998 Act"), a domestic statute that harmonizes national competition controls with the principal substantive rules on competition at the European level. A key mechanism harmonizing UK and EU law in this area is Section 60 of the 1998 Act, which imposes a duty on UK courts and the Competition and Markets Authority (CMA), the UK's national competition agency, to handle questions of competition law consistently with the European approach. This paper seeks to examine the consequences of Brexit for competition law by focusing on a narrow question: what is the future of the principle of consistency, embodied by Section 60 of the 1998 Act, once the UK withdraws from the EU?

Competition law in the contemporary European Union reaches far and wide. Even casual observers of EU business and politics are likely familiar with the high-profile actions of the European Commission in this area, which have touched the world's largest industries and companies—from the Commission's review of Facebook's planned acquisition of WhatsApp to fines levied on Apple for allegedly illegal tax benefits received in Ireland. In the United Kingdom, the CMA has pursued recent investigations or cases in areas such as pharmaceuticals, energy, and the toy market, among many others. Whether or not UK law will remain consistent with EU precedent in the area of competition is thus potentially consequential for a diverse range of industries, companies, and consumers within and outside of the UK.

This paper will explore UK competition law after Brexit by examining the relationship between the EU and UK legal systems and the possibility that the two will diverge following the UK's withdrawal from the EU. First, a description of the EU and UK competition law regimes will be given, emphasizing the close alignment of the two

---

[1] Competition Act 1998, c. 41.

systems as currently constituted. Second, this paper will examine the consistency principle contained in Section 60 of the 1998 Act and describe the implications should this principle be discarded as a result of Brexit: potential divergence between the UK and EU approaches to competition law. Third, the practical consequences of divergence will be illustrated through a discussion of Advocate General Nils Wahl's 2016 opinion in *Intel Corp. v. European Commission*,[2] a recent case that addressed the regulation of allegedly "abusive" conduct in discount pricing and rebate schemes. Fourth, this paper will describe the robust debate, still developing, on whether to allow UK competition law to depart from the EU approach following Brexit.

This paper will conclude by sounding a cautious note on divergence. While proponents of divergence have offered compelling reasons for a "reset" of UK competition law following Brexit,[3] these arguments should be tempered by recognition of the significant potential costs and unpredictability of allowing the UK's approach to competition law to diverge from that of the EU.

II.   COMPETITION LAW IN THE EU AND UK

Competition law and policy is a cornerstone of the European project[4] and is integral to the EU's vision for an integrated internal market. Following the European Commission's "modernization" reform in 2003,[5] competition rules in the EU have been enforced by a decentralized network of National Competition Authorities (NCAs) and courts, alongside the European Commission, primarily through the Director General for Competition and through EU courts. This section will offer a brief description of the EU and UK competition law regimes and introduce the principle of consistency, which plays an important role in aligning UK and EU law.

---

[2] Case C-413/14 P, Intel Corp. v. Eur. Comm'n, 2016 EUR-Lex ECLI:EU:C:2016:788 (Opinion of Advocate General Wahl) (Oct. 20, 2016).
[3] *See, e.g.*, Oliver Bretz, UK *Competition Policy and Brexit– ime for a Reset*, Competition Pol'y Int'l (July 2016), http://www.competitionpolicyinternational.com/uk-competition-policy-and-brexit-time-for-a-reset.
[4] The centrality of competition policy and law to the European project is evident, for example, in the treaties constituting the EU. *See, e.g.*, Consolidated Version of the Treaty on European Union art. 3(3), Dec. 13, 2007, 2016 O.J. (C 202) 17 (stating that the EU "shall establish an internal market."); Consolidated Version of the Treaty on the Functioning of the European Union protocol 27, Dec. 13, 2007, 2016 O.J. (C 202) 308 [hereinafter TFEU] (stipulating that this "internal market" shall "include[] a system ensuring that competition is not distorted.").
[5] Council Regulation 1/2003, 2003 O.J. (L 1) (EC).

The EU Competition Law Regime

Market integration is a central aim of the EU and is facilitated by competition law and policy, which together create a "unified competitive environment" and prevent private companies from establishing barriers to trade between member states.[6] Competition law and policy in the EU address several major issues: abuse of a dominant position (monopolist behavior), anti-competitive agreements, mergers, and state aid.

Following the ratification of the Treaty of Lisbon,[7] the principal substantive rules on anti-competitive agreements and abuse of dominant market positions are contained in Articles 101[8] and 102[9] of the Treaty on the Functioning of the European Union (TFEU), respectively, while state aid is addressed in Article 107. Mergers are dealt with in the European Merger Control Regulation, a separate regulation.[10] This paper will focus on the main rules on anti-competitive agreements and dominant market players as embodied by Articles 101 and 102 TFEU.

Article 101 TFEU prohibits agreements between "undertakings" which may affect trade between EU member states and which "have as their object or effect the prevention, restriction or distortion of competition within the internal market."[11] In practice, this provision may cover conduct such as price fixing, limiting or controlling production, and other forms of cartel-like conduct.[12] Article 102 TFEU prohibits the "abuse" of a "dominant position" within the EU internal market so far as it "may affect trade between member states."[13] This provision seeks to prevent businesses with significant market power from impeding competition through actions such as limiting output, increasing prices, and offering unfair discounts or rebates.[14]

The UK Competition Law Regime

Competition law and policy in the UK is closely aligned and modeled on the law of the EU. The Competition Act 1998 harmonized UK competition controls with the principal substantive EU competition rules. Chapter I of the 1998 Act prohibits anti-competitive agreements

---

[6] Barry J. Rodger & Angus MacCulloch, COMPETITION LAW AND POLICY IN THE EU AND UK 21, 25 (5th ed. 2015).

[7] The Treaty of Lisbon is an international agreement signed in December 2007 that amended the core treaties constituting the European Union.

[8] TFEU, *supra* note 4, art. 101.

[9] TFEU, *supra* note 4, art. 102.

[10] Council Regulation 139/2004, 2004 O.J. (L 024) (EC).

[11] TFEU, *supra* note 4, art. 101.

[12] *Id.*

[13] TFEU, *supra* note 4, art. 102.

[14] Rodger and MacCulloch, *supra* note 6, at 93.

and Chapter II prohibits abuse of a dominant position.[15] The Chapter I
and II prohibitions thus parallel Articles 101 and 102 TFEU (although
Chapter I and II apply only to conduct affecting trade within the United
Kingdom, while Articles 101 and 102 TFEU apply to conduct that has
an economic effect on trade between EU member states[16]). Notably, the
Labour Government that enacted the 1998 Act was not obligated to
establish this framework but did so because of the perceived benefits of
closely aligning the UK's competition law regime with that of the EU,
including the benefit of avoiding a "double compliance burden" on UK
businesses.[17] Similar to the EU regime, merger control in the UK is
addressed apart from the other two competition pillars through a
separate law, the Enterprise and Regulatory Reform Act of 2013.
Domestic UK law does not reach state aid, which is monitored and
enforced by the European Commission under EU state aid rules.

Consistency between UK and EU Law

Because EU competition law is enforced at both the European
Commission and national levels, a series of rules exist to ensure the
consistent application of EU competition law.[18] Under the doctrine of
precedence, which governs the EU legal order generally, directly
applicable EU rules are supreme over the national laws of member
states.[19] In other words, EU legal rules take precedence over national law.
This doctrine is established in the UK by the European Communities
Act 1972 (ECA 1972).[20] In the event of a conflict between UK and EU
competition law, EU law trumps any conflicting provisions of UK law.

The convergence of EU competition law with the competition rules
of member states is further solidified by Council Regulation 1/2003.[21]
Regulation 1/2003 requires the national courts and authorities of
member states to apply Articles 101 and 102 TFEU when interpreting
domestic competition laws in cases where there is an effect on interstate
trade.[22] The goal of this provision is to "ensure a clearer substantive rule
of precedence in the application of EU law and national law."[23] Finally,

---

[15] Competition Act 1998, *supra* note 1.

[16] Commission Notice–Guidelines on the effect on trade concept contained in Articles
81 and 82 of the Treaty, 2004 O.J. (C 101).

[17] Rodger and MacCulloch, *supra* note 6, at 27.

[18] *Id.* at 37.

[19] Case 26/62, Van Gend en Loos v Nederlandse Administratie der Belastingen, 1963
E.C.R. 2.

[20] European Communities Act 1972, c. 68, §§ 2(1), 3(1).

[21] Council Regulation 1/2003, *supra* note 5.

[22] *Id.*

[23] Rodger and MacCulloch, *supra* note 6, at 38.

the consistent application of EU competition law by national courts and authorities is enhanced by Article 267 TFEU. Article 267 enables national courts to request a preliminary ruling from the Court of Justice of the European Union (CJEU) on questions of EU law. While Article 267 opinions are not binding on national courts, they provide authoritative guidance as to how the CJEU can be expected to rule on a specific question regarding the interpretation of EU law. Given the increasing role of national courts and authorities in enforcing EU competition rules, the Article 267 procedure is an important mechanism ensuring the uniform interpretation of EU law by the legal systems of the various member states.[24]

The above description provides a sense of the important legal mechanisms that ensure consistency when the supranational legal order of the EU interacts with the national legal systems of EU member states. In the UK, the principle of consistency between UK and EU competition law is set forth in Section 60 of the 1998 Act, which is discussed below.

III. SECTION 60 AND BREXIT

Under Section 60 of the 1998 Act, UK courts and competition authorities have a duty to interpret the provisions of the Act consistently with EU jurisprudence. The purpose of this consistency principle is to

> ensure that so far as is possible (having regard to any relevant differences between the provisions concerned), questions arising under [Part I of the 1998 Act] in relation to competition within the United Kingdom are dealt with in a manner which is consistent with the treatment of corresponding questions arising in Community law in relation to competition within the Community.[25]

In order to achieve this goal, Section 60 requires the CMA and UK courts considering questions under the 1998 Act to ensure that there is consistency between "the principles laid down by the Treaty and the European Court, and any relevant decision of that Court."[26] Section 60 also imposes a duty on the CMA and UK courts to "have regard to any relevant decision or statement of the Commission."[27]

---

[24] *Id.* at 53.
[25] Competition Act 1998, *supra* note 1, § 60.
[26] *Id.*
[27] *Id.*

Brexit and the Consistency Principle

Section 60 of the 1998 Act has helped to ensure the consistent application of EU competition law within the UK. However, after Brexit, the principle of consistency will need to be reevaluated in light of the UK's new relationship to the EU legal order. A key question is thus: what will become of Section 60's consistency principle once the UK is no longer a part of the EU?

The UK government has proposed to address the post-Brexit challenge of what to do with UK legislation that implements EU law with a "Great Repeal Bill," through which the UK Parliament will repeal the ECA 1972, while transposing EU law into domestic law "wherever practical."[28] These changes will take effect on "Brexit Day," the day that the UK officially leaves the EU.[29] The Great Repeal Bill will also enable Parliament or government ministers to amend or repeal UK legislation that was enacted to give effect to the UK's obligations under the treaties constituting the EU.[30] Thus, in the realm of competition law, the Great Repeal Bill could provide the UK government with the opportunity to alter the focus of UK competition law by adapting or repealing provisions of the 1998 Act such as Section 60.

It should be noted that revisiting the Section 60 consistency principle will only be necessary if the UK undertakes a "hard Brexit" and leaves the Single Market and the EU legal order. In the alternative, if the UK follows the "Norwegian model" and joins the European Economic Area (EEA), Brexit's impact on competition law will be less substantial. Joining the EEA would require the UK to accept a continued role for EU law, the CJEU, and the Commission. If the UK follows the "Swiss model" and joins the European Free Trade Association, the UK would similarly need to accept a continued role for EU law (although the UK could in theory try to negotiate for more autonomy through a bilateral treaty with the EU). However, neither the Norwegian model nor the Swiss model appears likely to happen. The UK government under the leadership of Prime Minister Theresa May has announced its preference for a "hard Brexit."[31] In this scenario, it is less probable that the UK will continue to adhere to the consistency principle of Section 60. As one

---

[28] HOUSE OF COMMONS LIBRARY, BRIEFING PAPER NO. 7793 23, LEGISLATING FOR BREXIT: THE GREAT REPEAL BILL (Nov. 21, 2016), http://researchbriefings.parliament.uk/ResearchBriefing/Summary/CBP-7793.

[29] Competition Act 1998, *supra* note 1.

[30] *Id.*

[31] *Theresa May to Say UK Is 'Prepared to Accept Hard Brexit,'* THE GUARDIAN (Jan. 15. 2007), https://www.theguardian.com/politics/2017/jan/15/theresa-may-uk-is-prepared-to-accept-hard-brexit.

prominent observer has remarked, "[m]any Brexiteers hold the utmost contempt for the Court of Justice."[32] For this reason, it is "unlikely that [they] would be willing to leave [S]ection 60 in place since Brexit is about the restoration of national sovereignty and freedom from the 'meddling' in internal affairs by the Courts in Luxembourg and Strasbourg."[33] As a "hard Brexit" appears far more probable than the alternative scenarios, this paper assumes a "hard Brexit" for the purpose of examining the consequences of Brexit for the Section 60 consistency principle.

The Potential for Divergence between EU and UK Competition Law

Following a "hard Brexit" and the enactment of the Great Repeal Bill, it is probable that the UK will retain the Chapter I and Chapter II competition provisions of the 1998 Act, which are modeled on Articles 101 and 102 TFEU. Outright repeal of these "central pillars of antitrust law and policy" is unlikely and would risk "years of uncertainty" and harm to businesses, consumers, and the economy.[34] However, gradual divergence in the interpretation of UK and EU law could occur. As noted above, repeal of the ECA 1972 would eliminate the requirement that UK courts treat EU law as supreme in the event of a conflict between UK and EU law. Moreover, upon the UK's exit from the European legal order, UK courts would no longer be able to request rulings from the CJEU to clarify issues of EU competition law under the Article 267 provision. This would eliminate another of the principal mechanisms that have kept EU and UK competition law consistent.

As one eminent commentator has suggested, one option for the UK in this situation would be to amend Section 60 to "require UK authorities and courts to 'have regard to' EU case law rather than necessarily to act consistently with it."[35] This amendment of the Section 60 consistency principle would allow UK courts and authorities to treat EU law as persuasive authority while avoiding the awkwardness of allowing a non-UK court to determine the content of a UK statute (which would occur if Section 60's consistency requirement were left in place following the UK's withdrawal from the EU).[36]

---

[32] Richard Whish, *Brexit and EU Competition Policy*, 7 J. of Eur. Competition L. & Prac. 297 (2016).

[33] *Id.*

[34] Sir John Vickers, *Consequences of Brexit for Competition Law and Policy* 8 (Paper for British Academy Conference on 'The Economic Consequences of Brexit,') (Dec. 7, 2016), http://www.bclwg.org/wp-content/uploads/2016/12/Vickers-British-Academy-7-Dec-16.pdf.

[35] *Id.*

[36] *Id.*

What would the divergence of EU and UK competition jurisprudence look like? It is likely that any change would be gradual, as UK courts would still seek guidance from prior UK competition cases, which were decided under the consistency principle of Section 60 and thus reflect the approach to competition law of the CJEU and other relevant EU bodies. However, over time, UK courts could use the UK's departure from the EU to reshape domestic competition law according to UK-specific legal concepts and policy objectives.

As has been noted, "market integration"—the control of barriers to trade within the EU internal market—has exerted significant influence on the development and direction of competition law in the EU.[37] Following a "hard Brexit," the cohesion of the EU internal market will no longer be a goal of UK jurisprudence, thus creating the potential for divergence where the "market integration" objective had previously helped determine the answer to specific legal questions. However, despite its centrality in the formation of EU competition law, "market integration" has ceased to be the "predominant principle" in EU competition law.[38] For this reason, the detachment of UK jurisprudence from the "market integration" principle will be unlikely to be the primary driver of divergence between the EU and UK competition law regimes.

Instead, the gradual separation of UK and EU competition law could occur if EU and UK courts begin to approach legal and policy questions from broadly divergent philosophies regarding the nature and objectives of competition law. Specifically, the UK is currently regarded as a leader in promoting the "modernization" of EU competition law through the use of cutting edge economics and a preference for legal analysis focusing on the "effects" of allegedly anticompetitive conduct. By contrast, the traditional EU competition law regime is associated with a more formalist approach focusing on the form rather than the "effects" of conduct.[39] The departure of the UK from the EU legal order presents the possibility that UK courts could seek to develop the "effects"-oriented approach to competition law. Conversely, the legal authorities of the EU, free from the "modernizing" influence of the UK, could pursue a more traditional approach. The following section will examine this dynamic through the example of *Intel Corp. v. European Commission*, a

---

[37] Rodger and MacCulloch, *supra* note 6, at 25.

[38] *Id.* at 26.

[39] While neither the UK nor the EU competition law regimes directly parallel the approach of the United States, the "modernizing" impulse of some UK competition lawyers can be seen in similar developments in the US, including the use of behavioral economics and other cutting edge economic tools to analyze antitrust problems. On this aspect of US antitrust law, *see id.* at 19-20.

recent case that illustrates the difference between the formalist and effects-based approaches in the context of Article 102 TFEU's prohibition of the abuse of a dominant market position.

IV. CASE STUDY: *INTEL CORP. V. EUROPEAN COMMISSION*

On October 20, 2016 Advocate General Nils Wahl of the CJEU issued an opinion in *Intel Corp. v. European Commission*,[40] the latest step in Intel's quest to overturn a record-setting €1.06 billion fine imposed on it by the European Commission in 2009 for alleged abuse of its dominant position in the market for computer microprocessors. In addition to the massive fine at issue, the *Intel* case has inspired wide interest because its outcome may determine whether the EU follows a formalist or "effects-based" approach to the analysis of allegedly anticompetitive rebate schemes.[41]

At issue in the case is an incentive scheme under which Intel offered rebates to computer manufacturers under the condition that they buy a set percentage of computer processors from Intel. [42] Following its investigation, the Commission found that Intel had violated EU competition rules on abuse of a dominant position through the rebate scheme, which the Commission concluded was aimed at foreclosing a competitor, AMD, from entering the market for x86 CPU microprocessors.[43] The Commission subsequently levied its record €1.06 billion fine on Intel. On appeal, the General Court rejected Intel's argument that the Commission's fine should be set aside.[44] The General Court found that Intel's rebates were "exclusivity rebates," rebates that are conditional on the customer obtaining all or nearly all of its requirements from the dominant company.[45] The General Court found such "exclusivity rebates" to be presumptively illegal because they are intrinsically anticompetitive and capable of preventing the entrance of a competitor to the market.[46]

Advocate General Wahl's recent opinion cogently critiques the General Court's analysis and provides compelling grounds for the CJEU to ultimately overturn the earlier decision in the case and the €1.06 billion fine of Intel. Advocate General Wahl sets out several grounds for

---

[40] Case C-413/14 P, Intel Corp. v. Eur. Comm'n, *supra* note 2.

[41] Advocate General Wahl himself recognizes the potential impact of the *Intel* case. *See id.* at para. 3 ("[This] case offers the Court an opportunity to refine its case-law relating to the abuse of a dominant position under Article 102 TFEU.").

[42] *Id.* at paras. 25-29.

[43] *Id.* at para. 18.

[44] *Id.* at para. 34.

[45] *Id.* at para. 44.

[46] *Id.* at paras. 44, 46.

rejecting the General Court's approach. Most relevant to the discussion here are his conclusions that: (1) it was improper for the General Court to create a category of rebates—"exclusivity rebates"— that are per se illegal because of the form of the rebate, instead of its effects;[47] and (2) a court's analysis of the alleged abuse of a dominant position in rebate cases must show more than the "mere theoretical possibility of an exclusionary effect" for a violation to be found.[48]

Both of the above arguments constitute a forceful critique of the formalist approach to rebate cases. First, Advocate General Wahl finds that the General Court's prohibition of "exclusionary rebates" was improper because it was "based on the *form* of the conduct instead of its *effects*."[49] That is, the General Court and the Commission before it focused on the Intel rebate scheme's formal structure (that it was conditional on consumers meeting Intel's requirements) instead of whether the rebate scheme had actual anti-competitive effects. This analysis was improper, according to Advocate General Wahl, because it prevented Intel from presenting evidence that the rebate scheme at issue might actually have beneficial effects on competition[50] and because it ignored "experience and economic analysis," which show that loyalty rebates do not always harm competition.[51]

Under the new approach to analyzing rebate schemes articulated by Advocate General Wahl, a court must look to "all the circumstances" surrounding a case to determine effects.[52] Ultimately, to find that a rebate scheme constitutes a violation of Article 102 TFEU, a court must find that the "likelihood [is] considerably more than a mere possibility that [the conduct at issue] may restrict competition."[53] Advocate General Wahl notes that to accept the General Court's standard, which would find a violation due to the "mere theoretical possibility of an exclusionary effect," one would "have to accept that EU competition law sanctions form, not anticompetitive effects.[54]

Advocate General Wahl's Opinion and the "Effects-Based" Approach

Advocate General Wahl's opinion has been heralded by the proponents of the "modernization" of competition law because it points

---

[47] *Id.* at paras. 84-86.
[48] *Id.* at para. 117-120.
[49] *Id.* at para. 86.
[50] *Id.* at para. 87.
[51] *Id.* at para. 89.
[52] *Id.* at para. 101.
[53] *Id.* at para. 117.
[54] *Id.* at para. 118.

the way toward an effects-based analysis of rebate schemes, whereas the earlier General Court opinion had utilized a traditional, formalist approach. As the opinion of an Advocate General, Wahl's decision is not binding but will be considered as persuasive by the CJEU in reaching its final judgment. It is thus unknown at this stage whether the CJEU will follow Advocate General Wahl's reasoning. Whatever the ultimate outcome at the CJEU, however, the Wahl opinion demonstrates how the "effects-based" and formalist approaches can lead to profoundly different outcomes when applied to concrete questions of competition law. The UK's departure from the EU legal order will enable UK courts, should they choose to, to chart a new course in competition law jurisprudence by embracing an effects-based approach. If the CJEU rejects Advocate General Wahl's call for a modernized, effects-based approach to competition law, UK courts after Brexit would be free to adopt the Wahl analysis for rebate cases in the UK. Indeed, given the trend toward emphasizing effects-based tests and economic analysis in UK competition law, it seems probable that UK courts may follow this path.

Advocate General Wahl's opinion was issued amidst a robust debate over the future of competition law in the UK following Brexit. Some commentators have advocated for a "reset" of competition policy following Brexit.[55] This "pro-reset" camp emphasizes the potential salutary effects of allowing UK competition law to develop independently of EU law, which would allow the UK competition regime to drive innovation by serving as a "test-bed for new economic theories and methods."[56] Further, these commentators note that the UK's departure from the EU may result in a "more Franco-German approach" to competition law at the European Commission, including reduced emphasis on economic analysis in the interpretation of competition rules.[57] On the other side, some observers have argued that "it is in the UK's interests to remain broadly aligned with current EU [c]ompetition [p]olicy and to avoid a divergence in substantive antitrust rules."[58] Such broad alignment will minimize uncertainty and "avoid unnecessary increases in the regulatory burden for firms operating in the UK."[59]

---

[55] Bretz, *supra* note 3.

[56] *Id.*

[57] *Id.*

[58] Bruce Lyons, David Reader & Andreas Stephan, *UK Competition Policy Post-Brexit: In the Public Interest?* 20 (Centre for Competition Policy, Working Paper No. 16-12, 2016), https://papers.ssrn.com/sol3/papers.cfm?abstract_id=2864461.

[59] *Id.*

CONCLUSION

The future of the consistency principle embodied by Section 60 of the UK's Competition Act 1998 is uncertain. A "hard Brexit" presents the probability that UK courts may use the UK's departure from the EU legal system to reshape their approach to competition law. This paper will conclude by concurring with those commentators urging caution with respect to this potential divergence. The reasoning of Advocate General Wahl's opinion in *Intel* persuasively shows that there may be significant benefits to pursuing a modernized, effects-based approach to questions of competition law, such as how rebate schemes are analyzed under competition rules. However, notwithstanding the potential benefits of divergence, allowing the UK's legal regime to radically depart from that of the EU could increase both risk and costs for UK businesses and regulators.

It is notable that the UK first modeled its domestic competition law on the EU system due to the perceived benefits of alignment. These benefits, which include minimizing compliance costs for UK businesses, will still exist after Brexit. This is particularly true in light of the "effect on trade" concept, which guides the extraterritorial application of EU competition law.[60] Under the "effect on trade" concept, EU competition law applies to conduct that has an effect on interstate trade between member states.[61] Following Brexit, EU law will thus continue to apply to the many UK businesses whose activities will still impact trade between EU member states. If a sharp break between UK and EU competition law and policy occurs, compliance costs and risk for these businesses will swell due to the need to comply with two potentially conflicting systems of competition law. Moreover, divergence would increase the burden on the UK competition authorities, tasked with enforcing a less stable and predictable competition law regime. This increased risk and cost militate strongly in favor of limiting the divergence of UK and EU competition law and maintaining the spirit of Section 60's consistency principle.

This paper has explored the impact of Brexit on competition law in the UK through the lens of Section 60 of the Competition Act 1998. Section 60 imposes a duty on UK courts and the national competition authority to handle questions of competition law consistently with the European approach. Following Brexit, courts in the UK have the opportunity to discard the "consistency principle" of Section 60 and to progressively develop UK competition law away from the formalist orthodoxies of EU precedent. As Advocate General Wahl's opinion in

---

[60] Commission Notice, *supra* note 16.
[61] *Id.*

the *Intel* case shows, powerful substantive arguments exist for a modernized, effects-based approach to competition law. However, notwithstanding these arguments, courts and policymakers in the UK should approach divergence from the EU competition regime with caution. Such divergence would entail significant uncertainty and an increased burden on both UK businesses and regulators.

CHAPTER 8: STATE AID REGULATIONS AFTER BREXIT: A GOOD DEAL FOR THE UK?

ANNA WEINBERGER

INTRODUCTION

In this paper, I intend to primarily analyze the consequences of Brexit on the UK. For this purpose I will examine advantages and disadvantages of this UK exit from the European Union (the "EU"). Finally, because some impacts on the EU cannot be ignored, I will briefly raise few negative effects of Brexit affecting EU companies.

On August 30, 2016, the *Washington Post* titled its story, "How the E.U.'s ruling on Apple explains why Brexit happened."[1] This headline, although outrageous, has truth to it. Apple had benefited for years from illegal state aid granted by the Irish government through a low corporate-tax. But what is the link with Brexit? It seems that the interventionism[2] of the EU institutions convinced a majority of UK voters to leave the EU on June 23.

When creating the single market based on a free circulation of goods, services, and peoples, the EU also introduced limits to protect and balance this freedom. Nowadays, parts of this protection are composed of EU competition rules, including State aid rules (the "State aid rules" or "State aid regime"). In this respect, the EU State aid regime relies exclusively on direct effect regulation[3] (TFEU and Council/Commission regulations), which will cease to apply after Brexit and has no equivalent at a national level.[4]

Article 107 TFEU[5] defines what a state aid is and which state aid is allowed. Four cumulative conditions need to be fulfilled in order for the European Commission to qualify a state aid: (i) there must have been an intervention by the State or through State resources, (ii) the measure gives the investor an advantage on a selective basis, (iii) which would

---

[1] Max Bearak, *How the E.U.'s ruling on Apple explains why Brexit happened*, The *Washington Post*, August 30, 2016

[2] *Id.*

[3] Jonathan Branton et al., *Brexit: what happens to the law on State aid*, DWF.LAW, Jun. 9, 2016, at 3.

[4] Slaughter and May, *Brexit Essentials: The legal and business implications of the UK leaving the EU*, at 14.

[5] Consolidated Version of the Treaty on the Functioning of the European Union art. 107(1), Oct. 26, 2012, O.J. C 326/91 [hereinafter TFEU].

have resulted in the distortion of the competition and (iv) would have affected the trade between the EU Member States (the "Member States"). Aiming to avoid any subsidy race, [6] protectionism [7] and anticompetitive market distortions, all arising from governmental support, [8] the EU created these rules and gave the control and enforcement power exclusively to the European Commission [9] (the "EC"). As a matter of fact, the EU State aid regime is based on a "restrictive" approach: each Member State, willing to grant a state aid, is subject to an *a priori* control by the EC (notification, subject to approval). Also, Member States are subject to an *a posteriori* control. When allegations of illegal aid are expressed, the EC also has a power of investigation to determine whether a Member State breached the EU State aid rules. In case of breach, the EC will order this Member State to recover the illegal aid granted. Otherwise, the dispute will be brought before the Court of Justice of the European Union (the "CJEU").

Despite the weightiness and ascendency of the EC, the UK has always been a strong supporter of the State aid rules.[10] First, it provides a high level of playing field across Europe.[11] Second, the UK has never subsidized its industries and companies as much as some of its neighbors.[12] Nonetheless, the broad authority of the EC over UK governmental decisions appeared as a major concern for the British last June and becomes part of a more global European criticism.[13] For instance, the French President has "also demanded a rewriting of EU merger control rules and restrictions on state aid to industry to enable the creation of 'European Champions.'"[14] Indeed, difficulties faced by the UK steel industry and the current Italian banking industry crisis raised indignation from Member States, and European citizens pointed out limits to the EU State aid regime.

---

[6] Albert Sanchez Graells, *Brexit may have negative effects for the control of public expenditure particularly regarding subsidies to large companies*, University of Bristol Law School Blog, Jun. 28, 2016, at 1.

[7] Slaughter and May, *supra* note 4, at 14.

[8] *Id.*

[9] *Id.. See also* TFEU art. 108, Oct. 26, 2012, O.J. C 326/92.

[10] James Webber et al., *Brexit: State Aid Implications*, Shearman & Sterling LLP, Client Publication, Antitrust, Jul. 5, 2016 at 2.

[11] Mark Poulton, *Brexit: What does it mean for multinationals*, Clifford Chance, Client Briefing, Aug. 24, 2016, at 11.

[12] James Webber et al., *supra* note 10, at 2.

[13] *Id.*

[14] *The EU's authority is fraying in reaction to Brexit vote*, Reuters, Jul. 5, 2016, at 2, *available at* Fortune.com.

Although the EU State aid rules remain applicable to the UK until it formally leaves the EU,[15] different legal schemes post-Brexit are envisaged. Rather than joining the EEA/EFTA or signing a new FTA with the EU (at least in a short run), I believe that only a hard Brexit is realistic. For this reason, I focused my research on the applicable regime post-Brexit where only the World Trade Organization[16] (the "WTO") rules will apply to the UK. In this respect, the Subsidies and Countervailing Measures Agreement (the "SCM Agreement") will substitute for the EU State aid rules.

While in a first part of this paper I will try to determine why Brexit represents a good opportunity for the UK (I), in a second part I will briefly examine some consequences damageable for EU companies (II).

I.   A BENEFIT FOR THE UK

When Brexit takes place, the EU laws will stop applying to the UK. However, as a WTO member state (the "member state"), the UK will still have to comply with the WTO rules,[17] which includes the SCM Agreement dealing with the subsidies.[18] The SCM Agreement will primarily apply to all relationships existing between the UK, the EU, and the 27 remaining Member States. Therefore, the central question is whether the SCM Agreement will provide to the UK the same protections/limitations regarding subsidy as the EU laws?

After comparing the EU State aid rules and the SCM Agreement (A), I will first highlight the reasons why I believe Brexit will benefit the UK (B), before pointing out some concerns that must be mitigated by the UK government after Brexit (C).

---

[15] Chris Rhodes, *Industrial Strategy*, House of Commons Library, Briefing Paper n°07682, Oct. 14, 2016, at 12 ("the UK will be a member of the EU until negotiations have been finalised so currently and until the formal exit, State Aid rules will still apply").

[16] Christian Duvernoy et al., *Brexit: Implications for State Aid/Control of Subsidies*, Wilmerhale, Regulatory and government affairs, Nov. 22, 2016, at 1 ("[u]ntil Britain leaves the EU, all of these types of subsidies—both within the UK and in the other 27 EU Member States—are subject to the discipline imposed by EU State aid law, briefly summarized below. If a "hard Brexit" occurs, with the UK leaving the EU without a customs or trade agreement in place that extends to subsidies, the fallback rules controlling subsidies granted by the UK will be the World Trade Organization's (WTO's) Agreement on Subsidies and Countervailing Measures, and EU State aid rules would no longer apply to the UK").

[17] David Unterhalter SC & Thomas Sebastian, *AFTER BREXIT: State Aid under WTO disciplines*, Monckton Chambers, Sep. 15, 2016, at 1.

[18] Agreement on Subsidies and Countervailing Measures, World Trade Organization, art. 1, at 229 [hereinafter SCM Agreement].

A. BETWEEN THE EU LAWS AND THE SCM AGREEMENT: WHAT ARE THE ACTUAL CHANGES?

The SCM Agreement and the EU State aid rules cover the same overall concepts, i.e., any subsidies granted by a member state to any undertakings through public funds. When comparing the two regimes, one perceives that both involve: (i) measures which are taken by governments or which are imputable to governments, (ii) the grant of benefits or advantages, and (iii) measures which are not generally applied but which are specific or selective.[19]

Although the concepts themselves seem very close, differences between these two regimes may substantially impact the protection and limitation to state aid granted within the UK. Among others, the requirements to qualify a state aid differ (1), and the two systems are based on different theories (2) which lead to different types of sanctions (3).

1. Different treatment according to the type of subsidies/state aid, and the different requirements therefor

Among the major differences observable between the two systems, the EU one provides a very consistent, uniform, and unique regime for all types of subsidies, whereas the WTO differentiates by the kind of subsidies.

First, regarding the purviews' regimes, the SCM Agreement covers only the subsidies on goods,[20] leaving the subsidies on services free from limitation. This means that the scope of the SCM Agreement is smaller than that of the EU rules, the latter of which applies to the state aid on services as well. In addition, the SCM Agreement prohibits *per se* export subsidies and import substitution subsidies, which is not so in the EU rules.[21]

Second, regarding the latitude of requirements, the complainant, willing to obtain a decision terminating the subsidy, must prove the existence of at least one adverse effect listed by the SCM Agreement. Within the EU, the conditions are less stringent than the WTO rules. Indeed, the complainant only has to prove a distortion of the competition and trade between the Member States. Thus, the WTO rules provide for a harder actionable regime on subsidies than the EU laws.

2. Two systems based on different theories: restriction v. freedom, control a priori v. a posteriori

The EU laws and the WTO rules are not built with the same approach. On the one hand, Article 107(2) and (3) TFEU provide for a

---

[19] David Unterhalter SC & Thomas Sebastian, *supra* note 17, at 2.

[20] Christian Duvernoy et al., *supra* note 16, at 3.

[21] David Unterhalter SC & Thomas Sebastian, *supra* note 17, at 3.

prior approval system, which does not exist under the SCM Agreement.[22] Indeed, the EU regime is based on the approval of state aid granted within the EU, by the EC. Each Member State is subject to prior notification to the EC and to a duty to cooperate with it during the investigation phase. In addition, the Member State must also comply with the EC's discretionary decision and cannot decide on its own to grant state aid, which would otherwise breach EU laws. By contrast, the WTO system is only based on trade sanctions *a posteriori*. Since there is no duty to obtain prior approval, the only potential negative consequence is that a WTO member state may apply countervailing measures and/or file a claim before the WTO Dispute Settlement Body ("the DSB") for breach of the SCM Agreement by another WTO member state. Therefore, the main theories underlying the two systems are radically opposite: one is based on freedom (WTO), whereas the other one is based on restriction (EU). This significant difference in practice also impacts the process of granting a subsidy. On the one hand, under EU laws, it is an *a priori* control mechanism, where the EU Member State needs to notify the EC of its will to grant state aid before the EC gives its decision. On the other hand, under WTO rules it is an *a posteriori* control mechanism where the WTO member state grants aid whenever it decides to do so (even though it is still supposed to comply with the SCM Agreement).

The EU system appears to be much slower and more burdensome than the WTO system. It may impact trade heavily in a world where all commercial exchange is getting faster by the minute.

3. Different enforcement mechanisms

Last but not least, there are significant differences between the two enforcement mechanisms. Again, these are two radically different approaches. Under EU law, the enforcement mechanism can be triggered by the EC itself, as well as by any Member State or any undertaking "interested," whereas under the SCM Agreement, only WTO member states can either apply countervailing measures and/or initiate proceedings before the WTO DSB.[23] The EU system therefore provides a far more comprehensive and stringent enforcement mechanism than the one given by the WTO rules.[24]

---

[22] *Id.*

[23] *Id.* at 5.

[24] *Id.* at 3 ("[t]hird, the enforcement mechanisms under both sets of treaty arrangements differ. EU law provides for far more comprehensive and stringent enforcement mechanism than that provided under WTO law. Under EU law, the grant of state aid can trigger enforcement proceedings by the European Commission as well as proceedings by private parties in domestic courts. Those proceeding can result in an order that the

Under the SCM Agreement, in the future, UK companies will have to request the support of the UK government to apply countervailing duties or trigger any proceeding to terminate a subsidy given to its competitor. Therefore, it will be more difficult for a company of that WTO member state to stop the grant of the subsidy and to obtain any damages, or compensation measures.

Moreover, under the EU laws, the EC has an important mission to investigate, which does not exist under the WTO rules. When determining the existence of a breach, the EC investigates in cooperation with companies and Member States. Under the SCM Agreement, the industry concerned is left alone and will have to investigate itself through its own funds before any proceedings begin. Thus, compared to the EC, the undertaking has a more limited access to information as well as a more limited financial power to investigate, which impacts the result of the investigation.

Finally, the types of remedies differ radically. The EU law is based on financial sanctions (the recovery of the state aid, plus interest); whereas the WTO system is based on trade sanctions (countervailing measures). That is to say, under EU law, the company subsidized will have to reimburse the illegal state aid to the Member State, while under the WTO rules, the subsidized industry's product will be subject to countervailing measures (higher tariffs) or the member state will be subject to a prospective recommendation to remove the adverse effects of the subsidy. On the one hand, there is an individual financial sanction, where on the other hand, there is a global trade sanction on an entire industry.

B. *WHY IS IT BETTER FOR THE UK?*

Because of the difference pointed out in the first part, the Brexit appears to be a good opportunity for the UK regarding state aid. Indeed, while the EC and CJEU will have no more rights over the UK governmental decisions (1), the UK companies will still be able to complain before the EC against state aid granted to their European competitors (2). In addition, it offers a leverage to mitigate the damageable consequences of Brexit on UK companies (3), and enable the UK government to rescue and support some of its injured industries such as the UK energy sector (4).

---

beneficiary must pay back illegally granted state aid. By way of contrast, under WTO law, affected enterprises have no standing and must seek remedies through their home states").

1. No more rights of the EC and CJEU over the UK government's decisions

Notwithstanding the long adherence to the EU State aid rules by the UK, the burdensome influence of the EC becomes problematic during social and economic crises, as the EU and the UK are currently facing. The EC's control of governments' decisions is particularly strict and broad when it comes to state aid compliance with EU rules. Indeed, the EC has broadened its jurisdiction and strengthened the rules since its creation, as explained by G. Peretz:

> [T]here is a concern that the Commission and the CJEU have tended to widen the scope of the State aid rules to catch measures that should not be the concern of a regime whose principal purpose (at least historically) was to protect competition in the internal market against distortions caused by unjustified subsidies. (...) Concerns have centered on lack of transparency, lack of economic rigour and, partly as a result of those failings, a concern that the Commission's approach is sometimes too 'political'. (...) [T]he delay caused by the time taken by the Commission to deal with individually notified measures, given the unlawfulness of proceedings with those measures before the Commission's approval has been obtained. (...) [I]n some cases those delays can stop a desirable project or make it more expensive.[25]

By leaving the EU, the UK breaks away from the EC and CJEU's jurisdiction. Namely, since the EC and the CJEU only have power over the Member State's decisions, the UK will no longer be subject either to the EC investigations, approvals, and decisions or to the CJEU's jurisdiction.

Regarding the EC *a priori* control, on the one hand, the UK will be relieved from its duty of cooperation since only "Member States are under an obligation to cooperate with the Commission and to provide it with all information required."[26] On the other hand, the UK will also relieve itself from its duty to notify any new state aid since "any plans to grant new aid shall be notified to the Commission in sufficient time by the Member State concerned,"[27] which the UK will not be anymore. As

---

[25] G. Peretz, *Paper on post-Brexit options for State aid*, UK State Aid Law Association, Nov. 16, 2016, at 3-4.

[26] Council Regulation (EU) 2015/1589 §6, Jul. 13, 2015, O.J. L 248/9.

[27] Council Regulation (EU) 2015/1589 art. 2, Jul. 13, 2015, O.J. L 248/14.

a result, the UK will be free from any *a priori* control of the EC, and therefore it will regain its freedom of decision (even if still subject to the SCM Agreement). The upshot might help the UK government to provide a second wind to injured industries needing subsidies to prosper.[28]

Regarding the EC *a posteriori* control, the EC will no longer have the power to order the recovery of state aid considered by itself as unlawful. In fact, "where negative decisions are taken in cases of unlawful aid, the Commission shall decide that the Member State concerned shall take all necessary measures to recover the aid from the beneficiary."[29] Hence, the EC has jurisdiction to order any recovery of the aid only to a Member State, which again will not be the case of the post-Brexit UK.

Regarding the CJEU jurisdiction, the EC, which can bring the dispute before the CJEU in the event of non-compliance with its order,[30] will not have this power over the UK anymore. Indeed, the CJEU only has jurisdiction when the EC or a Member State bring the case before it. Therefore, since the UK will have the status of a non-Member State, the CJEU will not have jurisdiction over it.[31]

Coupled all together, this disappearing "hat" over the UK's head appears to be a real benefit. Accordingly, the UK will regain flexibility in its decision-making process for state aid, which will enable it to fund UK business as it sees fit, and "to support 'national champions' if it wishe[s] to do so."[32] Nonetheless, I believe that the UK government will mainly use its new freedom of decision with regard to state aid to offset the consequences of Brexit on UK-based companies.

2. UK-based companies competing on the EU market will still have the right to complain to the EC

According to EU regulations, even if a non-Member State cannot complain before the EC, it is not the case for any "undertaking whose interests might be affected by the granting of aid,"[33] meaning that UK-based companies will still have the right to file a complaint before the EC according to the EC State aid rules. The EU State aid regulation provides:

Council Regulation (EU) 2015/1589 art. 24:
Rights of interested parties

---

28 Slaughter and May, *supra* note 4, at 14.
29 Council Regulation (EU) 2015/1589 art. 16, Jul. 13, 2015, O.J. L 248/20.
30 Council Regulation (EU) 2015/1589 art. 28, Jul. 13, 2015, O.J. L 248/24.
31 TFEU art. 263§2, Oct. 26, 2012, O.J. C 326/162.
32 Slaughter and May, *supra* note 4, at 14.
33 Council Regulation (EU) 2015/1589 art. 1(h), Jul. 13, 2015, O.J. L 248/14.

Any interested party may inform the Commission of any alleged unlawful aid and any alleged misuse of aid. To that effect, the interested party shall duly complete a form that has been set out in an implementing provision referred to in Article 33 and shall provide the mandatory information requested therein.[34]

Council Regulation (EU) 2015/1589 art. 1(h):
Definitions
(h) "interested party" shall mean any Member State and any person, undertaking or association of undertakings whose interests might be affected by the granting of aid, in particular the beneficiary of the aid, competing undertakings and trade associations.[35]

A UK-based company might use this right to offset any advantage that any EU Member State would have granted to one of its competitors within the single market. More precisely, the UK will no longer have rights before the EC, but UK-based companies will be able to: first, help the EC during a formal investigation opened against a competitor, but also to advise the EC of the existence of an illegal state aid granted inside the single market, since this company will be considered as an interested party (such as a competitor). The EU State aid rules provide:

Council Regulation (EU) 2015/1589 art. 12(1):
Examination, request for information and information injunction
1. Without prejudice to Article 24, the Commission may on its own initiative examine information regarding alleged unlawful aid from whatever source.[36]

Commission Regulation n°372/2014 clause (3):
(3) The Commission may, on its own initiative, examine information on unlawful aid from any source, in order to assess compliance with Articles 107 and 108 of the Treaty. In that context, complaints are an essential source of information for detecting violations of State aid rules. It is, therefore, important

---

[34] Council Regulation (EU) 2015/1589 art. 24, Jul. 13, 2015, O.J. L 248/22.

[35] Council Regulation (EU) 2015/1589 art. 1(h), Jul. 13, 2015, O.J. L 248/14.

[36] Council Regulation (EU) 2015/1589 art. 12(1), Jul. 13, 2015, O.J. L 248/18.

to define clear and efficient procedures for handling complaints lodged with the Commission.[37]

The EC takes into account any information obtained, no matter what the source is, to trigger formal investigations. However, complaints are the most important source of information, and the complaint form[38] does not require any proof of whether the complainant is a EU-based company; only minimum information about their identity and their interest in the outcome are required. These regulations and forms mean that the EC is not restricting the access to complaints, which enables future UK-based companies to file claims before the EC against their EU competitors, subject to proof that it will have affected their trade within the single market. Therefore, UK companies gain a significant advantage over their competitors in the EU, since they can themselves benefit from UK state aid but also trigger investigations over state aid granted to their competitors. They benefit from UK financial support and may offset their EU competitors' financial aid. These cumulative rights make UK companies likely to remain competitive on the EU market.

In any event, the "EU State aid law would continue to apply to UK companies with subsidiaries in the remaining EU/EEA Member States, either as beneficiaries or complainants."[39] Therefore, either through their EU subsidiaries or as parent companies based in the UK, UK companies will have a continuing right to complain to the EC.

3. A leverage to mitigate the consequences of the exit from the single market

a. *Why this leverage is essential to the UK economy*

Within the EU, the freedom of movement includes the movements of goods. Thereby, no EU tariffs are applied to products exported to Member States from a Member State. As a result, it reduces the product's final sale price for the end customer. In contrast, a non-EU product sold

---

[37] Commission Regulation (EU) 372/2014 (3), Apr. 9, 2014, O.J. L 109/14.

[38] Commission Regulation (EU) 372/2014 Annex IV cl. 5, Apr. 9, 2014, O.J. L 109/17, Annex IV, Form for the submission of complaints concerning alleged unlawful state aid or misuse of aid ("Please be aware that, by virtue of Article 20(2) of Council Regulation (EC) No 659/1999 of 22 March 1999 laying down detailed rules for the application of Article 108 of the Treaty on the Functioning of the European Union, only interested parties within the meaning of Article 1(h) of that Regulation may submit formal complaints. Therefore, in the absence of a demonstration that you are an interested party, the present form will not be registered as a complaint, and the information provided therein will be kept as general market information").

[39] Falk Schöning, *Together forever? How State aid law will affect the UK even after Brexit*, Kluwer Competition Blog, Jul. 2, 2016, at 3.

within the EU will be applied EU tariffs, which raises the final sale price. Hence, it does constitute a major market force for EU-based companies and a major weakness for non EU-based companies acting on the European single market. Likewise, after Brexit, UK-based companies will be weakened. To mitigate this flaw, subsidizing companies/industries will be considered by the UK government. A member of the Parliament stated: "[a]ccess to the single market is an important determinant of FDI but by no means the only one. Outside the EU, the UK may be able to establish a regulatory regime more favorable to overseas investors, which could offset the effect of its departure."[40] While there is an effective threat from UK-based multinationals willing to leave the UK, the UK government needs to find a solution to hold back its companies. Nissan Motor Manufacturing ("Nissan"), a UK-based company, is a good example of the struggle faced by these multinational corporations. Nissan exports to Member states represent about 55% of its total sales. Because the EU applies 10% tariffs to cars coming from outside the European single market, Nissan could face a 290 millions pounds annual Brexit bill (to be paid to the EU).[41] For this reason, Nissan is thinking to relocate its activity inside the European single market. To hold it back, the UK government offered blurry measures to offset the financial effect of the Brexit on Nissan exports. Indeed, according to Reuters, "the British government said last month that it had given Nissan assurances that its new investment in plant in Britain would remain competitive after Brexit but said the firm had not been given any explicit promise of compensation for EU tariffs."[42] Therefore, it "implie[s] some other form of support has been agreed for Nissan."[43] The question remaining is " whether a post-Brexit deal could free the UK Government from such State aid control, at least in the medium to long-run, so that it could engage in largely unchecked public subsidy policies, such as creating particularly beneficial tax conditions in order to try to retain or attract large multinational companies considering relocating elsewhere in the EU."[44]

---

[40] Vaughne Miller et al., *Brexit: impact across policy aeras*, UK Parliament, Commons Library briefing, papers CBP-7213, Aug. 26 2016, at 2.
[41] Rob Davies, *Q&A: why Brexit is so important to Nissan (and Britain)*, The Guardian, Business, Oct. 28, 2016, at 1.
[42] Alastair Macdonald, *EU queries UK Brexit assurances to Nissan*, Reuters, Nov. 7, 2016, at 1.
[43] Rob Davies, *supra* note 41, at 1.
[44] Albert Sanchez Graells, *supra* note 6, at 1.

b. How to retain these companies?

Following the Irish model, the UK might try to lower its corporate tax rate in order to offset the consequence of EU tariffs. The sizable change of its corporate tax regime would enable the UK to retain and attract multinationals trading within the European single market.[45] As a result, the UK will be competitive in the offshore low-tax states game. According to the former Chancellor George Osborne, to raise this level of competitiveness, the UK should "cut corporation tax to below 15%— five points lower than its current 20% rate and the lowest of any major economy."[46] Nonetheless, feared by the EU, the UK would become a corporate-tax haven grabbing international investments that would otherwise have gone to the EU.[47]

Within the EU, tax regime belongs to the Member States' prerogatives, except when tax benefits become subsidies. In this case, the EC has exclusive jurisdiction, especially when it comes to tax reduction/relief qualified as subsidies.[48] Post-Brexit, no longer subject to the EC's authority, the UK government will be free to increase corporate-tax incentive arrangements. [49] To retain and attract international companies, the UK government possesses a new significant power of leverage, a relative freedom to design a corporate-tax incentive regime.

4. More freedom to help some UK industries
a. In the long run, it will benefit the UK energy industry

The Energy Minister, Andrea Leadsom, stated, "'[t]here is an area of energy policy where leaving could help the UK bill payer…. And that is in getting away from the massive restrictions of EU State Aid rules.' She continued: 'We've seen only recently how help for our steel sector is subject to EU State Aid, making it not only difficult, but also painfully slow to save our steel!'"[50] Nowadays the UK energy sector is funded by limited and controlled subsidies whereas it would need more public support to survive competition and economic crisis. Taking into account also the international concerns about climate change and the will to

---

[45] Andrew Cave, *Apple and Brexit: An unintended consequence of the European Commission's tax ruling?*, Forbes, Aug. 31, 2016, at 1.

[46] Toby Ryland, *Could Brexit trigger a tax bonanza for UK business ?*, HK Fisher & Company, Aug. 2016, at 1; *See also* Jason Douglas, *Brexit may make UK more attractive to multinationals after EU's Apple ruling*, The Wall Street Journal, Business, Aug. 30, 2016, at 1.

[47] *Id.*

[48] *Id.*

[49] Richard Croker, *Benefits of Brexit for the U.K. and Other Countries*, Bloomberg NBA, International Tax Library, at 7.

[50] Will Yeates, *Leaving EU state aid rules could increase lobbying for Government 'hand-outs' on energy and climate policy*, Demoguk, Jul. 4, 2016, at 1.

transform themselves into green economies, Gary Clyde Hufbauer thinks that "[t]he steps are usually accompanied by public subsidies, product mandates and domestic procurement rules."[51] Under the EU system, as explained, the EC controls the grant of public subsidies. Among others, UK renewable energy subsidies, such as Renewables Obligation Certificated, Feed-in Tariffs and Contracts for Difference, are subject to the EC notification and approval.[52] The EU State aid regime gives an exclusive power of decision to the EC. The upshot is that the EC may neither have the same position on the need to subsidize a specific industry locally, nor the same interest as the UK government at that time. As a result, the UK energy sector has suffered from the EC's refusal to subsidize some projects, such as the Hinkey Point nuclear power station, which was considered a priority for the UK government at that time. This mechanism has damaged the UK energy sector by slowing/blocking the process of granting financial support to the injured industry.

Post-Brexit, the SCM Agreement alone will apply to the UK subsidies. Under the SCM system, only an *a posteriori* control takes place. The UK government will have to decide alone whether a subsidy should be granted, and whether this subsidy complies with the WTO rules. By comparing the WTO and EU dispute resolution system, the complainant bears the burden to prove either the existence of "adverse effects" on its own interest (WTO) or the existence of an "effect on intra-EU trade" (EU). Because the evidence of the latter is easier to produce, it is more arduous for the complainant to trigger a proceeding before the WTO Dispute Settlement Body (the "DSB") than before the EC. Thus and notwithstanding the duty to comply with the SCM Agreement, the number of potential proceedings triggered before the WTO DSB will likely be lesser than before the EC. As a consequence, the SCM regime will likely enable the UK government to largely increase its subsidies to the energy sector in the short term.

b. In the short run, a burdensome transitional period is expected

After the Brexit vote of last June, the EC has implicitly expressed its will to de-prioritize the treatment of UK requests for subsidies approval.[53] Accordingly, by slowing down the process of granting

---

[51] Gary Clyde Hufbauer, *The Definition of Subsidy and State Aid. By Luca Rubini*, 13(4) Oxford University Journal of International Economic Law, Book Review 1145, 1145 (2010).

[52] Totis Kotsonis, *Market view: the effect of Brexit on EU state aid rules*, Utility Week, Sep. 21, 2016, at 1.

[53] James Webber et al., *supra* note 10, at 1.

financial support to UK industries, the EC might weaken the UK during the transitional period. In addition, the EC continues to trigger formal investigations against alleged unlawful aid granted by the UK to UK-companies.[54] In this situation, two scenarios are foreseeable: It will either lead to a substantial injury of the UK energy industry, or alternatively, the UK, pressured to protect its energy sector, will breach the EU State aid rules and will subsidize energy companies, overriding the EC's authority.

C. SOME CONCERNS REMAIN

Having now assessed the benefit of the UK, it cannot be ignored that some concerns remain and come to balance the outcome of Brexit. For this purpose, first, the UK will lose protection against wrongful use of state aid due to a lack of transparency in its decision-making process (1), and second, the UK government will also lose its right to complain before the EC and challenge the EC's decision before the CJEU (2).

1. A future lack of transparency in the use of public funds

The *a priori* EC's control of state aid implies a subsidiary function in practice: to control the use of public funds regarding subsidies.[55] Once the UK leaves the EU, no more protection against the wrongful use of public funds through subsidies will remain. As a matter of fact, this lack of protection arising during a political/economic crisis leads to the increase of corruption. After Brexit, because the WTO rules do not provide any similar protection, the UK will rely on its domestic law. As a result, the protection will get back to the Parliament and the National Audit Office, which may be unlikely to prevent 'politicized' uses of public funds. 'Politicized' use of public funds usually goes against the pursuance of the taxpayer's best interest.[56] Therefore, the disappearance of a strict, fair, and neutral control of the use of public funds for subsidies, in addition to a total opacity in the decision-making process, might injure the UK public economy as well as UK taxpayers.

Coupled with the lack of control over public funds arises the increase of lobbying.[57] Lobbyists are acting on behalf of industries to influence legislators and governments on policy and regulatory issues, in order to protect their own interest. Even if the lobbying system in some countries, such as the USA, is supposed to be fully transparent and regulated, it is still not fully the case in the UK. In this situation, a foreseeable scenario

---

[54] Alex Barker, *EU: Brussels launches first post-Brexit vote state aid probe into UK,* The Financial Time, Sep. 19, 2016, at 1.

[55] Albert Sanchez Graells, *supra* note 6, at 1.

[56] *Id.,* at 1.

[57] Will Yeates, *supra* note 50, at 1.

could be that being pressured by lobbyists representing companies willing to leave the UK, the UK government would likely grant many unjustified subsidies, risking a shortage in the UK public funds.[58] Being conscious of this flaw, the UK enacted in 2014 the Transparency of Lobbying, Non-Party Campaigning and Trade Union Administration Act,[59] which is a first but insufficient step to lobbying transparency. To offer adequate protection against the wrongful use of public funds, UK government and Parliament should go further. Because the UK government "considered the State aid rules to be a useful discipline to restrain wasteful public spending in devolved regions or nations,"[60] I believe the UK will enact new regulations to create a strict control of the use of public funds. To protect the taxpayers' interests, prevent corruption and wrongful use/misuse of public funds, this regulation needs to provide a stringent decision-making procedure subject to full transparency.

2. The UK government loses its right to complain to the EC and to challenge EC's decisions before the CJEU

Outside the EU, any complaint filed to the EC by the UK government (1), and any challenge to the EC's decision brought to the CJEU by the UK government (2), will not be admissible anymore. These rights are strictly linked to the notion of "Member State," which the UK will not be any more post-Brexit.

a. No more complaints filed to the EC will be admissible

According to article 11(a) of the EU regulation (EU) 2015/1589 of July 13, 2015, only Member States or interested parties have the right to complain before the EC. As defined in article 1(h), "'interested party' means any Member State and any person, undertaking or association of undertakings whose interests might be affected by the granting of aid, in particular the beneficiary of the aid, competing undertakings and trade associations."[61] Neither a Member State, nor an interested party, the UK government will not be able to complain and therefore loses its rights over the EC.

However, as provided by clause (3) of the Regulation (EU) No 372/2014 of April 9 2014 amending Regulation (EC) No 794/2004, the

---

[58] Andrew Porter, "David Cameron warns lobbying is next political scandal," The Daily Telegraph, Feb. 8, 2010, at 1 ("David Cameron in 2010 said 'the next big scandal waiting to happen. It's an issue that crosses party lines and has tainted our politics for too long, an issue that exposes the far-too-cosy relationship between politics, government, business and money' in order to clarify 'who is buying power and influence'").

[59] Transparency of Lobbying, Non-Party Campaigning and Trade Union Administration Act (UK), Jan. 30, 2014, 2014 c.4.

[60] James Webber et al., *supra* note 10, at 2.

[61] Council Regulation (EU) 2015/1589 art. 1(h), Jul. 13, 2015, O.J. L 248/14.

EC can trigger a formal investigation regarding an alleged unlawful aid, based on information coming from "any source." [62] This article also states, "in that context, complaints are an essential source of information for detecting violations of State aid rules."[63] By analyzing the provision's wording, although the complaint is an essential source of information for the EC, it is not the exclusive one. Because the complaint is not the only means for providing information, while the UK government will lose its right to officially complain before the EC, it could still denounce to the EC the existence of unlawful aids granted by other Member States through "officious canal." To trigger an investigation, this denouncement, even if not a complaint, could fall under the concept of "any source" provided by clause (3) of the Regulation (EU) No 372/2014.[64] Nevertheless, this interpretation is weak and is likely to be unrealistic.

b. No more challenge of the EC's decisions before the CJEU will be admissible

Once the EC's has rendered its formal *a priori* approval (in case of notification) or *a posteriori* approval (in case of investigation), a challenge can be brought before the CJEU according to article 263(2) of the TFEU. [65] Usually, competitors of the subsidized company have an interest in challenging the EC's decision. Indeed, by challenging the EC's decision, the company tries to set aside the subsidies granted to one of its EU competitors by a Member State. However, the requirements provided by article 263§4 TFEU[66] are arduous to be fulfilled by a "legal person," thus the company requests the support of its Member State who will bring the challenge before the CJEU on its behalf. Indeed, any Member State has an automatic right to challenge the EC's decisions before the CJEU, as provided by Article 263§2 TFEU: the CJEU "shall for this purpose have jurisdiction in actions brought by a Member State."[67] Until the day of the UK exit, as a Member State, the UK government keeps its right to bring cases before the CJEU.[68] However, once the UK leaves the EU, as a non-EU Member State, the UK government will lose this right. Any challenge brought by the UK will not be admissible anymore. As a result, "this means that the companies will not be able to enlist the UK's support (or opposition) in legal

---

[62] Commission Regulation (EU) 372/2014 §3, Apr. 9, 2014, O.J. L 109/14.

[63] *Id.*

[64] *Id.*

[65] TFEU art. 263§2, Oct. 26, 2012, O.J. C 326/162.

[66] TFEU art. 263§4, Oct. 26, 2012, O.J. C 326/162.

[67] TFEU art. 263§2, Oct. 26, 2012, O.J. C 326/162.

[68] Christian Duvernoy et al., *supra* note 16, at 5.

proceedings concerning state aid before the EU courts." Beyond the UK government losing the right to challenge EC's decisions, it "could negatively affect UK competitors."[69] While Brexit gives a significant advantage to UK companies and the UK government, such a loss may balance the outcome.

II. MAJOR LOSS FOR THE EU COMPANIES

While the UK will benefit from Brexit regarding State aid policy, the EU companies will probably suffer from the massive subsidies granted by the UK. Close enough to be competitors in third-party markets, the EU companies will probably lose slices of market taken by UK companies. On the one hand, the EC companies will not rely anymore on the EC's control of UK state aids (A); on the other hand, EC companies will be subject to their Member State/EU discretionary decision to complaint before the WTO DSB (B). Weakened on both sides, EU companies will ultimately be injured by Brexit.

A. *EU COMPANIES WEAKENED IN THIRD-PARTY MARKET: NO MORE CONTROL FROM THE EC OVER THE UK STATE AID DECISIONS*

On June 23, 2015, UK voters expressed their will to avoid any form of control from the EU authorities.[70] Based only on EU Treaties and regulations, and subject mainly to the EC's control, state aid is an area particularly concerned. According to articles 108(2)[71] and 263(2)[72] TFEU, the EC and the CJEU have power only over the Member States. Post-Brexit, when the UK becomes a non-Member State, the EU will lose its prerogatives over the UK governmental decisions regarding state aid.[73] As a result, UK-based companies will gain advantage over EU-based companies: the EU companies subject to the EU laws and EC jurisdictions will not be able to obtain state aid as easily as their competitors in the UK.

This may have important implications for business, both in the UK and in the remaining 27 EU Member States. Notably, where UK and EU companies remain in close competition, EU companies will not benefit from the system of EU control of State aid with respect to aid granted by UK. However, both

---

[69] Slaughter and May, *supra* note 4, at 14.
[70] Alex Barker, *supra* note 54.
[71] TFEU art. 108(2), Oct. 26, 2012, O.J. C 326/92.
[72] TFEU art. 263§2, Oct. 26, 2012, O.J. C 326/162.
[73]Christian Duvernoy et al., *supra* note 16, at 5.

EU- and UK-based companies will still be able to make use of EU State aid control to challenge aid granted to their competitors by EU countries to the extent such aid impacts competition in the EU, provided that they fulfill applicable standing requirements[74]

The advantage shows up when both UK and EU companies compete in a third-party market, such as the USA. In this situation, although both companies will be subject to similar/close tariffs, the UK-based company will become more competitive than the EU-based company. Indeed, for the same cost of production/distribution, the UK-based company will be more likely subsidized, which will enable it to sell its products at a lower price than the EU-based company not subsidized, and thus become more competitive. As a consequence post-Brexit, the EU-based companies will likely lose market slices and thus will be weakened.

B. A WEAKENED PROTECTION OF EU COMPANIES SUBJECT TO AN ADDITIONAL LEVEL OF FILTER BEFORE THE WTO DSB

Radically different than the EU investigation process, the WTO dispute resolution mechanism is an interstate dispute system. In other words, any admissible complaint must be filed by a member state against another member state. In contrast with the EU mechanism, neither individuals nor companies have a right to bring a case before the WTO DSB. Because cases shall be brought by a member state, complaining before the WTO intertwines with the diplomatic position of the complainant government. The member state's interests might differ from those of the injured industry at the time the complaint is lodged. As a matter of fact, "WTO members always have reasons *not* to launch subsidy complaints against one another, and the European Commission is seldom eager to bring cases against member states."[75] Compared to the EU mechanism where companies are able to complain directly to the EC, under the WTO, the member state has the final decision whether to file a claim before the DSB. It constitutes an additional level of filter imposed on EU companies, which lower their protection against unlawful subsidies granted by the UK to their competitors on the EU market.

---

[74]*Id.*, at 5.
[75] Gary Clyde Hufbauer, *supra* note 51, at 1147.

CONCLUSION

Benefiting from its new freedom of decision regarding state aids, the UK government will be more likely to support and retain UK based companies. Through broad subsidies, the UK government will be able to offset, or at least mitigate, some of the damaging consequences for UK companies due to Brexit. Nevertheless, being realistic, a financial question must be raised: would the UK be able to fund all these injured companies/industries when Brexit happens? Furthermore, this financial concern must be coupled with the risk of wrongful use of public funds due to a lack of transparency in the decision-making process of subsidization. Hence, Brexit offers many assets to the UK government and to the UK companies; however, negative effects must not be ignored, and solutions should be prepared before the effective exit day.

With regard to the EU, Brexit will relatively weaken the EU companies competing with UK companies. On the one hand the UK companies subsidized will encroach on the actual market of EU companies outside the EU, and on the other hand, the EU companies' protection against unlawful state aid granted by the UK will be less efficient than before Brexit. Therefore, EU companies are the biggest losers in Brexit regarding state aid policy.

Finally, the EC's broad power regarding state aid seems to become incompatible with the will to create "European Champions." Whether to remodel the State aids policy is a current question raised by different western European governments.[76] These governments doubt of the opportunity to keep EU State aids rules. If a deregulation of the European system of state aid were achieved, it is likely that western European countries would grant massive subsidies. As a result, it might create a significant distortion of the market inside the EU, which would injure the eastern European industries. Therefore Brexit might be the first step towards a broad rewriting of the EU State aid rules, but it is likely that total deregulation would be a mistake for the EU.

---

[76] James Webber et al., *supra* note 10, at 2.

CHAPTER 9: THE UNITED KINGDOM'S PUBLIC PROCUREMENT REGIME IN A POST-BREXIT LANDSCAPE

JOSEPH T. LUMLEY

I. INTRODUCTION

On June 23, 2016, the United Kingdom voted to leave the EU, sending shockwaves throughout the international community. One of the criticisms most commonly lodged against membership in the EU is that compliance with EU directives costs the United Kingdom more than the benefits that have accrued.[1] Within this broader debate, an area ripe for criticism has been public procurement—the purchase by governments and state-owned enterprises of goods, services, and works.[2] As the United Kingdom navigates its departure from the EU, the future of its public procurement regime has been called into question.

The most vocal critics charge that the EU directives on public procurement create excessive red tape that hinders the award of contracts. All major legal tenders are to be advertised in the Official Journal of the EU, and contracting entities must comply with procedures outlined in EU directives, which in total span 128 pages.[3] Vote Leave, the official campaign for Britain to leave the EU, argued that compliance with the EU's directives on public procurement spending costs British companies approximately £1.69 billion per year and that an estimated 1.9 million work days were lost to red-tape delays.[4]

---

[1] Roger Bootle, *Three Reasons why Britain needs 'Brexit,'* TELEGRAPH (Nov. 1, 2015 6:38 PM), http://www.telegraph.co.uk/finance/comment/11968813/Three-reasons-why-Britain-needs-Brexit.html; Andrew Tyrie MP, *Giving Meaning to Brexit*, OPEN EUROPE, (Sept. 2, 2016), http://openeurope.org.uk/intelligence/britain-and-the-eu/giving-brexit-meaning/.

[2] OECD: PUBLIC PROCUREMENT, http://www.oecd.org/gov/ethics/public-procurement.htm (last visited: Jan. 3, 2017).

[3] *Quitting EU would be 'save billions' in procurement costs*, BBC (May 26, 2016), http://www.bbc.com/news/uk-politics-eu-referendum-36382197; Roger Newman, *EU Public Procurement Regulations – a Small but Valid Argument for Brexit?* DENOVE (Feb. 15, 2016), http://www.denove.com/eu-public-procurement-regulations-a-small-but-valid-argument-for-brexit/.

[4] Heather Stewart, *Vote Leave: EU Rules add almost £1.7 billion to the costs of Whitehall contracts*, GUARDIAN (May 26, 2016 12:01 AM), https://www.theguardian.com/politics/2016/may/26/vote-leave-eu-rules-add-almost-2bn-costs-whitehall-contracts.

Given the significant financial implications, it is understandable that the future of the UK procurement regime has generated much discussion. Accounting for 15–20 percent of global GDP, public procurement represents a substantial portion of the EU economy and the economy of many countries around the world.[5] Every year, over 250,000 public authorities in the EU spend around 14 percent of GDP on the purchase of services, works, and supplies. [6] Procurement regulation is now featured in almost all free trade agreements and has garnered increased attention from the international community.[7]

This Note attempts to provide a fuller assessment of the future of the United Kingdom's procurement regime post-Brexit, and adds to the debate by considering some specific changes that could be made to the legal framework. Part II of this Note will examine the public procurement regime under which the United Kingdom currently exists. Part III of this Note will examine the extent to which different models of transition would impact the United Kingdom's public procurement regime, focusing on the processes by which such changes would occur and the legal implications of each option with respect to procurement. This Part will specifically consider whether the United Kingdom should become a party to the WTO Government Procurement Agreement (GPA). Part IV will assess the extent to which the United Kingdom could and would realistically alter its procurement regime. Part V will offer some concluding remarks.

II. PROCUREMENT LAW IN THE UNITED KINGDOM
A. EU PROCUREMENT LAW

Public procurement law in the United Kingdom is almost entirely derivative of EU law, so an examination of the EU procurement directives is essential to understanding the framework of UK procurement legislation. Procurement has explicitly been a feature of the law of the EU since 1971, and today the EU has one of the most comprehensive bodies of procurement law in the world. Underlying the procurement regime are the principles of transparency, equal treatment, and non-discrimination stemming from the Treaty on the Functioning of the EU (TFEU).[8] By standardizing the process by which procurement occurs, the EU's procurement directives "seek to ensure that companies

---

[5]   EUROPEAN   COMMISSION: PUBLIC   PROCUREMENT, https://ec.europa.eu/growth/single-market/public-procurement_en (last visited: Jan. 3, 2017).
[6] *Id.*
[7] *Id.*
[8] Consolidated Version of the Treaty on the Functioning of the EU art. 18, 2008 O.J. C 115/47 [hereinafter TFEU].

from across the single market have the opportunity to compete for public contracts (above defined thresholds)…remove legal and administrative barriers to participation in cross-border tenders, [and] to ensure equal treatment and remove scope for discriminatory purchasing by ensuring transparency."[9]

1.   The Procurement Directives

In April 2004, the EU enacted two directives that attempted to consolidate and simplify the medley of directives governing the European procurement scheme at the time[10]: Directive 2004/18,[11] which applied to service, supply, or works contracts entered into by public bodies, excluding utilities (the "2004 Public Sector Directive"); and Directive 2004/17,[12] which applied to service, supply, or works contracts entered into by public and some private bodies in the utilities sector (i.e., electricity, gas, heat, water), and transport and postal sectors (the "2004 Utilities Directive"). Despite their ambitious goals, the directives quickly came under criticism for being opaque, overly burdensome, rigid, and favoring large firms over small and medium-sized enterprises (SME's) in procurement.

As part of its Europe 2020 strategy for smart, sustainable, and inclusive growth, the EU recognized that it needed to update the directives to, among other things, reduce complexity, increase efficiency in public spending, provide greater flexibility for contracting entities, and facilitate the participation of SMEs in public procurement. [13] Accordingly, it replaced the 2004 directives with three new directives that came into force in April 2014: Directive 2014/24 (the "2014 Public Contracts Directive), [14] which repeals the 2004 Public Contracts Directive; Directive 2014/25 (the "2014 Utilities Directive"),[15] which repeals the 2004 Utilities Directive; and Directive 2014/23 (the "2014 Concessions Contracts Directive"), [16] a new directive that sets out rules for concession contracts.

The directives' coverage is broad. The 2014 Public Contracts Directive applies to "the State, regional or local authorities, bodies

---

[9] EUROPEAN COMMISSION, EU PUBLIC PROCUREMENT LEGISLATION: DELIVERING RESULTS (2014).

[10] Sue Arrowsmith, *EU Public Procurement Law: an Introduction*, EU ASIA INTER UNIVERSITY NETWORK FOR TEACHING AND RESEARCH IN PUB. PROCUREMENT REG. 55-58 (2010).

[11] European Parliament and Council Directive 2004/18/EC, 2004 O.J. (L 134) 114-240.

[12] European Parliament and Council Directive 2004/17/EC, 2004 O.J. (L 134) 1-113.

[13] EUROPEAN COMMISSION, GREEN PAPER ON THE MODERNISATION OF EU PUBLIC PROCUREMENT POLICY TOWARDS A MORE EFFICIENT EUROPEAN PROCUREMENT MARKET (Jan. 1, 2011).

[14] European Parliament and Council Directive 2014/24/EC, 2014 O.J. (L 94) 65-242.

[15] European Parliament and Council Directive 2014/25/EC, 2014 O.J. (L 94) 114-240.

[16] European Parliament and Council Directive 2014/23/EC, 2014 O.J. (L 94) 1-64.

governed by public law, associations formed by one or several of such authorities or one of several of such bodies governed by public law."[17] Essentially, "all bodies that spend money are covered."[18] The Utilities Directive adds to its scope of coverage "public undertakings" (separate legal entities owned or controlled by a public body) and entities that "operate on the basis of special or exclusive rights granted by a competent authority of a Member State."[19] Despite the broad entity coverage, not all contracts are included; the regulations only apply to contracts above a specified financial threshold.[20] However, contracts below the threshold are still subject to the (TFEU) principles of transparency, non-discrimination, and equal treatment.

When conducting procurement, contracting authorities must follow one of six types of procedures outlined in the 2014 directives. At the outset, most contracts above the threshold, regardless of the procedure used, must be advertised in the OJEU.[21] The first type of procedure— the most commonly used under the 2004 directives—is the "open procedure," under which "all interested providers tender a single, fully priced offer in response to the advertisement."[22] The second type of procedure is the "restricted procedure," which "requires interested bidders to 'pre-qualify' before being invited to submit a fully priced tender."[23] The third type of procedure is the "competitive procedure with negotiation," which "involves a pre-qualification stage and then a negotiation stage with the pre-qualified group of tenderers to seek improved offers."[24] The fourth type of procedure is the "competitive dialogue," which is "flexible" and allows a dialogue to be conducted with potential bidders, to develop one or more suitable solutions for its requirements on which chosen bidders will be invited to tender.[25]

The 2014 Directives added the final two procedures. The first is the innovation partnership, which allows tenderers to submit a request to participate in response to a contract notice to establish a partnership for the development of an innovative product, service, or work aimed at meeting a need for which there is no suitable existing "product" on the

---

[17] Council Directive 2014/24/EC art. 2(1).

[18] Euan Burrows and Edward McNeill, *EU Public Procurement Rules, in* THE INTERNATIONAL COMPARATIVE LEGAL GUIDE TO PUBLIC PROCUREMENT 2017 (9th ed. 2016).

[19] *Id.*; Council Directive 2014/24/EC art. 2(2).

[20]   https://ec.europa.eu/growth/single-market/public-procurement/rules-implementation/thresholds_en.

[21] Burrows and McNeill, *supra* note 18.

[22] *Id.*

[23] *Id.*

[24] *Id.*

[25] *Id.*

market.[26] The second new procedure is the competitive procedure with negotiation.[27] This procedure involves negotiation with each tenderer with a view to improving the content of the tenders.[28]

Contracting authorities are free to choose between the open and restricted procedures.[29] The competitive dialogue and competitive procedure with negotiation are alternatives to each other, and they may be used only in certain circumstances, including where a contract is particularly complex, there is no ready solution available, or the technical specifications cannot be defined in specific detail.[30] Contracting authorities may also use a final procedure—the negotiated procedure without prior publication of a contract notice.[31] Under this procedure, the contracting authority may negotiate directly with one or more suppliers if, because of technical or artistic reasons or because of the protection of exclusive rights, the contract may only be carried out by those particular suppliers.[32]

Additionally, the procurement directives contain requirements for award criteria and disqualification. The 2014 Public Contracts Directive mandates that the contract shall be awarded to the "most economically advantageous tender" ("MEAT"), which must be based on "price or cost, using a cost-effectiveness approach," such as life-cycle costing.[33] The costs to be considered over the life-cycle of the contract include: (i) costs relating to acquisition; (ii) use, such as consumption of energy; (iii) maintenance; (iv) end of life, such as collection and recycling; and (v) environmental externalities whose monetary value can be determined and verified, such as emissions of greenhouse gases or other pollutants.[34] The cost-effectiveness approach may include the best price-quality ratio, which in turn can be based on "qualitative, environmental, and/or social aspects," such as the quality and training of the staff.[35] This represents a significant departure from the 2004 Public Contracts Directive, which required consideration of price only.[36] A contracting authority even has

---

[26] CROWN COMMERCIAL SERVICE, A BRIEF GUIDE TO THE EU 2014 PUBLIC PROCUREMENT DIRECTIVES 10 (Oct. 2016).

[27] *Id.*

[28] *Id.*

[29] *Id.*

[30] *Id.* For a general discussion regarding the conditions for use of the different procedures, see Pedro Telles and Luke R. A. Butler, *Public Procurement Award Procedures in Directive 2014/24/EU*, in NOVELTIES IN THE 2014 DIRECTIVE ON PUBLIC PROCUREMENT (Francois Lichere et. al. eds.,2015).

[31] CROWN COMMERCIAL SERVICE, *supra* note 26, at 10.

[32] *Id.*

[33] Council Directive 2014/24/EC art. 67(2).

[34] Council Directive 2014/24/EC art. 68(1).

[35] Council Directive 2014/24/EC art. 67(2).

[36] Burrows and McNeill, *supra* note 18.

the discretion to reject the most economically advantageous tender if it finds that the tender fails to comply with its applicable obligations in the fields of environmental, social, and labor law.[37] Moreover, a contracting authority is *required* to exclude an economic operator from participation in a procurement procedure if it is aware the economic operator has been convicted of certain crimes, such as corruption, fraud, child labor, or is in breach of certain obligations, such as those relating to the payment of taxes.[38]

Aggrieved public contractors may seek redress in national courts or by appealing to the European Commission. If a potential infringement comes to the attention of the European Commission either through a third-party complaint or on its own initiative, the Commission can exercise its powers under Article 258 of the TFEU, referred to as the "infringement procedure."[39] Should the Commission determine that an infringement has occurred, the Commission can request the violating party to comply with the directives. If the Member State fails to comply, the Commission can bring an action against the Member State in the Court of Justice of the EU (CJEU).[40] The CJEU can require the Member State to take "all necessary measures to comply" with a judgment against it, which might include rescission of a contract that has already been awarded.[41] With respect to national procedures, the 2008 Remedies Directive details remedies that must be made by domestic courts.[42] These include an injunction against award of the contract if the decision is challenged in court, and a post-contract award "ineffectiveness" remedy, which nullifies the contract.[43]

2. State Aid Rules

Overlapping with the procurement directives are the EU rules on State aid. A transaction qualifies as State aid if: (1) it is financed directly or indirectly through State resources; (2) it confers an economic advantage to undertakings exercising an economic activity; (3) the advantage is selective and distorts or threatens to distort competition; and (4) it has an effect on intra-Community trade.[44] EU member states are forbidden from providing state aid unless the entity provides notice

---

[37] Council Directive 2014/24/EC art. 55(1).

[38] Council Directive 2014/24/EC art. 57(1).

[39] Burrows and McNeill, *supra* note 18.

[40] *Id.*

[41] *Commission of the European Communities v. Federal Republic of Germany*, Case C-503/04, Judgment (July 18, 2007).

[42] European Parliament and Council Directive 2 2007/66/EC, 2007 O.J. (L 335) 31.

[43] *Id.*

[44] *See* TFEU, *supra* note 8, art. 107(1); Nóra Tosics and Norbert Gaál, *Public procurement and State aid control — the issue of economic advantage*, COMPETITION POL'Y NEWSL, Issue 3, 2007, at 15.

to the European Commission and receives approval for the grant[45] or the aid falls under an exception.[46] The European Commission has the authority to investigate potential violations of the State aid rules.[47]

There has been much debate regarding the application of State aid rules to public procurement, as most public procurement activities would qualify as State aid under the TFEU's definition of the term. Procurement is largely financed through state resources, the award is necessarily selective and potentially competition distorting, and certain lucrative public contracts have a significant effect on intra-EU trade.[48] The critical issue to consider is whether the procurement activity confers an economic advantage to a contractor that the contractor would not receive under normal economic conditions—that is, whether the same decision would have been made by a "disinterested buyer" or a "market economy buyer."[49] The European Commission takes the position that the use of a competitive procurement procedure which is in line with the EU public procurement rules and thus suitable to achieve best value for money, i.e., fair market price for the goods, services or infrastructure purchased, creates a presumption that no State aid will be involved to the economic operator concerned.[50] However, that presumption can be rebutted by showing that despite technical compliance with the regulations, the price paid for the contract exceeds market price.[51]

B. UK PROCUREMENT LAW

England, Wales, and Northern Ireland transposed the EU procurement directives in 2015 through three separate regulations: the Public Contracts Regulations 2015,[52] Concession Contracts Regulations 2016,[53] and Utilities Contracts Regulations 2016.[54] Scotland transposed

---

[45] Christian Duvernoy et al., *Brexit: Implications for State Aid/Control of Subsidies*, WILMERHALE   4   (Nov.   22,   2016), https://www.wilmerhale.com/uploadedFiles/Shared_Content/Editorial/Publications/ WH_Publications/Client_Alert_PDfs/2016-11-22-WilmerHale-Alert-Brexit-Implications-for-State-Aid-Control-of-Subsidies.pdf.

[46] *See* Albert Sanchez-Graells, *Public Procurement and State Aid: Reopening the Debate?* 21 PUB. PROCUREMENT L. REV. 205, 207 (2012)

[47] Christian Duvernoy et al., *supra* note 45, at 7.

[48] *See* Sanchez-Graells, *supra* note 46, at 207.

[49] Case T-14/96, BAI v. Comm'n, 1999 E.C.R. II-139 ¶¶ 71–76.

[50] EUROPEAN COMMISSION, COMMISSION NOTICE ON THE NOTION OF STATE AID AS REFERRED   TO   IN   ARTICLE   107(1)   TFEU, http://ec.europa.eu/%20community_law/state_aids/comp-2007/n046-07.pdf.

[51] Sanchez-Graells, *supra* note 46, at 208.

[52] Public Contracts Regulations 2015, SI 2015/102.

[53] Concession Contracts Regulations 2016, SI 2016/273.

[54] Utilities Contracts Regulations 2016, SI 2016/274.

the regulations independently.[55] The regulations are essentially a copy-out of the EU directives.[56] However, in a rare move, the United Kingdom also introduced purely domestic legislation to supplement the EU directives, in a practice known as "gold-plating." These bills included the Public Services (Social Value) Act, which requires public authorities to consider social value in procurement decisions, and the Lord Young reforms, which are aimed at facilitating participation in the procurement process for Small and Medium-sized Enterprises (SMEs).[57]

Challenges for breach of the Procurement Regulations in England and Wales are heard by the High Court, and sometimes "by specialist judges, in particular in the Administrative Court or the Technology and Construction Court of the Queen's Bench Division of the High Court or in the Chancery Division of the High Court."[58] However, challenges under the regulations are fairly rare.[59] In accordance with the 2008 Remedies Directive, there are a number of remedies available to bidders, including "damages, an automatic suspension where the contract has not yet been entered into and, in limited circumstances, a declaration of ineffectiveness."[60]

C. THE GOVERNMENT PROCUREMENT AGREEMENT

A third body of rules by which public entities in the United Kingdom must abide is the Government Procurement Agreement (GPA).[61] The GPA is a plurilateral agreement within the framework of the World Trade Organization (WTO), meaning that it is not binding on all WTO members, only those that have signed it.[62] The Agreement consists of

---

[55] Given the complexity of Scotland's own future within the United Kingdom, this Note focuses primarily on England, Wales, and Northern Ireland.

[56] Some have criticized the United Kingdom for its hasty transposition. *See* Albert Sanchez-Graells, *Would a Brexit significantly change the way the English public sector buys supplies and services?*, HOW TO CRACK A NUT: A BLOG ON EU ECONOMIC LAW (Apr. 23, 2016), http://www.howtocrackanut.com/blog/2016/4/22/would-a-brexit-significantly-change-the-way-the-english-public-sector-buys-supplies-and-services?rq=brexit.

[57] Sue Arrowsmith, *The implications of Brexit for the law on public utilities procurement*, ACHILLES 14, https://www.achilles.com/images/locale/en-EN/buyer/pdf/U.K./sue-arrowsmith-brexit-whitepaper.pdf.

[58] Sue Arrowsmith, *Competitive Dialogue in the United Kingdom*, in COMPETITIVE DIALOGUE IN EU PROCUREMENT 189 (Sue Arrowsmith and Steen Treumer, eds. 2012).

[59] *Id.*

[60] Fenella Morris and Rose Grogan, *The Implications of Brexit for Public Procurement*, in THE INTERNATIONAL COMPARATIVE LEGAL GUIDE TO PUBLIC PROCUREMENT 2017 (9th ed. 2016).

[61] Revised Agreement on Government Procurement, March 30, 2012, 1869 U.N.T.S. 508 (Text available at 1915 U.N.T.S. 103) [hereinafter GPA].

[62] WORLD   TRADE   ORGANIZATION, https://www.wto.org/english/tratop e/gproc e/gp gpa e.htm (last visited Jan. 3, 2016).

nineteen parties covering forty-seven WTO members (counting the EU and its twenty-eight member states as one party).[63] Currently, the EU procurement directives are in compliance with the provisions of the GPA. This is because the GPA is more basic and flexible than EU procurement legislation: it requires national treatment and non-discrimination in procurement of goods and services, and establishes baseline procedural requirements with respect to both the procurement process—which have the aim of ensuring transparency—and remedies.[64] Additionally, the GPA excludes defense procurement and procurement by private utilities, both of which are included in the EU directives. Parties to the GPA adopt a schedule of commitments specifying both what federal and sub-federal entities, and what goods and services (above the GPA threshold), are covered by the Agreement. The extent of these market access commitments depends on bilateral negotiations between the different parties.[65]

Critically, the United Kingdom is not a party to the Agreement in its own right, but only through its membership in the EU. As such, it does not have its own coverage schedule, but rather is governed by that of the EU. While Annexes 1-3 of the EU's coverage schedule identify specifically the federal and sub-federal entities that are covered for each member state (including the United Kingdom), Annexes 4-7 specify what goods and services are covered only on a general, EU-wide basis.[66] Thus, one of the effects of Brexit would be that the United Kingdom would have to either adopt the EU coverage schedule or negotiate its own coverage schedule. Part III takes up the question of whether the United Kingdom should join the GPA in its own right and what it would take to do so.

III: WHAT COMES AFTER BREXIT?

As of the time of this writing, the United Kingdom remains a member of the EU, which requires continued compliance with EU procurement directives. The directives will continue to apply during the two-year negotiation period that will be triggered when the United Kingdom gives notice to the European Council of its intention to leave.[67] Even after the United Kingdom leaves the EU, it is unlikely that UK

---

[63] *Id.*

[64] Arrowsmith, *supra* note 57, at 11.

[65] *Id.*

[66] *Id.*

[67] *The effect of "Brexit" on U.K. public procurement legislation and the application of EU State aid rules in the U.K.,* EVERSHEDS INT'L (June 30, 2016), http://www.eversheds.com/global/en/what/articles/index.page?ArticleID=en/Public Procurement/U.K.-public-procurement-legislation.

procurement law will change significantly within a short time period after departure. If it passes in Parliament, Prime Minister Theresa May's Great Repeal Bill, which repeals the European Communities Act 1972, would also convert the EU procurement directives, as transposed, into UK domestic law.[68] Thus, even in the event that the United Kingdom emerges from the negotiations with no preferential trade relationship with the EU, the EU directives will likely continue to apply, as a practical matter, in the wake of Brexit.

What UK procurement law will look like in the long term is a more challenging question. As with many questions regarding the future of the United Kingdom's legal regime, the answer largely depends on what model of relations with the EU the United Kingdom chooses to adopt.[69] An assessment of the merits of each model irrespective of procurement law is mostly outside the scope of this Note; rather, this Note assumes each model as the starting point of analysis. Several different models of UK-EU relations have been proposed: membership in the European Economic Arrangement (EEA), otherwise known as the "Norwegian Model," under which the United Kingdom would still be bound by the directives of the EU; a bespoke agreement, otherwise known as the "Swiss Model," under which most of the laws of the EU would continue to apply; and no trade agreement with the EU.[70] For the purposes of procurement, the last option would entail either joining the GPA or being part of no procurement agreements. This part considers each of these models in turn.

A. THE NORWEGIAN MODEL

Based on the rhetoric of UK politicians including Theresa May, joining the EEA, which would entail continued compliance with EU law, seems to be an increasingly unlikely option[71]; however, given that there

---

[68] The EU procurement directives were transposed into UK law as secondary legislation, in the form of regulations, pursuant to Section 2(2) of the European Communities Act 1972 (ECA). Thus, "any secondary legislation made under 2(2) alone would cease to have effect if the ECA were simply repealed." Jack Simson Caird, *Briefing Paper: Legislating for Brexit: the Great Repeal Bill*, HOUSE OF COMMONS LIBRARY (Feb. 23, 2017). Accordingly, "these instruments will need to be 'saved' by provisions in the Great Repeal Bill to ensure that they continue to operate." *Id.* at 17.

[69] Arrowsmith, *supra* note 57, at 4.

[70] *Id*; JEAN-CLAUDE PIRIS, CENTRE FOR EUR. REFORM, IF THE U.K. VOTES TO LEAVE: THE SEVEN ALTERNATIVES TO EU MEMBERSHIP (2016); *Five models for post-Brexit U.K. trade*, BBC NEWS: EU REFERENDUM, (June 27, 2016), http://www.bbc.com/news/uk-politics-eu-referendum-36639261.

[71] Anushka Asthana and Jennifer Rankin, *Brexit: U.K. government faces legal challenge over single market*, GUARDIAN (Nov. 28, 2016 2:17 PM), https://www.theguardian.com/politics/2016/nov/28/uk-government-faces-legal-challenge-over-single-market.

is little certainty as to the course of the negotiations, it is worth considering. If the United Kingdom joins the EEA, little would change in terms of the substance of the UK procurement regime. The EU procurement directives apply to all EEA members, and thus the United Kingdom would have minimal flexibility to alter its procurement regulations as currently transposed. Additionally, for contracts of "cross-border interest" that fall outside the directives' coverage, the general principles of transparency and equal treatment stemming from the TFEU would continue to apply. Although the United Kingdom would not be automatically bound by subsequent amendments to the procurement directives—they must be explicitly adopted by the Joint Committee of the EEA, comprised of both EU and non-EU EEA members—to date, all the EU procurement rules have been adopted in the EEA.[72] EFTA State aid rules would apply and be enforced by the EFTA Surveillance Authority, although these rules are nearly identical to the EU State aid rules.[73]

There are two notable ways in which joining the EEA would represent a departure from the United Kingdom's current procurement regime. First, the EFTA Court, rather than the CJEU, would be the ultimate court enforcing disputes arising from the procurement directives. However, this is more of a formal distinction than a practical one, as the EFTA Court follows the jurisprudence of the CJEU on matters of EU law wherever possible.[74] Second, the United Kingdom would lose its vote, and thus its capacity to influence future developments in EU procurement law would be significantly diminished.[75] This is a critical difference, as the United Kingdom has been instrumental in shaping procurement law by pushing for greater flexibility, particularly with respect to the development of the competitive dialogue procedure and framework agreements.[76] Future modifications of the procurement regulations that do not take into account the wishes of the United Kingdom could be detrimental to UK interests.

B. *THE SWISS MODEL*

A second option for the United Kingdom is to join EFTA and negotiate a bilateral trade deal with the EU that largely grants access to the single market but does not entail membership in the EEA.

---

[72] Arrowsmith, *supra* note 57, at 7.
[73] *Brexit: Implications for state aid rules*, OXERA: AGENDA (June 2016), http://www.oxera.com/getmedia/72c5742f-8018-4bfb-8be4-d2c408ae24d9/Brexit-implications-for-state-aid-rules_Final.pdf.aspx?ext=.pdf.
[74] Morris and Grogan, *supra* note 60.
[75] Arrowsmith, *supra* note 57, at 7.
[76] *Id.*

Switzerland currently has access to the single market for most of its industries, which has been granted through approximately 120 agreements concluded between Switzerland and the EU.[77] Switzerland must also provide for the free movement of people and contributes billions of dollars to EU projects.[78] In terms of procurement, the directives do not technically apply to Switzerland. Rather, the relationship between Switzerland and the EU is primarily governed by the schedules and award procedures of the GPA. A bilateral agreement specifies that in regards to procurement to which the GPA does not apply (such as private utilities), the contract shall be awarded in accordance with the principles of "non-discrimination, transparency, and fairness."[79]

Although this model theoretically presents the United Kingdom with the opportunity to change its procurement regime, in reality it is highly likely that the EU will insist on compliance with the procurement directives due to its leverage in negotiations. The United Kingdom currently imports more from the EU than vice versa—around 44 percent of UK exports go to the EU, while the reverse is around 8 percent.[80] Additionally, under recent practice and CJEU jurisprudence, the agreement would likely be a "mixed" agreement, which would require the consent of all EU members.[81] Several of these countries run a trade deficit with the United Kingdom,[82] so would have limited incentive to make concessions. Moreover, sentiment against the United Kingdom following Brexit is generally negative. Concerns other than procurement also make this option unlikely—Switzerland's nearly 120 agreements were reached over the course of decades and through much negotiation. Even if the United Kingdom and the EU were able to reach a more streamlined agreement, the negotiation and drafting periods would be long, costly, and create uncertainty for businesses as long as they were ongoing. Moreover, Theresa May has insisted that imposing border

---

[77] Aydan Bahadir and Fernando Garcés de los Fayos, *Fact Sheets on the EU: The European Economic Area (EEA), Switzerland and the North*, European Parliament (Sept. 2016), http://www.europarl.europa.eu/ftu/pdf/en/FTU_6.5.3.pdf.

[78] BBC News: EU Referendum, *supra* note 57.

[79] Arrowsmith, *supra* note 57, at 9.

[80] *Everything you might want to know about the U.K.'s trade with the EU*, Full Fact (June 20, 2016), https://fullfact.org/europe/uk-eu-trade/.

[81] For example, the free trade agreement between the EU and South Korea was treated as a mixed agreement, as is the free trade agreement between Canada and the EU ("CETA"). The CJEU recently ruled that the Singapore Free Trade Agreement was a mixed agreement. Court of Justice of the EU, Press Release No 147/16, Advocate General Sharpston considers that the Singapore Free Trade Agreement can only be concluded by the EU and the Member States acting jointly (Dec. 21, 2016).

[82] These countries are Croatia, Estonia, Bulgaria, Denmark, Malta, Luxemburg, and Ireland. Full Fact, *supra* note 77.

controls is of greater concern than any attempt to remain a member of the single market.[83]

A different iteration of the Swiss model would be a free trade agreement with the EU that does not permit full access to the single market—for example, the proposed EU-Canada Comprehensive Economic and Trade Agreement ("CETA"). The procurement provisions contained in CETA are very similar to those contained in the agreement between the EU and Switzerland.[84] The primary difference is that the dispute resolution method is arbitration.[85] Though perhaps this model would be easier to implement, the EU would likely still insist on compliance with the procurement directives for the same reasons mentioned above.

C. NO TRADE AGREEMENT

The most intriguing possibility for the United Kingdom in terms of its future procurement regime is foregoing a trade relationship with the EU. In this situation, the United Kingdom would have two options: not join any agreements on procurement and potentially scrap its domestic procurement legislation, or join the GPA and adhere to the Agreement's baseline requirements. This section contends that at a minimum, the United Kingdom should join the GPA in order to ensure that domestic contractors are given protection in the EU and in other countries around the world.

1. Going it Alone

At the heart of the debate over the future of the UK procurement regime is the contention that the EU procurement directives are overly complex, and the costs of compliance for government entities (and to a lesser extent, economic operators) are too high. It has been proposed that the United Kingdom would benefit by deregulating the procurement process entirely or almost entirely.[86] Under such a system, common law contract principles would govern the procurement process.[87] The High

---

[83] Anushka Asthana, Peter Walker and Jon Henley, *May on collision course with Conservative backbenchers over hard Brexit*, GUARDIAN (OCT. 3, 2016 7:12 AM), https://www.theguardian.com/politics/2016/oct/02/may-on-collision-course-with-backbenchers-seeking-soft-brexit.

[84] Morris and Grogan, *supra* note 60.

[85] *Id.*

[86] *See* Sue Arrowsmith, *The EC Procurement Directives, National Procurement Policies and Better Governance: The Case for a New Approach*, 27 EUR. L. REV. 3 (2002). However, Arrowsmith herself notes that more radical reforms would be politically difficult to achieve. Sue Arrowsmith, *Modernising the EU's Public Procurement Regime: A Blueprint for Real Simplicity and Flexibility*, 21 PUB. PROCUREMENT L. REV. 71, 72 (2012).

[87] Morris and Grogan, *supra* note 57; Michael Bowsher, QC, *Procurement law after Brexit?*, PUBLIC SECTOR BLOG (March 16, 2016), http://publicsectorblog.practicallaw.com/procurement-law-after-brexit/.

Court has held that there can be an implied contract that gives rise to a duty to consider a tender submitted in accordance with the requirements of an invitation to tender[88]—at least where the procurement regulations do not apply.[89] In the absence of detailed regulations, then, the High Court would likely develop a more robust body of contract law related to procurement.[90]

This would be both imprudent and unlikely for several reasons. First, it would create much uncertainty for contracting entities and contractors alike. Second, arguments that the costs of compliance and the delay in contract awards are too high overlook the transaction costs that would be imposed in the absence of regulations. Many studies have examined the link between weak or ineffective procurement laws and corruption in the procurement process.[91] Corruption would cause inefficiencies that could have a more detrimental economic effect than the cost of compliance with regulations. Second, the cost of compliance is a trade-off of the important policy objectives served by the procurement directives, including openness, transparency, and ensuring value for money. Third, doing away with the regulations would leave UK contractors exposed to discriminatory practices abroad. Although contracts awarded abroad represent a relatively small portion of those secured by UK firms—0.8 percent by value[92]—several billion dollars a year is not an economically insignificant figure. Finally, from a practical perspective, given the international community's increased focus on comprehensive procurement regulation, doing away with procurement regulation entirely seems improbable.

2. The GPA Option

Joining the GPA would be a critical step in ensuring that UK firms operating abroad receive protection in foreign markets. The EU and its major trading partners, including the United States, Japan, and Canada, are parties to the Agreement. Not to join the GPA could mean "losing access to important procurement markets of both current GPA Parties and those of the increasing number of countries that are interested in acceding [including China]…It could also mean losing the opportunity

---

[88] *Blackpool & Fylde Aero Club v Blackpool Borough* Council, EWCA Civ 13 (1990).

[89] *Lion Apparel Systems Limited v. Firebuy* EWHC 2179 (Ch) (2007); *Varney v. Hertfordshire County Council* EWHC 1404 (QB) (2010).

[90] Morris and Grogan, *supra* note 60.

[91] *See*, e.g., OECD, Fighting Corruption and Promoting Integrity in Public Procurement (2005).

[92] Lorna Booth, *Briefing Paper: Public Procurement*, House of Commons Library (July 3, 2015),
http://researchbriefings.parliament.uk/ResearchBriefing/Summary/SN06029#fullrepo
rt.

to influence the future direction of the GPA under the forthcoming review of the Agreement."[93]

It would likely be relatively easy for the United Kingdom to join the GPA by applying the same schedule as that currently applied by the EU. The EU's GPA schedule currently covers entities in the United Kingdom at the federal and sub-federal level, and thus no new negotiations would have to occur. One minor point is that the EU's GPA schedule references the EU's procurement directives, not the United Kingdom's national legislation.[94] However, revising the agreement to reference UK national law would likely be little more than a formality, given that, as noted, the United Kingdom's procurement regulations largely track those of the EU procurement directives. Moreover, the United Kingdom's remedies procedure would continue to be in compliance with the GPA.

If the United Kingdom wishes to reform its procurement regime and provide for more limited coverage, i.e., by excluding certain sectors, the process of joining the GPA will be more complicated. The United Kingdom will need to negotiate its own concessions, for which it will need approval from other GPA parties.[95] This could potentially be a long and costly process, and WTO members may be disinclined to negotiate new concessions with the United Kingdom. An additional concern is that it may be difficult to disentangle the United Kingdom's accession to the GPA from the ongoing negotiations with the EU.[96] For example, if the EU is insistent on strict compliance with EU laws in whatever arrangement is achieved, the United Kingdom will not be able to include less in its schedules.

However, even if the United Kingdom chooses to adopt the EU schedules, accession to the Agreement will probably not be automatic. The GPA is an agreement within the WTO framework, meaning that only WTO members may sign it. Although the United Kingdom is a member in its own right, its membership terms are intertwined with those of the EU, and establishing new membership terms will require the consent of the WTO's 162 members. The WTO's Director General has said that agreeing on the UK's position in the WTO "would likely take years."[97] It is not clear whether the United Kingdom can operate as a WTO member and sign the GPA without agreed upon schedules, and

---

[93] Arrowsmith, *supra* note 57, at 12.
[94] GPA, *supra* note 61, at EU apps. 1-5.
[95] Morris and Grogan, *supra* note 60.
[96] Arrowsmith, *supra* note 57, at 13.
[97] Shawn Donovan, *WTO warns on torturous Brexit trade talks*, FINANCIAL TIMES (May 25, 2016), https://www.ft.com/content/745d0ea2-222d-11e6-9d4d-c11776a5124d

there is no precedent for such a situation.[98] If, as a formal matter, the United Kingdom's status as a party to the GPA cannot be finalized until its membership terms in the WTO are consented to by other members, it could be a very long time before the United Kingdom becomes a party to the GPA.

Two notable changes would result from the United Kingdom relying solely on its status as a party to the GPA. First, in addition to requiring that domestic challenge procedures be available to foreign contractors, the GPA permits parties to bring challenges against other parties through the WTO dispute settlement mechanism.[99] This would expose UK government entities to another potential source of liability but also provide an additional layer of protection for UK contractors operating abroad. An important point to note is that, whereas under the EU enforcement regime private parties may challenge procurement activities, only states may access the WTO dispute settlement process.[100] With respect to national procedures, the GPA requires parties to establish an independent administrative or judicial tribunal for complaints.[101] While the High Court would likely continue to serve as the forum for procurement disputes, it has been suggested that the United Kingdom should take the opportunity to establish a Procurement Appeals Tribunal, which could reduce the costs of litigation.[102]

Another potential area of change under this option is regulation of State aid. Although the United Kingdom would no longer be bound by EU State aid rules, it would be subjected to the requirements of the Agreement on Subsidies and Countervailing Measures (SCM Agreement) as a member of the WTO.[103] The SCM Agreement is less restrictive than EU state aid rules.[104] Although it requires WTO members to provide

---

[98] *Id.* Shawn Donovan, *Brexit and the WTO option: Key questions about a looming challenge,* FINANCIAL TIMES (July 11, 2016), https://www.ft.com/content/5741129a-4510-11e6-b22f-79eb4891c97d.

[99] GPA, *supra* note 61, at art. XX.

[100] *Id.*

[101] *Id.* at art. XVIII.

[102] David Gollancz, *Brexit: What next for public procurement?,* PUBLIC SECTOR BLOG, (Oct. 18, 2016), http://publicsectorblog.practicallaw.com/brexit-what-next-for-public-procurement/. For a general discussion of how establishing such a system would work in practice, see *Xinglin Zhang, Construction a system of challenge procedures to comply with the Agreement on Government Procurement, in* THE WTO REGIME ON GOVERNMENT PROCUREMENT: CHALLENGE AND REFORM (Sue Arrowsmith and Robert D. Anderson eds., 2011).

[103] Agreement on Subsidies and Countervailing Measures, Apr. 15, 1994, Marrakesh Agreement Establishing the World Trade Organization, Annex 1A, 1869 U.N.T.S. 14. Unlike the GPA, the SCM Agreement is a multilateral agreement, meaning that it is binding on all WTO members. *Id.*

[104] Christian Duvernoy et al., *supra* note 45, at 7.

notice of subsidies to the Committee on Subsidies and Countervailing Measures and Subsidiary Bodies (SCM Committee), the SCM Committee does not approve subsidies *ex ante*. Rather, there is only *ex post* relief granted through the dispute settlement mechanism in the form of a recommendation to bring the offending measure into compliance.[105] Unlike the European Commission's enforcement regime, the dispute settlement body does not have the authority to order remuneration for illegal subsidies.[106] Alternatively, an affected WTO member can enact a countervailing duty on exports from the subsidizing country without resorting to the WTO dispute resolution mechanism.

Despite the potential hurdles that the United Kingdom might face, joining the GPA is a prudent decision. Even if the United Kingdom opts for EEA or EFTA membership, it should join the GPA independently to affirm its commitment to honoring procurement procedures and in order for its firms abroad to receive reciprocal benefits.

IV: OPPORTUNITIES FOR REGIME CHANGE

Opting out of EEA or EFTA membership and relying simply on the GPA as a baseline would give the United Kingdom latitude to restructure its procurement regime free of the oversight of the European Commission, provided that it complies with the requirements of the GPA and WTO. Some scholars and practitioners who have long pushed for reform recognize this as a significant opportunity to improve UK procurement law, while others caution that making changes to the regime could have significant consequences for firms both domestically and abroad. This section argues that, while the United Kingdom would no longer be constrained by EU rules, the welfare of UK businesses in the EU post-Brexit must provide the backdrop for any consideration of regime reform.

A. REFORMING THE PROCUREMENT DIRECTIVES

It has already been argued that stripping UK procurement directives would be both impractical and unlikely. A more realistic possibility is that the United Kingdom would retain some form of procurement regulation while streamlining or making more moderate changes to its current regime. For example, Professor Sue Arrowsmith has suggested a simplified bill based on the Utilities Directive.[107] Instead of three different directives, each with its own detailed set of requirements and conditions under which procurement procedures can and cannot be used, there would only be one directive. There is often confusion as to

---

[105] *Id.*

[106] *Id.*

[107] Arrowsmith, *Modernising the EU's Public Procurement Regime, supra* note 86, at 73.

what directive applies in the case of procurement for mixed goods and services. The question has not only vexed procuring entities, but also the CJEU. [108] Consolidating the different regimes into one could add simplicity and clarity to the regulations. Additionally, the Utilities Directive offers flexibility to procuring entities, for example by providing for the use of "qualification systems," which are closed lists of contractors that meet certain requirements, instead of requiring notice of every specific procurement.[109] Another criticism commonly levied at the EU procurement regime is that the directives do not go far *enough* in permitting procuring entities to consider social objectives in making procurement decisions. One reproach is that the directives do not include any mandatory provisions regarding sustainable public procurement—for example, contracting authorities have the discretion to exclude tenderers for violations of social and labor law.[110]

Adding simplicity and flexibility would not be inconsistent with international law. The GPA is based on the same principles underlying the EU procurement directives, but the entire Agreement comprises only twenty-two articles printed on twenty-nine pages. Nor would it be inconsistent with the practices of some of its major trading partners. The United States, for example, permits the use of qualification systems and buy-local policies in certain sectors.[111] With respect to greater inclusion of social policy concerns in the procurement process, the OECD has recently recognized the importance of integrating sustainable public procurement.[112]

Despite the attractiveness of a more simple and flexible regime, or one that takes into account a wider range of social factors, the United Kingdom must bear in mind the consequences of creating a different set of legal rules for both its domestically-based multinationals and the subsidiaries of foreign contractors operating in the United Kingdom. Given the statistics, it may seem that amending the procurement regulations would have little impact—between 2009 and 2011, only 1.3 percent of UK public contracts were awarded to foreign contractors,[113] and it is estimated that 0.8 percent of public contracts secured by UK

---

[108] For a list of relevant cases, see Grith Skovgaard Ølykke and Albert Sanchez-Graells, *Introduction*, *in* REFORMATION OR DEFORMATION OF THE EU PUBLIC PROCUREMENT RULES n. 36 (Grith Skovgaard Ølykke and Albert Sanchez-Graells eds., 2016).

[109] Arrowsmith, *Modernising the EU's Public Procurement Regime*, *supra* note 86, at 74.

[110] Abby Semple, *Reform of the EU Procurement Directives and WTO GPA: Forward Steps for Sustainability?*, *in* CHARTING A COURSE IN PUBLIC PROCUREMENT INNOVATION AND KNOWLEDGE SHARING (G.L. Albano et. al. eds., 2012).

[111] *Brooks Act*, 40 USC §1101.

[112] *Implementing the OECD Recommendation on Enhancing Integrity in Public Procurement*, OECD (2012), http://www.oecd.org/gov/ethics/combined%20files.pdf.

[113] Booth, *supra* note 92, at 16.

firms are awarded abroad.[114] However, neither of these figures takes into account *indirect* cross-border procurement—contracts awarded to domestic economic operators for which a substantial part of the contract is performed by a foreign firm (i.e., contracts secured by domestic subsidiaries of foreign firms). Across the EU, direct-cross border procurement accounts for approximately 3.5 percent of contracts awarded by value, while indirect cross-border procurement through affiliates accounts for 13.4 percent of contracts awarded by value.[115] Although UK-specific statistics are unavailable, presumably the percentage of indirect-cross border procurement by UK-based firms is higher than that of direct cross-border procurement, particularly given the prevalence of UK financial services companies in the EU and the importance of consulting contracts to these companies.

Forcing entities to comply with a set of legal rules different than those in the EU could impose costs that ultimately outweigh the benefits of reforming the domestic regime. For UK subsidiaries based throughout the EU, this could mean markups for products or services provided to EU contracting entities, which could reduce the competitiveness of those businesses.[116] If the United Kingdom fails to conclude a free trade deal with the EU, these costs would be added to the additional duties placed on goods and services. The divergent regulations may also result in a decrease in foreign direct investment from EU-based contractors, particularly if amendments to the regulations include implementing "buy-local" policies, which are currently prohibited under the EU directives. Though the pro-Brexit camp might desire such an effect, it must also be considered that this would offer fewer choices to contracting entities and potentially result in decreased efficiency.[117]

While the United Kingdom might hope that simplifying its own regime would nudge the EU to consider doing so as well, this is unlikely to happen. Streamlining the procurement process and allowing procuring entities greater flexibility was a major focus of the 2014 Regulations.

---

[114] *Id.*

[115] EUROPEAN COMMISSION: FINAL REPORT: CROSS-BORDER PROCUREMENT ABOVE EU THRESHOLDS 36 (March 2011), http://ec.europa.eu/internal_market/publicprocurement/docs/modernising_rules/cross-border-procurement_en.pdf.

[116] Albert Sanchez-Graells, *Additional Thoughts on Brexit and Public Procurement*, HOW TO CRACK A NUT: A BLOG ON EU ECONOMIC LAW (Nov. 30, 2016), http://www.howtocrackanut.com/blog/2016/11/30/brexit-and-public-procurement-some-thoughts-after-kcl-seminar.

[117] Luke Snelling, *EU Referendum: British Procurement Needs the EU*, LINKEDIN (MAY 31, 2016), https://www.linkedin.com/pulse/eu-referendum-british-procurement-needs-european-union-luke-snelling?trk=pulse_spock-articles.

Moreover, the European Commission has recognized that at this point, any improvements to the directives are not to come from future legal reform, but rather from "develop[ing] a culture of legal compliance, which will require further training, professionalization and exchange of information and best practices within the public sector."[118] The United Kingdom would also be wise to place its focus on working within the current framework to streamline processes—for example, by more fully implementing e-procurement platforms at every level of government, and training contracting entities to focus more on social objectives in procurement decisions—rather than expending resources to reform the legal regime.[119] In any event, as the United Kingdom attempts to negotiate thorny innumerable issues as it sorts out its future relationship with the United Kingdom, it likely will not want to expend political capital reopening the issue of procurement law when the directives only came into effect two years ago.

B. STATE AID

Brexiting without joining the EEA or EFTA would also permit the United Kingdom to create State aid rules that allow for greater latitude to provide public financing than the EU State aid rules, or at least conduct procurement without running afoul of the rules. Critics have been particularly vocal about the rigidity of the EU State aid rules with respect to the United Kingdom's failing steel industry.[120]

However, the United Kingdom should exercise restraint in making any changes to its State aid regime, and in any event is unlikely to do so. For one, the substantive definition of a subsidy contained in the SCM Agreement is very similar to the EU definition of State aid, so the United Kingdom would have to be cautious of violating its WTO obligations and risking challenge from another WTO member. Second, in the same vein as the above analysis, the United Kingdom should consider the welfare of its multinational corporations. Any subsidy could result in countervailing duties against exports from the United Kingdom that could injure subsidiaries abroad. Finally, State aid "has always been a fundamental pillar of domestic Competition Law," and "the United Kingdom has always been a driving force for State aid regulation in the

---

[118] Grith Skovgaard Ølykke and Albert Sanchez-Graells, *supra* note 108, at 8.

[119] Sanchez-Graells, *supra* note 116.

[120] Lianna Brinded, *China is not to blame for the destruction of Britain's steel industry*, BUSINESS INSIDER U.K. (March 31, 2016), http://uk.businessinsider.com/uk-steel-industry-failure-eu-state-aid-rules-imports-exports-prices-2016-3.

EU."[121] Therefore, it is unlikely to implement a regime that would be much more conducive to granting state aid.

CONCLUSION

For the United Kingdom, the beginning of 2017 signals that the formal commencement of the Brexit process is right around the corner, at least if Theresa May intends to stick to her plan of giving notice to the EU by the end of March. For the United Kingdom's public procurement regime, little will change in the short term, but the future of the legal framework largely depends on the outcome of the negotiations with the EU. To protect the interests of its public contractors operating abroad, the United Kingdom should at a minimum join the GPA. Relying solely on this Agreement will present an opportunity to reform the domestic regime, but in a period of great uncertainty for businesses, the United Kingdom should be cautious about upheaving the system that it has played an important role in designing when asymmetrical regulations could pose significant costs for businesses.

---

[121] Jonathan Branton, *Brexit: what happens to the law on State aid?*, DWF (Sept. 6, 2016), https://www.dwf.law/news-events/legal-updates/2016/06/will-brexit-free-the-uk-from-state-aid-rules/.

CHAPTER 10: BREXIT AND HUMAN RIGHTS: IMPLICATIONS FOR THE LAWS AND PEOPLE OF THE UNITED KINGDOM

⟩ FRANCIE N. BERGER

I. INTRODUCTION

Following the vote of the United Kingdom (UK) to leave the European Union (EU) in June 2016, varying concerns about the future of human rights of those in the country have arisen. While some see "Brexit" as an opportunity for beneficial legal reform, others have emphasized what losses may result.[1] There are also potential ripple effects on other human rights instruments at home and abroad, as the British Government has signaled that leaving the EU could just be the first step in a series of reforms to human rights frameworks.[2] In any case, there is ambiguity about what protections for these rights will look like following Brexit, and what real effects will be felt in the UK by citizens and non-citizens.

There has been resultant investigation by public and private parties into the implications for human rights. Overall, there are likely to be negative implications for human rights protections from Brexit, because legal enforcements will be circumscribed, and the EU will no longer have a constraining influence on the UK. Part II of this Essay provides a high-level overview of the state of UK human rights prior to Brexit, including a discussion of what falls under the category of "human rights" law. Part III examines some of the most significant potential changes that may arise after Brexit in human rights laws and trade provisions, and it concludes that it seems more likely that Brexit will have detrimental effects on human rights protections.

II. AN OVERVIEW OF UK HUMAN RIGHTS LAW BEFORE BREXIT

The current framework of rights in the UK is a patchwork of international, domestic, and regional structures that intersect and diverge in their scope of application. Some conceptual grounding is provided

---

[1] *See generally* JOINT COMMITTEE ON HUMAN RIGHTS, THE HUMAN RIGHTS IMPLICATIONS OF BREXIT, 2016, HC 695 (UK) (providing expert testimony on both sides of this debate).
[2] Will Worley, *Theresa May 'will campaign to leave the European Convention on Human Rights in 2020 election'*, THE INDEPENDENT (Dec. 29, 2016), http://www.independent.co.uk/news/uk/politics/theresa-may-campaign-leave-european-convention-on-human-rights-2020-general-election-brexit-a7499951.html.

regarding what human rights are to narrow the structures at issue. This section is followed by an overview of what positive human rights law affects the UK.

A. WHAT WE TALK ABOUT WHEN WE TALK ABOUT RIGHTS: ACQUIRED VS. HUMAN RIGHTS

First, there has been some ambiguity about what rights are "human rights" at stake in Brexit, because there are concurrent discussions about whether or not acquired rights are also implicated in the withdrawal process. Distinguishing these two types of rights, with their varying bases in the law, will likely be significant in withdrawal negotiations. Overall, I recommend that the two kinds of rights be analyzed separately in considering the impact of Brexit, and this Essay will discuss only the implications of human rights as defined below.

Human rights in the post-World War II period are exemplified by the Universal Declaration on Human Rights (UDHR). While the UDHR does not update with ongoing changes in human rights thinking, it remains a prominent representation of contemporary human rights, and parts are considered customary international law. [3] The UDHR underscores that human rights follow from people's inherent possession of dignity, which allows them to hold inalienable rights that are afforded equally. [4] These rights are considered universal, in that "violations of human rights were [and are] offenses of concern to humankind generally, and not just matters between a people and their sovereign." [5] Finally, despite emanating from individual personhood, human rights are actualized through law, and "[s]tates must take positive action to facilitate the enjoyment of basic human rights." [6] Accordingly, the UK has taken on such human rights obligations through domestic, regional, and international instruments.

Acquired rights (or "vested rights"), by contrast, tend to encompass "those rights not automatically revoked if a treaty or law no longer applies . . . once a person/organisation has exercised them, they cannot

---

[3] See DAVID LUBAN ET AL., INTERNATIONAL AND TRANSNATIONAL CRIMINAL LAW 34 (2d ed. 2014).

[4] G.A. Res. 217 (III) A, Universal Declaration of Human Rights (Dec. 10, 1948) [hereinafter UDHR] ("the inherent dignity and of the equal and inalienable rights of all members of the human family").

[5] JENNY MARTINEZ, THE SLAVE TRADE AND THE ORIGINS OF INTERNATIONAL HUMAN RIGHTS LAW 149 (2012).

[6] See What are human rights?, UNITED NATIONS HUMAN RIGHTS OFFICE OF THE HIGH COMMISSIONER, http://www.ohchr.org/EN/Issues/Pages/WhatareHumanRights.aspx (last visited Jan. 14, 2017).

Sionaidh Douglas-Scott

be removed—even in the event of a change in the ultimate power over a country. . . ."[7] As a result, people in the UK would gain acquired rights by exercising them in the country—rather than by being human—should these rights be recognized post-Brexit. Despite some substantive overlap, the "most pressing issues of EU acquired rights are not strictly speaking human rights."[8] For example, while the right to health is a commonly cited human right,[9] the potential acquired right at stake in Brexit is the right to free National Health Service healthcare "using the European Health Insurance Card."[10] Moreover, there is unique controversy about whether or not these acquired rights should exist at all after Brexit, because these rights do not have a legal grounding as well-defined as human rights. As Sionaidh Douglas-Scott has concluded, "absent a Withdrawal Agreement which gives clear protection of acquired rights, existing national, EU and international law does not offer a great deal of protection."[11] Considering the differing legal conception and basis undergirding acquired rights, they deserve separate treatment from the dignity-based human rights described above.

B. PRE-BREXIT HUMAN RIGHTS PROTECTIONS AT THE EU, INTERNATIONAL, AND DOMESTIC LEVELS

Pre-Brexit human rights law involves several legal instruments at the EU, international, and domestic levels. Each of these types of obligations are examined below in order to facilitate an understanding of what laws Brexit may or may not change in the short- and long-term. First, the human rights law most implicated in the Brexit process is the EU Charter of Fundamental Rights (EUCFR or Charter), which is the EU agreement that "lays down the fundamental rights that are binding upon the EU

---

[7] Sionaidh Douglas-Scott, *What Happens to 'Acquired Rights' in the Event of a Brexit?*, UK CONSTITUTIONAL LAW ASS'N (May 16, 2016), https://ukconstitutionallaw.org/2016/05/16/sionaidh-douglas-scott-what-happens-to-acquired-rights-in-the-event-of-a-brexit/.

[8] *Id.*

[9] *See, e.g.,* UDHR, *supra* note 4, at art. 25.

[10] The following may also fall under the umbrella of acquired rights during Brexit negotiations: "the right to live, work and own property in all 28 countries of the EU," "the ability to retire to another EU country," "the right to vote in local elections in other EU countries mutual recognition of child custody decisions across the EU," "the use of the European Small Claims Procedure to reclaim up to €2,000 from individuals in other EU countries," and "the right to use public services in other EU countries." *See* Tim Eicke QC, *Could EU citizens living in the UK claim 'acquired rights' if there is a full Brexit?*, LexisPSL (Apr. 11, 2016).

[11] Douglas-Scott, *supra* note 7.

institutions and bodies." [12] These fundamental rights include many traditional human rights, as well as some more expansive social and economic rights.[13]

While the EUCFR came into force with the 2009 Treaty of Lisbon, there has been ongoing debate about how it actually legally applies in the UK.[14] This debate stems from Protocol 30 to the Treaty,[15] which states that the "Charter does not extend the ability of the Court of Justice of the European Union, or any court . . . of the [UK], to find that the laws . . . of the [UK] are inconsistent with the fundamental rights, freedoms and principles that it reaffirms."[16] At the time of its drafting, this Protocol appeared to provide the UK an opt-out from the EUCFR's application.[17] However, some of the Court of Justice of the European Union's (CJEU) decisions in 2011 underscored that this Protocol was not an opt-out.[18] Rather, the Protocol was just a reassurance that was meant to emphasize explicitly that the Charter would "not create new rights."[19] The UK judiciary also seems to have fallen in line with this CJEU reasoning, as the UK High Court stated, "[n]otwithstanding the endeavours of our political representatives at Lisbon it would seem that the much wider Charter of Rights is now part of our domestic law."[20] This conclusion has been echoed in Parliamentary reporting[21] and expert opinion.[22] Thus, it seems well-established that, despite the plain wording of Protocol 30,

---

[12] *Human Rights*, EUROPEAN UNION, https://europa.eu/european-union/topics/human-rights_en (last visited Jan. 14, 2017).

[13] *See* THE HUMAN RIGHTS IMPLICATIONS OF BREXIT, *supra* note 1, at 10.

[14] *Id.* at 20.

[15] *Id.*

[16] Protocol on the Application of the Charter of Fundamental Rights of the European Union to Poland and to the United Kingdom to The Treaty of Lisbon Amending the Treaty on European Union and the Treaty Establishing the European Community, Dec. 17, 2007, 2007 O.J. (C 306) 157.

[17] THE HUMAN RIGHTS IMPLICATIONS OF BREXIT, *supra* note 1, at 20.

[18] *Id.* at 21.

[19] *Id.* at 21–22.

[20] AB v. Secretary of State for the Home Department [2013] EWHC (QB) 3453 (Admin) CO/11191/2010 [14].

[21] EUROPEAN SCRUTINY COMMITTEE, THE APPLICATION OF THE EU CHARTER OF FUNDAMENTAL RIGHTS IN THE UK: A STATE OF CONFUSION, 2014, HC 979, at 5 (UK) ("Protocol 30 was designed for comfort rather than protection: it is in no sense an opt-out Protocol; consequently, the Charter is directly effective in the UK with supremacy over inconsistent national law.").

[22] JOINT COMMITTEE ON HUMAN RIGHTS, ORAL EVIDENCE: WHAT ARE THE HUMAN RIGHTS IMPLICATIONS OF BREXIT?, Oct. 26, 2016, HC 695, at 15–16 (UK) ("Protocol 30, which was intended to enshrine the UK's understanding of the limited reach of the charter, has been rendered a dead letter . . . .") [hereinafter ORAL EVIDENCE Oct. 26].

the Charter is still applicable to the UK (while a Member State of the EU).

Procedurally, the Charter does have bite with regard to enforcement. UK courts are able to find that British legislation is incompatible with provisions of the Charter and then disapply the domestic legislation.[23] Complaints may also go up to the CJEU, the ultimate decision-maker on EU law that has the ability to make binding decisions on EU Member States[24] (though individuals are typically not allowed to bring their claims in the CJEU directly).[25] It should be noted that substantively, however, the Charter applies only to state/EU conduct in carrying out EU law.[26]

There is appreciable overlap between the EUCFR and the other major multinational human rights instrument applicable to the UK: the European Convention on Human Rights (ECHR or Convention).[27] Unlike the Charter, the Convention is not related to the European Union, and the UK will remain party to the ECHR after Brexit unless it decides to withdraw from both.[28] The Charter is considered more expansive than the ECHR, because the Charter includes additional rights, such as "the right to fair and just working conditions, the right to preventive healthcare, the right to good administration, the right to access to documents and a more wide ranging right to privacy."[29] However, the ECHR is not limited in its application to EU law like the Charter.[30] Overall, the substantive features of the ECHR may not be as expansive as the Charter, but they can be applied in more situations.

There are also some notable procedural differences with the ECHR. Individual or state petitions are allowed in the European Court of Human Rights (ECtHR), the international body that adjudicates alleged violations of the ECHR.[31] Decisions by the ECtHR, however, do not

---

[23] The Human Rights Implications of Brexit, *supra* note 1, at 20–21 (citing Benkharbouche v. Embassy of the Republic of Sudan [2015] EWCA Civ 33).

[24] *Id.* at 20 ("CJEU is not a court of individual petition. This restricts the right of access by individuals.").

[25] *Id.* at 10.

[26] *Human Rights*, European Union, https://europa.eu/european-union/topics/human-rights_en (last visited Jan. 14, 2017).

[27] Council of Europe, European Convention for the Protection of Human Rights and Fundamental Freedoms, as amended by Protocols Nos. 11 and 14, art. 7, Nov. 4, 1950, E.T.S. 5 (entered into force Sept. 3, 1953) [hereinafter ECHR].

[28] Simultaneous withdrawal seems unlikely, given the current statements of the Government. Post-Brexit withdrawal, though, seems possible (if unlikely). *See* Worley, *supra* note 2.

[29] The Human Rights Implications of Brexit, *supra* note 1, at 10.

[30] *Id.* at 21.

[31] *European Court of Human Rights*, Council of Europe, http://www.coe.int/t/democracy/migration/bodies/echr_en.asp (last visited Jan. 14,

have the same strong effects as the CJEU or UK courts with regard to the Charter.[32] Instead of courts disapplying laws, violations of the ECHR lead to "a declaration of incompatibility." [33] In response to such declarations, "Parliament has the capacity to fast-track changes to that legislation, but if Parliament wishes to carry on in wilful denial of this declaration of incompatibility, it can."[34] Such denial has indeed occurred (and continues) in the UK with regard to its ban on prisoner voting. Despite being considered a violation of the ECHR, the ban persists due to a domestic unwillingness to grant prisoners the vote.[35] As a result, enforcement of the ECHR is often considered less powerful in comparison to the Charter.[36]

There are also a number of domestic instruments that aim to secure human rights in the UK. While these acts may be aligned with EU law, they remain separately implemented at the domestic level and would not come to an end following the UK's withdrawal from the EU. One of the most relevant is the Human Rights Act 1998 (HRA), which "give[s] further effect to rights and freedoms guaranteed under the [ECHR]" within UK law.[37] Accordingly, ECHR rights may be enforced through UK courts (instead of requiring complainants to go to the ECtHR, though appeals to the ECtHR remain available to potential petitioners).[38] British courts, however, are also mostly limited to the same "declaration of incompatibility" in addressing incompatibilities at the legislative

---

2017); *see also* ECHR, *supra* note 27, at art. 35(1) (highlighting the procedural caveat that domestic remedies must first be exhausted).

[32] EUROPEAN UNION COMMITTEE, THE UK, THE EU AND A BRITISH BILL OF RIGHTS, *Chapter 5: The enforcement of the ECHR and EU Charter in national law*, 2016, HL 139 (UK), http://www.publications.parliament.uk/pa/ld201516/ldselect/ldeucom/139/13908.htm.

[33] *Id.*

[34] *Id.*

[35] *Id.*

[36] It should be noted, however, that Prime Minister May has previously objected the strength of ECHR enforcement more than that of the EU. *See* Anushka Asthana & Rowena Mason, *UK must leave European convention on human rights, says Theresa May*, THE GUARDIAN (Apr. 25, 2016), https://www.theguardian.com/politics/2016/apr/25/uk-must-leave-european-convention-on-human-rights-theresa-may-eu-referendum ("The ECHR can bind the hands of parliament, adds nothing to our prosperity, makes us less secure by preventing the deportation of dangerous foreign nationals—and does nothing to change the attitudes of governments like Russia's when it comes to human rights.").

[37] Human Rights Act 1998, Introductory Text (UK).

[38] *A Guide to the Human Rights Act 1998: Third Edition*, DEPARTMENT FOR CONSTITUTIONAL AFFAIRS 8 (Oct. 2006), https://www.justice.gov.uk/downloads/human-rights/act-studyguide.pdf.

level—aside from secondary legislation, which judges may disapply.[39] Should the ECHR right violation come from actions of public authorities, though, judges can award damages and take injunctive measures.[40] Thus, while some individuals may receive a remedy, broader impacts on country-wide legislation can remain inaccessible.

Finally, there are some specialized UK legislative acts that address individual topics within the human rights realm, such as the Modern Slavery Act 2015 and Equality Act 2010. The Modern Slavery Act takes aim not only at the eponymous issue of slavery, but also forced labor and human trafficking.[41] One of the most notable provisions in the Act is the requirement for certain commercial organizations to "prepare a slavery and human trafficking statement for each financial year of the organisation."[42] This requirement for the private sector is considered a step toward advancing the United Nations Guiding Principles on Business and Human Rights. [43] The Equality Act 2010 provides protections[44] for "people from discrimination in the workplace and in wider society."[45] This Act consolidated existing anti-discrimination law, expanded select provisions,[46] and brought the UK into line with EU Directives.[47] Like the HRA, these acts would not be affected by Brexit per se.

III. POST-BREXIT HUMAN RIGHTS OUTCOMES

There are a number of procedural avenues by which the Brexit negotiations and withdrawal process may transpire, but the British Government can only start formal withdrawal by triggering Article 50 of the Lisbon Treaty. [48] Prime Minister May has announced the

---

[39] *Id.*

[40] *Id.*

[41] Modern Slavery Act 2015, Part 1 (UK).

[42] *Id.* at Part 6.

[43] *See* Freshfields Bruckhaus Deringer LLP, *Brexit: What It Means for Human Rights*, LEXOLOGY (July 6, 2016), http://www.lexology.com/library/detail.aspx?g=9daa145c-3468-4e99-9f89-881027791a55.

[44] Protection is afforded on the bases of "age; disability; gender reassignment; marriage and civil partnership; pregnancy and maternity; race; religion or belief; sex; sexual orientation." Equality Act 2010, c. 1, §4 (UK).

[45] *Equality Act 2010: Guidance*, GOV.UK (June 15, 2015), https://www.gov.uk/guidance/equality-act-2010-guidance.

[46] *Id.*

[47] Colm O'Cinneide & Kimberly Liu, *Defining the limits of discrimination law in the United Kingdom: Principle and pragmatism in tension*, 15 INT'L J. OF DISCRIMINATION AND THE LAW 80, 83–84 (2015).

[48] Consolidated Version of the Treaty on European Union art. 50, 2010 O.J. C 83/01 [hereinafter Lisbon Treaty].

Government's intention to do so by March 2017.[49] Britain's treaties with the EU will then formally cease when either of the following happens: 1) the EU and UK conclude withdrawal agreement(s), which could cover human rights issues and the incorporation of Charter rights in the UK, or 2) two years pass from the triggering of Article 50, regardless of the status of a withdrawal agreement between the EU and UK.[50] With the withdrawal, the EUCFR "would not apply and the Court of Justice of the European Union (CJEU) would most probably cease to have jurisdiction over the UK."[51] With regard to UK courts, the immediate legal effect of withdrawing from the EU would be the elimination of their ability to disapply that UK law which they find in violation of the Charter. [52] Additionally, the UK will not be obligated to keep up legislatively or judicially with ongoing changes in the EU with regard to human rights.[53]

Currently, the Government has proposed a stopgap "Great Repeal Bill" that would "annul the 1972 European Communities Act (ECA), which gives EU law instant effect in the UK," and then "give Parliament the power to absorb parts of EU legislation into UK law and scrap elements it does not want to keep."[54] A question for the Government going forward is whether or not the Charter's rights would be absorbed into UK law in the passage of the Great Repeal Bill. While the Prime Minister has underscored a commitment to continuing workers' rights protections over from the EU, there has not been clarity regarding other rights from the Charter. [55] For example, when Parliament's Joint Committee on Human Rights questioned Sir Oliver Heald about whether or not the Government planned to incorporate the Charter into the Great Repeal Bill, he replied that it "was not [his] understanding"

---

[49] *Brexit: Theresa May to trigger Article 50 by end of March*, BBC NEWS (Oct. 2, 2016), http://www.bbc.com/news/uk-politics-37532364.

[50] *See* Lisbon Treaty, *supra* note 48, at art. 50. The two year period can only be extended where "the European Council, in agreement with the Member State concerned, unanimously decides to extend this period." *Id.*

[51] THE HUMAN RIGHTS IMPLICATIONS OF BREXIT, *supra* note 1, at 8.

[52] *Id.* at 23 (quoting the Human Rights Centre at the University of Essex).

[53] *Id.* at 7.

[54] Alexandra Sims, *What is the Great Repeal Bill? The Brexit law to end all EU laws (that we don't like)*, THE INDEPENDENT (Oct. 3, 2016), http://www.independent.co.uk/news/uk/politics/great-repeal-bill-brexit-law-eu-law-theresa-may-david-davis-a7343256.html.

[55] THE HUMAN RIGHTS IMPLICATIONS OF BREXIT, *supra* note 1, at 6.

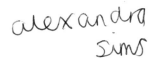

that the Charter would come over with the Bill.[56] As a result, the Joint Committee has pressed for more clarity of what human rights would actually be represented in the Bill.[57] Furthermore, there is significant concern that even if Charter rights would come over with the Bill, they could be stricken without due consideration via Henry VIII clauses, which "enable Ministers to make changes to primary legislation by way of secondary legislation." [58] With the ambiguity around the Government's plans and what issues may arise during the negotiations with the EU, it is difficult to say just how human rights may expand or contract in the Brexit process. However, assuming the Government abides by its current plan not to incorporate the Charter into the Great Repeal Bill, it appears that the implications of Brexit on human rights will be substantial.

A. *IMMEDIATE HUMAN RIGHTS IMPACTS*

While Brexit may affect several human rights, two of the most evidently implicated are the right to private and family life and the right to anti-discrimination. While these rights remain protected under other international and domestic laws, Brexit still has appreciable negative implications through reductions in unique legal provisions and European influence.

1. The Right to Private and Family Life and Residence Rights

Potential changes to residency laws, which implicate the right to private and family life, are among the most concerning in the Brexit debate. Following the withdrawal, non-British EU citizens will no longer have the same rights to reside in the UK, leaving a popular question of whether the UK could and would deport previously-lawful residents.[59] Professor Colm O'Cinneide provided the following representative anecdote of what situation can face UK residents:

> Let me give you an example . . . [an author] has two children, and . . . [multiple sclerosis]. Her partner is a French national. He has not worked since he came to the UK because he looks after

---

[56] JOINT COMMITTEE ON HUMAN RIGHTS, ORAL EVIDENCE: WHAT ARE THE HUMAN RIGHTS IMPLICATIONS OF BREXIT?, Nov. 23, 2016, HC 695, at 5 (UK) [hereinafter ORAL EVIDENCE Nov. 23].

[57] THE HUMAN RIGHTS IMPLICATIONS OF BREXIT, *supra* note 1, at 6.

[58] *Id.*

[59] In addition to issues of residency and movement, data privacy is another major issue with implications for a right to private and family life. Shannon Togawa Mercer's Essay in this volume provides a detailed explanation of impacts of Brexit on data privacy; therefore, data privacy is not covered in this Essay.

the children while she writes and copes with her medical treatment. That has all sorts of implications under EU law, which I will not go into the detail of, but basically his right to free movement under EU law is extremely restricted because he is not here for employment as such. He has been living in north London looking after the kids for five or six years now.[60]

So, how might the French national here assert a right to private and family life (in the face of deportation or lack of access to state services)?[61]

First, the right to private and family life, even if the Charter were not brought over with the Great Repeal Bill, could still be asserted by such a claimant through the ECHR and HRA mechanisms. Unlike the language of the Charter,[62] though, "interferences with [ECHR] Article 8 rights can be justified under Article 8(2) of the ECHR in circumstances where they are in accordance with the law, in pursuit of a legitimate aim and a proportionate means of achieving that aim."[63] Thus, the protections of the ECHR appear to be less robust in comparison with the Charter on a textual basis, because the government can justify its actions violating the right.

Several legal scholars, however, have concluded that despite the differences in the rights law between the Charter and Convention, EU citizens in the UK could likely have strong claims based on Article 8 violations, including before domestic courts.[64] This conclusion arises from previous legal decisions that made Article 8 determinations on the basis of how "embedded" one is in the community—i.e., the more embedded one is in the community, the greater one's right to private and family life.[65] Considering the ties of the French national in the aforementioned example, it is likely such a person would have a powerful Article 8 claim on account of his personal relationships and caretaking role.[66] The Parliament Joint Committee on Human Rights has rightly pointed out that considering this is a fact-specific inquiry for which many will seek relief, "such claims could potentially overwhelm the courts and tribunals system."[67] Overall, it appears that without further government

---

[60] ORAL EVIDENCE Oct. 26, *supra* note 22, at 14.

[61] *See id.*

[62] Article 7 of the Charter states that "[e]veryone has the right to respect for his or her private and family life, home and communications." Charter of Fundamental Rights of the European Union, Dec. 18, 2007, 2007 O.J. (C 364) 10.

[63] THE HUMAN RIGHTS IMPLICATIONS OF BREXIT, *supra* note 1, at 15.

[64] *Id.* at 15–16.

[65] *Id.*

[66] ORAL EVIDENCE Oct. 26, *supra* note 22, at 14.

[67] THE HUMAN RIGHTS IMPLICATIONS OF BREXIT, *supra* note 1, at 16.

action, there will be popular confusion and judicial backlog as residents assert Article 8 rights to remain in the UK where no individual can be certain of winning in a fact-specific inquiry.

A blanket government reply seems desirable in response to this situation.[68] As it is hard to say that all persons after a certain point of time should leave (because embeddedness does not always correspond with time in a country), using a blanket cut-off *before* formal Brexit would be difficult.[69] Groups like the Immigration Law Practitioners Association, therefore, have recommended a cut-off at formal withdrawal at the earliest.[70] This proposal seems more advisable and probable, because it heads off costly litigation and wide-scale uncertainty. Furthermore, it allows for negotiation room with the EU in regard to securing the protection of UK citizens who reside in EU countries. Thus, while the impact of Brexit on the right to private and family life will likely face contraction due to the more limited scope of the ECHR provision and revocation of EU citizenship rights, there can be measures to help mitigate the changes.

2. Discrimination Protections

Human rights advocates have also underscored the effect of Brexit on the frequency of discrimination, particularly with regard to hate crimes against marginalized groups. Human Rights Watch (HRW) highlighted an increase in xenophobia following the Brexit vote, noting that there was "a 42% rise in [hate crime] incidents in the last two weeks of June compared to the same period in 2015."[71] While HRW applauded the efforts of government officials in responding to these incidents, it also cautioned against a "watering down" of the Charter discrimination provisions by Parliament after Brexit.[72] This Essay concludes that while many legal protections against discrimination will continue after Brexit, there will likely be a negative loss in the constraining influence of the EU.

The Charter's provisions on anti-discrimination, and any resultant CJEU precedent, will disappear after Brexit; however, provisions in the domestic Equality Act 2010 and ECHR Article 14 will still provide a legal basis for challenges to discrimination in most instances. One notable

---

[68] *See id.* at 17.
[69] ORAL EVIDENCE Oct. 26, *supra* note 22, at 14.
[70] THE HUMAN RIGHTS IMPLICATIONS OF BREXIT, *supra* note 1, at 17.
[71] Benjamin Ward, *What Brexit Means for Human Rights*, HUMAN RIGHTS WATCH (July 11, 2016), https://www.hrw.org/news/2016/07/11/what-brexit-means-human-rights; *see also 'Record hate crimes' after EU referendum*, BBC NEWS (Feb. 15, 2017), http://www.bbc.com/news/uk-38976087 ("In the three months to September 2016, 33 of the 44 forces in England and Wales saw their highest levels of hate crimes since comparable records began in 2012.").
[72] Ward, *supra* note 71.

exception is the example of *Benkharbouche v. Embassy of the Republic of Sudan*.[73] In that case, "the Court of Appeal disapplied the law on state immunity, which prevented the claimants from accessing the courts" on the basis of the Charter for a complaint that included racial discrimination allegations (alongside workers' rights claims). [74] Opponents of the Charter have underscored that avoiding case law like *Benkharbouche* will be a positive implication of Brexit, because European standards will not supersede British legislation, and judges will not have free rein to interpret European standards more expansively than British ones.[75] However, it appears that *Benkharbouche* is an isolated decision, and courts are not regularly using Charter provisions in practice to disapply British law.[76] Overall, *Benkharbouche* shows a gap in rights coverage that is constrained but meaningful.

Perhaps more concerning than the gap between the Charter and other laws, though, is the loss of the EU's influence over discrimination protections, as the UK will no longer have to keep up with EU precedent and directives. [77] Historically, "[t]he scope of coverage of UK anti-discrimination legislation has been shaped in response to civil society advocacy from below and EU obligations from above rather than arising in unified fashion through a central principle."[78] This alignment between civil society groups, who alone may face difficulty in making political change, and the EU has helped in ensuring that the marginalized and democratically-unrepresented receive protections.[79] As a result, there is concern about whether UK legislation and judicial decision-making would advance appropriately or even regress over time without the EU's influence.[80] In response to these concerns, the Government currently points to past progress in lawmaking as a sign of future success,[81] but "gave [Parliament's Joint Committee on Human Rights] no commitment that the Government would monitor or take account of EU law developments."[82] Brexit, therefore, is more likely to have the problematic

---

[73] Benkharbouche v. Embassy of the Republic of Sudan [2015] EWCA Civ 33.

[74] THE HUMAN RIGHTS IMPLICATIONS OF BREXIT, *supra* note 1, at 21; *Benkharbouche*, [2015] EWCA Civ 33, ¶ 5.

[75] ORAL EVIDENCE Oct. 26, *supra* note 22, at 19.

[76] *Id.*

[77] *See* THE HUMAN RIGHTS IMPLICATIONS OF BREXIT, *supra* note 1, at 7.

[78] O'Cinneide & Liu, *supra* note 47, at 85.

[79] ORAL EVIDENCE Nov. 23, *supra* note 56, at 5.

[80] THE HUMAN RIGHTS IMPLICATIONS OF BREXIT, *supra* note 1, at 26–28.

[81] ORAL EVIDENCE Nov. 23, *supra* note 56, at 6, 13.

[82] THE HUMAN RIGHTS IMPLICATIONS OF BREXIT, *supra* note 1, at 28.

effect of "creating points of vulnerability" for discrimination rights,[83] as a model for UK law on discrimination will probably be disregarded.

B. TRADE AND ISSUES IN HUMAN RIGHTS ENFORCEMENT

In addition to lawmaking that is specifically aimed at promoting human rights in the UK, there is also human rights enforcement through trade regulation. There are questions of how this practice will affect those in the UK, both in its potential agreements with the EU and free trade agreements with non-EU countries. Notably, EU "agreements on trade or cooperation with non-EU countries include a human rights clause stipulating that human rights are central to relations with the EU."[84] As a result, the possible Brexit withdrawal agreement on trade may place stipulations on human rights enforcement. The UK may also include such agreements in its future free trade agreement with non-EU countries.[85] Such provisions could affect the human rights practices of UK business entities at home and abroad. For example, human rights impact assessments could be integrated into their due diligence procedures.[86] Thus, the UK might choose to include more robust human rights protections via due diligence requirements in trade agreements. The UK could also decide *not* to continue implementing human rights provisions in trade agreements or to water down the provisions in comparison with the EU. Considering that these provisions are unpopular and the government will be "under pressure to achieve quick free trade clauses," it seems more likely that these clauses will be weaker than they are under the EU.[87] This would create an "imbalance between the EU standards and the UK standards, and that will certainly prove controversial."[88] Thus, the impact of new trade agreements could be positive or negative with regard to human rights, and more information from the negotiation process is needed.

---

[83] ORAL EVIDENCE Nov. 23, *supra* note 56, at 5.

[84] Ciarán McGonagle, *Timing, Tax and Human Rights – 3 reasons why Brexit negotiations may fail*, CIARANMCGONAGLE.COM (Jan. 3, 2017), https://ciaranmcgonagle.com/2017/01/03/timing-tax-and-human-rights-3-reasons-why-brexit-negotiations-may-fail/.

[85] THE HUMAN RIGHTS IMPLICATIONS OF BREXIT, *supra* note 1, at 7.

[86] *Id.* at 31.

[87] ORAL EVIDENCE Nov. 23, *supra* note 56, at 31.

[88] *Id.*

C. THE CLOUDS ON THE HORIZON: POTENTIAL OVERHAULING OF INTERNATIONAL AND DOMESTIC HUMAN RIGHTS INSTRUMENTS

While an in-depth discussion of what the UK legal landscape would look like without instruments like the ECHR and the HRA would require its own essay,[89] the potential domino effect of Brexit on other human rights instruments should not go unmentioned as a consequence of the withdrawal. Repealing other human rights measures would likely mean that several of the backstops on human rights discussed above could be lost. Proponents of removing these obligations believe that the country would benefit from increased national autonomy and security. For example, Prime Minister May has previously criticized the ECHR for preventing extradition and deportation of criminals and terrorists.[90] Recent reporting indicates that her Government may be planning to utilize the leaving the ECHR as part of the 2020 political campaign.[91] The Human Rights Act could also be dissolved in this process, likely to be replaced with a British Bill of Rights.[92] Indeed, there are already some moves to dismantle some of the obligations of the Convention, as Conservatives have proposed "introducing a 'presumption to derogate' from the ECHR in warfare."[93] Charles Falconer of Gibson Dunn has emphasized that the enormity of Brexit makes other changes, like

---

[89] See *The legal implications of a repeal of the Human Rights Act 1998 and withdrawal from the European Convention on Human Rights* (Kanstantsin Dzehtsiarou & Tobias Lock eds., 2015), http://ssrn.com/abstract=2605487, for an in-depth discussion of the repeal of the ECHR and Human Rights Act.

[90] Charlie Cooper, *Theresa May says UK should leave European human rights convention*, THE INDEPENDENT (Apr. 25, 2016), http://www.independent.co.uk/news/uk/politics/european-convention-human-rights-eu-referendum-brexit-theresa-may-a6999701.html.

[91] *See* Worley, *supra* note 2. *But see* Steven Swinford, *Theresa May is preparing to abandon plans for a British Bill of Rights, sources suggest*, THE TELEGRAPH (Jan. 26, 2017), http://www.telegraph.co.uk/news/2017/01/26/theresa-may-preparing-abandon-plans-british-bill-rights-sources/.

[92] Jon Stone, *Plans to Replace Human Rights Act with British Bill of Rights will Go Ahead, Justice Secretary Confirms*, THE INDEPENDENT (Aug. 22, 2016), http://www.independent.co.uk/news/uk/politics/scrap-human-rights-act-british-bill-of-rights-theresa-may-justice-secretary-liz-truss-a7204256.html.

[93] Peter Walker and Owen Bowcott, *Plan for UK military to opt out of European convention on human rights*, THE GUARDIAN (Oct. 4, 2016), https://www.theguardian.com/uk-news/2016/oct/03/plan-uk-military-opt-out-european-convention-human-rights; *see also* Letter from Harriet Harman to Michael Fallon regarding The Government's proposed derogation from the ECHR (Oct. 13, 2016), https://www.parliament.uk/documents/joint-committees/human-rights/correspondence/2016-17/HH_to_MF_re_derogation.pdf (providing a Parliamentary response to the Government's announcement of derogation).

withdrawing from the ECHR, "feel a very minor step by comparison with leaving the EU."[94] Thus, there may be not only a will but a way for the overhaul of other human rights agreements as a result of Brexit.

The withdrawal agreement between the EU and UK may also address this potential departure from the ECHR. Ciarán McGonagle has underscored that because all agreements with the EU include a provision on the importance of human rights in relationship to the EU, "[a] British Bill of Rights that either sought to limit human rights protections to British citizens or the scope of the rights granted by the ECHR themselves would likely infringe upon this policy objective."[95] As a result, the Government rhetoric about withdrawing from the ECHR in the wake of leaving the EU is likely to bring this topic to the Brexit negotiations table. McGonagle acknowledged that the EU does have agreements with countries that have problematic human rights records, perhaps making it less likely that ECHR withdrawal would impact negotiations. Still, he concludes that it seems problematic that the EU could meet its human rights policy objective when making agreements with a country that is actively knocking down human rights instruments (when compared to making agreements with countries where the EU can use "soft power with the objective of promoting gradual reform in these nations").[96]

Less commentary has circulated regarding specialized human rights legislation, like the Modern Slavery Act. Considering the relative newness and domestic crafting of such acts, it seems less probable that these will face active dismantling in the wake of Brexit.[97] During the Parliamentary inquiry into the human rights implications of Brexit, Sir Oliver Heald underscored that such domestic measures help to show that "we [the UK] do really press on human rights issues."[98] Consequently, it seems unlikely that these domestic measures are on the chopping block following Brexit.

CONCLUSION

While many of the human rights instruments that apply to people in the UK would remain after Brexit, there are likely to be appreciable negative implications from the withdrawal. Overall, Brexit is predicted to

---

[94] Charles Falconer, *Human Rights are under Threat–Just When We Need Them Most*, THE GUARDIAN (Jan. 3, 2017), https://www.theguardian.com/commentisfree/2017/jan/03/european-convention-human-rights-threat.

[95] McGonagle, *supra* note 84.

[96] *Id.*

[97] *See* Freshfields Bruckhaus Deringer LLP, *supra* note 43.

[98] ORAL EVIDENCE Nov. 23, *supra* note 56, at 13.

circumscribe human rights protections in the UK, because there will be the simultaneous loss of EU human rights provisions and influence on domestic law and trade provisions. There are a number of ways that the British state may go about mitigating the real world impact of these changes, particularly through negotiating rights in a potential EU withdrawal arrangement and pre-arranging protections in the Great Repeal Bill. At the same time, it seems that the Government may be driving forward a much more dramatic change in the future: withdrawal from the ECHR and repeal of the HRA. This potential consequence seems especially concerning, because it is unclear what rights protections would come in their stead, and there would be an additional loss of a model for human rights action in the ECtHR. Consequently, while Brexit per se is likely to do some harm to human rights, it may be most impactful for its facilitation of future human rights law repeals.

CHAPTER 11: THE COMMON TRAVEL AREA BETWEEN IRELAND AND THE UNITED KINGDOM AFTER BREXIT

ALEXIS A. BAKER

INTRODUCTION

The news that spread across the world on the morning of June 24, 2016, shocked many as they learned the United Kingdom (UK) citizens voted to leave the European Union (EU) by a slim majority of 51.9%.[1] The legal questions and implications span far and wide. When will Article 50 of the Lisbon Treaty be triggered, and was Article 50 intended to be triggered? Will the four freedoms continue to apply to those living in the UK? How will a business in both the UK and EU continue to operate? What will the UK and EU negotiate once Article 50 is triggered? Will the UK be better off leaving the EU? The list of legal questions is endless. This paper, however, will focus on the legal issues that loom over many minds concerning the Common Travel Area (CTA) between the UK and The Republic of Ireland (Ireland). The future of the border in the event of a Brexit is a major concern among individuals living and working in Ireland and the UK.[2] My objective will be to address the current laws and practices surrounding the CTA in the UK, EU and Ireland. Additionally, I will try to resolve whether the CTA will continue to exist after Brexit. Finally, I will conclude by presenting possible scenarios and factors that could contribute to the future of the CTA following Brexit.

In short, it is unlikely that the CTA will cease to exist between Ireland and the UK for legal, practical and political reasons. While Ireland and the UK are the only two parties to the CTA agreement, EU law recognizes the arrangements between the two countries.[3] Legal concerns would be inexistent if both countries intended to leave the EU. Ireland, however, will retain its membership in the EU while the UK will leave, presumably. Whether EU law will continue to recognize Ireland's arrangements with the UK after Brexit is at the core of the legal discourse

---

[1] *EU Referendum Results*, Brit. Broad. Corp., (Nov. 15, 2016), http://www.bbc.com/news/politics/eu_referendum/results.
[2] Northern Ireland Affairs Committee, Northern Ireland and the EU referendum, 2016-17, HC 26 (UK).
[3] Consolidated Version of the Treaty on the Functioning of the European Union Protocol 20, May 9, 2008, 2008 O.J. (C 115) 47 [hereinafter TFEU].

concerning the CTA. It would be unreasonable and unfair for EU law to cease recognizing the CTA and revoke the benefits Ireland currently enjoys from its relationship with the UK. Simply, there is no legal reason the CTA law would be removed from EU law solely because of the UK's departure.[4]

Practically, border control and passport checks at seaports and airports in Ireland would be feasible, but the land border between Ireland and Northern Ireland presents its own difficulties. The land border is not linear nor is it well defined.[5] Implementation of border controls would be costly, burdensome and impractical due to the length and intermingled nature of the border as it crosses between the two countries.[6] Finally, political desires to continue the arrangements between the two countries are evident.[7] In 1998, Ireland and the UK signed the Good Friday Agreement, and have vigorously worked for almost a decade to establish and maintain a virtuous relationship.[8] Political figures from both the UK and Ireland have stated their desire to continue to maintain the CTA.[9] Creating border barriers between the two countries would cripple the peace and cooperation towards which the two countries have worked. Thus, retention of the good relations between two countries is extremely desirable.[10] While legally, practically and politically it may be unforeseeable that border controls between the two countries would be implemented, EU law may mandate the establishment of border and passport controls.

---

[4] Bernard Ryan, *The implications of UK withdrawal for immigration policy and nationality law: Irish aspects*, Immigration Law Practitioners' Association, May 18, 2016, at 2.

[5] Bernard Ryan, *The Common Travel Area between Britain and Ireland*, 64 Modern L. Rev. 855, 869 (2001).

[6] *Id.*

[7] Amanda Ferguson, *Britain does not want return to Northern Ireland border controls says May*, Reuters (Dec. 16, 2016), http://www.reuters.com/article/us-britain-eu-nireland-idUSKCN1050J5; *Brexit could be triggered within weeks, warns Irish premier Enda Kenny*, Belfast Telegraph (Nov. 20, 2016), http://www.belfasttelegraph.co.uk/news/northern-ireland/brexit-could-be-triggered-within-weeks-warns-irish-premier-enda-kenny-35182052.html.

[8] The Northern Ireland Peace Agreement, Ir.-U.K., Apr. 10, 1998.

[9] Amanda Ferguson, *Britain does not want return to Northern Ireland border controls says May*, Reuters (Dec. 16, 2016), http://www.reuters.com/article/us-britain-eu-nireland-idUSKCN1050J5; *Brexit could be triggered within weeks, warns Irish premier Enda Kenny*, Belfast Telegraph (Nov. 20, 2016), http://www.belfasttelegraph.co.uk/news/northern-ireland/brexit-could-be-triggered-within-weeks-warns-irish-premier-enda-kenny-35182052.html.

[10] Bernard Ryan, *The Common Travel Area between Britain and Ireland*, 64 Modern L. Rev. 855, 870 (2001).

I. HISTORY OF THE COMMON TRAVEL AREA

The Common Travel Area informally commenced on December 6, 1922, when Ireland became a free state.[11] Since then, British and Irish citizens have enjoyed the luxury of traveling by air, car, boat and train among Ireland, the UK, the Channel Islands and the Isle of Man absent passport checks, subject to a few exceptions.[12] Once Ireland became free, the UK Home office stated it[13] "would not [] require, under the Aliens Order, a passport system between [the UK] and Ireland, and could not make any use of such requirement if they were asked to impose it."[14] In practice, the UK agreed to lift passport and border controls between the two countries, but Ireland was required to agree to participate in the British system of immigration control, which it did.[15] Ireland thought that the "co-operation" was the most effective means for the Free State to control aliens in general and "Bolshevists" in particular. [16] Unbeknownst to many, only British and Irish citizens possessed the benefit of the CTA until Ireland and the UK joined the EU.[17] Now, legally, British, Irish and EEA/Swiss nationals benefit from the CTA.[18]

Two reasons sparked the desire to form the CTA. First, operating effective immigration control between Ireland and Northern Ireland has always been and remains extremely difficult.[19] The land border between the two countries extends for 280 miles and "does not follow natural boundaries but rather cuts across 180 roads."[20] Most commonly, one only knows he or she has crossed the border into either Northern Ireland or Ireland by small sign posts that show the speed limit change in kilometers or miles per hour.[21] "The portioned island, jurisdictionally

---

[11] *Id.* at 856.

[12] *Id.*

[13]   Gov.UK,   *Home*   *Office*,   (Jan.   3,   2016), https://www.gov.uk/government/organisations/home-office. Home Office is the lead government department for immigration and passports, drug policy, crime, fire, counter-terrorism and police in the UK.

[14] 'Aliens Restriction Passports for Ireland' memorandum of Mar. 2, 1922 (PRO, HO 45/ 14630).

[15] Bernard Ryan, *The Common Travel Area between Britain and Ireland*, 64 Modern L. Rev. 855, 856 (2001).

[16] *Id.*

[17] European Affairs Committee, Report on Visa systems, 2016-17, British-Irish Parliamentary Assembly 4-5, (UK).

[18] *Id.*

[19] Bernard Ryan, *The Common Travel Area between Britain and Ireland*, 64 Modern L. Rev. 855, 869 (2001).

[20] *Id.*

[21] Joe O Murchadha, *The Common Travel Area Between Ireland and the UK*, (Dec. 21, 2016), http://migrationireland.blogspot.com/2012_06_05_archive.html.

speaking, is borderless, with no boundary controls of any kind."[22] It would take rigorous measures to control the land frontier between Ireland and Northern Ireland. [23] The physical difficulty and impracticability of establishing a border between Northern Ireland and Ireland was at the heart of the creation of the CTA, and it is the main reason the CTA has continued until today.[24] Secondly, once Ireland became a free state, there was a strong desire to enable freedom of travel between the two countries due to the extent of social and economic connections. [25] Naturally, this sparked the status quo to allow movement between the two countries to progress as if the island were one whole country without passport checks.[26]

Free movement and absent border checks between the two countries continued until World War II.[27] Ireland was neutral during WWII, which led both countries to desire controls on movement.[28] Britain primarily wanted border controls "out of fear of espionage and subversion, and Ireland, primarily to prevent influx of refugees."[29] Consequently, a travel permit was necessary during the war and "travel was restricted to those who went to Great Britain for the purposes of employment."[30] In addition, all individuals needed "the permission of both the British and Irish authorities" to travel. [31] When traveling between Ireland and Northern Ireland, however, one only needed to present proof of identification, but a permit was needed for longer stays.[32]

Conclusion of the war led the UK to lift the permit requirement in 1947 for those traveling from Ireland.[33] Ireland, however, had to again agree to a similar UK immigration policy. [34] Ireland conceded. The agreement between the two states "concerning co-operation in control

---

[22] Graham Butler, *Not a "real" common travel area: Pachero v. Minister for Justice and Equality*, Irish Jurist, 54, 155-164 (2015).

[23] Bernard Ryan, *The Common Travel Area between Britain and Ireland*, 64 Modern L. Rev. 855, 869 (2001).

[24] *Id.* at 870.

[25] Bernard Ryan, *The implications of UK withdrawal for immigration policy and nationality law: Irish aspects*, Immigration Law Practitioners' Association, May 18, 2016, at 2.

[26] The EU referendum and the Irish border (Dec. 4, 2016), https://fullfact.org/europe/eu-referendum-and-irish-border/.

[27] Bernard Ryan, *The Common Travel Area between Britain and Ireland*, 64 Modern L. Rev. 855, 857 (2001).

[28] *Id.* at 857.

[29] *Id.*

[30] *Id.*

[31] *Id.* at 858.

[32] *Id.*

[33] *Id.*

[34] *Id.*

over entry by aliens" was not made public.[35] Ireland feared their citizens would object to the control that the UK possessed over them concerning the UK immigration policy.[36] Long strides had been taken to make Ireland a free state in 1922, and Ireland feared the control by the UK would scare citizens that they were reverting back to prior times when their country was not free.[37] Additionally, no formal agreements were signed between the two countries, but the "'status quo' of allowing citizens of either state to travel and reside unhindered" continued.[38]

II. THE CTA ACKNOWLEDGED IN UK AND IRISH LAW

While no formal agreement has been made between the two countries, the UK, EU and Ireland acknowledge the existence of the CTA in their own laws, respectively. The Immigration Act 1971, a UK law, addresses the CTA in Section 1(3):

> Arrival in and departure from the United Kingdom on a local journey from or to any of the Islands (that is to say, that Channel Islands and Isle of Man) or the Republic of Ireland shall not be subject to control under this Act, nor shall a person require leave to enter the United Kingdom on so arriving, except in so far as any of those places is for any purpose excluded from this subsection under the powers conferred by this Act; and in this Act the United Kingdom and those places, or such of them as are not so excluded, are collectively referred to as "the common travel area."[39]

Section 3(1) of the Immigration Act states that immigration officers are permitted to examine any individual who is seeking to embark to the UK.[40] This includes determining whether said individual is patrial[41] and, if not, to determine the individual's identity by means of checking one's identification and/or passport.[42] However, as noted above in Section 1(3), individuals arriving from Ireland, or any of the Islands, are not subject to control under the UK's Immigration Act 1971, so long as they have been examined when they initially entered the CTA.[43]

---

[35] *Id.*

[36] *Id.*

[37] *Id.*

[38] Joe O Murchadha, *The Common Travel Area Between Ireland and the UK*, (Dec. 21, 2016), http://migrationireland.blogspot.com/2012_06_05_archive.html.

[39] Immigration Act 1971, c. 77, § 1 (3).

[40] Immigration Act 1971, c. 77, § 3 (1).

[41] A patrial is a native from the UK.

[42] Immigration Act 1971, c. 77, § 3 (1).

[43] Immigration Act 1971, c. 77, § 1 (3).

Generally, the law reads that no one entering the UK from Ireland is subject to border controls or passport checks. Immigration (Control of Entry through the Republic of Ireland) Order 1972,[44] however, lists individuals that do require immigration controls when entering the UK from Ireland.[45] This includes: persons, except Irish citizens, who merely passed through Ireland to embark to the UK; persons requiring visas; persons who entered Ireland unlawfully; persons who entered Ireland from the UK and Islands after entering there unlawfully, provided that he has not subsequently been given leave to enter or remain in the UK or any of the Islands; or persons who are subject to directions given by the Secretary of State to not be given entry to the UK on the ground that his exclusion is conducive to the public good.[46] If an individual is encompassed under any of these restrictions, the individual will be subject to immigration controls when entering the UK from Ireland and will not benefit from Section 1(3) of the Immigration Act.[47] If the individual is an Irish citizen and falls under one of the restrictions above, however, they will still be able to enter the UK without immigration controls because they are Irish.[48]

The Immigration Act 1971 and the Immigration Order 1972 provide written guidelines of the UK immigration law and those subject to immigration controls. It is a common misconception, however, that if an individual is not included under one of the five exceptions above, they will be able to enter the UK freely without immigration controls. Unfortunately, that is false. A Report on Visa Systems from the European Affairs Committee in the British-Irish Parliamentary stated:

> The concept of the CTA is not well understood outside of specialist immigration fields. Callers to our advice line are often surprised to hear that, while the CTA is a "free movement zone" for CTA and EEA nationals, it is not so for other nationals. This lack of awareness can result in people committing an offence by crossing the land border. In some cases, this can lead to

---

[44] www.parliament.uk, (Jan. 5, 2016), http://www.parliament.uk/site-information/glossary/orders-in-council/. "Orders of Council are decisions of the Privy Council which have the force of law. Unlike Orders in Council, these do not require personal approval by the monarch and can be made by government ministers."

[45] Immigration (Control of Entry through the Republic of Ireland) Order 1972 (SI 1972 No. 1610).

[46] *Id.*

[47] European Union Committee, Brexit: UK-Irish Relations, 2016-17, HL 27-32, 24 (UK).

[48] *Id.*

detention and removal. Clearly, this brings with it a high human cost as well as the economic cost of immigration enforcement.[49]

Before Ireland and the UK joined the EU, only British and Irish nationals enjoyed the lack of immigration controls when traveling from Ireland to the UK.[50] The extension to EEA/Swiss nationals developed after Ireland and the UK joined the EU to ensure equal treatment is given to all EU nationals, as required by EU law.[51] This rule, however, is not legally acknowledged in legislation.

Legally, EEA/Swiss, Irish and British citizens are not subject to immigration controls when traveling to the UK from Ireland.[52] In practice, however, it is common for no one to be subject to passport checks when entering the UK from Ireland. Thus, while it is legally required for third party nationals, for example, a U.S. citizen, to be subject to passport checks when traveling from Ireland to the UK, in practice it is unlikely that controls will be executed. If, however, an individual is not an EEA/Swiss, Irish or British citizen and is stopped by a random check point at an airport, seaport or while traveling by car or train from Northern Ireland to Ireland, one would need to present a form of identification.[53] If an individual does not have their identification, the individual risks breaking the law if randomly checked.[54]

Ireland's law on immigration presents differences for those who enjoy the benefits derived from the CTA. The Immigration Act 2004, Ireland's immigration law, requires border controls to apply automatically to all "non-nationals" who arrive from the UK by air or sea.[55] Therefore, passport controls must be legally applied to everyone but Irish and British citizens because neither are classified as "non-nationals" per Irish Immigration Law.[56] Different from UK law, legally

---

[49] European Affairs Committee, Report on Visa systems, 2016-17, British-Irish Parliamentary Assembly 4-5, (UK).

[50] *Id.*

[51] TFEU art. IV.

[52] European Affairs Committee, Report on Visa systems, 2016-17, British-Irish Parliamentary Assembly 4-5, (UK).

[53] *Id.*

[54] *Id.*

[55] Immigration Act (Northern Ireland) 2004 § 4.

[56] European Union Committee, *Brexit: UK-Irish Relations*, Sept. 30, 2016, HL. The Immigration Act 2004 states that "non-national" has the meaning assigned to it by the Immigration Act 1999. Immigration Act 1999 states "non-national" means an alien within the meaning of the Alien Act of 1935. "Alien" in the Aliens Act 1935 means a person who is not a citizen of Saorstat Eirann. Aliens (Exemption Order, 1935) states, "Every person who is a citizen, subject or national of any of the countries set out in the Schedule to this Order is hereby exempted from the application of Sections 8 and 9 of the Aliens Act, 1935 (No. 14 of 1935), and from the application of all the provisions of

under Irish law, EEA/Swiss nationals *are* subject to passport checks when traveling from the UK to Ireland.[57]

Like UK law, in practice, passport checks at airports, seaports and all entry points for all individuals traveling from the UK to Ireland are not commonly exercised. Passport checks are not enforced between the land border of Ireland and Northern Ireland, but similar to UK practice, passport checks at the land border "may be applied to those who arrive from Northern Ireland."[58] "While it is not true to say that the border is completely open—as there is number plate-monitoring technology in place—it is the case that individuals can travel across the border by land unimpeded."[59] If an individual is driving, flying or arriving by boat from the UK to Ireland, an individual could be subject to a random check where passports will be assessed, but it is not a guarantee. Therefore, if an individual is stopped by the Garda National Immigration Bureau (GNIB)[60], the Bureau may carry out checks on all persons, even Irish and British nationals who are not required to carry identification.[61] To prevent breaking the law, it is a safe measure to always carry a passport or form of identification.

It is a common misconception that anyone can travel freely through the CTA without passport checks once initially examined upon entry into the CTA.[62] That is false. The UK and Ireland have differing laws concerning those who profit from the CTA. To reiterate, every passport entering the UK from Ireland except Irish, British or EEA/Swiss nationals must legally be checked. Conversely, all non-nationals traveling from the UK to Ireland will be subject to passport checks. Thus, per Irish Immigration Act 2004, everyone, excluding British or Irish nationals, will be subject to passport examination.[63] In practice, however, no passport or border checks are implemented when traveling by air, sea or car between Ireland and the UK. While passport checks are not

---

the Aliens Order, 1935." The United Kingdom and Northern Ireland are listed and thus are not subject to the Irish Immigration Act. Further, Aliens (Amendment)(No. 2) Order, 1999 states that "the word 'alien' does not include a British citizen."

[57] *Id.*

[58] European Union Committee, *Brexit: UK-Irish Relations*, Sept. 30, 2016, HL.

[59] Northern Ireland Affairs Committee, Northern Ireland and the EU referendum, 2016-17, HC 26 (UK).

[60] Garda National Immigration Bureau is Ireland's border control.

[61] Joe O Murchadha, *The Common Travel Area Between Ireland and the UK*, (Dec. 21, 2016), http://migrationireland.blogspot.com/2012_06_05_archive.html.

[62] European Union Committee, *Brexit: UK-Irish Relations*, Sept. 30, 2016, HL.

[63] Immigration Act (Northern Ireland) 2004 § 4.

enforced, individuals who are not Irish, British or EEA nationals must carry identification on his or her person to avoid violating the law.[64]

III. THE CTA ACKNOWLEDGED IN EU LAW

The Common Travel Area has existed well before the creation of the EU and before Ireland and the UK joined the EU in 1973.[65] The formation of the EU in 1950 commenced to prevent frequent and bloody wars that had previously disturbed Europe.[66] The six founding countries desired to create a common community of neighboring countries by establishing one sovereign organization comprised of several individually sovereign nations.[67] Free trade and joint control over food production were some of the first issues the Union addressed while uniting the coal and steel communities.[68] Treaties establish the "objectives of the European Union, the rules for the EU institutions, how decisions are made and the relationship between the EU and its members states."[69] The most recent treaty, the Lisbon Treaty, was signed on December 13, 2007, and comprises the Treaty on the Functioning of the European Union (TFEU) and the Treaty on European Union (TEU).[70]

Three Protocols annexed to the TFEU reflect the arrangements between the UK and Ireland. Particularly, Protocol 20 acknowledges the Common Travel Area.[71] Article 1 within the Protocol states that the UK and Ireland are entitled to exercise control over their own borders on all persons and are not subject to Article 26 nor 77 of the TFEU.[72] Article 26 states that the Union shall adopt measures to establish an "internal market without internal frontiers in which the free movement of goods, persons, services and capital is ensured. . . ."[73] Article 77 proceeds by stating that a policy should be developed with a view of ensuring the absence of any controls on persons, whatever their nationality, when crossing internal borders and carrying checks on persons at external

---

[64] Joe O Murchadha, *The Common Travel Area Between Ireland and the UK*, (Dec. 21, 2016), http://migrationireland.blogspot.com/2012_06_05_archive.html.
[65] European Commission & Directorate-General Communication, *How the European Union works: your guide to the EU institutions*, at 3 (2014).
[66] *Id.*
[67] *Id.*
[68] *Id.*
[69] *Id.*
[70] *Id.*
[71] TFEU Protocol 20.
[72] *Id.*
[73] TFEU art. 26.

borders.[74] Consequently, Ireland and the UK, by EU law (Protocol 20), are not subject to creating a market without internal frontiers for people to move, creating absence of control on persons at internal crossing or creating checks at external borders.[75]

Article 2 in Protocol 20 continues by expressing that Ireland and the UK "may continue to make arrangements between themselves relating to the movement of persons between their territories, 'the Common Travel Area.'"[76] Thus, not only does the UK and Ireland domestic law acknowledge the CTA, but EU law also recognizes the CTA. The CTA is further identified in the Schengen Agreement.

All but six EU countries have created a similar agreement among themselves regarding absent internal borders and a common policy on external borders.[77] In 1985, separate from the EU, five of the six founding countries of the EU (the Netherlands, Belgium, Luxembourg, France and Germany) comprised the Schengen Agreement.[78] Border checks at internal borders between the five countries were to be abolished.[79] Consequently, no passport checks would be exercised. By 1990, the Agreement was implemented, and in 1995, internal borders among the contracting countries were abolished. A single external border with a set of applicable rules was then executed.[80]

Since its creation, the Schengen Agreement has become more detailed regarding the absence of internal borders and expanded to include 22 Member States of the EU and four non-EU Member States: Switzerland, Iceland, Norway and Liechtenstein.[81] Ireland and the UK, conversely both EU Member States, declined to participate in the Schengen Agreement.[82] The UK opted out of the Schengen Agreement to maintain its own borders.[83] Ireland opted out to keep its free movement and lack of border control arrangements with the UK.[84] The

---

[74] TFEU art. 77.

[75] TFEU Protocol 20.

[76] *Id.*

[77] Council Regulation 562/2006, art. 27-8, Mar. 15, 2006, Schengen Borders Code, 2006 O.J. (L 105) (EC).

[78] Schengen and the management of the EU's external borders, Parl. Eur. Doc. PE 581 (2016).

[79] *Id.*

[80] *Id.*

[81] Council Regulation 562/2006, art. 27-8, Mar. 15, 2006, Schengen Borders Code, 2006 O.J. (L 105) (EC).

[82] Schengen and the management of the EU's external borders, Parl. Eur. Doc. PE 581 (2016).

[83] *Id.*

[84] *Id.*

Schengen Agreement explicitly notes that Ireland and the UK "do not take part in" the Agreement.[85]

The Treaty of Amsterdam, which preceded the Lisbon Treaty, initially incorporated the Schengen Agreement into EU law in 1999.[86] Protocol 19, annexed in the TFEU, continues to implement the Schengen Agreement into EU law today. It continues to recognize the Agreement as providing a frame work for an external border and a policy for the absence of controls at internal frontiers.[87] Furthermore, Protocol 19 acknowledges unambiguously that the UK and Ireland do not participate in the provisions of the Schengen acquis.[88] Protocol 19, however, gives the ability for either country to join in some or part of the Schengen provisions at any time.[89] Lastly, Protocol 21 provides that the UK or Ireland may choose to provide input to EU immigration, or asylum legislation or any similar legislation except for legislation concerning the Schengen Agreement.[90] In conclusion, the recognition of the CTA between Ireland and the UK is explicitly annexed in EU law Protocols.

IV. LEGAL AND POTENTIAL IMPLICATIONS FOLLOWING BREXIT FOR THE CTA

The laws implementing and governing the CTA provide a background and set a foundation for the agreement between the UK and Ireland. The extensive and intertwined laws of the EU, UK and Ireland regarding the CTA have legitimized the CTA and recognized its importance. The recognition however, creates uncertainty to its result following Brexit. While the CTA is recognized in Irish and British domestic law, Ireland will be subject to the laws of the EU as it will retain its membership following Brexit.[91] Thus, the legal implications and questions regarding the CTA following Brexit concern mainly EU law, not British or Irish law. Illustrated below are possible outcomes pertaining to the CTA in EU law that could ensue from the departure.

The most radical scenario would result in the EU completely revoking its recognition of the CTA. Practically, Protocol 20, which is

---

[85] Council Regulation 562/2006, art. 27-8, Mar. 15, 2006, Schengen Borders Code, 2006 O.J. (L 105) (EC).
[86] TFEU Protocol 19.
[87] *Id.*
[88] *Id.*
[89] *Id.*
[90] Bernard Ryan, *The implications of UK withdrawal for immigration policy and nationality law: Irish aspects*, Immigration Law Practitioners' Association, May 18, 2016, at 2.
[91] European Commission & Directorate-General Communication, *How the European Union works: your guide to the EU institutions*, at 3 (2014).

annexed in the TFEU and recognizes the arrangements between Ireland
and the UK, would be removed from EU law. If Protocol 20 were
completely removed from EU law, it would be unlikely that Ireland (a
member state of the EU) would be allowed to continue to make
arrangements with the UK freely. As a result, Ireland would have to
either join the Schengen Agreement or negotiate an agreement with the
EU concerning border and passport checks for EU nationals entering
and traveling within Ireland.[92]

The physical and practical result from EU law failing to recognize
the arrangements between the UK and Ireland would be implementation
of passport and border checks at every entry point into Ireland from the
UK. Airports, seaports and rail stops would need heightened border and
passport checks. The implementation of more and new border checks at
airports and seaports could be obtained easily, but the additional security
measures would be costly. A harder task would be erecting a land border
between Ireland and Northern Ireland. The land border between Ireland
and Northern Ireland would become an external border for the EU.
Thus, Ireland would have to implement the EU policy on external
borders at all external land crossings from Northern Ireland. [93]
Consequently, border controls and passport checks would need to be
executed at every entry. The cost and practicality of executing physical
border checks along the 280-mile long border that cuts across 180 roads
between the two countries would be high.[94] Further, individuals who
work and reside on different sides of the border would feel an effect.
Data from 2001 revealed that 18,000 people cross the Northern
Ireland/Ireland border daily, 9,000 in each direction. [95] While it may be
burdensome, costly and impractical to erect a physical border between
Ireland and Northern Ireland, there may be no other option if the EU
does not continue to recognize the CTA.

A second but slightly far-fetched scenario may result in Protocol 20
remaining annexed in EU law, while only acknowledging Ireland's
arrangements with the UK. Presumably, this would be the most desirable
for the UK but the least desirable for the EU. Subsequently, the UK's
rights would be removed from Protocol 20, but Protocol 20 would
continue to recognize Ireland's agreement with the UK. Thus, Ireland
could continue its arrangements with the UK, and its citizens would

---

[92] TFEU Protocol 19.
[93] TFEU art. 77.
[94] Bernard Ryan, *The Common Travel Area between Britain and Ireland*, 64 Modern L. Rev.
855, 869 (2001).
[95] Northern Ireland Affairs Committee, Northern Ireland and the EU referendum, 2016-
17, HC 27 (UK).

enjoy the fruits and benefits from the CTA. No land border would need to be executed, and border controls by air and sea would remain the same.

If the EU agreed to allow Ireland to continue its arrangements with the UK and Ireland, it would be likely that the UK would refine its immigration laws respectively. One of the main reasons the UK desired to leave the EU was to regain control over its borders and decrease the number of people embarking to the UK.[96] It would be improbable that the UK would continue to allow absent border checks for all Irish and EEA/Swiss nationals traveling from Ireland. If the UK did not refine their immigration law, EEA/Swiss individuals seeking to embark to the UK could use Ireland as a "back door" to obtain their objective of traveling to the UK.[97] The relaxed nature of the borders when flying from Ireland to the UK would possibly increase the amount of people obtaining access to the UK. Thus, it is likely that Ireland and the UK would amend their agreement to revert to the original arrangements they had before either were members of the EU. Thus, only Irish and British nationals would receive preferential treatment when traveling between countries.

The second scenario would be the least desirable for the EU. If the EU refrained from negotiating special arrangements for the remaining EU nationals, the UK and Ireland would amend their agreement to only benefit British and Irish citizens. Thus, EU nationals would be prevented from exercising the free movement into the UK that they once enjoyed.

Perhaps more realistically, it may be plausible that the EU continues to acknowledge the CTA between Ireland and the UK, but it is foreseeable that the EU would mandate that all EU nationals receive the same treatment as Irish citizens in the agreement with the UK. This would result in Protocol 20 remaining annexed in the TFEU with a possible amendment to ensure that EEA/Swiss nationals are treated the same as Irish nationals when traveling between Ireland and the UK. The UK will likely resist this potential agreement out of fear that EU nationals would use Ireland, again, as a "back door" into the UK. Because of the UK's desire to leave the EU, it is likely that the UK will want stricter

---

[96] Reihan Salam, *Why Immigration Pushed Britons to Brexit*, Slate (Nov. 28, 2016), http://www.slate.com/articles/news_and_politics/politics/2016/06/immigration_and_brexit_how_a_rising.

[97] This would be the same result if the EU left Protocol 20 in EU law and took zero measures to regulate the arrangements between the UK and Ireland. Thus, if the EU is silent on the future CTA agreements, it is likely that the UK and Ireland would amend their agreements to return to the way the agreement was before either joined the EU. Resulting, only British and Irish citizens would receive preferential treatment and would not be subject to border checks between countries.

border controls to police the influx of individuals coming to the UK from Ireland.

To maintain good relations with the EU, the UK could provide alternatives for the EU if the EU is persistent on retaining rights for their nationals. If Protocol 20 remained in EU law, it is unlikely the UK would continue to allow EEA/Swiss nationals to enjoy the free movement currently exercised. Thus, instead of treating Irish and EEA nationals equally, the UK may want to negotiate an agreement where EEA nationals would not receive the free movement benefits but could be exempt from UK visa requirements.[98] "Alternatively, persons with [EU] nationalities, and potentially their family members, with residence documents issued in the Republic of Ireland, might be permitted to enter the UK without a visa, even if they would otherwise be visa nationals."[99] These are two other potential arrangements that could derive from the negotiations.

Pending the EU's stance regarding the CTA during negotiations, Professor Dagmar Schiek, Jean Monnet Chair of EU Law and Policy at Queens University Belfast, stated: "Under EU law, any future relation between the Republic of Ireland and the UK would be subject to agreement not only with the Republic of Ireland, but with the whole of the EU."[100] While it is likely that the CTA remains in EU law, the UK will face the obstacle of not only conversing with Ireland but the entire EU; complete agreements by all or a majority of members will be needed.[101]

V. POLITICAL RESPONSES CONCERNING THE CTA

Political figures from both countries have expressed their opinion regarding the future arrangements, giving context to the surrounding law and potential outcomes of the CTA. The Taoiseach,[102] Enda Kenny, of Ireland stated:

> I have agreed with the Prime Minister that there will be no return to the borders of the past. Therefore, the retention of an open border is critical. Neither I, nor the Prime Minister, desire to limit the freedom of people on both sides of the Irish Sea to

---

[98] Bernard Ryan, *The implications of UK withdrawal for immigration policy and nationality law: Irish aspects*, Immigration Law Practitioners' Association, May 18, 2016, at 3.

[99] *Id.*

[100] Northern Ireland Affairs Committee, Northern Ireland and the EU referendum, 2016-17, HC 34 (UK).

[101] European Commission & Directorate-General Communication, *How the European Union works: your guide to the EU institutions*, at 3 (2014).

[102] Taoiseach is the head of the government in Ireland, also known as the Prime Minister.

trade, to live, to work, to travel freely across these islands. We have agreed that the benefits of the Common Travel Area be preserved.[103]

In agreement, Prime Minister Theresa May, on her first visit to Ireland after the vote to leave the EU, stated: "We had a common travel area between the United Kingdom and the Republic of Ireland many years before either country was a member of the European Union. Nobody wants to return to the borders of the past."[104] May and Kenny's desires for the CTA to remain as the status quo is one thing. Having the EU intertwined into the negotiations between the two countries is another. Only time will tell how the negotiations will develop.

Academics have also commented on the future of the CTA following Brexit. Bernard Ryan, a Professor of Migration Law at the University of Leicester stated, "There is no apparent legal reason why the Republic of Ireland should not retain the benefit of Protocols 19 and 20 after Brexit, so as to permit bilateral co-operation with the United Kingdom outside the Schengen zone."[105] Further, Ambassador Mulhall stated that there was "no pressure from other Member States for Ireland to join Schengen, because of their recognition of the unique circumstances in Northern Ireland." [106] Lastly, Dr. Etain Tannam, Assistant Professor, Irish School of Economics, Trinity College Dublin, noted "that the fact that Ireland was not part of the Schengen area would make it possible to continue with the CTA."[107] These comments by academics and professions in the field stoutly boosts the probability of retention, legally and practically, of the CTA.

CONCLUSION

The Common Travel Area is only one issue in the queue of issues the EU and UK will negotiate when Article 50 is triggered. Just like many other legal issues surrounding Brexit, the CTA affects daily travel for individuals. Currently under UK law, UK, Irish and EEA/Swiss nationals enjoy the ability to travel within the CTA without being subject

---

[103] *Brexit could be triggered within weeks, warns Irish premier Enda Kenny*, Belfast Telegraph (Nov. 20, 2016), http://www.belfasttelegraph.co.uk/news/northern-ireland/brexit-could-be-triggered-within-weeks-warns-irish-premier-enda-kenny-35182052.html.

[104] Amanda Ferguson, *Britain does not want return to Northern Ireland border controls says May*, Reuters (Dec. 16, 2016), http://www.reuters.com/article/us-britain-eu-nireland-idUSKCN1050J5.

[105] European Union Committee, Brexit: UK-Irish Relations, 2016-17, HL 27-32 ¶112 (UK).

[106] *Id.* at ¶ 116.

[107] *Id.* at ¶ 113.

to passport checks. Under Irish law, solely UK and Irish citizens enjoy the benefits of the CTA. In practice, passport checks are rarely implemented for anyone traveling to or from either the UK or Ireland. When the UK "brexits" the EU, however, the status given to Irish, British and EEA/Swiss nationals may cease to exist. It is unlikely that the EU will fail to acknowledge the CTA. The history and strides for peace between the UK and Ireland, the establishment of the CTA before the EU was created, and the impracticability and difficulty of actually establishing a land border will deter the minds of EU officials to revoke the CTA from EU law. Additional arrangements concerning EU nationals, in addition to Irish nationals, may face the UK officials as part of the negotiations. While there are many factors pointing in the direction of retaining the CTA, the EU may stop recognizing the CTA. The fact is, only time will tell the impact Brexit will have on the CTA.

CHAPTER 12: BREXIT AND THE ENGLISH PREMIER LEAGUE: IMPLICATIONS FOR PLAYERS AND BROADCASTING RIGHTS

CODY M. KERMANIAN

INTRODUCTION

As Brexit looms, its impact is expected to pervade Britain's principal institutions, leaving few untouched. Premier League ("PL") football, perhaps the UK's most sacred and globally renowned export, is among those likely affected. The league boasts broadcast rights in over 150 countries, its players represent sixty-four nationalities, and a majority of its club owners hail from abroad.[1]

This note analyzes Brexit's legal impact on the Premier League. Its scope is limited to assessing the disengagement's legal implications and does not independently consider its economic ramifications. Part I examines the PL's transfer system. The system is subject to change in three primary areas: work permitting regulations, free transfers and quotas, and the international transfer of minors. Part II explores the Premier League's broadcasting structure. The framework's future will depend on the post-Brexit force of European Commission ("Commission") decisions.

PART I: PLAYER TRANSFERS

BACKGROUND: RELEVANT ASSOCIATIONS AND TRANSFER SYSTEM

The Fédération Internationale de Football Association (FIFA) is world football's governing body. It is composed of regional Confederations, which regulate national associations.[2] The Union of European Football Associations (UEFA)[3] is Europe's regional Confederation, which overseas the continent's national associations, including England's Football Association (FA).[4] Although the FA is authorized to impose its own regulations upon English leagues, it must

---

[1] *The global game: The Premier League's international reach, broken down*, EUROSPORT (Nov. 8, 2015, 1:25PM), http://www.eurosport.co.uk/football/premier-league/2015-2016/the-global-game_sto4853526/story.shtml.
[2] *Associations*, FIFA, http://www.fifa.com/associations/ (last visited Jan. 10, 2017).
[3] *UEFA*, FIFA, http://www.fifa.com/associations/uefa/index.html (last visited Jan. 10, 2017).
[4] *Associations*, FIFA, http://www.fifa.com/associations/ (last visited Jan. 10, 2017).

comply with applicable FIFA and UEFA rules, including those regarding domestic and international transfers.[5]

The structure of international football's transfer system is unlike the customary format employed by American professional sports, where players are typically acquired as free agents or via trades, during the off season or before the league's trade deadline. In football, clubs across the globe engage in a "transfer market," which facilitates the movement of players domestically and abroad. A club may only transact during its league's biannual "transfer window," [6] in which players are most commonly acquired by purchase, loan, or free transfer.

WORK PERMITS

As a result of the UK's European membership, foreign players from within and beyond the European Economic Zone (EEA)[7] face separate work permitting requirements based on their nationalities. Article 45 of the Treaty on the Functioning of the EU (TFEU) guarantees the free movement of workers within the EU.[8] Footballers are considered "workers" for these purposes. Consequently, players of nationalities within the EU (and EEA) are not required to obtain work permits in order to participate in the PL.

In contrast, footballers of non-EEA nationalities must apply for and receive work permits from the Home Office before competing in the league. The application process is twofold. First, a player must obtain a governing body endorsement (GBE) from the FA, then he may apply for a work permit from the Home Office. Automatic eligibility for a GBE requires a player to have participated in a minimum percentage of senior competitive international matches for his national team over the two years preceding the date of his application.[9] The required percentage

---

[5] *See Regulations on the Status and Transfer of Players*, FIFA http://www.fifa.com/mm/document/affederation/administration/regulations_on_the _status_and_transfer_of_players_en_33410.pdf (last visited Jan. 10, 2017) [hereinafter Regulations on the Status and Transfer of Players]; *UEFA Club Licensing and Financial Fair Play Regulations*, UEFA, http://www.uefa.org/MultimediaFiles/Download/Tech/uefaorg/General/02/26/77/ 91/2267791_DOWNLOAD.pdf (last visited Jan. 10, 2017).

[6] *Worldwide Transfer Windows Calendar*, FIFA (Jan. 3, 2017), https://www.fifatms.com/itms/worldwide-transfer-windows-calendar/.

[7] The EEA includes all twenty-eight EU Member States plus Iceland, Liechtenstein, and Norway.

[8] European Union, *Treaty on the Functioning of the European Union*, Art. 45, 26 Oct. 2012, OJ L. 326/47-326/390; 26.10.2012 [hereinafter TFEU].

[9] The FA, *Governing Body Endorsement Requirements for Players 2016/2017 Season*, 3 (2016); Carol Couse & Jake Cohen, *Brexit and the FA's work permit criteria*, MILLS & REEVE (May 2016), http://www.mills-reeve.com/files/Publication/8d514783-243d-444d-9f61-

varies depending on the national team's FIFA ranking.[10] A player whose national team is ranked beyond the FIFA top fifty is ineligible to receive an automatic GBE.[11] If a player fails to qualify for an automatic GBE, he may appeal to the FA Exceptions Panel for reconsideration.[12] The Panel then makes a points-based judgment upon consideration of certain objective criteria.[13] After receiving a GBE from the FA, the player must apply for a work permit from the Home Office. Depending on his grasp of the English language, he may apply for a Tier 2 or Tier 5 work permit, which differ in duration.[14]

The concern that Brexit harbors is the risk that EEA non-UK players will be required to undergo the same permit process as their non-EEA counterparts. If the UK terminates its European membership and elects not to protect the free movement of labor in its subsequent negotiations with the EU, European footballers will likely face work permit requirements of some sort. Last season, the PL employed 161 EEA non-UK players.[15] A study estimated that 111 of those players

---

c79312846f48/Presentation/PublicationAttachment/9f737130-5a06-4bc6-af57-9fc1b2cf7167/BrexitBriefing_May16.pdf.

[10] The FA, *Governing Body Endorsement Requirements for Players 2016/2017 Season,* 3 (2016). The required percentage for national associations ranked 1-10 is 30% and above; the required percentage for national associations ranked 11-20 is 45% and above; the required percentage for national associations ranked 21-30 is 60% and above; and the required percentage for national associations ranked 31-50 is 75% and above. *Id.* Players under 21 need only fulfill the required percentage over the preceding 12 months. *Id.*

[11] *Id.* at 7.

[12] *Id.* at 14.

[13] *Id.* at 15. Such criteria include the player's transfer fee, his wages, his current club's ranking. *Id.*

[14] *Id.* at 9. The duration of a Tier 2 permit is the shorter of three years or the length of the player's contract and can be extended a maximum of three years. *Id.* The maximum duration of a Tier 5 permit \ twelve months. *Id.* If a club wishes to employ a Tier 5 permitted player for a period of longer than twelve months, the player must return overseas to make a new application and obtain entry clearance for a further twelve-month period under Tier 5. *Id.* Though Tier 2 permits are longer in duration, they impose more stringent English language requirements. Tier 2 applicants who are not nationals of majority English speaking countries must prove their knowledge of the English language by satisfactorily completing English language tests or proving that they hold the equivalent of a UK Bachelor degree or higher that was taught in English. Tier 2 of the Points Based System – Policy Guidance, 35-37, https://www.gov.uk/government/uploads/system/uploads/attachment_data/file/571090/Tier_2_Policy_Guidance_11_2016.pdf (last visited Feb. 9, 2017). Tier 5 applicants may not be required to satisfy English language requirements. *See* The FA, *Governing Body Endorsement Requirements for Players 2016/2017 Season,* 9 (2016).

[15] Kate Lyons, George Arnett, C. Fardel, Carlo Zapponi, Alberto Nardelli, *How Brexit could drive out European Premier League Footballers,* THE GUARDIAN (Sept. 11, 2015, 5:00PM), https://www.theguardian.com/world/2015/sep/11/brexit-europe-eu-decimate-premier-league-footballers-data.

would not have met the criteria used for automatic GBE eligibility.[16] Among those were key talents such as David de Gea, Juan Mata, Anthony Martial, and Dimitri Payet.[17] Although it is likely that 75 of the 111 could have made strong cases to receive GBEs upon appeal, 36 of them (22% of all European players in the PL), would have struggled to meet the minimum standards.[18] Because the permit process is intended to limit the issuance of work permits to players who are internationally established at the highest level, the requirements disproportionately impact developing prospects.[19]

Application of the current work permit requirements to EEA non-UK players would considerably disadvantage the PL. Doing so would strengthen top European clubs by diminishing the competition for and price of elite European talent.[20] Constraining free movement may also preclude dual nationals (particularly South Americans of European heritage) from securing PL transfers.[21] Additionally, the restrictions would exacerbate the existing power imbalance within the PL, as small market clubs, whose sporting and financial success often depends on developing undiscovered talent, will face greater difficulty in securing work permits for those players.

Despite the risks of applying the existing work permitting requirements to EEA non-UK players, it is unclear whether the FA will react to offset the foreseeable reduction of Europeans in the league. In a 2015 op-ed, Greg Dyke, then Chairman of the FA, affirmed the FA's duty "to protect and promote the interests of English football at all levels," claiming that the English national team's decline in prominence is a consequence of the diminished quantity of Englishmen in the league.[22] In the PL's inaugural 1992/93 season, Englishmen composed 73% of first-day starting elevens.[23] By 2015, the percentage dwindled to

---

16 *Id.*

17 *Id.*

18 *Id.*

19 *See Id.*

20 *See* Couse & Cohen, *supra* note 9; George Parrett, *Premier League transfer spending reaches a new record of £870m*, DELOITTE (Sept. 2, 2015), https://www2.deloitte.com/uk/en/pages/press-releases/articles/premier-league-transfer-spending-870m.html. PL clubs' gross and net spending over the summer of 2015 was more than double that of any other European league. *Id.*

21 Carol Couse & Jake Cohen, *The potential impact of Brexit on European football*, MILLS & REEVE (May 2016), http://www.mills-reeve.com/files/Publication/a8160952-2df7-4d33-bb77-12781c308f33/Presentation/PublicationAttachment/09acac2d-e736-478b-a9f7-85fe27737051/216791132_1.pdf.

22 *Id.*

23 Louise Taylor & Mike Adamson, *Revealed: The Premier League reaches an all-time low of English players*, THE GUARDIAN (Aug. 19, 2013, 6:02PM),

33%.[24] To combat the trend, Dyke created a commission aimed at increasing the percentage of English players in the league to 45% by 2020.[25] In recent years, the FA has accordingly limited the number of "non-homegrown" players per club and imposed more stringent requirements for GBE eligibility.[26] Therefore, although it is possible that the FA will modify its regulations to mitigate the impact of applying work permitting requirements to EEA non-UK players, the FA's interest in the matter conflicts with the PL's, and it has proven that its priority is to promote the development of domestic talent rather than preserve the existing European footprint in the league.

FREE TRANSFERS AND QUOTAS

Prior to 1995, European football was different in two significant ways. First, the laws of some Member States allowed clubs to prevent their players from securing transfers, even upon the expiration of their contracts, unless the acquiring clubs paid satisfactory transfer fees.[27] Second, "many national football associations [and UEFA] introduced rules... restricting the extent to which foreign players could be recruited or fielded in a match."[28] In its landmark 1995 *Bosman* opinion, the European Court of Justice (ECJ) found both the restriction on free transfers and the existence of nationality based quotas incompatible with

---

https://www.theguardian.com/football/2013/aug/19/england-qualified-players-premier-league.

[24] Couse & Cohen, *supra* note 9.

[25] *Premier League home-grown percentage not bad, says FA*, BBC (Aug. 12, 2015), http://www.bbc.com/sport/football/33892349.

[26] The PL instituted the Homegrown Player Rule for the 2010/11 season, which requires teams to include a minimum of eight players older the age of 21, who have spent at least three years between the ages of 16 and 21 with a club in the English football league system. Thomas Wachtel, *The Premier League's Home Grown Player Rule, Explained*, SB NATION (Sept. 3, 2014), http://theshortfuse.sbnation.com/2014/9/3/6101699/premier-league-home-grown-player-rule-arsenal-welbeck-chambers-wilshere. In 2015 Chairman Dyke attempted, but failed, to increase the number of homegrown players required from 8 to 12. Owen Gibson, *FA chief Greg Dyke plans to get tough on overseas-player quotas*, THE GUARDIAN (Mar. 23, 2015, 7:23PM), https://www.theguardian.com/football/2015/mar/23/greg-dyke-fa-overseas-player-quotas. Instead, the FA modified its GBE criteria, making eligibility for automatic endorsements more difficult to obtain. *England FA seek tougher rules for foreign players to obtain work permits*, ESPNFC (Mar. 23, 2015) http://www.espnfc.com/english-premier-league/story/2363598/england-fa-seek-tougher-rules-for-work-permits-for-foreign-players.

[27] Case C-415/93, Union Royale Belge des Sociétés de Football Association ASBL v. Bosman, 1995 E.C.R. I-4921, ¶¶6-24; THE OXFORD HANDBOOK OF SPORTS ECONOMICS 261 (LEO KAHANE & STEPHEN SHMANSKE, Vol. 1, 2012).

[28] Bosman at ¶25.

the freedom of movement of workers.[29] Consequently, transfer fees for out of contract players were prohibited where players moved within the EU and clubs were no longer bound by quotas limiting the number of EU nationals they could field.[30] The ECJ subsequently expanded *Bosman*'s scope by applying its protections to non-EU nationals who were lawfully residing within the EU when their disputes arose and whose countries of origin had applicable Association or Partnership Agreements with the EU.[31]

The *Bosman* decision has had a profound impact on European football. For some, it marked the "day on which football stopped being a sport and became a business."[32] The abolition of nationality-based quotas increased the demand for foreign talent among the wealthiest European sides.[33] Clubs, particularly those less affluent, faced greater difficulty retaining their players who were now guaranteed free transfers upon the expiration of their contracts.[34] Since the decision, Europe's power balance has shifted substantially in favor the continent's four wealthiest leagues (PL, Bundesliga, Serie A, and La Liga).[35] Over the

---

[29] Bosman at ¶¶100, 116-120.

[30] *See Id.*

[31] *See* Case C-438/00, Deutcher Handballbund eV v. Marcos Kolpak, 2003 E.C.R. I-4153 (holding that citizens of countries which have Association Agreements with the EU and who are lawfully working within an EU country, have equal rights to work as EU citizens, and cannot have restrictions such as quotas placed upon them); Case C-265/03 Igor Simutenkov v. Ministerio de Educación y Cultura and Real Federación Española de Fútbol, 2005 E.C.R. I-2596 (holding that a national of a state, who has already obtained the status of lawful resident and worker within an EU member state, and whose country of origin has an applicable Partnership Agreement with the EU, enjoys "a right to equal treatment in working conditions of the same scope as" nationals of member states, which precludes limitations based on nationality). The EU currently has twenty-three Association Agreements, with countries such as Chile, Turkey, Serbia, and Bosnia and Herzegovina, under which the *Koplak* protections would apply. In contrast, the applicability of *Simutenkov* protections depend upon the specific language of the Partnership agreements at issue. In *Simutenkov*, the ECJ reviewed Article 23(1) of the EU-Russia Partnership and Cooperation Agreement, which specifically addressed employment discrimination.

[32] Mark Doyle, *The Bosman Ruling may have freed footballers from 'slavery' – but the elite now own football*, GOAL (Dec. 15, 2015, 9:00AM), http://www.goal.com/en-gb/news/2601/features/2015/12/15/18368182/the-bosman-ruling-may-have-freed-footballers-from-slavery.

[33] *Id.*

[34] *Id.*

[35] *Premier League wages dwarf those around Europe with top-flight players in England earning an average of £2.3million a year...almost 60 per cent more than in Germany*, DAILY MAIL (Nov. 14, 2014, 7:21AM) http://www.dailymail.co.uk/sport/football/article-2833020/Premier-League-wages-dwarf-Europe-flight-players-England-earning-average-2-3million-year.html.

twenty years preceding the *Bosman* decision, (1975-1995) clubs from
leagues outside Europe's top four reached the UEFA Champions League
Finals[36] thirteen times. Since then, only three have. The impact has
similarly pervaded national associations, particularly the FA, where wage
gaps between the top and lower level domestic leagues have widened to
unprecedented extents.[37]

As Brexit nears, the concern is whether *Bosman*'s free transfer and
quota precedents will persist, in any form, within the UK. Though it is
unlikely that ECJ decisions will retain binding force in British post-Brexit
jurisprudence,[38] *Bosman*'s impact on the PL appears indelible.[39] Neither
nationality-based quotas nor free transfer restrictions appear set for
reinstitution.

First, the FA's homegrown player rule has considerably obviated the
need for nationality based quotas.[40] The rule limits PL clubs to including
a maximum of seventeen non-homegrown players[41] in their first team

---

[36] Known as the European Champions' Cup until 1997.

[37] *Mind the gap… Premier League wages soar with average salaries during 2014-15 season around £1.7million as the rest creep along*, DAILY MAIL (Feb. 20, 2016, 5:49PM) http://www.dailymail.co.uk/sport/football/article-3456453/Mind-gap-Premier-League-wages-soar-average-salaries-2014-15-season-1-7million-rest-creep-along.html; *Premier League average salaries soar to £1.7MILLION as gap to lower league clubs widens*, MIRROR (Feb. 20, 2016, 11:57PM), http://www.mirror.co.uk/sport/football/news/premier-league-average-salaries-soar-7410264.

[38] *See* Joosje Hamilton & Andrew Sheftel, *Brexit – UK and EU legal framework*, NORTON ROSE FULBRIGHT (June 2016), http://www.nortonrosefulbright.com/knowledge/publications/136975/brexit-uk-and-eu-legal-framework. It should be noted however, that Prime Minister Theresa May, stated her intention that the UK adopt the European aquis. Prime Minister Theresa May, *Theresa May – her full Brexit speech to Conservative conference*, INDEPENDENT (Oct. 2, 2016), http://www.independent.co.uk/news/uk/politics/theresa-may-conference-speech-article-50-brexit-eu-a7341926.html,while addressing a Conservative Party Conference in October 2016.

[39] Couse & Cohen, *supra* note 21.

[40] *Id. See Protection of young players*, UEFA (Jan. 2, 2014, 12:26PM) http://www.uefa.com/news/newsid=943393.html. UEFA requires clubs to include a minimum of eight "locally trained" (or "homegrown") players in their twenty-five player squad lists. *Id.* Among the eight, four must be "club trained" and four must be association trained. *Id.* A club trained player is one who, between the age of fifteen and twenty-one, has been registered with his current club for a period of three years. *Who can play in the Champions League group stage?*, UEFA (Sept. 1, 2015) http://www.uefa.com/uefachampionsleague/news/newsid=2277105.html. An association trained player is one who, between the age of fifteen and twenty-one, has been registered with his current club or a club within the same association for three years. *Id.*

[41] *FA Chairman's update on England Commission*, The FA (Mar. 2015) http://www.thefa.com/news/2015/Mar/23/greg-dyke-england-commission-homegrown-players-work-permits-march-2015. Homegrown players are defined as those

squads of twenty-five.[42] Although homegrown status is based on a player's youth experience in the FA or Football Association of Wales, rather than on his nationality, the rule encourages PL clubs to promote domestic talent rather than acquire prospects from overseas.[43] Therefore, it is unlikely that the FA would impose nationality-based quotas because doing so would further restrict PL clubs' access to foreign talent and disadvantage them in international play.

Next, the likelihood that the FA would impose limitations upon free transfers is similarly improbable. The FA has already established procedures which address the issue domestically. The Professional Football Compensation Committee sets compensation terms for players under twenty-four years of age.[44] Those beyond the threshold are granted free transfers upon the expiration of their contracts.[45] Additionally, preventing free international transfers for out of contract players would put PL clubs at a competitive disadvantage with their European counterparts. Foreigners, particularly those at the outset of their careers, would be deterred from signing with PL clubs in fear that their transfers could be blocked upon contract expiration.

Therefore, whether *Bosman* remains instructive in British jurisprudence,[46] the FA is unlikely to depart from its precedent regarding nationality-based quotas and free transfers.

---

who have been registered with the FA or FAW for three years before the age of twenty-one. *Id.*

[42]   *Home-grown   quota   for   Premier   League,*   http://www.epfl-europeanleagues.com/quota_for_Premier_League.htm (last visited Jan. 12, 2017, 9:59PM); *FA Chairman's update on England Commission,* The FA (Mar. 2015) http://www.thefa.com/news/2015/Mar/23/greg-dyke-england-commission-homegrown-players-work-permits-march-2015.

[43] Timothy Rapp, *Premier League Homegrown Rules: Explaining EPL Player Quotas* (July 22, 2014) http://bleacherreport.com/articles/2137974-premier-league-home-grown-rules-explaining-epl-player-quotas#.

[44] *Id.*

[45] *Id.*

[46] The continued applicability of ECJ decisions in the UK is currently unclear. Some, including Prime Minister May, seek to grandfather the EU acquis (the accumulated legislation, legal acts, and court decisions in EU law), and adopt that body of law as part of the UK's. Others however, prefer a post-Brexit UK that is independent from and unconstrained by the acts of foreign legislators and courts. If the acquis is grandfathered, ECJ decisions will initially remain binding precedent in the UK. Nevertheless, the decisions are subject to change if they are challenged in subsequent cases raising similar issues in British courts. Therefore, *Bosman*'s immediate and enduring force in British jurisprudence is currently unpredictable.

TRANSFERS OF MINORS

Article 19 of FIFA's Regulations on the Status and Transfer of Players prohibits the international transfer of players below the age of eighteen.[47] However, the rule contains three exceptions, one of which allows the transfer of players aged between sixteen and eighteen, provided the transfer takes place within the EEA.[48] In the event of Brexit, it is expected that the UK will lose both its EU and EEA memberships,[49] depriving British clubs of access to the Article 19 loophole.[50] Although FIFA may amend the exception to include a post-Brexit UK within its ambit, the likelihood of such action is unforeseeable. If the exception ceases to apply, the PL will be impacted on several fronts: PL player quality may moderately diminish, top flight clubs will be disadvantaged in the European transfer market, and English clubs will face greater difficulty satisfying FA and UEFA home grown player requirements.

PL clubs have exploited the Article 19 exception to actuate hundreds of transfers in recent years, including the acquisitions of Adnan Januzaj, Hector Bellerin, and Cesc Fabregas.[51] The exception currently allows them to compete on a level playing field with their European counterparts when acquiring youth prospects between the ages of sixteen and eighteen. If Brexit impedes British clubs from accessing that talent class, the league may experience a marginal decline in the quality of play as these youth prospects play important roles in both their academy and professional sides.

The Article 19 exception is also fundamental to how clubs procure cost effective talent.[52] It enables them to acquire prospects across the continent before they blossom into high profile players.[53] The loophole's continued application is particularly imperative for the financial viability of small and middle market clubs which are more heavily impacted by high transfer costs. Furthermore, access to lower priced talent is significant for PL clubs participating in European play in light of UEFA's

---

[47] *Regulations on the Status and Transfer of Players*, Art. 19.
[48] *Id.*
[49] Simon James, *Brexit: will the UK remain in the EEA despite leaving the EU?*, CLIFFORD CHANCE (Dec. 1, 2016) https://www.cliffordchance.com/briefings/2016/12/brexit_will_the_ukremainintheeeadespit.html.
[50] Gabriele Marcotti, *Could EU Brexit significantly limit European Premier League players?*, ESPNFC (Mar. 9, 2016), http://www.espnfc.us/blog/marcotti-musings/62/post/2825545/eu-brexit-impact-on-european-premier-league-players.
[51] Couse & Cohen, *supra* note 21; Marcotti, *supra* note 49.
[52] Couse & Cohen, *supra* note 21.
[53] *Id.*

Financial Fair Play regulations ("FFP"). FFP seeks to mitigate the impact of football's monetary imbalance by imposing sanctions upon clubs which exceed a level of financial losses.[54]

Finally, absent access to the Article 19 exception, PL clubs face greater difficulty satisfying the FA's homegrown player rule and UEFA's locally trained player requirements. The FA's home grown player rule prohibits clubs from including more than seventeen non-homegrown players in their twenty-five player squad lists.[55] UEFA similarly prohibits clubs from including more than seventeen non-locally trained players in their twenty-five player squad lists during European competition.[56] Under each regime, squads must contain a certain number of players who have been registered with their current clubs, or clubs within the same association, for three years before the age of twenty-one.[57] The Article 19 exception has effectively granted PL clubs an additional two years to fashion newly acquired EU prospects into home grown and locally trained players by enabling clubs to sign such players at the age of sixteen rather than eighteen. If Brexit renders the exception unavailable, top flight clubs will have a shorter window to satisfy the applicable FA and UEFA requirements.

In conclusion, if Brexit strips the UK of its EEA membership and thereby deprives PL clubs of access to FIFA's Article 19 exception, the PL may endure a moderate decrease in the quality of play, PL clubs will experience increased transfer costs, and clubs will face greater difficulty in satisfying domestic and European homegrown player requirements.

---

[54] *UEFA Club Licensing and Financial Fair Play Regulations*, UEFA (Ed. 2015), http://www.uefa.org/MultimediaFiles/Download/Tech/uefaorg/General/02/26/77/91/2267791_DOWNLOAD.pdf .

[55] *FA Chairman's update on England Commission*, The FA (Mar. 2015) http://www.thefa.com/news/2015/Mar/23/greg-dyke-england-commission-homegrown-players-work-permits-march-2015.

[56] *Who can play in the Champions League group stage?*, UEFA (Sept. 1, 2015) http://www.uefa.com/uefachampionsleague/news/newsid=2277105.html. See footnote 40 above for a more detailed description of UEFA's locally trained player rule.

[57] *FA Chairman's update on England Commission*, The FA (Mar. 2015) http://www.thefa.com/news/2015/Mar/23/greg-dyke-england-commission-homegrown-players-work-permits-march-2015; *Who can play in the Champions League group stage?*, UEFA (Sept. 1, 2015) http://www.uefa.com/uefachampionsleague/news/newsid=2277105.html.

Part II: Broadcasting

Background: Premier League Broadcasting Structure

The PL's broadcasting rights are owned centrally by the FA Premier League (FAPL),[58] which maintains the exclusive right to negotiate media rights agreements on behalf of PL clubs.[59] This centralized structure provides the FAPL with substantial bargaining leverage[60] as it licenses its media rights to broadcasters on exclusive territorial bases.[61]

In February 2016, the FAPL completed its most lucrative sale of broadcasting rights, a windfall exceeding £8.3 billion over the following three seasons.[62] The figure includes both domestic and overseas revenues.[63] While each club is entitled to an equal share of overseas broadcasting funds, domestic prize money is allocated on a different basis.[64] Each club is guaranteed a minimum share (50%) of the domestic revenue, with the remainder distributed by virtue of a club's league performance (25% "merit payment") and the number of times its matches featured live in the UK that season (25% "facility fees").[65]

European Commission Applies Competition Rules to Sport

Though the FAPL independently negotiates its domestic and international licensing agreements, those taking place within the EU are subject to European competition law. Article 101(1) of the TFEU (previously Art. 81(1)) prohibits commercial undertakings which

---

[58] *About the Premier League*, Premier League, https://www.premierleague.com/about (last visited Jan. 12, 2017, 10:26PM).

[59] European Commission, 22 March 2006, Case COMP/C-2/38.173, *Joint selling of the media rights to the FA Premier League*, ¶5 [hereinafter *FAPL joint selling*]

[60] Matt Bonesteel, *Massive new English Premier League TV deal has the rest of European soccer worried*, Washington Post (Feb. 13, 2015) https://www.washingtonpost.com/news/early-lead/wp/2015/02/13/massive-new-english-premier-league-tv-deal-has-the-rest-of-european-soccer-worried/?utm_term=.f457825b27d0.

[61] Cases C-403/08 and C-429/08, *FAPL and Others v QC Leisure and Others and K. Murphy v Media Protection Services Ltd*, ECR 2011 I-0000, ¶¶33-34 [hereinafter *Murphy*].

[62] Ben Rumsby, *Premier League clubs to share £8.3 billion TV windfall*, The Telegraph (Feb. 4, 2016, 8:02PM) http://www.telegraph.co.uk/sport/football/12141415/Premier-League-clubs-to-share-8.3-billion-TV-windfall.html.

[63] *Premier League Prize Money Table 2015/16 Season (Confirmed)*, Totalsportek (May 9, 2016) http://www.totalsportek.com/football/premier-league-prize-money-table-2015/.

[64] *Id.* Of the record setting £8.3 billion 2016-2019 sale of broadcasting rights, approximately £5.136 billion is derived from domestic sales and over £3 billion from overseas. *Id.*

[65] Ben Rumsby, *Arsenal finally top Premier League table – for prize money*, The Telegraph (May 24, 2016, 10:08PM) http://www.telegraph.co.uk/football/2016/05/24/arsenal-finally-top-premier-league-table---for-prize-money/.

"prevent[], restrict[] or distort[] . . . competition" within the EU market.[66] Article 101(3) (previously Art. 81(3)) however, provides an exemption for undertakings which improve the production or distribution of goods or promote technical or economic progress, while allowing consumers a fair share of the resulting benefit and which do not substantially eliminate competition.[67]

Until 2003, UEFA, like the FAPL, held the exclusive right to sell its Champions League media rights.[68] It distributed them to individual broadcasters in single bundles, long-term contracts, and on territorial bases.[69] In its 2003 *UEFA Champions League* decision, the EU Commission "for the first time expressly recognized that joint selling of broadcasting rights by sports leagues could create efficiencies."[70] Though the decision led UEFA to unbundle its rights into several packages (allowing multiple broadcasters to purchase Champions League rights) and to shorten the duration of its contracts to three year periods, UEFA was ultimately permitted to retain the exclusive right to sell.[71] The Commission noted that "UEFA's joint selling arrangement [led] to the improvement of production and distribution by creating a quality branded league focused product sold via a single point of sale" and that the arrangement was "unlikely to eliminate competition," thereby exempting the arrangement from Article 81(1) noncompliance.[72] Two years later, the Commission reinforced its position, deciding that the centralized distribution of Bundesliga broadcasting rights was similarly exempted, provided that it unbundled the rights into separate packages.[73]

DECISIONS REGARDING FAPL BROADCASTING RIGHTS

The existing FAPL broadcasting structure is a product of recent EU Commission and ECJ decisions. In 2001, the Commission opened an investigation into the FAPL's joint selling arrangements and concluded

---

[66] TFEU Art. 101(1).

[67] TFEU Art. 101(3)

[68] *See* European Commission, 23 July 2003, Case 37.398, *Joint selling of the commercial rights of the UEFA Champions League*, OJ 2003 L 291/25 [hereinafter *UEFA joint selling*].

[69] *Id.*

[70] Ken Daly & Jessica Walch, *Sports and competition law: An overview of EU and national case law,* e-Competitions, http://www.sidley.com/~/media/files/publications/2012/02/sports-and-competition-law-an-overview-of-eu-and /files/view-article/fileattachment/k--daly-j--walch-ecompetitions-n-42447.pdf (last accessed Jan. 15, 2017). *See UEFA joint selling.*

[71] Daly & Walch, *supra* note 69.

[72] *UEFA joint selling* at ¶201.

[73] Daly & Walch, *supra* note 69; European Commission,19 January 2005, Case COMP/C.2/37.214, *Joint selling of the media rights to the German Bundesliga,* ¶41.

that they restricted competition within the meaning of Article 81(1).[74] After applying for and being denied an exemption under Article 81(3), the FAPL submitted a provisional set of commitments in a renewed effort to obtain the exemption.[75] The 2003 commitments offered to: (a) increase the overall output of media rights; (b) sell TV rights in several balanced packages and prevent a single buyer from purchasing all the rights; (c) reduce the embargoes for mobile and internet rights; (d) sell UK and Ireland rights separately; (e) limit the duration of the agreements to three years; (f) sell the rights in a transparent and non-discriminatory tendering procedure; and (g) revert unused rights to clubs for their exploitation.[76] In light of the FAPL's commitments, the Commission concluded that its arrangements were no longer prohibited by Article 101(1) and confirmed that the commitments were binding upon the FAPL. [77] In doing so, the Commission extracted several notable concessions. From 2007 onwards, no single broadcaster could buy every live rights package; clubs were given the right to provide internet and mobile video content of the matches they participated in as of matchday at midnight; the EPL increased radio broadcasting; and it allowed two matches to be broadcast live nationally on Saturday afternoons.[78]

More recently, the ECJ has considered the legality of territorial restrictions included in FAPL licensing contracts. The FAPL generally requires licensees to ensure that the signals are only transmitted to subscribers within the licensed territory.[79] At the time, these contractual limitations were supported by national legislation in the UK.[80] In order to avoid paying costly British subscription fees, several British pubs purchased decoder cards from Greek licensees, allowing them to access and display live PL match feeds being broadcasted in Greece.[81] Upon suit by the FAPL against one such pub owner, the ECJ considered the legality of the FAPL's licensing agreements. The *Murphy* court held that the FAPL's contractual provisions, which prohibited broadcasters from selling and supplying decoder cards to viewers in other Member States, violated the TFEU's protection of free movement of services and were

---

[74] *FAPL joint selling* at ¶¶11-12.

[75] Id. at ¶¶13-17.

[76] Id. at ¶32.

[77] Id. at ¶¶38-39.

[78] Ian Blackshaw, *Collective sale of sports television rights in European Union: competition law aspects*, South African Legal Information Institute, http://www.saflii.org/za/journals/DEJURE/2013/21.html (last accessed Jan. 15, 2017).

[79] Daly & Walch, *supra* note 69.

[80] *Murphy* at ¶97.

[81] *Murphy* at ¶¶38-43.

anticompetitive in practice.[82] Additionally, the court found that the FAPL could not copyright football matches themselves because they did not constitute original works.[83] However, the court found copyright in the opening credits and graphics, EPL anthem, and match highlights.[84] Therefore, the display of PL matches on pub TV screens, which constitutes communication to the public, nonetheless requires the FAPL's authorization.[85] Accordingly, the FAPL may still prohibit the public display of PL matches when accessed via decoder devices.[86] The decision merely affirmed the FAPL's practice of territorially segmenting the market and assuring that those seeking to publically display its content have paid for the right to do so. Thus, *Murphy* did not tangibly impact the distribution or value of FAPL broadcast rights.

BREXIT'S IMPACT ON FAPL BROADCASTING

Much like its effect on club rosters, the magnitude of Brexit's impact on the FAPL's broadcasting regime depends on whether the UK adopts the European acquis. In any case, the FAPL will remain bound by the relevant Commission and ECJ decisions within the EU. The laws will continue to govern economic practices in Europe despite the UK's disengagement. Therefore, the legal framework in which FAPL currently operates within Europe will remain unchanged post-Brexit. As a result, the extent of any potential change is limited to the UK market. Nevertheless, the domestic market alone comprises £5.1 billion of the FAPL's £8.3 billion 2016-19 contracts, compared to £771 million for the remainder of Europe.[87]

Though the continued application of ECJ judgements will not meaningfully impact FAPL broadcast rights, the fate of EU Commission decisions will. If Commission decisions cease to be enforceable, the FAPL will no longer be bound by its 2003 commitments. Among its guarantees, the commitments obligate the FAPL to sell TV rights in

---

[82] Id. at ¶¶. *See* TFEU Arts. 57, 101.

[83] *Murphy.*

[84] *Id.*

[85] *Id.*

[86] In a new wave of actions, the FAPL succeeded in preventing two further publicans from using decoder devices to display live PL matches. *See FAPL Ltd. v. Luxton and Barclays Bank Ltd.* [2014] *EWHC 253 (Ch); FAPL Ltd. v. Berry and Barclays Bank Plc* [2014] EWHC 726 (Ch).

[87] Nick Harris, *Premier League set for £3bn windfall from global TV rights as rival broadcasters slug it out to screen England-based superstars,* Daily Mail (Oct. 8, 2015, 5:56AM) http://www.dailymail.co.uk/sport/football/article-3264606/Premier-League-set-3bn-windfall-global-TV-rights-rival-broadcasters-slug-screen-England-based-superstars.html.

several balanced packages and to prevent a single buyer from purchasing them all. The commitments effectively limit the price that the FAPL can demand by increasing the supply of products in the market.[88] In the absence of that constraint, the FAPL will be able to negotiate more lucrative deals in the future.[89] Any increases will directly benefit the clubs, which are entitled to portions of the prize money. The significance of such an impact cannot be overstated. The PL's greatest strength is its wealth. Broadcast revenues currently constitute 49% of the average PL club's revenue.[90] For reference, "average domestic broadcast revenues in England exceeded €100m per club in FY2015, comfortably more than double the Italian and triple the Spanish and German average." [91] Accordingly, PL clubs accounted for 17 of the top 20 UEFA clubs by broadcast revenue in 2015.[92] If Brexit renders EU Commission decisions inapplicable and enables the FAPL to realize a more favorable bargaining position in licensing its broadcast rights, PL managers, players, trainers, and groundskeepers can expect a bump in their salaries come 2020.

CONCLUSION

TRANSFERS

Brexit's impact on PL player transfers is primarily confined to three aspects of the transfer system: work permit regulations, free transfers and quotas, and the transfer of minors.

The extent to which Brexit will inhibit European players from participating in the PL is highly dependent upon the course of action pursued by British rule makers. Though the Home Office and FA may alter their regulations to mollify the impact of imposing work permit requirements upon EEA non-UK players, the FA has evinced a clear

---

[88] Assuming the packages are in fact balanced (of equal value), that the FAPL need only guarantee that they are purchased by a minimum of two licensees (such is the case with the 2016-19 rights, sold entirely to Sky and BT), and that all other market conditions are perfect, the price per package will be that which the second highest bidder offers. In contrast, where the FAPL need neither unbundle its packages nor sell to multiple buyers, and all other market conditions are perfect, the rights will be sold at the highest price offered. Therefore, the 2003 commitments limit the monopoly power that the FAPL may exert in distributing its broadcast rights.

[89] *Id.*

[90] *Club Licensing Benchmark Report Financial Year 2015*, 74, UEFA (2015) http://www.uefa.org/MultimediaFiles/Download/Tech/uefaorg/General/02/42/27/91/2422791_DOWNLOAD.pdf.

[91] *Id.* The divide will likely sharpen as the revenues from the FAPL's new record setting are yet to kick in until the 2016/17 season. Note however, that the relative value of the contracts will be moderately diluted by the pound's recent decline in strength.

[92] *Id.* at 75. The three exceptions were Barcelona (1), Real Madrid (2), and Juventus (11).

intention to protect and promote English youth prospects at the expense of their foreign counterparts. Therefore, it is possible that a post-Brexit PL will feature fewer foreign players, particularly Europeans, resulting from the broader application of work permit requirements upon them and the FA's reluctance to self-correct. In contrast, the current standing of free transfers and the inexistence of nationality-based quotas will likely remain unaltered. Modifying either policy would greatly disadvantage PL clubs in international play. Lastly, it is expected that Brexit will terminate both the UK's EU and EEA memberships, depriving PL clubs of FIFA's Article 19 exception. If so, and if FIFA decides not to amend the provision to include an isolated UK, British clubs will be unable to sign European players below the age of eighteen. The league may consequently experience a moderate decline in the quality of play; clubs will be hindered in signing European youth targets, either foregoing acquisition or waiting until they reach eighteen and likely paying higher prices; and clubs will face greater difficulty satisfying the FA and UEFA's home grown player requirements.

BROADCASTING

Brexit's impact on the distribution and value of FAPL broadcast rights depends on the continued force of EU Commission decisions in British post-Brexit jurisprudence. If such decisions are no longer enforceable, the FAPL will not be bound by its 2003 commitments, which have effectively limited the price of its rights. Consequently, the FAPL will be able to negotiate more advantageous domestic licensing contracts, providing PL clubs with greater broadcast revenues, a source they heavily depend on.

Chapter 13: Scot-In Even Through Brexit? Scotland's Legal Options in the Wake of the UK Referendum to Leave the EU

Nour M. El-Kebbi

I. Introduction

On June 23, 2016 the United Kingdom (UK) voted on whether to leave or remain in the European Union (EU)—a referendum that proved highly divisive, politicizing, and shocked the world's consciousness when the UK voted to leave after nearly 50 years of membership.[1] While a slight majority of the country voted to leave,[2] in Scotland the resounding answer to the vote was to remain—evidenced by the fact that no Scottish county voted majority leave and 62% of Scots voted to remain, the highest percentage of any of the four nations that make up the UK.[3] The official position of the Scottish Government at Holyrood, currently held by the Scottish National Party (SNP) headed by Nicola Sturgeon, was also strongly to remain.[4]

The drivers of this position are of paramount economic, political, and legal significance. Scotland losing access to the European Union will have significant effects on its economy; 42% of Scottish trade is with other EU member states, and is valued at £11.6 billion; leaving is also expected to result in an estimated loss of 80,000 Scottish jobs and a fall of £2,000 in wages.[5] In terms of the UK's relationship with the EU, in 2001 Westminster and Holyrood worked out an agreement by which Scotland received certain devolved rights and responsibilities in shaping and implementing EU regulations and protocols in Scotland (the Memorandum of Understanding).[6] This also increased Scotland's presence and involvement in Brussels, placing Scottish politicians at the fore of certain areas of EU lawmaking and empowering them to lobby

---

[1] Simon Lewis, *U.K. Votes to Leave European Union in Historic Vote*, TIME (June 24, 2016, 6:26 AM), http://time.com/4381042/leave-eu-referendum-brexit-vote/.
[2] *Id.*
[3] *EU Referendum: Scotland Backs Remain as UK Votes Leave*, BBC (June 24, 2016), http://www.bbc.com/news/uk-scotland-scotland-politics-36599102.
[4] Scottish National Party. *Manifesto 2016*. Glasgow: Saltire Print, 2016.
[5] Scottish Government. *Scotland's Place in Europe*. Edinburgh: APS Group Scotland, 2016.
[6] Memorandum of Understanding and Supplementary Agreements Between the United Kingdom Government Scottish Ministers, the Cabinet of the National Assembly for Wales and the Northern Ireland Executive Committee, Dec. 2001, CM 5240, at 5-11 [hereinafter "Memorandum of Understanding"].

more effectively in Scotland's interest.[7] The terms of that non-binding agreement expanded on the scope of Scotland's devolved powers,[8] a significant political victory that Holyrood is understandably fiercely opposed to relinquishing. From a legal perspective, while the Memorandum of Understanding is a non-binding agreement, it has served as the basis and justification for actual lawmaking—i.e. implementation of EU regulations and directives in the form of Scottish laws.

These laws, having been made under the auspices of this agreement, explicitly state within their text that their purpose is to implement certain EU directives or regulations. Therefore, they will be robbed of their legal foundation if the UK, and consequently Scotland, leave the EU—which will have a material effect on Scottish lawmaking powers under the devolution agreement with Westminster. The legal implications of the Brexit vote to these laws and the devolved powers of Scotland with regards to the EU, as well as to spirit of devolution generally, are both illustrative of the extent to which Scotland is directly linked to the UK's EU membership and, this paper argues, form the basis for its strongest arguments as to why Westminster must receive some form of Scottish approval for the terms of the UK's EU withdrawal under Article 50.

In assessing Scotland's legal options in the wake of Brexit, this paper will first examine the existing devolution agreement between Scotland the UK government, the Memorandum of Understanding and the role it allocates to Scotland within the UK-EU relationship, and the status of existing Scottish laws that have been passed that are implementations of EU law. The purpose of this examination is to determine whether Westminster will need to attain Scottish consent or at least acquiescence to the terms of the UK's withdrawal from the EU, or conversely, the extent to which, if at all, Scotland can block or significantly delay achieving a Brexit agreement. — ▶ Will this happen?

The next portion of this paper will consider the legal viability of the SNP's plans to find a way to keep Scotland within the EU's single market, even if the rest of the UK leaves. This portion of the paper will use as reference certain precedents, such as Greenland's exit from the EU despite the Netherlands' remaining within the EU, which may provide at least a theoretical framework for Scotland's aspirations. The paper will conclude with a brief contextualization of these legal theories in the current political climate of post-Brexit Europe and the reception Scotland's proposal received as of early January 2017, non-legal elements that ultimately will be highly determinative of the prospects of Scotland's ambitions to remain within the EU.

---

7   Scottish   Government,   *Scottish   Government   EU   Office—Brussels*, http://www.gov.scot/Topics/International/Europe/Offices.
8 Memorandum of Understanding, *supra* note 6, at 5-9, 33-34.

II. SCOTLAND'S RELATIONSHIP WITH THE EU

Scotland cannot "veto" Brexit, as some members of the Scottish government and press had initially alleged.[9] It is clear that from the Memorandum of Understanding and the laws of devolution that ultimately the UK government at Westminster has the final say over not only the terms of Brexit, but also the Scottish laws implementing any EU law. This is due to the fact that Scottish laws only become effective in Scotland after having received royal assent, which can only be granted once a bill has successfully undergone all the parliamentary stages in both Houses of Parliament.[10] Therefore, these laws only exist with Westminster's support. Nevertheless, the principles Westminster and Holyrood historically agreed to in terms of devolution and Scotland's involvement in the EU have created clear, binding Scottish law. These laws will have to be materially altered if and when the UK leaves the EU, changes that must be effected by Holyrood, and therefore Westminster is obliged to seek Scottish agreement to the terms of the UK's withdrawal. To ignore such an obligation would strike at the very heart of devolution and therefore the constitutional make-up of the UK, as the devolved institutions (the Scottish Parliament at Holyrood, the Northern Ireland Assembly at Stormont, the National Assembly for Wales at Senedd) are accepted as "established components of the UK's constitution."[11]

A. DEVOLUTION: SCOTLAND ACT OF 1998

The Scotland Act of 1998 reestablished the Scottish Parliament,[12] which had been dissolved when Scotland became part of the UK in 1707. The 1998 Act not only reestablished the Scottish Parliament in Edinburgh, but also devolved (the transfer or delegation of power to lower level, typically by central government to local or regional administrative bodies) certain areas of governance that had previously been reserved for Westminster.[13] The devolved areas of particular importance in Scotland concern agriculture and food production, fisheries and the fishing industry, both terrestrial and marine

---

[9] Christopher Hope, *Sturgeon: I can block UK exit from Europe*, TELEGRAPH (July 17, 2016), http://www.telegraph.co.uk/news/2016/07/17/nicola-sturgeon-accepts-she-has-a-veto-over-brexit-timing-in-com/.

[10] UK Parliament, *Royal Assent*, http://www.parliament.uk/about/how/laws/passage-bill/lords/lrds-royal-assent/.

[11] House of Lords, *The Union and devolution*, HL Paper 149, 4, http://www.publications.parliament.uk/pa/ld201516/ldselect/ldconst/149/149.pdf.

[12] Scotland Act 1998, 1998, c. 46, §§ 1-43, UK.

[13] *Id.*

environmental protection, certain areas of civil and criminal law, healthcare, and education.[14]

Both the 1998 Act and the 2001 Memorandum of Understanding explicitly state that while negotiation and relations with the EU are reserved for the UK Government, the implementation of EU legislation relevant to the aforementioned devolved areas remains with the Scottish Government, such as EU directives concerning fishing, environmental standards, and agricultural production. One of the Scottish Government's primary forms of implementation has been the designing and passing of Scottish laws putting such EU legislation into effect. Therefore, if Scotland remains in the UK and the UK ceases to be part of the EU, the Scottish Parliament and Government will be charged with replacing or modifying current Scottish legislation to replace EU law in devolved areas. These are powers and responsibilities reserved to Scottish Parliament under the Sewel Convention,[15] which can only be overridden with the consent of Scottish Parliament, which is highly unlikely to be granted given the SNP's current dominance and its staunch commitment to maintaining the devolution of powers to Scotland and its advocacy for increased devolution in the wake of Brexit.[16]

B. 2001 MEMORANDUM OF UNDERSTANDING

The 2001 Memorandum of Understanding is a statement of political intent between the UK Government on one hand and the Scottish Ministers and parallel institutions in Wales and North Ireland on the other, collectively referred to as "the devolved administrations."[17] The Memorandum stipulates that all the parties will give "appropriate consideration to the views of the other administrations," and only provides for statutory consultation by the UK Government with the devolved administrations with regard to "certain specific matters."[18] These include matters "with an EU dimension" and "international relations touching on the responsibilities of the devolved administrations." [19] The Memorandum states that the devolved administrations are "responsible for implementing international, ECHR, and EU obligations" which concern devolved areas of competence.[20] Therefore, this Memorandum and the understanding between the UK

---

[14] Scottish Government Report, *Scotland's Place in Europe*, 2016. Edinburgh: APS Group Scotland, 42.

[15] Scotland Act 2016, 2016, c. 11, § 2, UK.

[16] *Scotland's Place in Europe*, *supra* note 13, at 39-44.

[17] Memorandum of Understanding, *supra* note 6, at 5.

[18] *Id.* at 6.

[19] *Id.* at 6-7.

[20] *Id.* at 9.

and Scottish Governments enshrined within it explicitly provide the basis upon which the Scottish Parliament produced Scottish legislation, policy, and other governing instruments with regard to implementing EU legislation. EU legislation is explicitly cited to within these Scottish laws.[21]

The Memorandum explicitly states that it is not to be interpreted as a binding agreement, nor does it create legal obligations between the parties, but is "binding in honour only."[22] While "honour" is not legally enforceable in court, the political implications for ignoring such an extralegal arrangement could be disastrous—especially given the SNP's strong advocacy for a second Scottish independence referendum in the wake of Brexit.[23] Brazenly ignoring the clear desire of the Scottish people as well as their government could fan the flames of Scottish dissatisfaction with Westminster into a blaze of secessionism, creating yet another constitutional crisis that the UK can hardly afford as it attempts to negotiate Brexit.

C. SCOTLAND ACT OF 2016 AND THE SEWEL CONVENTION

The 2016 Scotland Act[24] was passed to amend the 1998 Scotland Act, to explicitly include the Sewel Convention (also known as the "Legislative Consent Convention"), and to enumerate the functions and related responsibilities of the Scottish Ministers. [25] The Sewel Convention, as stated in the 2016 Act, amended section 28 of the 1998 Act by adding "But it is recognized that the Parliament of the United Kingdom will not normally legislate with regard to devolved matters without the consent of the Scottish Parliament."[26] The 2016 Act also made explicit that the Scottish Parliament and Government "are a permanent part of the United Kingdom's constitutional arrangements,"[27] enshrining the devolution, its related powers, and areas of responsibility with both constitutional legitimacy and protection. Derivatively, the legislative competence and executive power by Scotland's devolved

---

[21] See for example the Preamble to the Environmental Assessment (Scotland) Act 2005, which states: "An Act of the Scottish Parliament to make provision for the assessment of the environmental effects of certain plans and programmes, including plans and programmes to which Directive 2001/42/EC of the European Parliament and of the Council relates; and for connected purposes." 2005, asp 15, Preamble, UK. Similar language and explicit references to relevant EU regulations, directives, and decisions are included in all other pieces of Scottish legislation and governing instruments implementing such EU legislation.

[22] Memorandum of Understanding, *supra* note 6, at 5.

[23] *Scotland's Place in Europe, supra* note 13, at 38.

[24] Scotland Act 2016, 2016, c. 11, § 2, UK.

[25] *Id.* at §§ 1-12.

[26] *Id.* at §§ 13-21.

[27] *Id.* at §§ 1-12.

Parliament and Government are also established features of the UK's constitution.[28] If the Scottish Parliament or Government deems that Westminster is violating its devolved rights, it is this amendment to the 1998 Act that can provide the jurisdictional nexus to take the UK government to UK court.

D. 2010 INTERPRETATION AND LEGISLATIVE REFORM (SCOTLAND) ACT

In further complication of the extent to which Holyrood can claim some power over the Brexit decision-making is an additional, brief provision in the Interpretation and Legislative Reform (Scotland) Act 2010, whose Section 20 states: "An Act of Scottish Parliament of a Scottish instrument binds the Crown except in so far as the Act or instrument provides otherwise."[29] The explanatory notes for this section elucidate that this provision is a substantive shift in the law. Whereas previously the Crown could only be bound by express statutory provision or by necessary implication of such statutory language, Section 20 sets the new default position that the Crown is bound by acts of Scottish Parliament or Scottish instruments *unless* there is an express exemption within the statute's or instrument's provisions.[30]

While this provision only applies to the Crown and therefore not to Parliament, the provision is relevant to the decision of the appeal in the UK Supreme Court concerning whether an act of Parliament is necessary to trigger Art. 50, or whether the Crown can act without Parliamentary approval.[31] The lower court ruled that Parliamentary approval was necessary to trigger Article 50; if that is the case, then the aforementioned 1998 and 2016 Scotland Acts, along with possibly the Sewel Convention, could have provided the constitutional justification for obtaining Scottish consent to the Brexit terms.

However, in its decision the UK Supreme Court found that neither the Scotland Acts nor the Sewel Convention legally oblige the UK Government to obtain Scottish consent to leave the EU. The Court reasoned that relations, negotiations, and entering into agreements with the EU are responsibilities that fall outside of the legislative competences

---

[28] *Written Case of Lord Advocate On Appeal From the High Court of Justice Queen's Bench Division* at 2, Various Interested Parties and Interveners v. The Queen and Secretary of State for Exiting the European Union, Nos. CO/3809/2016 and CO/3821/2016 (Div. Ct. 2016).

[29] Interpretation and Legislative Reform Act (Scotland), 2010, asp 10, § 20(1).

[30] Explanatory Note 43, Interpretation and Legislative Reform Act (Scotland), 2010, asp 10, § 20(1).

[31] Shehab Khan, *Everything you need to know about the Supreme Court judgment on Brexit,* INDEPENDENT (December 4, 2016), http://www.independent.co.uk/news/uk/politics/brexit-supreme-court-ruling-when-is-it-article-50-a7455146.html.

devolved to Scottish Parliament under the Scotland Acts.[32] The court also notes that these responsibilities are explicitly reserved for the UK Parliament in the Sewel Convention, and asserts that the Convention's expectation that "Westminster would not normally legislate with regard to devolved matters in Scotland without the consent of the Scottish Parliament" has been met in the case at hand because prior UK legislation implementing changes to EU institutions that thereby affected devolved competencies had not required the consent of devolved legislatures.[33] The underlying assumption is that any UK legislation to pull out of the EU qualifies as legislation implementing changes to EU institutions (in this case the change is the UK's withdrawal) and therefore, according to past practice, such legislation would not require Scottish Parliament's consent. However, the court also emphasized that it is beyond the "constitutional remit of the judiciary" to enforce or police the scope and the manner of the Sewel Convention's operation, as it is a political convention and therefore not a legal instrument.[34] However, Section 20, which was not discussed in the Supreme Court's opinion, may yet provide Scotland with another legal nexus by which it can insert itself into the Brexit decision-making process.

The argument to be made is that because the Crown, and therefore the UK Government, is bound by Scottish Acts of Parliament and Scottish instruments under Section 20, and Brexit will necessarily alter such acts and instruments that reference or implement EU legislation, then the Crown would be ignoring Section 20 and the 1998 and 2016 Acts by essentially overwriting, materially altering, or invalidating these Scottish legislative instruments; allowing such unilateral action by the Crown or the UK Government would establish a dangerous precedent whereby the Crown could gut Scottish legislation of its legitimacy and enforceability, despite its own Royal Assent to being bound to such acts of Scottish governance.

Allowing the Crown to disregard Scottish legislation to which it is bound could trigger a constitutional crisis by substantively corroding the very essence of devolution, and therefore a fundamental aspect of the UK constitution. Disturbingly, a January 2016 pamphlet prepared by the Office of the Parliamentary Counsel, which was intended for use by the members of said Office, stated that the presumption remains that the Crown is not bound by Acts unless expressly or by necessary implication

---

[32] R (on the application of Miller and another) v. Secretary of State for Exiting the European Union, [2017] UKSC 5, para. 136.

[33] Id. at para. 137, 140.

[34] Id. at para. 141.

throughout the United Kingdom.[35] This assertion runs directly counter to Section 20 of the 2010 Interpretation and Legislative Reform Act, particularly as the pamphlet also states that the House of Lords settled that it also applies in Scotland in *Lord Advocate v. Dumbarton District Council*[36] by determining that the presumption "applies to all parts of the United Kingdom." [37] In *Dumbarton*, two Scottish local authorities attempted to assert Scottish law against construction contractors of the UK Ministry of Defense, who had placed an obstruction on a Scottish highway; the House of Lords reversed the Scottish court decision against the contractors, holding that the Scottish Acts were not binding on the Crown because they neither contained any such express provision nor include any necessary implication that the Crown should be bound.[38]

However, *Dumbarton* was decided in 1990; presumably, the 2010 Act and its Section 20, which received Royal Assent, overrides this decision and the presumption it reinforced. The pamphlet therefore cannot be compatible with current UK law, which makes it all the more troubling that it is meant to be used as a guidance document to the Office for Parliamentary Counsel in 2016. This pamphlet may be only one of other such guidance documents that cite to no longer effective law, a lapse in accuracy that could lead to serious misunderstandings and legal conflict between the UK Government and Scottish Parliament over to what extent the Crown and Her Majesty's Government are beholden to Scottish legislation. A more careful review for legal inconsistencies in the current operating practices, presumptions, and guidelines is necessary to ensure avoidance of unnecessary conflict.

The Crown's necessary Royal Assent to all of the enacted Scottish Acts of Parliament and other Scottish instruments, as well as the 2010 Act, further binds the Crown. While the Queen's giving of Royal Assent is primarily a formality, [39] it nevertheless reflects the Crown's acknowledgement of the act and the provisions therein. This would include the Section 20 provision, which explicitly binds the Crown to Scottish laws and instruments. Since the proposed Great Repeal Bill[40]

---

[35] Office of the Parliamentary Counsel, *Crown Application*, January 2016. https://www.gov.uk/government/uploads/system/uploads/attachment_data/file/493665/Crown_Application.pdf.

[36] [1990] 2 AC 580.

[37] *Crown Application*, *supra* note 31, at 1.

[38] Duncan Berry, "Crown Immunity from Statute: *Bropho v. The State of Western Australia*" STATUTE LAW REV 1993; 14(3): 204-222, 204.

[39] UK Parliament, *Royal Assent*, http://www.parliament.uk/about/how/laws/passage-bill/lords/lrds-royal-assent/.

[40] House of Commons, *Legislating for Brexit: the Great Repeal Bill*, House of Commons Library Research Briefing, http://researchbriefings.parliament.uk/ResearchBriefing/Summary/CBP-7793.

and subsequent acts of Parliament to navigate the Brexit process will also require Royal Assent to become an official Act of Parliament, and such Acts will certainly materially affect Scottish legislation such that it must be altered or replaced, according to Section 20 the Crown will have an additional duty to consider the Scottish legislation to which it is bound and to not act to contravene such legislation.

Therefore, despite the Supreme Court's final decision, the Scottish Parliament and Government may have a few legal claims from which to choose to argue that the Brexit terms, decision-making, and consequent legislation will require some form of Scottish consent, or some other form of official agreement with Westminster, the Crown, or the UK Government.

E.   CAN SCOTLAND TAKE THE UK GOVERNMENT TO COURT?

It is unlikely that the UK Government will completely disregard Scottish interests and demands in their negotiations and final decisions regarding Brexit. However, if the Scottish Parliament and Government feel that their legal rights under the UK Constitution have been violated or otherwise compromised, the Scottish government may be able to take the UK Government to court. The principal determination of such a proceeding would be whether the UK Government can agree to certain terms of the UK's exit from the EU even if Scotland believes they violate the devolution agreement that is part of the UK Constitution.

There are both UK and EU dimensions to this query. On the UK side, it is a question of to what extent the devolution agreements can be overridden by Westminster in the name of conducting foreign policy and foreign relations with the EU, which are exclusively reserved for Westminster.[41] From an EU perspective, the language of the Lisbon Treaty's Article 50 explicitly states that "Any Member State may decide to withdraw from the Union in accordance with its own constitutional requirements." Therefore, the UK is bound to withdraw from the EU in a manner that does not violate its constitution. As devolution and the rights and responsibilities it confers upon the Scottish Parliament and Government as devolved institutions are part of the UK's constitution, then however the UK withdraws from the EU must be in accordance with such devolution arrangements. In theory there could be a question of to what extent the language of Art. 50 constrains the UK Government in its withdrawal process as it relates to devolution, a question that involves interpretation of EU law, and therefore one that Scotland could submit to the Court of Justice of the European Union.[42]

---

[41] Memorandum of Understanding, *supra* note 6, at 23.
[42] The Court of Justice of the European Union is the EU's judicial instrument to interpret EU law and ensure that it is applied in the same way in all EU countries, and to settle any

However, as primarily this is a question of UK constitutional law, a more appropriate forum is the UK's Supreme Court; they will be best positioned and most informed to make a determination of to what extent the devolution agreements shape the UK's process of EU withdrawal. A decision from the UK Supreme Court would have a profound impact on the UK Government as its paramount domestic legal institution. Additionally, the decision would continue to be binding regardless of the UK's membership in the EU, whereas a decision of the Court of Justice would in theory cease to bind the UK once they are no longer a party.

The UK Supreme Court, in addition to its role as the final court of appeal in the UK, focuses particularly on cases of greatest public and constitutional importance.[43] The question of to what extent the UK Government is constitutionally bound to obtain consents from other UK bodies—be it the UK Parliament, as the High Court held,[44] or even the Scottish Parliament and Government, as Scotland contends—certainly constitute questions of public and constitutional importance. When the case being brought against the UK Government triggering Article 50 without the UK Parliament's consent was announced, Scottish First Minister Nicola Sturgeon publicly endorsed the case against the UK Government. She stated:

> The Scottish Government is clear that triggering Article 50 will directly affect devolved interests and rights in Scotland. And triggering Article 50 will inevitably deprive Scottish people and Scottish businesses of rights and freedoms which they currently enjoy…[i]t simply cannot be right that those rights can be removed by the UK Government on the say-so of a Prime Minister without parliamentary debate, scrutiny or consent. So legislation should be required at Westminster and the consent of the Scottish Parliament should be sought before Article 50 is triggered.[45]

From this quote it is evident that from the very beginning of the Brexit process, the Scottish Government was keenly aware of the legal, constitutional, and democratic concerns that would affect Scotland in the

---

legal disputes between national governments and EU institutions. Court of Justice of the European Union, Europa, https://europa.eu/european-union/about-eu/institutions-bodies/court-justice_en.

[43] Supreme Court, *Role of the Supreme Court*, https://www.supremecourt.uk/about/role-of-the-supreme-court.html.

[44] *Supreme Court judgment on Brexit, supra* note 30.

[45] Angela Dewan, *Brexit: Scotland backs legal case against UK government*, CNN (Nov. 8, 2016), http://www.cnn.com/2016/11/08/europe/brexit-scotland-legal-case/.

event of a UK exit from the EU, concerns Holyrood has consistently and strongly communicated to Westminster since the outcome of the referendum was announced. The legal issues the statement highlights are the constitutional issues at play ("devolved interests and rights in Scotland"), the material deprivation of certain economic and political rights of the Scottish people should they be forced to leave the EU against their will by the UK Government, and the inevitable impact it will have on Scottish legislation, such that it forces the Scottish Parliament to act, and therefore it should be necessary to obtain their consent.

In line with these concerns, in December 2016 the Scottish Government released its proposal to the UK Government with Scotland's positions on Brexit and the terms it seeks in whatever Brexit agreement is reached with the EU. The proposal states the Scottish Government's full intent and desire to remain within the EU Single Market, a legal and political rat's nest that will be deeply dependent upon the UK Government's willingness to support such an arrangement. The final section of this paper scrutinizes the legal underpinnings of the Scottish Government's claims and terms in this proposal, and assesses their legal validity and viability.

III. SCOTLAND'S ABILITY TO REMAIN IN THE EU SINGLE MARKET: THE SCOTTISH GOVERNMENT'S PROPOSAL

The Scottish Government's proposal, "Scotland's Place in Europe," is prefaced by the restatement that the SNP continues to believe that Scotland's best option is to leave the UK and join the EU as an independent country.[46] The First Minister states that Scotland is entitled to another independence referendum in light of the fact that the SNP was elected on the platform that "The Scottish Parliament should have the right to hold another referendum [...] if there is a significant and material change in the circumstances that prevailed in 2014, such as Scotland being taken out of the EU against our will."[47] The Brexit vote certainly meets these conditions.

However, this does not legally entitle Scotland to another referendum—only some agreement with the UK Government can confer the right on Scotland to hold such a referendum, and while this manifesto provision is a compelling political justification, it does not create a legal right to hold a referendum nor does it compel or obligate Westminster to comply with Scotland's request. Under Section 30 of the Scotland Act 1998, an Order in Council must be agreed between the

---

[46] *Scotland's Place in Europe, supra* note 13, at vi.
[47] *Id.*

Scottish and UK Government in order for another referendum to be legislated by the Scottish Parliament, a decision that is entirely up to the discretion of "Her Majesty" and by implication Her (the UK's) Government.[48] While it may be politically damaging and inadvisable for the UK Government to refuse Scotland a second independence referendum, their hands are not tied to do so as the Scottish proposal implies. The remainder of the proposal is framed as a compromise against the SNP's threat, more political than legal, to request a second referendum.[49]

The proposal then advocates that even if the UK leaves the EU, it should remain a member of the EU Single Market through the European Economic Area and remain within the European Customs Union.[50] However, the Scottish Government also recognizes that Theresa May has indicated this will not be something the UK Government is willing to do;[51] in that case, the proposal puts forward "differentiated options for Scotland" that will allow Scotland to remain both a part of the UK and the EU Single Market by becoming a member of European Free Trade Association (EFTA) and then the European Economic Area (EEA), but outside the EU Customs Union, in order to avoid creating an external border between the rest of the UK and Scotland.[52]

As the proposal admits, this suggestion is legally, practically, and politically difficult; additionally, it is entirely reliant on not only the political will of the UK Government to support such a relationship, but on EU Member States' willingness to accept a Scotland that is both within the UK and the EU Single Market.[53] The proposal points to Denmark as an example, and reasons that just as Denmark is an EU Member State but parts of its territory—Greenland and the Faroe Islands —are not part of the EU, then it must be possible for a differentiated agreement to be reached whereby Scotland, as part of the UK's territory, can remain within the EU or at least its Single Market while the other parts of the UK—England, Wales, and Northern Ireland—remain outside.[54]

The crucial, evident hurdle in this reasoning is that Scotland is not an independent country. Membership in the EU, EFTA, and consequently the EEA is predicated on the applicant nation being a

---

[48] Scotland Act 1998, §30.
[49] *Scotland's Place in Europe, supra* note 13, at viii.
[50] *Id.* at vi, 24-26.
[51] *Id.* at 26.
[52] *Id.* at 26-39.
[53] *Id.* at 29.
[54] *Id.* at 26.

recognized state.[55] The proposal recognizes this legal obstacle on several levels; it is characterized as one involving "the capacity of Scotland to operate within the single market framework without being an independent country," and the admission that the UK would likely have to sponsor Scotland's application to join EFTA or the EEA (and similarly to join the EU, which would also require the UK remain in the EU—no longer a likely possibility).

However, the proposal states that Scotland could directly seek "full or associate membership of EFTA and subsequently the EEA Agreement," without the UK's sponsorship. This poses two interesting legal questions—firstly, whether in fact a nation not recognized as a state can directly apply for full or associate membership in EFTA, and the secondly, if such an application were successful, whether it would qualify the nation to join the EEA. The Scottish Government's proposal fails to answer these legal questions—it merely makes the assertion, but then does not verify its legal validity. EFTA Article 56(1) clearly states that only a "State" may accede to the EFTA Convention, and that the EFTA Council must approve this accession;[56] this would seemingly disqualify Scotland from acceding to the Convention, as it is not a state but rather a nation within a state (the UK). Though Art. 56 (2) states that the EFTA Council may negotiate an agreement between the EFTA Member States and "any other State, union of States, or international organization" to create an "association embodying such reciprocal rights and obligations, common actions and special procedures as may be appropriate," once again this would not provide an opportunity for Scotland as a Scotland within the UK would not fall within the categories of "any other State, union of States, or international organization."[57] *BUT*.

Art. 56(3) poses a further complication that even if Scotland were somehow able to sidestep the statehood requirement obstacle, Scotland would then be required to "apply to become a party to the free trade agreements between the Member States on the one hand and third states, unions of states or international organisations on the other."[58] These required actions fall within the purview of international relations and entering into international treaties and agreements, which are areas of governance not devolved to Scotland and exclusively within the

---

[55] See Treaty of Lisbon Amending the Treaty on European Union and the Treaty Establishing the European Community, Dec. 13, 2007, 2007 O.J. (C 306) 1, art. 49; Convention Establishing the European Free Trade Association (EFTA), Jan. 4, 1960, 1960 c. 1 art. 2; Agreement on the European Economic Area, Mar. 17, 1993, 1993 O.J. (No L 1, 3.1.1994), pt. 1 art. 2.

[56] EFTA Covention, *supra* note 51, at art. 56(1).

[57] EFTA Covention, *supra* note 51, at art. 56(2).

[58] EFTA Covention, *supra* note 51, at art. Art. 56(3).

competence of the UK Government.[59] Therefore, the plain reading of EFTA Art. 56 does not support the Scottish Government's claim that it can directly seek EFTA membership, full or associate. Because Scotland does not qualify for ascension to the EFTA Convention nor the EU, seeking EEA membership without the UK's sponsorship is also untenable.

CONCLUSION

While the Scottish Government enumerates several proposals for how to work around its lack of statehood and the consequent disqualification for direct membership in the aforementioned European economic institutions, treaties, and conventions, there are a multitude of internal UK constitutional and political arrangements that must first be achieved, to say nothing of the international negotiations that the UK must then enter into on Scotland's behalf. As discussed, according to the texts of the Lisbon Treaty, the EFTA Convention, and the EEA Agreement, Scotland cannot directly seek membership in any of these international bodies. While the proposal earnestly presents several creative differentiated options for a Scotland within the UK to remain in the EU Single Market, the legal texts underpinning these institutions do not support the contention that Scotland can qualify for membership as a non-state.

While this could be construed as a question of treaty interpretation that could be submitted to the relevant judicial arms of these three international bodies, even if it were legally possible for Scotland as a non-state to seek membership, it would also require the consent of the Member States to approve a non-state's ascension. The likelihood that both a legal finding that Scotland can join the EFTA and the EEA and a political agreement between their respective Member States to allow Scotland's ascension is extremely unlikely. Spain's firm objections to the Scottish Government's proposal nearly immediately after its release and the UK Government's refusal to facilitate Scotland's continued membership in the EU Single Market if it means that the four freedoms would still apply in Scotland are indicative of the political climate's intractability to Scotland's ambitions to remain in the EU or its Single Market.

Ultimately, the extent of Scotland's legal right to demand Westminster gain its consent to the terms of Brexit is a question of UK constitutional law interpretation, according to the present devolution structure. Therefore, while Scotland may appeal to the EU or its

---

[59] See Scotland Act 1998, *supra* note 11; Scotland Act 2016, *supra* note 14; and Memorandum of Understanding, *supra* note 6.

institutions for assistance in its fight against being taken out of the EU against its democratically demonstrated will, strategically Scotland will be better served by securing a UK court decision that establishes its constitutional, devolved right to be at the Brexit negotiating table. According to the UK Supreme Court's decision, Scotland has no constitutional or legal right to demand its consent be attained. However, perhaps the question of Scottish consent or involvement can be raised again on different legal grounds, as discussed above. While such a finding may be difficult to achieve and ultimately unlikely, any court decision in this area may still prove beneficial as it would address what appears to be a clear lacunae in UK constitutional law on the legal inner workings of devolution within the UK.

Chapter 14: The Fate of Scotch Whisky Post Brexit—Implications for Geographical Indications

Christine Zhao

Background Information

Champagne, Roquefort cheese, Port, Cornish pasties, Scotch whisky.... These are examples of geographical indications (GIs), a *sui generis* category of intellectual property that is tied to the culture of the geographic region where the products originate. Protection means that no one else can call their product by the same name. There can be no "Scotch" that isn't proper Scotch whisky. GIs are offered protection based on the way that the products are made, where they are made, and where the components come from. Currently, qualifying products may apply under EU law for a protected GI designation. In general, the three categories of protection are: protected designation origin (PDO), protected GI (PGI), traditional specialties guaranteed (TSG).[1] PDOs and PGIs are offered full protections as GIs, whereas TSGs are given non-GI level quality schemes.[2] Protected status requires that products include a quality label that signifies whether a product is a PDO, a PGI, or a TSG.[3] PDOs are entitled to protection based on a tie to a specific place, where its quality and characteristics are "essentially or exclusively due to a particular geographical environment."[4] PGIs are protected based on a specific "quality, reputation or other characteristics1 attributable to that

---

[1] Roland Herrmann, *The Socio-Economics of Geographical Indications* (WIPO Worldwide Symposium on Geographical Indications, Lima, Peru, 2011), http://www.wipo.int/edocs/mdocs/geoind/en/wipo_geo_lim_11/wipo_geo_lim_11_8.pdf.

[2] EUIPO Infringement of Protected Geographical Indications for Wine, Spirits, Agricultural Products and Foodstuffs in the European Union (April 2016), https://euipo.europa.eu/tunnel-web/secure/webdav/guest/document_library/observatory/documents/Geographical_indications_report/geographical_indications_report_en.pdf [hereinafter EUIPO GI Report].

[3] *Agriculture and rural development*, European Commission, http://ec.europa.eu/agriculture/quality/schemes_en (last visited Dec. 27, 2016).

[4] Luc Berlottier and Laurent Mercier, *Protected Designations of Origin and Protected Geographical Indications* (European Commission Agriculture and Rural Development – Wine, alcohol, tobacco, seeds and hops 2010), http://ec.europa.eu/internal_market/iprenforcement/docs/observatory/gi-designations_en.pdf.

geographical origin."[5] TSGs are protected if they carry a "specific character," including production with traditional raw materials, a traditional composition, and a traditional mode of production and/or processing.[6] Scotch is a PGI, meaning that not every step of the process needs to take place in the designated origin in order to qualify for protection: having certain parts of the process be done in Scotland and having a good reputation is enough. Reputation is critical for GIs and the consequences of damage to a GI's reputation (as a result of fraudulent goods, for example) can be dire for producers.

A number of bodies of law cover GI rights for each product. On an international scale, the Trade Related Aspects of Intellectual Property Rights (TRIPS) agreements of the World Trade Organization (WTO) Agreement and European Union (EU) laws govern. On a local level, national laws can be used to create and enhance intellectual property rights. Earning protected status means that products must pass particular tests in order to be labelled a certain way. You cannot, for example, label whiskey from Ireland "Scotch whisky," or vice versa. In order to qualify as a GI, a product must have an essential connection to its place of origin.[7] Unlike the United States, where GIs are protected under trademark law, European GIs are dependent on the concept of *terroir*.[8] Terroir fundamentally refers to a specific property of the geographic region that determines whether a product can qualify for protected GI status, and therefore whether or not others can use the name and label. Emphasizing the importance of terroir means that many GIs may include common food names, which further restricts what products can be called.[9] These requirements and restrictions mean that products that successfully register as GIs are likely to benefit from robust protection.

Since 1972, when it joined the EU, the United Kingdom (UK) has enjoyed protections for GIs offered by the supranational organization. These protections and the additional protections for wines and spirits are extended to Scotch whisky, an important UK GI. But once Article 50 is triggered and the UK leaves the EU, Scotch whisky's protection might change or come to rely on different bodies of law. There may be new regulatory schemes required to guarantee that Scotch retains the level of protection necessary for it to thrive as a lucrative product. The UK may

---

[5] *Id.*

[6] Herrmann, *supra* note 1.

[7]   *Geographical   Indications—What   is   a   geographical   indication?*,   WIPO, http://www.wipo.int/geo_indications/en/ (last visited Dec. 24, 2016).

[8] K. William Watson, *Reign of Terroir: How to Resist Europe's Efforts to Control Common Food Names   as   Geographical   Indications*,   CATO   Institute   (Feb.   16,   2016), https://www.cato.org/publications/policy-analysis/reign-terroir-how-resist-europes-efforts-control-common-food-names.

[9] *Id.*

also have to re-negotiate agreements with countries that already agreed to protect GIs registered under EU law, but not to protect GIs from the UK as an individual member state.

The fate of Scotch is of particular importance because spirits make up a significant portion of exports from the UK. Beyond that, Scotch also enjoys a rich, lengthy history that, unlike some of its fellow GIs, is well-known beyond the UK. The whisky industry has seen newcomers, such as Japanese whisky producers, ready to compete with European producers, making it all the more important to ensure that Scotch whisky remains protected. Scotch's PGI status under EU law, which it has enjoyed since 2008, means that certain parts of the whisky production process may be performed outside of Scotland, subject to careful scrutiny by national and supranational law. EU law requires that the production of GIs be carefully regulated and verified in order to defend the GI's reputation and quality. In order to produce Scotch whisky, businesses performing each step of the process must be registered with Her Majesty's Revenue & Customs (HMRC). Producers must list every site within and outside Scotland from distilleries to bottling plants. In 2014, a verification scheme called the Scotch Whisky Verification Scheme was introduced at the behest of the Scotch Whisky Association (SWA) and industry leaders.

The variety of tactics employed to protect Scotch whisky's reputation and integrity speaks to Scotch's importance to the UK economy. Each year, Scotch accounts for almost £4 billion in exports, making it a crucial product for the UK.[10] In a 2014 study, hard liquor accounted for 28% of the United Kingdom's overall exports, totaling about $8.5 billion, and it is likely that Scotch, given its clout, accounts for a large portion of the total amount.[11] Europe as a whole is the largest importing continent of hard liquor, with $11.6 billion in imports, followed by North America with $8.32 billion in imports and Asia with $8.09 billion.[12] In September 2016, exports of Scotch to EU countries totaled around 208 million bottles in the first half of the year, though the value of the imports decreased slightly.[13] The latest numbers show that almost 40% of exports of Scotch go to the rest of the EU, while the USA accounted for £357.4 million in sales.[14] UK sales account for about 7%

---

[10] *Hard Liquor Export Data*, OEC, http://atlas.media.mit.edu/en/profile/hs92/2208/ (last visited Dec. 17, 2016).

[11] *Id.*

[12] *Id.*

[13] *Scotch whisky exports 'up for first time in three years'*, BBC News (Sep. 16, 2016), http://www.bbc.com/news/uk-scotland-scotland-business-37379947.

[14] *Id.*

of Scotch production.[15] These numbers demonstrate the importance of Scotch as a product for the UK, both domestically and abroad. Continuing to protect the reputation of a product like Scotch whisky will continue to ensure that it remains overall profitable for the UK, even after it leaves the EU.

I. OVERVIEW OF PROTECTED STATUS

A. PROTECTIONS UNDER INTERNATIONAL LAW

The Paris Convention, administered by the World Intellectual Property Organization (WIPO), prohibits the use of false indications of origin and has been modified to offer this protection even where fraudulent intent is not shown, which reinforces the strength of measures taken to prevent infringement.[16] The Paris Convention has 176 contracting parties, offering broader protection than many other international agreements. The United Kingdom is a signatory to the Paris Convention, as are a number of other EU Member States.[17] The Lisbon Agreement expands on the Paris Convention's protection of GIs by providing for the protection of appellations of origin. The Lisbon Agreement also states that if a GI is protected at a national level, the interested Member State can register the GI with the WIPO.[18] As of 2016, the Lisbon Agreement has 28 contracting parties. The UK is not currently a party to the Lisbon Agreement. Moving forward, negotiations may also need to clarify whether there would be different protections for GIs than for intellectual property rights in general, though on an international level they appear to be treated the same for legal purposes.

The WTO's TRIPS agreements allow for intellectual property to be entitled to special protections, enforceable by the individual member states of the WTO. TRIPS requires that member states protect GIs from: (a) the use of any means in the designation or presentation of a good that indicates or suggests that the good in question originates in a geographical area other than the true place of origin in a manner which misleads the public as the geographical origin of the good, and (b) any use which constitutes an act of unfair competition within the meaning of Article 10*bis* of the Paris Convention.[19] Article 23 offers enhanced

---

[15] *Id.*

[16] CATHERINE SEVILLE, EU INTELLECTUAL PROPERTY LAW AND POLICY 291 (2009).

[17] *WIPO-Administered Treaties – Contracting Parties – Lisbon Agreement*, WIPO, http://www.wipo.int/treaties/en/ShowResults.jsp?lang=en&treaty_id=10 (last visited Dec. 24, 2016).

[18] Seville, *supra* note 16 at 291.

[19] TRIPS: Agreement on Trade-Related Aspects of Intellectual Property Rights, Apr. 15, 1994, Marrakesh Agreement Establishing the World Trade Organization, Annex 1C, THE LEGAL TEXTS: THE RESULTS OF THE URUGUAY ROUND OF

protection for wines and spirits, prohibiting the use of a GI even if a non-GI product acknowledges the true origin of the goods, is used in translation, or is accompanied by a qualifier such as "style."[20] For instance, a whisky that is not authentic Scotch whisky could not be labelled "Scotch-style" or "Scotch-imitation." TRIPS are likely to be more effective than any other international treaty for GIs because of the number of parties that have agreed to honor it. The UK is a member of the WTO in its own right, meaning it would have to fulfill its obligations under TRIPS regardless of its EU membership, and would probably receive the same courtesy in return from other WTO members. When the UK joined the EU, Scotch was a protected GI, and therefore able to register right away under EU law. The UK's national level protections, however, may not be as important as the EU protections because the EU Member States' GIs, including the UK's, are primarily protected at the EU level. The EU's benefits from TRIPS also benefit the current Member States of the EU, including the UK. But once the UK departs, it may have to re-negotiate some of the agreements that the EU was a party to as a supranational entity but not its individual Member States.

B. CURRENT PROTECTIONS UNDER THE EUROPEAN UNION

Under EU law, GIs may be offered *sui generis* intellectual property rights if there is an essential link between the quality and the geographical region where the product originates.[21] Under EU law, a product may have PDO status or PGI status.[22] Protected status ensures that rival companies cannot sell "knock-offs" by leveraging the fame of the product's name or engage in other fraudulent behavior. Producers of spirits that are GIs, such as Scotch whisky, must follow additional guidelines. For Scotch whisky, the protection is of particular importance given its extensive popularity, which attracts a slew of copycats across the globe. Its prominent place in culture as well as international trade has inspired a number of competing producers to seek the opportunity to break into the market of producing Scotch.

The EU Enforcement Directive, introduced in 2004, provides that all Member States must protect intellectual property rights within the EU in addition to fulfilling their international obligations under TRIPS. The Directive has been transposed into the national laws of the Member

---

MULTILATERAL TRADE NEGOTIATIONS 320 (1999), 1869 U.N.T.S. 299, 33 I.L.M. 1197 (1994) [hereinafter TRIPS Agreement].

[20] TRIPS Agreement, Art. 23.

[21] EUIPO GI Report

[22] Agriculture, *supra* note 3.

States, including the United Kingdom.[23] Article 9 of the Directive provides the judicial remedies available where infringement is suspected.[24] Remedies include interlocutory injunctions and civil remedies. National law can require additional elements before offering an injunction remedy: the UK, for example, requires that (a) damages alone will not be adequate, and that (b) equitable remedies such as injunctions keep conscionability in mind.[25]

Scotch is currently protected under Regulation (EC) 110/2008, which applies to GIs for spirit drinks. 110/2008 works in tandem with the UK's verification scheme, and retaining future protection for Scotch within TRIPS relies on a successful negotiation of the UK's GI protections within the EU. 110/2008 is complemented by Regulation No 2006/510, which regulates foodstuffs and agricultural products. 110/2008 fine-tunes the protections offered to GIs by tailoring them to fit the specific needs of spirit drinks like Scotch. Article 15 of 110/2008 defines covered GIs as "an indication which identifies a spirit drink as originating in the territory of a country, or a region or locality in that territory, where a given quality, reputation or other characteristic of that spirit drink is essentially attributable to its geographical origin."[26] 110/2008 includes detailed information about what is and is not covered, as well as treatment of "generic" names. Annex III contains a list of products that cannot become generic (essentially meaning the product will always retain protection) because they were established as GIs at the time of implementation. Scotch whisky is among the products listed in Annex III. Given that Scotch was included in 110/2008 as a registered GI, there's a possibility that there would not be a need for Scotch to be re-registered.

110/2008 also offers guidance for third countries (those who are not within the European Union) wishing to register GIs. In order to register, the product must clear a number of requirements, all of which are detailed in Article 17.[27] Products may qualify for protected status by demonstrating that they have earned national protection through their country of origin and by submitting a technical file detailing the products' qualifications for protection and production requirements.

Article 6 provides that member states can require more stringent legislation, which would indicate that the national law can preempt EU

---

[23] *National Transposition,* http://eur-lex.europa.eu/legal-content/EN/NIM/?uri=CELEX:32004L0048&qid=1483162406763 (last visited Dec. 27, 2016).

[24] Council Directive 2004/48/EC, art. 9, 2004 O.J. (L 157) 45.

[25] JUSTINE PILA ET. AL., EUROPEAN INTELLECTUAL PROPERTY LAW 590-591 (2016).

[26] Council Regulation 110/2008, art. 15, 2008 O.J. (L 39), 13.2.2008 (EC).

[27] Council Regulation 110/2008, art. 17, 2008 O.J. (L 39), 13.2.2008 (EC).

law where it is more stringent. For Scotch, this means that any protections offered through Scotland and the United Kingdom would be respected by the EU. Once the UK ceases to be a member state and becomes a third country, it is unlikely that the Article would still apply, as the language of the Article clearly specifies "Member State." This means that if the Commission accepted post-Brexit UK's application to register Scotch as a GI of a third country, it may not benefit from the additional protections offered by national laws. The enforcement process in the EU for GIs is based on agreements,[28] and does not typically require judicial action by rights-holders in order to act against infringement.[29] The European Union Intellectual Property Organization (EUIPO) enforces intellectual property rights for trademarks, designs, patents, and copyrights. They offer mediation for these forms of protections, but with GIs, most of the burden of enforcement shifts to the Member States responsible for the GIs. Article 24 of 110/2008 says that "Member States shall be responsible for the control of spirit drinks."[30] Compliance checks must be performed by the Member States or any country wishing to have their GIs protected within the EU. Member States, including the UK, are responsible for putting in place a verification scheme to ensure the quality and authenticity of their GIs and market controls to prevent injury to consumers and the product's reputation.[31] Verification schemes ensure that producers abide by the requirements set forth in GI technical files while market controls provide ex officio[32] protection in the Member State.

The EU trademark reform efforts launched in March 2016 introduced new pieces of legislation that increase cooperation between the EUIPO and the Member States, creating a more unified system for granting and protecting intellectual property rights. Regulation 2015/2424 allows third parties to oppose trademarks that interfere with GIs[33] and Directive No. 2015/2436 sets forth methods to invalidate marks that conflict with GIs.[34] These recent developments may also need to be re-established post-Brexit, given that they currently concern the Member States. The UK may have to adopt these regulations or

---

[28] National schemes such as the UK's Spirit Drinks Regulations 2008 work to ensure that EU Regulations, including Regulation 110/2008, are adequately enforced. In addition, HMRC's Scotch verification scheme acts as an additional safeguard from counterfeiting and unauthorized production.

[29] EUIPO GI Report.

[30] Council Regulation 110/2008, art. 24, 2008 O.J. (L 39), 13.2.2008 (EC).

[31] *Id.*

[32] *Id.*

[33] Council Regulation 2015/2424, 2015 O.J. (L 341) 21 (EU).

[34] Council Directive 2015/2436, 2015 O.J. (L 336) 1 (EEA).

complete additional registration requirements for Scotch and its other GIs.

C. CURRENT PROTECTIONS UNDER NATIONAL LAW

UK national law offers few specific protections for GIs. The Department for Environment, Food and Rural Affairs (DEFRA) is responsible for issuing policy concerning GIs. [35] The protections established by 110/2008 are enforced by DEFRA's Spirit Drinks Regulations 2008, and the Scotch Whisky Regulations 2009 provide additional Scotch labelling requirements.[36] The Spirit Drinks (Cost of Verification) Regulations 2013 provide HMRC with the power to charge producers under certain circumstances for verification.[37] UK law also controls the bulk movement of Scotch (other than Single Malt Scotch) by requiring that recipients of bulk orders of Scotch provide HMRC with an "undertaking."[38] An undertaking is a form that is submitted to the HMRC if the recipient, typically a "bulk importer" who will complete the bottling, blending, or labelling process outside of Scotland, has registered for the Spirit Drinks Verification (SDV) Scheme.[39] As of January 2015, verification must be secured before bulk orders can be completed.[40] This process ensures that aspects of Scotch production that can be completed outside of Scotland, as provided by the technical file, are carefully regulated.

Under UK national law, spirit drinks, including Scotch, apply for verification under the Spirit Drinks Verification Scheme through the HMRC. The requirements for verification are included in the technical files provided as part of the application and registration process detailed in 110/2008. The HMRC launched a verification scheme for Scotch whisky in January 2014.[41] The verification scheme allows producers of Scotch whisky to apply for and receive verification of the authenticity of their product as Scotch whisky. In order to qualify, producers must fulfill the requirements regarding various aspects of the process of making Scotch as well as certain characteristics that must be present (color, aging process, materials used throughout the production steps). [42] Scotch whisky is differentiated from other whiskies by differences in the

---

[35] *Scotch whisky Technical File* (October 2014), https://www.gov.uk/government/uploads/system/uploads/attachment_data/file/380284/techincal-guidance.pdf.
[36] *Id.*
[37] *Id.*
[38] *Id.*
[39] *Id.*
[40] *Scotch whisky, supra* note 27.
[41] *Id.*
[42] *Id.*

production process, the unique characteristics of Scotland's geology and geography, certain characteristics of the appearance, including color, and the specific skills of the distiller and blender.[43] These requirements result in an increased emphasis on the process of making, bottling, and labelling Scotch.

The first step to applying for verification is to fill out an application on the HMRC website for each production facility. If the application is approved, then the HMRC will conduct their verification process, either on the premises (if a producer is within Scotland) or after an undertaking has been submitted (if the producer is bottling, blending, or labelling outside Scotland). The verification system involves checking the producer's processes against those detailed in the technical file and ensuring compliance. During biennial verification visits (cleverly timed to precede the 3-year minimum aging requirement of Scotch), the HMRC will review: (1) fermentation, (2) distillation, (3) maturation, (4) blending, and (5) bottling/labelling. The production facility's processes must match those listed in the technical file in order to pass inspection. If blending, bottling and labelling takes place outside of Scotland, then HMRC must also ensure that those facilities (after the facilities' undertaking forms are approved) are compliant with the technical file. The burden falls on the producer to ensure that, if they receive materials from external sources that are not owned by the producer, all of the supplies used in the production of Scotch are compliant with the technical file's standards. Once a facility (or facilities, if a single producer completes the process inside and outside Scotland) is verified, it will be listed as "assured" on HMRC's website.[44]

The verification scheme's voluntary system of compliance means that, while there is no financial penalty for failing to secure verifications, if the Scotch produced is not verified it is considered to be illegally produced.[45] Both the producers and their customers may be liable and subject to enforcement actions.[46] Enforcement, however, is not within the purview of HMRC's duties: food authorities and port health authorities are responsible for enforcing the verification scheme and other protections, including those offered by EU law. [47] If the circumstances call for it, the HMRC will forward information to the

---

[43] *Id.*

[44]   *HMRC   Scotch   whisky   verification,*   HMRC,
https://www.gov.uk/government/consultations/how-hmrc-propose-to-verify-scotch-whisky (last visited Dec. 1, 2016).

[45] *Scotch whisky, supra* note 27.

[46] *Id.*

[47] *Id.*

relevant enforcement bodies. While the UK remains a part of the EU, the EU Enforcement Directive also applies.

Under UK common law, the tort of "passing off" offers another avenue for those who suffer injury from a GI being misrepresented or creating confusion. The elements of passing off are: (1) reputation or goodwill in the mind of the consumer connected with the goods or services supplied and such goods or services are known to the consumer to have some distinctive feature, (2) the defendant has, whether or not intentionally, made misrepresentations to the public leading them to believe that the defendant's goods or services are the plaintiff's, and (3) the plaintiff has suffered or is likely to suffer damage because of the erroneous belief engendered by the defendant's misrepresentation.[48] The 1970 "Scotch whisky Case" allowed the description of Scotch as "Scotch" to be protected because it was determined that "there were no blenders of Scotch whisky outside of Scotland or England."[49] England also has the Trade Descriptions Act, which applies to Scotch and prohibits traders from proffering a "false trade description to any goods," meaning no indications of the place of production or the identity of the producer can be fraudulently used.[50] The Trademark Act of 1994, much like 110/2008, allows GIs to register for protection. GIs can register as certification marks, collective marks, or based on a "distinctive character." A certification mark is defined as "a mark indicating that the goods or services in connection with which it is used are certified by the proprietor of the mark in respect of origin, material, mode of manufacture of goods or performance of services, quality, accuracy or other characteristics," while a collective mark is defined as "a mark distinguishing the goods or services of members of an association which is the proprietor of the mark from those of other undertakings."[51] Under the Trademark Act, GIs can apply to register with the Trademark Registry, and offer protection to GIs that kicks in even before any injury takes place, thus working to avoid infringement.[52]

The SWA is a UK trade organization that has a great deal of influence over the fate of Scotch as a PGI.[53] The SWA has two offices: one in Edinburgh, Scotland, and one in London, UK. Established in October 1912 as the Wine & Spirit Brand Association, the organization grew to be a major player in ensuring Scotch retains all benefits of GI

---

[48] *Passing Off*, In Brief UK, http://www.inbrief.co.uk/intellectual-property/passing-off/ (last visited Dec. 24, 2016).
[49] BERNARD O'CONNOR, THE LAW OF GEOGRAPHICAL INDICATIONS 214 (2004).
[50] O'Connor, *supra* note 50. at 215.
[51] O'Connor, *supra* note 50 at 217.
[52] *Id.*
[53] SCOTCH WHISKY ASSOCIATION, http://www.scotch-whisky.org.uk/.

and IP regulatory schemes. Because of the importance of geography to Scotch's reputation and worth, the SWA's role will be sure to increase in importance following the start of negotiations between the EU and the UK. The SWA advocates for the continued protection of Scotch across the globe, ensuring that Scotch retains not only its reputation, but its valuable protection against counterfeit products. The SWA's remarkable influence means that it will likely have a say in how negotiations impact Scotch as a PGI.

The SWA also provides updates on the status of Scotch in terms of culture, economy, and advancements in new markets. These updates include insights into where Scotch is being exported while emphasizing the importance of Scotch's reputation, something that is reliant on its status as a GI. A news section keeps interested readers and Scotch enthusiasts apprised of the latest figures for exports by volume and the overall conditions of the Scotch industry. Following the Brexit vote, the SWA published an overview of what they believed would happen to Scotch's protections, as well as tariff implications, market impacts, and new requirements. One of the key uncertainties cited by the SWA was the potential need for national-level rules on the "definition of whisky, food labelling, bottle sizes, and so on," all of which had been determined at the EU level.[54] Should there be a need for UK-level rules, the SWA will probably have a fairly active role in how protections are administered and enforced.

On the national scale, post-Brexit political plans contribute to growing concerns over how EU law and UK law will progress. In early October 2016, Prime Minister Theresa May unveiled the Great Repeal Bill as a solution for the preemptive reconciliation of EU laws and UK national laws. The Great Repeal Bill would terminate the European Communities Act of 1972, meaning that EU law will no longer have instant effect in the UK.[55] But the Bill also purports to keep all Regulations in place by transposing all EU laws, "wherever practical," into UK legislation. "Wherever practical" would probably include 110/2008 because it makes sense to preserve protection of intellectual property rights for significant products such as Scotch. If this is the case, then the Prime Minister may be able to retain all the current protections

---

[54] *Brexit – what now for Scotch whisky?*, SCOTCH WHISKY ASSOCIATION (Aug. 3, 2016), http://www.scotch-whisky.org.uk/news-publications/news/brexit-what-now-for-scotch-whisky/#.WGcno7YrK8o (last visited Nov. 28, 2016).

[55] Alexandra Sims, *What is the Great Repeal Bill? The Brexit law to end all EU laws (that we don't like)*, THE INDEPENDENT (Oct. 3, 2016), http://www.independent.co.uk/news/uk/politics/great-repeal-bill-brexit-law-eu-law-theresa-may-david-davis-a7343256.html; *see also Taking Back Control*, THE ECONOMIST (Nov. 6, 2016), http://www.economist.com/news/britain/21709589-high-court-rules-parliament-must-vote-trigger-brexit-process-taking-back-control.

by transposing 110/2008 to national law. But how the Great Repeal Bill will transfer each EU law remains to be seen, as it's unlikely to be as simple as a copy and paste, nor does it seem to be that different than keeping the European Communities Act in place.

II. POST-BREXIT PREDICTIONS

One of the biggest questions to answer post-Brexit is: what gets lost? The current protections are a series of intertwined agreements between the EU, the WTO, individual countries, and WIPO. Currently, under TRIPS, the UK fulfills its obligations by honoring GIs from other countries in return for its own GIs being honored. As a result, Scotch whisky is protected by the force of both the EU and the WTO. The ongoing WTO Doha negotiations may amend TRIPS and change the way protections are handled on an international and national scale. At the time of writing, there is an ongoing debate concerning how GIs should be protected within individual member countries. Following a number of roadblocks, the impact of the Doha Round remains uncertain.[56] The EU has influence and power as a whole, but the individual Member States have less bargaining power.

Unlike the United States, where there is a central agency enforcing intellectual property rights, the EU does not yet have a centralized system for enforcing protections. Regulation 110/2008 is still likely to offer Scotch its protections once the UK re-registers. Presumably, given the importance of Scotch, this process of ensuring that there is no gap in protection is likely to be fairly painless, if it is necessary in the first place. There is a strong likelihood that, assuming negotiations go well, Scotch will remain protected as-is under 110/2008. If the UK does have to re-register Scotch, it can do so according to Article 17 of 110/2008. The UK would submit an application directly to the Commission, and include proof that the GI is protected in its country of origin, meaning national protection for GIs, including Scotch, might have to be more clearly defined.[57] At the international level, the UK may consider becoming a party to the Lisbon Agreement to secure further protections. The UK may also, as part of Article 50 exit negotiations, enter into a bilateral agreement with the EU. This action is not unprecedented, as the EU has bilateral agreements with a number of third countries to protect their GIs.[58]

Post-Brexit, the UK may need to re-negotiate free trade agreements that were made between the EU and third countries. The UK may also

---

[56] Tehelka Web Desk, *Slow Doha talks hurt business planning*, TEHELKA (Dec. 20, 2016), http://www.tehelka.com/2016/12/slow-doha-talks-hurt-business-planning/.
[57] Council Regulation 110/2008, art. 17, 2008 O.J. (L 39), 13.2.2008 (EC).
[58] EUIPO GI Report

seek to enter into new agreements with additional countries, including the United States. Because the United States has the United States Patent and Trademark Office (USPTO) for registering and enforcing the protection of trademarks, the UK may have to work around the USA's regulations should an agreement be made, paying close attention to the relationship between GIs and trademarks.[59] Because trademarks are distinctive identifiers of "goods by an enterprise" and not limited by geographical links, they are not impacted in the same way by the concerns over terroir that are inherent in GIs.[60] This difference can lead to complications in trade agreements where views differ on how trademarks and GIs should be protected. For instance, the USA protested the effect of Article 4(3) of Regulation No 2006/510 allowing new GIs to be registered even if they are identical or similar to an existing trademark, so long as the coexistence of the new and old would not mislead consumers.[61] The USA felt that this allowance violated Article 16 of TRIPS, and the ensuing Panel Report declared that while prior marks and new GIs could coexist, it "did not allow unqualified coexistence of trademarks and GIs…to broaden the scope of protection actually granted to a GI by using translations that are not covered by the registration as entered into the Commission's registry."[62] In light of an agreement between the UK and the USA, these guidelines would have to be modified to accommodate the national laws of both the UK and the USA concerning spirits, which are regulated in the USA by the USPTO.

There is also the relationship between national law and Community law: unlike 2006/510, 110/2008 does specify that national protection systems can offer parallel protection by enforcing additional, more stringent regulations.[63] In one case concerning protection of a designation for beer, the ECJ held that "no protection on the basis of a bilateral agreement can be claimed for a geographical indication in case that the opportunity has been missed during the available time period to apply for protection under the GI Regulation, although the designation would have qualified for such protection."[64] The disallowance of double protection would be another issue that needs to be addressed. A feasible solution might be that, because the UK would no longer be subject to

---

[59] ANNETTE KUR ET. AL., EUROPEAN INTELLECTUAL PROPERTY LAW: TEXT, CASES AND MATERIALS 349 (2013).

[60] *Id.*

[61] Kur, *supra* note 60 at 347.

[62] Kur, *supra* note 60 at 348.

[63] Kur, *supra* note 60 at 349; *see also* Council Regulation 110/2008, art. 6, 2008 O.J. (L 39), 13.2.2008 (EC).

[64] Kur, *supra* note 60 at 350 (referencing *Budejovicky Budvar v. Ammersin*, [2009] ECR I-7721).

the same rules as it was while an EU Member State, it can create and leverage national laws to bolster the protections offered to Scotch in any new trade agreements.

One other important consideration is the scenario in which Scotland votes to leave the UK and rejoin the EU independently. While a close analysis of the consequences is beyond the scope of this paper, a Scotland departure is not beyond belief given the growing tensions between Scotland and the UK. The 2014 referendum came down to just above 55% stay and just above 44% leave, but at that point, Brexit seemed to be an improbable occurrence. [65] Nicola Sturgeon, Scotland's First Minister, announced that because most of Scotland voted to remain in the EU during the Brexit referendum, Scotland deserved a second chance to vote for independence.[66] In this case, an entirely different set of issues would take place, including the fate of whether Scotch remains with Scotland or goes with the rest of the UK. There would certainly be a great deal of negotiating to be done given the much longer history between Scotland and the rest of the UK versus Scotland and the EU. Despite all these ambiguities, even after Article 50 is triggered and negotiations begin, Scotch is undoubtedly going to maintain its place at the table, both literally and figuratively.

CONCLUSION

As post-Brexit negotiations ramp up, it is clear that the UK will need to consider which of the possibilities is most desirable. In a recent *Telegraph* piece, officials speculated that UK GIs and protected names would remain protected in the European Union "if the commission decisions granting this protection are not repealed."[67] At the time of writing, it is unclear whether or not the UK intends to return the favor: according to the article, there would need to be additional agreements and "a 'new relationship' would have to be drawn up" to include mutual recognition. These EU protections will probably be most valuable to Scotch because of their depth and influence across the continent (compared to WTO protections, which hold water but are not as likely to make a difference day-to-day). The UK should, at a minimum, aim to (1) clarify and fine-tune existing national protections (both on the UK level and the Scotland level) for GIs to ensure that, should it be necessary to re-

---

[65] *Scotland Decides*, BBC News, http://www.bbc.com/news/events/scotland-decides/results.

[66] *Brexit: Nicola Sturgeon says second Scottish independence vote 'highly likely'*, BBC News (Jun. 24, 2016), http://www.bbc.com/news/uk-scotland-scotland-politics-36621030.

[67] Henderson, Barney, *EU 'worried English Champagne will flood into continent after Brexit'*, The Telegraph (Feb 15, 2017 11:16 P.M.), http://www.telegraph.co.uk/news/2017/02/15/eu-worried-english-champagne-will-flood-continent-brexit/

register through the processes defined in 110/2008, it is clear what protections will be available to Scotch, (2) prioritize the preservation of existing protections under EU law by agreeing to a mutual recognition of GIs, particularly spirit drinks, and (3) clearly define what protections they are guaranteed through the WTO and TRIPS once they exit, and if their individual Member State status through the WTO would mean they can retain all protections currently available without modification. By guaranteeing continued protection for highly valuable products like Scotch, the UK may find a smoother path for trade post-Brexit.

PART III:

Cross-Cutting and EU Issues

CHAPTER 15: THE RIGHT OF RESIDENCY OF EU CITIZENS IN THE UK AFTER BREXIT

EVELYN EDERVEEN

INTRODUCTION

The British have voted for Brexit. The UK is preparing itself to leave the European Union; however, does this mean all its nationals must do so too? In addition, since European countries did not vote for Brexit, an even more important question to ask is what will happen to EU nationals who currently live in the UK.

Imagine the hypothetical of the representative Nowak family in the UK. Marek Nowak came to the UK in the summer of 2014 to help a farmer near Canterbury with harvesting strawberries. He decided to stay in the UK and live with his brother who emigrated in 2010. Half a year later his fiancé Ewa finished her education in Poland and decided to move to the UK as well. In January 2015 Ewa gave birth to their child Agnieszka. They now live together in a little apartment in a suburb of London. This is just one example of many; approximately 2.9 million EU citizens live in the UK. The future position of these citizens has now become uncertain.

This paper will examine the legal position that EU nationals as Marek are in. The scope of the paper will be narrowed down to EU nationals who have been living in the UK for longer than one year. After one year, every EU citizen that is exercising his rights regarding free movement of persons becomes eligible to request a registration certificate that proves his position under EU law.[1] Changes to the position of this group of citizens can be even more impactful, especially since these nationals often relied upon EU rights to make life-changing decisions as, for example, the decision to start a family in the UK.

Furthermore, the paper will focus on *the right of residency* of EU nationals who have been living in the EU for longer than a year. Will EU nationals as Marek be allowed to remain in the UK after Brexit? Firstly, to answer this question a closer look should be paid to UK law. It must

---

[1] The Immigration (European Economic Area) Regulations 2006, SI 2006/1003, art. 16, ¶1 (UK); Milieu Ltd. Et al., National Conformity Study: Conformity Study for the United Kingdom Directive 2004/38/EC on the right of citizens of the Union and their family members to move and reside freely within the territory of the Member States (2008), 36, https://200438ecstudy.files.wordpress.com/2013/05/uk_compliance_study_en.pdf.

be established if the UK is free to change the law and take (former EU) rights away from people. It is important to know the exact status of the transposed EU law in the UK legal order to establish how strong the rights generated by this law will be in a post-Brexit situation. Will immediate gaps in the law emerge? Secondly, the future position of the right of residency will be examined. Can the way in which this EU-based right is implemented guarantee a strong post-Brexit position? Lastly, the question remains of how stable the right of residency, regardless of how it has been implemented, would be in a post-Brexit situation. To what extent can EU nationals rely on human rights law and UK law to ensure the protection of this particular right? In this context, it is also important to know how one could use current EU based law in a beneficial way.

Providing certainty to EU nationals who have been living in the UK for longer than a year and who fear for their future right of residency should remain a priority for the UK government.[2] From a human right point of view I believe that making dramatic changes to the right of residency of EU citizens who have been living in the UK for longer than a year could violate the human right of family life of individuals. I furthermore argue that significant changes to the current position of EU citizens who have been living in the UK for longer than a year could and should lead to an interference with the legitimate expectations doctrine of UK law. I therefore believe that EU nationals, including those individuals who are not living in the UK for much longer than a year but still relied on EU rights implemented in the UK legal order to make life changing decisions, should be allowed to stay in the UK under similar rights as before.

I.   THE POSITION OF EU LAW IN THE UK LEGAL ORDER

Since EU nationals who live in the UK cannot (automatically) rely on EU law after Brexit, examining the UK's approach towards EU-law is important. For EU nationals living in the UK, it is important to know if gaps in UK law can emerge and how vulnerable their EU-based rights can become to changes after Brexit.

To start with, an overall examination of the status of transposed EU law in the UK legal order. The UK is, as some other countries in the EU are too, a dualist country.[3] This means that the UK believes EU law

---

[2] The White Paper, *The United Kingdom's exit from and new partnership with the European Union*, HM   GOVERNMENT   (Feb.   2nd   2016),   29 https://www.gov.uk/government/uploads/system/uploads/attachment_data/file/589 191/The_United_Kingdoms_exit_from_and_partnership_with_the_EU_Web.pdf.
[3] Margot Horspool et al., European Union Law 178-187 (Oxford University Press 7th ed. 2012); *See also* Ramses Wessel et. al., Multilevel Regulation and the EU 346 (Brill, 2008)

belongs to a different sphere of law than UK law. While in monist European countries the EU legal order is regarded as supreme to their national system, the UK as a dualist country needs to define its relationship with the EU legal order explicitly.

Defining this relationship has been quite challenging for the UK. Firstly, the EU requires Member States to give direct effect to EU laws that are clear, precise and unconditional.[4] Secondly, EU law must be treated with priority over national laws.[5] It is difficult for the UK to meet these requirements while not losing its dualist view. For the UK, it is impossible to let EU law decide its position in the UK legal system since this would violate Parliament's supremacy. The view that the ECJ had established a higher principle of the supremacy of EU law thus had to be rejected.[6]

To meet the requirements of the EU, the UK Parliament in 1972 adopted the European Communities Act (ECA). Through this act Parliament automatically gives effect to the duties the EU imposes on the Member States in the UK's law.[7] It is a unique act because it allows directly applicable EU law to be a part of the UK legal system without the need of implementation (article 2(1)).[8] The ECA also allows EU law that is not directly applicable to become part of the UK legal order. This can happen through either primary or secondary legislation (article 2(2)).[9] The secondary legislation, Statutory Instruments (SIs), can however, also amend an act of Parliament (primary legislation).[10] Furthermore, courts are obligated to give effect to these ECA-based laws and to interpret them in accordance with the ECJ jurisprudence. Courts can even overturn provisions of primary legislation that conflict with EU law.

The ECA is thus a very special act that determines the UK's relationship with the EU. The UK's Supreme Court found that the ECA makes EU law an independent source of UK law. Because of the ECA, rights and rules that are laid down in EU treaties thus too are an

---

– dualist countries are considered to be: Hungary, Italy, Finland, Denmark, Malta, Sweden, Ireland, Germany and the UK.

[4] Case 26/62, van Gend & Loos, 1963, E.C.R. 1.

[5] Case 6/64, Costa v. Enel, 1964, E.C.R. 585.

[6] EUROPEAN SCRUTINY COMMITTEE, The EU Bill and Parliamentary Sovereignty, 2010, HC 633 – I, ¶2.

[7] Id.

[8] European Communities Act 1972, c. 68 (UK), http://www.legislation.gov.uk/ukpga/1972/68/section/2 (rule 2(1)).

[9] HOUSE OF COMMONS BRIEFING PAPERS, 2010, RP10-62, at 19 (UK).

[10] EUROPEAN SCRUTINY COMMITTEE, The EU Bill and Parliamentary Sovereignty, 2010, HC 633 – I, ¶2; European Communities Act 1972, c. 68 (UK), http://www.legislation.gov.uk/ukpga/1972/68/section/2 (rule 2(2)).

independent source of UK law. Since withdrawal from the EU treaties would be a direct consequence of Brexit, Brexit would cut off a source of UK law. This was one of the core reasons for the court to rule that Parliament had to be involved in triggering Article 50 (the article which starts the process of leaving the EU). [11] Despite this ruling, which shows that EU-based law that became part of the UK's law through the ECA enjoys a quite strong position in the UK legal order, Parliament gave its consent on triggering Article 50.[12] The ECA and the EU-based rights that are applicable in the UK will now become subject to change after Brexit.

It is questionable however, if Brexit will have immediate consequences for EU-based law that has been incorporated through the ECA. Some argue that directly applicable EU law (article 2(1) ECA), which does not require implementation in the UK legal order, will immediately cease to apply.[13] Others think that both Articles 2(1), direct applicable EU law and 2(2), implementation by SIs, first have to be repealed. It has been argued that *all* EU law that became part of UK law because of Article 2(1) and 2(2) will then cease to apply. A repeal would, in this view, take away the legal basis of direct applicable EU law and SIs based EU law. [14] All SIs-based EU law for example, would lose force of law because its legal basis, Article 2(2) would not apply any more. Since acts of Parliament implementing EU law (primary legislation) would not lose their legal basis with a repeal of the ECA, these acts would most likely have to be individually repealed, even after the ECA is repealed.

However, the announced Great Repeal bill, which will repeal the ECA, is likely going to end the discussion mentioned above. SIs-based law and EU-based law that is directly applicable in the UK because of the ECA, will most likely continue to have a legal basis in the UK's legal system after Brexit. The Great Repeal bill will allow Parliament to give EU-based law that became part of the UK legal order through the ECA the status of UK law. From this point the process of repealing, amending

---

[11] Owen Bowcott et. al., *Supreme Court rules that parliament must have vote to trigger article 50*, THE GUARDIAN, Jan 24th, 2017, https://www.theguardian.com/politics/2017/jan/24/supreme-court-brexit-ruling-parliament-vote-article-50.

[12] UK politics, *Brexit: MPs overwhelming back Article 50 bill*, Feb 1st, 2017, http://www.bbc.com/news/uk-politics-38833883.

[13] Rt Hon Sir Richard Aikens et al., *Brexit - amending UK domestic law before withdrawal*, LAWYERS FOR BRITAIN http://www.lawyersforbritain.org/revise-uk-law.shtml (last visited Dec. 20th, 2016).

[14] Catherine Barnard, *The constitutional practicalities of leaving the EU*, KING'S COLLEGE LONDON: Analysis (May 18 2016), http://ukandeu.ac.uk/the-constitutional-practicalities-of-leaving-the-eu/.

and keeping the former EU laws can start. The Great Repeal bill will probably allow more SIs to be made to change current laws.[15] What the exact process of law changing will look like still remains unclear.[16] Teresa May, UK's prime minister, might be following a similar law changing strategy to the one that was explained by lawyers-for-Britain in their article *Amending UK domestic law before withdrawal*. In the article it is suggested to, at the same time as repealing the ECA, draft a new Act that would allow the SIs-based law making system as laid down in section 2(2) ECA, to continue to exist. By adopting such an act, SI-based law would not lose its legal force. The idea is that the SIs system could then be used to gradually and easily unravel the implemented EU law.[17]

The government states that the Great Repeal Bill will: "..enable changes to be made by secondary legislation to the laws that would otherwise not function sensibly once we have left the EU, so that our legal system continues to function correctly outside the EU."[18] The government thus too wants to use secondary legislation, (SIs form the majority of this legislation),[19] to change current EU-based legislation.

This previously mentioned SIs based system of law reform has major implications.[20] The question that comes to my mind when thinking about using SIs to repeal implemented EU law is what the democratic basis to amend/repeal these former EU laws would be. Who would for example determine if an EU-based law could not function sensibly once the UK

---

[15] Ian Dunt, *Don't be fooled: May's big EU law announcement is just admin*, The London School of Economics and Political Science: Brexit Blog (Oct. 3rd 2016) http://blogs.lse.ac.uk/brexit/2016/10/03/dont-be-fooled-mays-big-eu-law-announcement-is-just-admin/.

[16] The White Paper, *The United Kingdom's exit from and new partnership with the European Union*, HM Government (Feb. 2nd 2016), https://www.gov.uk/government/uploads/system/uploads/attachment_data/file/589191/The_United_Kingdoms_exit_from_and_partnership_with_the_EU_Web.pdf.

[17] Alexandra Sims, *What is the Great Repeal Bill? The Brexit law to end all EU laws (that we don't like)*, Independent, Oct. 3rd, 2016, http://www.independent.co.uk/news/uk/politics/great-repeal-bill-brexit-law-eu-law-theresa-may-david-davis-a7343256.html.

[18] The White Paper, *The United Kingdom's exit from and new partnership with the European Union*, HM Government (Feb. 2nd 2016), https://www.gov.uk/government/uploads/system/uploads/attachment_data/file/589191/The_United_Kingdoms_exit_from_and_partnership_with_the_EU_Web.pdf.

[19] Parliamentary business – Bills & legislation, Secondary Legislation, http://www.parliament.uk/business/bills-and-legislation/secondary-legislation/.

[20] Steve Peers, *Who exactly will 'take back control'? Parliament vs executive after Brexit and the 'Great Repeal Bill'*, EU Law Analysis Blog (Oct. 2, 2016), http://eulawanalysis.blogspot.com/2016/10/who-exactly-will-take-back-control.html.

leaves the EU?[21] Changing law without a debate and legislation in Parliament seems undemocratic to me. The UK Parliament had reasons for giving implied consent to EU law. While implementing EU law through SIs has some democratic basis because directives are drafted with the consent of the European Parliament, it is questionable if *repealing/amending* former SIs using SIs would as well.

In addition, the recent ruling of the Supreme Court of the UK shows how important parliamentary involvement is when it comes to changing UK law as a consequence of Brexit.[22] It is therefore questionable if the White Paper on the Great Repeal bill, which will explain the governmental approach in more detail, will continue to support this current idea about the law changing process after Brexit.[23]

The parliamentary vote on the triggering of Article 50 shows that the UK's approach to EU law after Brexit will likely leave the government room for change. It is quite certain that the UK will face a long process of law changing after Brexit. I do not think however, that many gaps in the UK's law would emerge in this period of time since it is unlikely that any proposal that would allow for such gaps would get voted through. [24]

Parliament will likely have an important say about the UK's approach to the different forms of implemented EU law in the near future. A current prediction of this approach, still assuming there is uncertainty about the exact content of the Great Repeal bill, could be that implemented EU law by primary legislation will enjoy a more stable position than implemented EU law by SIs or automatic implementation. Unlike EU law that is implemented using these instruments (which find their legal basis in the ECA), primary legislation exists regardless of the

---

[21] The White Paper, *The United Kingdom's exit from and new partnership with the European Union,* HM   GOVERNMENT   (Feb.   2nd   2016),   10 https://www.gov.uk/government/uploads/system/uploads/attachment_data/file/589 191/The_United_Kingdoms_exit_from_and_partnership_with_the_EU_Web.pdf.

[22] Owen Bowcott et. al., *Supreme Court rules that parliament must have vote to trigger article 50,* THE   GUARDIAN,   Jan   24th,   2017, https://www.theguardian.com/politics/2017/jan/24/supreme-court-brexit-ruling-parliament-vote-article-50.

[23] The White Paper, *The United Kingdom's exit from and new partnership with the European Union,* HM   GOVERNMENT   (Feb.   2nd   2016),   9 https://www.gov.uk/government/uploads/system/uploads/attachment_data/file/589 191/The_United_Kingdoms_exit_from_and_partnership_with_the_EU_Web.pdf.

[24] Ian Johnston, *Brexit loophole? MPs must still vote in order for Britain to leave the EU, say top lawyers,* INDEPENDENT,   June   27th,   2016, http://www.independent.co.uk/news/uk/politics/brexit-loophole-eu-referendum-mps-law-legal-legislation-constitution-a7105181.html.

ECA.[25] UK-based legislation will most likely be the least vulnerable to post-Brexit law reform. It has to be kept in mind however that many domestic legislation is amended by implemented EU law. For example, the British Nationality Act on which some EU nationals may rely, contains UK law and is amended by SIs.[26] The certain future approach towards EU-based law will be determined when the Great Repeal bill will get voted through.

II.   THE IMPLEMENTATION OF THE EU DIRECTIVE ON THE FREE MOVEMENT OF PERSONS IN THE UK LEGAL ORDER

How is the EU right of residency implemented in the UK legal order? Is this right based on primary legislation, SIs or is it based on directly applicable EU law which has not been implemented in the UK legal order? The great bill of repeal will likely transform most SIs-based EU law into UK law but the position of unimplemented EU law is more difficult to predict.

It is clear that the right of residency is laid down in the directive 2004/38/EC on the movements of persons. This directive, since it is related to immigration and nationality law, was one of "reserved matters," which means that it had to be implemented by the Westminster Parliament. Therefore, there are no changes in implementation by the different devolved parliaments.[27] Most of the directive was transposed by the Immigration (European Economic Area) Regulations 2006 which is SIs-based law. Also, provisions in the Immigration Acts 1971/1988, Immigration rules and procedural rules were amended to make UK's law comply with the EU directive.[28] It must be kept in mind that the UK has

---

[25] Charles Brasted, Susan Bright, Christopher Thomas et al., *Brexit: What now?*, HOGAN LOVELL   4-6   (Jul.   29th   2016), http://www.hoganlovellsbrexit.com/ uploads/downloads/11075 CM BREXIT-whatnow INFO E.pdf.

[26]   British   Nationality   act   1981,   c.   61   (UK), http://www.legislation.gov.uk/ukpga/1981/61/pdfs/ukpga 19810061 en.pdf;   The British Nationality (General) (Amendment No. 2) Regulations 2015, SI 2015/681 (UK), http://www.legislation.gov.uk/uksi/2015/681/pdfs/uksi 20150681 en.pdf.

[27]   Devolved   Parliaments   and   Assemblies, http://www.parliament.uk/about/how/role/devolved/; Alan Page, *The implications of EU withdrawal for the devolution settlement* 12 (CULTURE, TOURISM, EUROPE AND EXTERNAL RELATIONS   COMMITTEE) http://www.parliament.scot/General%20Documents/The implications of EU withd rawal for the devolution settlement.pdf.

[28] Milieu Ltd. Et al., National Conformity Study: Conformity Study for the United Kingdom Directive 2004/38/EC on the right of citizens of the Union and their family members to move and reside freely within the territory of the Member States (2008) https://200438ecstudy.files.wordpress.com/2013/05/uk compliance study en.pdf.

not always succeeded in making its law fully in compliance with the EU directive. Generally speaking, the UK has had difficulties with adapting its immigration control law and with changing its policy towards non-EU citizens who are family members of EU citizens. This is important to know since after Brexit SIs-based law as it is effective *currently* will become UK law.

Furthermore, even if the text of the law seems legitimate the EU has pointed out some difficulties in practice with complying with the directive. [29] The UK Border Agency has the power to make most decisions about the Status of EU citizens and their family members. The Secretary of State in addition has some, (in the opinion of the EU sometimes too wide), discretion in decisions about providing residence cards. Also, certain powers in the field of immigration are given to the executive in the name of the Crown. No legislation is needed to, for example, issue, refuse or revoke passports. [30]

Lastly, it has to be pointed out that the UK *succeeded* in setting up its own court systems to ensure that implemented rights under the directive and other rights concerning immigration are respected by executive bodies. Executive decisions taken under immigration law can be appealed outside the ordinary court system, residence and settlement matters can be appealed to the Asylum and Immigration Tribunal and the ordinary courts can function as a safeguard too. This court system will become even more important in the case SIs-based law becomes binding UK law because it means that an existing authority can remain checking UK's compliance with the rules. [31]

Even though the UK might not have implemented the directive in complete conformity, it can be said that the core rights are ensured. The right of residency as stated in the 2004/38 directive is one of these rights. The right of residency for more than three months is formulated as follows:

EU citizens with a valid identity card or passport may: [32]

- Live in another EU country for longer than 3 months subject to certain conditions, depending on their status in the host country. Those who are employed or self-employed do not need to meet any other conditions. Students and other people not working for payment, such as those in retirement, must have

---

[29] *Id.*

[30] *Id.*

[31] *Id.,* at 17.

[32] EU freedom of movement and residence, http://eur-lex.europa.eu/legal-content/EN/TXT/HTML/?uri=URISERV:l33152&from=EN.

sufficient resources for themselves and their family, so as not to be a burden on the host country's social assistance system, and comprehensive sickness insurance cover.

- Have to register with the relevant authorities if living in the country longer than 3 months. Their family members, if not EU nationals, require a residence card valid for 5 years.

- Be entitled to permanent residence if they have lived legally in another EU country for a continuous period of 5 years. This also applies to family members.

The UK has effectively transposed this legislation into its legal system in articles 6 and 14 of the Regulations 2006, except for that citizens of A8 (Czech Republic, Estonia, Hungary, Latvia, Poland, Slovakia, Slovenia) and A2 (Bulgaria, Romania) countries cannot require a proof of their status earlier than after a year of continuous work in the UK.[33]

Nationals who are jobseekers, workers, self-employed persons, self-sufficient persons or students are qualified persons who are entitled to reside in the UK for as long as they remain in the UK.[34] The UK did not choose to make registration certificates obligatory which is why it is important to see if in practise the process of obtaining proof of a certain registration status is also in conformity with EU law. This appears not always to be the case. For example, more documents must be provided in request for a registration certificate than required under the directive. This practise can be burdensome for EU nationals and family members who are applying for this card.[35]

EU citizens who have been living in the UK thus rely, for their right of residency, on the 2006 Regulation that implements the 2004/38 directive. After Brexit, it is likely that this SIs-based right as implemented,

---

[33] Milieu Ltd. Et al., National Conformity Study: Conformity Study for the United Kingdom Directive 2004/38/EC on the right of citizens of the Union and their family members to move and reside freely within the territory of the Member States (2008), 36, https://200438ecstudy.files.wordpress.com/2013/05/uk_compliance_study_en.pdf.

[34] The Immigration (European Economic Area) Regulations 2006, SI 2006/1003, art. 6 jo 14, ¶1 (UK).

[35] Milieu Ltd. Et al., National Conformity Study: Conformity Study for the United Kingdom Directive 2004/38/EC on the right of citizens of the Union and their family members to move and reside freely within the territory of the Member States (2008) https://200438ecstudy.files.wordpress.com/2013/05/uk_compliance_study_en.pdf.

will become domestic law through the Great Repeal bill.[36] SIs-based rights in general, however, can be subject to law reform.[37]

III. THE STRENGTH OF THE RIGHT OF RESIDENCE OF EU NATIONALS LIVING IN THE UK FOR LONGER THAN A YEAR

Although most EU nationals who have been living in the UK for longer than a year rely on the SIs-based right of residency, some might be able to rely on UK law itself after Brexit. Also, differences in the duration of exercising the SIs-based right of residency could possibly lead to a different post-Brexit situation. To see how individuals could ensure themselves a strong post-Brexit position it is thus important to examine the different positions that an EU national could be in after Brexit.

This paper will discuss the following positions of EU citizens living in the UK (it is assumed that they are currently exercising their EU-based rights of free movement of persons):

- European nationals living in the UK for at least 6 years *(potentially eligible to apply for UK citizenship)*

- European nationals living in the UK for longer than 5 years

- European individual living in the UK for less than 5 years.

To start with, the position of EU nationals living in the UK for at least 6 years. In my opinion their position can be the most stable after Brexit, provided that the nationals who meet the requirements apply for British citizenship. When they successfully go through the process of naturalisation, which requires them first to obtain a permanent residence card, they will become British citizens and will have their rights secured under British law after the Brexit.[38] This process however, can be quite burdensome for individuals. The UK's immigration policy, generally speaking, makes it quite difficult for immigrants to receive acknowledgements of their rights according to Jan Doerfel, a British immigration lawyer. For example, while immigrants in the UK must go

---

[36] Theresa May, Prime Minister UK, Conservative Party Conference at The ICC, Birmingham: Britain after Brexit: A Vision of a Global Britain (Oct. 2nd 2016), http://press.conservatives.com/post/151239411635/prime-minister-britain-after-brexit-a-vision-of.

[37] Rt Hon Sir Richard Aikens et al., *Brexit - amending UK domestic law before withdrawal*, LAWYERS FOR BRITAIN http://www.lawyersforbritain.org/revise-uk-law.shtml (last visited Dec. 20th, 2016).

[38] Colin Yeo, *EU nationals must apply for permanent residence card for British nationality applications*, EU FREE MOVEMENT (Aug. 1st 2016), https://www.freemovement.org.uk/eu-nationals-must-apply-for-permanent-residence-card-for-british-nationality-applications/.

through 85 pages in order to request a residence permit, immigrants in Belgium just have to fill out one single page.[39]

In addition, citizens who are considering becoming a British national should in my opinion make sure that they will keep the citizenship of their home country as this allows them to still be an EU citizen. The rights that come with EU citizenship can then still be enjoyed and protected when a citizen reaches the territory of the European Union again.[40] Citizens of the UK would, in the event of a hard Brexit, find themselves in the bad position of losing their EU citizenship. To prevent this from happening some UK residents living in Belgium have already applied for Belgian citizenship.[41] Also, many UK citizens try to apply for Irish citizenship since this is quite easy to acquire.[42] It has to be kept in mind however, that obtaining citizenship can also hold (legal) obligations towards the country of citizenship.[43]

Although the future position of European nationals who have obtained their status of permanent residency is not completely certain, I think their right of residence in a post-Brexit situation is one of the strongest. Firstly, the UK government has stated in the recently published White paper on Brexit that those who have lived lawfully in the UK for 5 years under the 2004/38 directive, will automatically have a permanent right to reside in the UK after Brexit.[44] It is questionable however, if these words, written in the paragraph about the UK's policy before Brexit, also have consequences for the situation after Brexit. Secondly however, it is argued that the right of permanent residency is connected to human rights law and can therefore not be taken from an

---

[39] Tim de Wit, *'Ik voelde me altijd een EU burger in een EU-Land, nu een immigrant'*, NOS NIEUWS, Feb 7th, 2017, http://nos.nl/artikel/2157001-ik-voelde-me-altijd-eu-burger-in-een-eu-land-nu-een-immigrant.html.

[40] Dimitry Kochenov, *EU Citizenship and Withdrawals from the Union: How Inevitable Is the Radical Downgrading of Rights?* 16 (UNIVERSITY OF GRONINGEN FACULTY OF LAW RESEARCH Paper No. 111, 2016), https://papers.ssrn.com/sol3/papers.cfm?abstract_id=2797612.

[41] Need British Citizenship?, https://www.rt.com/uk/348954-brexit-belgian-citizenship-requests/.

[42] Patricia Mindus, *European citizenship after Brexit* 18 (UPPSALA UNIVERSITY, Working Paper, 2016), https://papers.ssrn.com/sol3/papers.cfm?abstract_id=2842500.

[43] *See generally* Matthias Bieri, *Military conscription in Europe: New Relevance* 1-4 (CSS ETH ZURICH, CSS ANALYSES IN SECURITY POLICY No. 180, 2015), http://www.css.ethz.ch/content/dam/ethz/special-interest/gess/cis/center-for-securities-studies/pdfs/CSS-Analyse180-EN.pdf.

[44] The White Paper, *The United Kingdom's exit from and new partnership with the European Union*, HM GOVERNMENT (Feb. 2nd 2016), 30 par. 6.2. https://www.gov.uk/government/uploads/system/uploads/attachment_data/file/589191/The_United_Kingdoms_exit_from_and_partnership_with_the_EU_Web.pdf.

individual.[45] The right to permanent residence can in the opinion of Jean-Claude Piris even be derived from the ECHR.[46] However, it must be kept in mind that the UK did not ratify protocol No. 4 (as it did not ratify protocols No. 7 and 12) and the UK therefore ensures immigrants less human rights protection under the ECHR. In addition, it is still uncertain if the UK will remain part of the European Convention of Human Rights (ECHR) after the elections in 2020. What exact consequences the choice to opt out would have is still unclear. Teresa May has already announced that she wants to transfer the rights that are laid down in the ECHR into UK law. This might imply that the UK, in the case of leaving the ECHR, would aim for a continuity in the level of protection of human rights.[47]

It is clear that the right of family life as ensured in the UK at this time can protect people from changes being made to their right of residency in certain cases. The ECtHR case *Kuric* might indicate that the UK has the obligation under 8 ECHR to regulate the status of applicants with a lawfully established right of residence in the country.[48] The court in *Kuric* states that, "the failure to pass appropriate legislation and to issue permanent residence permits to individual applicants, constitutes an interference with the exercise of the applicant's rights to respect for their private lives, especially in cases of statelessness."[49] It therefore does not rule out that there could be an interference in cases where there is no statelessness. The UK, by taking away the permanent right of residency at once, would impact the personal lives of individuals tremendously. It therefore appears to be the case that the right of residency will become a "frozen" right after Brexit.[50] The UK has to be careful when enacting new legislation in regard to the right of permanent residency to ensure that the legislation respects the right of family life of individuals.

---

[45] Interview by Kate Beaumont with Tim Eicke, QC, UK government, *Could EU citizens living in the UK claim 'acquired rights' if there is a full Brexit?*, (Apr. 11, 2016) https://georgetownlaw.instructure.com/courses/21679/files/779987?module_item_id=461509.

[46] Jean-Claude Piris, *If the UK votes to leave The seven alternatives to EU membership* 12 (CENTRE FOR EUROPEAN REFORM), https://www.cer.org.uk/sites/default/files/pb_piris_brexit_12jan16.pdf.

[47] Will Worley, *Theresa May 'will campaign to leave the European Convention on Human Rights in 2020 election'*, INDEPENDENT, Dec. 29th, 2016, http://independent.co.uk/news/uk/politics/theresa-may-campaign-leave-european-convention-on-human-rights-2020-general-election-brexit-a7499951.html.

[48] Laura van Waas, *Fighting statelessness and discriminatory nationality law in Europe*, 14 EU JOURNAL MIGRATION AND LAW 243, 252-253 (2012) (Explaining the Kuric case), https://pure.uvt.nl/ws/files/1459239/EJML_article.pdf.

[49] Kuric and others v. Slovenia, No. 26828/06, Eur. Ct. H.R., 70-72 (2012).

[50] Patricia Mindus, *European citizenship after Brexit* 13-14 (UPPSALA UNIVERSITY, Working Paper, 2016), https://papers.ssrn.com/sol3/papers.cfm?abstract_id=2842500.

The case *Uner* shows too that a change in the status of residency can lead to an interference with the right of family life; "the totality of social ties between settled migrants and the community in which they are living constitute part of the concept of 'private life' irrespective of whether family ties have been developed."[51] This sentence makes it clear that no family in the traditional sense has to be established in order for the right of family life under 8 ECHR to become applicable. It is this broader perspective on the right of family right that must be taken into account when assessing the impact of removal or refusal to renew a residence permission.

It must be kept in mind that, when assessing if removal would be legitimate, a fair balance has to be struck between the competing interests of the individual and of the community as a whole.[52] In both cases the State enjoys a margin of appreciation. For individuals who, under EU-based law, already obtained a permanent right of residence it is not self-evident that the balance would result in a favourable outcome.

For most individuals who have been living in the UK shorter than 5 years, the fair balance test between their interests and the interests of the government would probably not result in a desirable outcome. Also, it is questionable how much the right of residency of this group would be protected by the right of family life if the UK develops a new policy, which would gradually change the right of residency for people with resident cards.[53] The group of people who will not have a permanent right of residency by 2019 will therefore still be more vulnerable to major changes being made to their position. However, it has still to be examined individually if removal or change in residence status would violate the right of family life.

In contrast, the statement that the right of residency cannot be easily amended seems to be a view that is supported within the domestic legal order of the UK.[54] BBC news cites diplomat and civil servant Mark Sedwill about this issue. He argues that even without specific confirmation from Parliament it can be said that people who have the five-year residence, have in effect had a guarantee in regard to their rights.[55] Also, precedents in the UK show legal implications of changing

---

[51] Cathryn Costello, The Human Rights of Migrants and Refugees in European Law 114 (Oxford University Press, 1st ed. 2016).

[52] Boultif v. Switzerland, No. 54273/00, Eur. Ct. H.R., 48 (2001).

[53] Kuric and others v. Slovenia, No. 26828/06, Eur. Ct. H.R., 70-72 (2012).

[54] Helena Wray, *What would happen to EU nationals living or planning to visit or live in the UK after a UK exit from the EU?*, EU LAW ANALYSIS BLOG (Jul. 17, 2016), http://eulawanalysis.blogspot.com/2014/07/what-would-happen-to-eu-nationals.html.

[55] Interview with Mark Sedwill, Top official at the home office, Government (Jul. 20th, 2016), http://www.bbc.com/news/uk-politics-36849071.

the rights on which people relied.[56] These precedents could indicate that the UK legal order can protect both individuals with a right of permanent residence and individuals who rely only on a registration certificate to their position after Brexit.

The courts argue that there exists a principle in legitimate expectation cases. It is thought of as a legal standard, which cannot be directly deprived from the ECHR. It is interrelated to rights as fair trial and no punishment without law. It is regarded as a principle that is difficult to depart from since a limitation would have to be in accordance with the criteria set out by the ECHR. It thus has to be prescribed by law, have a legitimate aim and be necessary in a democratic society.'[57] The court in the principle case in which this approach is laid down explicitly states that, "The principle that good administration requires public authorities to be held to their promises would be undermined if the law did not insist that any failure or refusal to comply is objectively justified as a proportionate measure in the circumstances."

One of the cases that is especially relevant in this context is a case where the UK government tried to make changes to extensions and settlements criteria of immigrants that were in the UK under the old immigration rule.[58] The court held that part of the immigrants entering under the old scheme only did so because they had a legitimate expectation that if they would meet the criteria, they would be able to stay for longer or even remain in the UK. Since the immigrants who qualified for those rights under the old scheme could fail the new test, applying the new test to everyone would lead to unfairness in individual circumstances. The government in the old scheme did not make clear that the procedures and requirements of the scheme could change. Therefore, the government is under the obligation to respect the rights upon which immigrants that entered under the old scheme relied. The court ruled that in this case it was "unable to see a sufficient public interest which outweighs the unfairness, which I am satisfied the changes visit upon those already admitted under the programme. In the circumstances, I am satisfied that the terms of the original scheme should

---

[56] HSMP Forum Limited v. Secretary of State for the Home Dep. [2008] EWHC 644 (appeal taken from Eng. & Wales) (UK).

[57] Steven Greer, *The exceptions to article 8 to 11 of the European Convention on Human Rights*, 15 COUNCIL OF EUROPE PUBLISHING 5, 9-15 (1997) (Established case law ECtHR on restrictions on human rights), http://www.echr.coe.int/LibraryDocs/DG2/HRFILES/DG2-EN-HRFILES-15(1997).pdf.

[58] HSMP forum limited v. Secretary of the State for the Home Department [2008] EWHC 664 (appeal taken from Eng. & Wales) (UK).

be honoured and that there is no good reason why those already on the scheme shall not enjoy the benefits of it as originally offered to them."

The main reasons for the court to rule as it did is that the government is under an obligation to have a good administration and to be straightforward towards the public. Changing certain rights that one could reasonably rely upon can lead to unfairness and abuse of power. In this case, it was also an important fact that individuals who relied upon the rights of the old scheme would face hardship if their rights would be taken from them. Also, they had to go through much effort to again establish their rights under the new scheme.

For EU citizens who have been living in the UK for longer than a year it is thus wise to rely on UK law apart from relying on international human rights law. The case mentioned above seems relevant in this case because it shows an obligation of the government to ensure the rights upon one could reasonably rely in the context of permanent residency. In this case the immigrants, as the EU nationals in the case of Brexit, expected to receive the right of permanent residency. The question remains if in the case of EU nationals there would be a prevailing public interest for the government to change the rights. Having regard to the hardship EU nationals would have to face if they would have to leave their lives in the UK behind, I think that this would be difficult to argue, especially having regard to the broader approach on this issue expressed by the UK courts.[59]

IV. WHAT CITIZENS SHOULD DO TO CREATE A STABLE POST-BREXIT POSITION[60]

Those citizens who are eligible to become British citizens and would like to go through the process of obtaining citizenship should in my opinion do so now that EU law still applies, especially because the procedures in regard to providing a permanent residence card could change. After becoming a British citizen, individuals would have their post-Brexit right of residency ensured under UK law.

Since the right of permanent residence is perceived as a strongly grounded right in the UK legal order, European citizens who are eligible for this right should also consider applying for a permanent residence

---

[59] Nadarajah and Abdi v Secretary of State for Home Department [2005] EWCA (appeal taken from Eng. & Wales).

[60] *See generally* Jean Lambert, *The rights of EU nationals in the UK*, JEAN LAMBERT LONDON'S GREEN MEP (Nov. 2016), http://www.jeanlambertmep.org.uk/wp-content/uploads/2016/11/FACTSHEET-rights-of-EU-nationals-in-the-UK-FINAL.pdf.

card now that EU law is still applicable in the UK.[61] Because of the nature of the right of residency, both international human rights law and UK law might ensure its protection where UK's law changing system would allow for changes.

However, since international human rights law is likely to give less protection to most individuals who have been living in the UK for a rather short period of time, for those individuals it is wise to rely on the UK law on legitimate expectations. [62] Furthermore, this group should obtain registration certificates. Although this is not obligatory under UK law, it provides a proof for residence in the UK.[63]

CONCLUSION

In my opinion EU nationals who have been living in the UK for longer than a year do not have to fear for immediate changes in their living position. What is likely to happen to their right of residency is as follows.

The Great Repeal bill, if voted through, will make the SIs-based *Regulations 2006*, UK law. It is highly unlikely that the Great Repeal bill would get voted through if gaps in the law could emerge which makes it almost certain that implemented EU law will become UK law.

Since the right of residency is also protected under the human right of family life, an abrupt ending of the right of residency after Brexit will probably lead to an interference with article 8 ECHR. The case *Kuric* points out that the UK government can be under an obligation to adopt a straightforward system in regard to citizens who are vulnerable to changes in their residency position. Their current right of residency must therefore firstly be "frozen" after Brexit and the government should go from there.

However, in a post-Brexit situation, human rights do not prohibit the government from making changes to the position of individuals who have been living in the UK for longer than a year. For each individual case it has to be determined if the rules which could end their right of

---

[61] *Statement: the   status   of   EU   nationals   in   the   UK,* GOV.UK, https://www.gov.uk/government/news/statement-the-status-of-eu-nationals-in-the-uk.
[62] Helena Wray, *What would happen to EU nationals living or planning to visit or live in the UK after a UK exit from the EU?,* EU LAW ANALYSIS BLOG (Jul. 17, 2016), http://eulawanalysis.blogspot.com/2014/07/what-would-happen-to-eu-nationals.html.
[63] OTS Solicitors, http://otssolicitors.co.uk/brexit,-eu-and-eea-applications,-permanent-residence-card-and-appeals; Milieu Ltd. Et al., National Conformity Study: Conformity Study for the United Kingdom Directive 2004/38/EC on the right of citizens of the Union and their family members to move and reside freely within the territory   of   the   Member   States   (2008) https://200438ecstudy.files.wordpress.com/2013/05/uk_compliance_study_en.pdf.

residency in the future are fair. In each case a balance must be struck between the interest of an individual and the community as a whole. While this balance could lead to a desirable outcome for individuals who have been living in the UK for years, it is unlikely that every individual living in the UK for longer than a year would benefit.

It will therefore probably be more safe for individuals to rely on UK law. UK precedents shows that the country acknowledges the principle of "legitimate expectation." The fact that the courts believe that "the principle that good administration requires public authorities to be held to their promises would be undermined if the law did not insist that any failure or refusal to comply is objectively justified as a proportionate measure in the circumstances" shows that there is limited room for the government to make changes to the right of residency of EU nationals who are living in the UK. Although the UK government could say that it was EU law on which nationals relied, I believe that the UK government did not do anything to make the public aware of possible changes being made to their rights.

Parliament, by adopting the ECA, allowed EU law to be implemented/automatically applicable in the UK and nothing showed the public that this approach might change. EU nationals such as Marek often moved to the UK because implemented EU law would eventually give them the right to become a permanent resident of the UK. As in the case between *the Queen on the application of HSMP forum limited* and *secretary of the state for the home department* EU nationals too would face hardship if the right of residency upon which they relied would be taken from them. Also, they would have to go through a lot of procedures to try to ensure this right.

Having regard to all these facts it is clear in my opinion that the government made a promise to EU nationals that were considering coming to the UK. If they would meet certain criteria they would be ensured of a permanent right of residency. Many nationals therefore made a life-changing decision to move to the UK. Therefore, in my view the UK is now responsible to ensure that these individuals will still have the chance to obtain this right under the same conditions as before.

So, I believe that Marek and his family must be allowed to stay in the UK under the current criteria regarding residency. They should still have the chance to fulfil the dream that they had when moving to the UK.

CHAPTER 16: EXPLORING THE POTENTIAL FOR COALESCENCE AND DIVERGENCE IN UK—EU DATA POLICY AFTER BREXIT

SHANNON TOGAWA MERCER

On June 23, 2016, nearly fifty-two percent of the United Kingdom voted to leave the European Union.[1] Overnight, the political and legal machines of an entire continent began to whirr in response to a question few had previously thought to ask: "What now?" To some audiences, the "Brexit" vote was an inevitable act of autonomy, but to many more it was an improbable sea change. Half a year later, some answers exist but few policy makers and legal experts report that the future of UK-EU relations is clear or simple. While it is not the intention of this author to address all, or even the majority, of the legal issues relevant to the United Kingdom's exit from the EU, this paper seeks to clarify the dynamics surrounding one of the more important elements of the coming negotiations: UK-EU data relations.

Pre-dating the 2013 revelations of Edward Snowden, data protection and data privacy have been integral to European conceptions of human rights. The European Continent began the work to clarify and ensure the individual's right to security in her data as early as 1981 and has continued through the European Union's Charter of Fundamental Rights and the European Convention on Human Rights.[2] Simultaneously, commerce, technology and crime have evolved so dramatically that the cross-border transfer of data is indispensable to many industries, including services, and governments.

It follows that consistency, or at least cooperation, in data regimes between the United Kingdom and the EU is integral to the sustenance of commerce and security in the post-Brexit world. This paper aims to clarify the future of data relations between the United Kingdom and the

---

[1] EU REFERENDUM: FINAL RESULTS, BLOOMBERG, https://www.bloomberg.com/graphics/2016-brexit-referendum/ (last visited Feb. 12, 2017).

[2] The Convention for the Protection of Individuals with Regard to Automatic Processing of Personal Data, or Convention 108, guaranteed the individual's right to the protection of personal data. It was adopted by the Council of Europe in 1981. *See* EUROPEAN UNION DATA PROTECTION LEGISLATION, https://secure.edps.europa.eu/EDPSWEB/edps/EDPS/Dataprotection/QA/QA2 (last visited Jan. 16, 2016).

EU and ultimately, to predict and recommend post-Brexit courses of action for the UK Government. In Part I, this paper provides a brief introduction to data security parlance and themes. Part II catalogues current international, European and UK data security law. In Part III, this paper details the data security laws most recently implemented and therefore central to the uncertainty surrounding post-Brexit policy. In light of this uncertainty, Part IV outlines the legal and political options available to the United Kingdom, providing a recommendation for the best option presented. Part V proceeds to briefly detail the costs and contingencies that Brexit introduces into the data security landscape. Ultimately, this paper predicts that the United Kingdom will align its domestic policy with standing EU regulations in an effort to avoid serious disruption to industry and law enforcement efforts. Additionally, it predicts that the United Kingdom will, and should, as part and parcel of larger negotiations, seek a means through which it will have some say in rapidly evolving data protection policy on the continent.

I. WHAT IS DATA SECURITY?

With much of international commerce and law enforcement dependent on the exchange of information between countries, the future of cross-border data protection could implicate millions of dollars for corporations, and national security consequences for countries. As a result, data security is an inestimably important issue in domestic and international political dialogues. This is largely because the conditions surrounding the gathering, aggregation, and dissemination of information about individuals invokes the tension between the individual right to privacy, the collective right of security, and the need for efficient transactions: on one hand, companies and governments need to transfer data about individuals in order to deal with global consumption and global threat; on the other hand, the individual right to privacy is both viscerally felt and legally recognized by many governments.

The individual data exchanged by companies and governments include, but are not limited to, demographic data, criminal information, biological data, health records, location, and internet browsing or purchasing behavior.[3] The United Kingdom's Information Commissioner's Office (ICO) defines personal data as "data which relate to a living individual who can be identified (a) from those data, or; (b) from those data and other information which is in the possession of, or is likely to come into the possession of, the data controller, and includes any

---

[3] *See* INFORMATION COMMISSIONER'S OFFICE, KEY DEFINITIONS OF THE DATA PROTECTION ACT, https://ico.org.uk/for-organisations/guide-to-data-protection/key-definitions/ (last visited Jan. 16, 2016) [hereinafter *DPA Definitions*].

expression of opinion about the individual and any indication of the intentions of the data controller or any other person in respect of the individual." A data processor, according to the EU, is the entity that "processes personal data on behalf of the controller."[4] The UK ICO defines a data processor similarly.[5] A data controller, according to the EU, is "the entity that determines the purposes, conditions and means of the processing of personal data."[6] The UK ICO defines a data controller as, "a person who (either alone or jointly or in common with other persons) determines the purposes for which and the manner in which any personal data are, or are to be, processed."[7]

II. HOW DATA TRANSFERS ARE CURRENTLY REGULATED

A. *INTERNATIONAL LAW AND DATA SECURITY*

There is no binding global regulatory regime for data security.[8] There are, however, guidelines and principles that have been promulgated by some international organizations. The United Nations has addressed the issue in resolution 68/167.[9] Adopted by the General Assembly on December 18, 2013, resolution 68/167 enshrines the right to privacy under Article 12 of the Universal Declaration of Human Rights and Article 17 of the International Covenant on Civil and Political Rights,[10] in the digital age by "affirm[ing] that the same rights that people have offline must also be protected online, including the right to privacy."[11] Resolution 68/167 calls on States to respect and protect this right by implementing domestic procedures, reviewing existing domestic procedures and establishing domestic oversight mechanisms.[12] Notably, nowhere in the resolution does the United Nations call for cross-border

---

[4] EU GENERAL DATA PROTECTION REGULATION, FREQUENTLY ASKED QUESTIONS, http://www.eugdpr.org/gdpr-faqs.html (last visited Jan. 16, 2016) [hereinafter GPDR FAQs].

[5] As "any person (other than an employee of the data controller" who processes the data on behalf of the data controller. *See DPA Definitions, supra* note 3.

[6] *See* GDPR FAQs, *supra* note 4.

[7] *DPA Definitions, supra* note 3.

[8] *See generally* Kriangsak Kittichaisaree & Christopher Kuner, "The Growing Importance of Data Protection in Public International Law," EJIL: TALK!: BLOG OF THE EUROPEAN JOURNAL OF INTERNATIONAL LAW (Oct. 14, 2015), http://www.ejiltalk.org/the-growing-importance-of-data-protection-in-public-international-law/.

[9] *See generally* G.A. Res. 68/167 (Dec. 18, 2013).

[10] *Id.*

[11] *Id.*

[12] *Id.*

cooperation to help safeguard and protect the individuals' right to privacy in the transfer of data between States. The United Nations has also promulgated two resolutions, 55/63 and 56/121, addressing the criminal misuse of information technology.

Additionally, the Organization for Economic Co-operation and Development (OECD) has compiled privacy principles[13] intending that they be used as tools to help "us think about and frame discussions about privacy."[14] The OECD claims that their Privacy Principles synthesize the privacy frameworks most commonly used in "existing and emerging privacy and data protection laws."[15] These principles have much in common with current EU regulations.

B. APPLICABLE EUROPEAN LAW

The EU traces the beginning of its recognition of the protection of personal data through its establishment of the respect for private life via the 1950 adoption of the Council of Europe Convention for the Protection of Human Rights and Fundamental Freedoms.[16] The EU cites the evolution of information and communication technologies in the 1960s and 70s as the impetus for more specific protection of personal data from increased government surveillance ability.[17] What followed was the first acknowledgement of a separate individual right to security in personal data through the 1981 Convention for the Protection of Individuals with regard to Automatic Processing of Personal Data (Convention 108).[18]

Now, the EU Charter of Fundamental Rights encompasses the rights established and defended in the case law of the European Court of Justice (CJEU), the European Convention on Human Rights (ECHR) and other rights common to member states in the EU.[19] In *KU v. Finland*, the European Court of Human Rights has read Article 8 [20] of the

---

[13] OECD PRIVACY PRINCIPLES, http://oecdprivacy.org/ (last visited Jan. 16, 2016).

[14] *Id.*

[15] *Id.*

[16] *See* EUROPEAN UNION DATA PROTECTION LEGISLATION, *supra* note 2.

[17] *Id.*

[18] *Id.*

[19] EUROPEAN COMMISSION, EU CHARTER OF FUNDAMENTAL RIGHTS, http://ec.europa.eu/justice/fundamental-rights/charter/index_en.htm (last visited Jan. 16, 2016).

[20] Article 8 includes the following protections: "(1) Everyone has the right to the protection of personal data concerning him or her; (2) Such data must be processed fairly for specified purposes and on the basis of the consent of the person concerned or some other legitimate basis laid down by law. Everyone has the right of access to data which has been collected concerning him or her, and the right to have it rectified; (3) Compliance with these rules shall be subject to control by an independent authority." EU

European Convention of Human Rights to apply to data privacy. A recent UK House of Commons Briefing Paper confirms this perspective, stating more conclusively that "the right to the protection of personal data is explicitly recognized by Article 8 of the European Union's Charter of Fundamental Rights and by the Lisbon Treaty...[which] provides a legal basis for rules on data protection...under Article 16 of the Treaty of the Functioning of the European Union."[21]

Data privacy in the EU is regulated by the Data Protection Directive 95/46/EC of 1995 (DPD).[22] The DPD was a framework directive which dictated the structure of national privacy laws.[23] The supplemental E-Privacy Directive, 2002/58/EC governs electronic communications.[24] Furthermore, Framework Decision 2009/977/JHA governs the protection of personal data in the context of cooperation in criminal matters.[25] These regulations have offered guidelines for domestic legislation, but neither have created full consistency across states. In 2012, the European Commission proposed reforming the existing legislation for several reasons, namely: (1) to make the legislation more relevant to current technology, and (2) to create data protection rights across Europe.[26] The General Data Protection Regulation and the Directive 2016/680 resulted from this reform effort, and they will be discussed in more detail below.

CHARTER OF FUNDAMENTAL RIGHTS, ARTICLE 8 PROTECTION OF PERSONAL DATA, http://fra.europa.eu/en/charterpedia/article/8-protection-personal-data (last visited Jan. 16. 2016).

[21] United Kingdom Parliament, Brexit and Data Protection, 2016, Commons, 7838, at 4 [hereinafter Brexit and Data Protection Report].

[22] See generally Council Directive 95/46/EC, 1995 O.J. (L 281) 31-50 (EC) [hereinafter The Directive].

[23] W. Scott Blackmer, GDPR: Getting Ready for the New EU General Data Protection Regulation, INFORMATION LAW GROUP (May 5, 2016), http://www.infolawgroup.com/2016/05/articles/gdpr/gdpr-getting-ready-for-the-new-eu-general-data-protection-regulation/.

[24] Id.

[25] See Brexit and Data Protection Report, supra note 21, at 3.

[26] EUROPEAN COMMISSION REFORM OF EU DATA PROTECTION RULES, http://ec.europa.eu/justice/data-protection/reform/index_en.htm (last visited Jan. 16, 2016); see generally EUROPEAN COMMISSION: LEGISLATION, http://ec.europa.eu/justice/data-protection/law/index_en.htm (last visited Jan. 16, 2016) (offering a comprehensive list of European legislation relating to data privacy).

1. Recent European Court of Justice Cases

Several recent cases characterize the EU perspective on data privacy, especially insofar as it may conflict with the United Kingdom's privacy policy inclinations.

In its 2015 decision in *Maximillian Schrems v. Data Protection Commissioner*, the CJEU held, *inter alia*, that "legislation permitting the public authorities to have access on a generalized basis to the content of electronic communications must be regarded as compromising the essence of the fundamental right to respect for private life." [27] Furthermore, the CJEU established that national supervisory authorities may review the level of protection provided by a data recipient country even if that country's system has been deemed adequate by the European Commission. Maximillian Schrems, a citizen of Austria, brought a case with the Irish Data Protection Commissioner, claiming that the laws and practice of the United States do not allow for adequate protection against surveillance of data transferred into America.[28] The *Schrems* decision is most often noted for its invalidation of the U.S.-EU Safe Harbor Agreement, but the case also establishes the EU's right to review a third state's data security policies and foreshadows viable challenges to the UK's treatment of EU data subjects.

More recently, the CJEU held that indiscriminate data retention laws are impermissible under EU privacy legislation.[29] The judgment was addressed to two cases, the first brought by David Davis and Tom Watson in 2014, concerning the UK Investigatory Powers Act's predecessor, the Data Protection and Investigatory Powers Act of 2014 (DRIPA),[30] and the second, a challenge to a Swedish order mandating that a company retain data relating to its users.[31] On DRIPA, the CJEU stated that the law "exceeds the limit of what is strictly necessary and cannot be considered to be justified, within a democratic society."[32] The judgment, however, did not preclude an EU member state from

---

[27] Court of Justice of the European Union Press Release No 177/15, The Court of Justice declares that the Commission's US Safe Harbour Decision is invalid (Oct. 6, 2016).

[28] *Id.*

[29] Andrew Keane Woods, *Implications of the EU's Data Retention Ruling*, LAWFARE BLOG (Dec. 22, 2016), https://www.lawfareblog.com/implications-eus-data-retention-ruling; *see also* Joined Cases C-203/15 and C-698/15, *Tele2Sverige AB and Watson and Others*, 2016, ¶ 107, ECLI:EU:C:2016:970.

[30] *CJEU Judgment in Watson*, INDEPENDENT REVIEWER OF TERRORISM LEGISLATION (Dec. 21, 2016), https://terrorismlegislationreviewer.independent.gov.uk/cjeu-judgment-in-watson/.

[31] Referred to as *Tele2Sverige and Watson and Others*.

[32] Joined Cases C-203/15 and C-698/15, *Tele2Sverige AB and Watson and Others*, 2016, ¶ 107, ECLI:EU:C:2016:970.

"adopting legislation permitting, as a preventative measure, the targeted retention of traffic and location data, for the purpose of fighting serious crime, provided that the retention of data is limited with respect to the categories of data to be retained, the means of communication affected, the persons concerned and the retention period adopted, to what is strictly necessary."[33] The core of this judgment echoes the *Schrems* decision in that the court reasserts that general and indiscriminate data retention is impermissible in the EU.[34]

Given that this decision concerned law enforcement surveillance, there is a very good chance that both corporate and government data transfers will be subject to a high level of scrutiny under the CJEU. Discussed in more detail below, the UK Investigatory Powers Act will be particularly susceptible to challenge and require revision if the UK desires an adequacy determination from the EC.[35]

For a complete list of cases that weigh on the definitions and scope of data privacy and security, the EC has provided an online catalogue accessible at http://ec.europa.eu/justice/data-protection/law/index_en.htm.

C. APPLICABLE LAW IN THE UNITED KINGDOM

The United Kingdom's membership in the EU requires, in most cases, that it incorporate EU law into its domestic regime. This is accomplished under the authority of the European Communities Act of 1972.[36] In the United Kingdom, the EU's DPD is implemented by the Data Protection Act of 1998 (DPA).[37] The Information Commissioner's Office is the arm of the UK government entrusted with upholding information rights in the public interest.[38] Alongside the DPA, the UK's Privacy and Electronic Communications Regulations (PECR) grant specific privacy rights to individuals.[39] The PECR regulate varied sectors such as marketing, the use of cookies or tracking technologies, the security of public electronic communications services and the privacy of

[33] *Id.* ¶ 108.
[34] *Id.* ¶ 97.
[35] Woods, *supra* note 29.
[36] *See generally* European Communities Act, 1972, http://www.legislation.gov.uk/ukpga/1972/68/introduction.
[37] *See* Brexit and Data Protection Report, *supra* note 21, at 3.
[38] *See generally* INFORMATION COMMISSIONER'S OFFICE: WHAT WE DO, https://ico.org.uk/about-the-ico/what-we-do/ (last visited Jan. 16, 2016).
[39] *See* INFORMATION COMMISSIONER'S OFFICE: WHAT ARE PECR?, https://ico.org.uk/for-organisations/guide-to-pecr/introduction/what-are-pecr/ (last visited Jan. 16, 2016).

customers using communications networks regarding location data, billing, identification services, and directories.[40] Both the DPA and the PECR apply simultaneously. In other words, neither supplants the other.[41]

Of all of the current legislation in place in the United Kingdom, the Investigatory Powers Act of 2016 (IPA) has been most frequently cited as a potential wrench in data security relations between the UK and the EU. The IPA, granted royal assent on November 29, 2016, consolidates the powers available to government agencies to aggregate communications, creates an Investigatory Powers Commissioner to oversee how surveillance powers are used, establishes a requirement for judicial approval of interception and other warrants, enables the government to use a range of surveillance tools domestically, and provides for law enforcement's retention of internet connection records.[42] The Guardian has characterized the IPA as granting "the most sweeping surveillance powers in the western world," while the Independent characterizes it as giving the UK's intelligence services "the 'most extreme spying powers ever seen'."[43] Liberty, a civil liberties group, has said that the law is a "beacon for despots everywhere."[44] Edward Snowden tweeted: "The UK has just legalized the most extreme surveillance in the history of western democracy. It goes farther than many autocracies."[45]

Last, the Digital Economy Bill of 2016-17 was proposed to help the UK meet modern digital technology needs through increased connectivity, infrastructure and protection from nuisance communications and inappropriate materials. [46] While not directly

---

[40] *Id.*

[41] *Id.*

[42] Ewen MacAskill, *'Extreme surveillance' becomes UK law with barely a whimper*, THE GUARDIAN (Nov. 1, 2016) https://www.theguardian.com/world/2016/nov/19/extreme-surveillance-becomes-uk-law-with-barely-a-whimper; *see also* UK GOVERNMENT: INVESTIGATORY POWERS ACT https://www.gov.uk/government/collections/investigatory-powers-bill (last visited Jan. 16, 2106).

[43] Andrew Griffin, *Investigatory Powers Bill Officially Passes Into Law, giving Britain the 'most extreme spying powers ever seen'*, INDEPENDENT (Nov. 29, 2016) http://www.independent.co.uk/life-style/gadgets-and-tech/news/investigatory-powers-bill-snoopers-charter-passed-royal-assent-spying-surveillance-a7445276.html (last visited Jan. 16, 2016); *see also* MacAskill, *supra* note 42.

[44] Griffin, *supra* note 43§.

[45] Edward Snowden (@snowden), Twitter (Nov. 17, 2016, 1:59 PM), https://twitter.com/snowden/status/799371508808302596.

[46] UK GOVERNMENT: DIGITAL ECONOMY BILL OVERVIEW, https://www.gov.uk/government/publications/digital-economy-bill-overview (last visited Jan. 16, 2016).

applicable to data protection, debate about the bill has considered its compliance with the GDPR in anticipation of Brexit.[47]

III. FUTURE REGULATION OF DATA TRANSFERS: GDPR AND THE DIRECTIVE

As mentioned above, the General Data Protection Regulation, Reg. 2016/679 (GDPR) and the Directive on data transfers for policing and judicial purposes 2016/680 (the Directive) are new pieces of EU legislation resulting from reform efforts begun in 2012. Both the GDPR and the Directive will most likely come into effect during the process of Brexit negotiations and most likely before the effective date of Brexit.[48] This creates a unique problem: businesses interacting with the United Kingdom will have to comply with the EU regulations in place during the negotiations, but there is uncertainty as to which regime they will find themselves subject after the official Brexit.

The European Council adopted the GDPR and the Directive in April of 2016. The GDPR will repeal and replace the DPD and be directly applicable in all EU member states by May 25, 2018. [49] Additionally, the Directive is currently in force and EU states are obligated to give it effect in national law by May 2018.[50]

The GDPR presents several fundamental changes to current data regulation in the EU. First, the GDPR extends extraterritorially to apply to any companies, within or without the EU, holding individual data (or, controllers) and those using individual data (or, processors) if those controllers and processors are offering goods or services or monitoring behavior of EU data subjects.[51] Second, the GDPR establishes legal obligations for data processors. The processors must maintain a written record of the processing activities of each controller, they must designate a data protection officer (DPO), they must conduct a data impact assessment for risky processing actions, implement data protection monitoring by default and they must notify controllers when there are instances of personal data breaches.[52] Additionally, explicit consent is now required for the processing of sensitive data. The controller has to prove that consent was obtained. Consent must also be as easy to withdraw as it is to give, and the "right to erasure (the right to be

---

[47] *See* Brexit and Data Protection Report, *supra* note 21, at 11.
[48] *Id.*
[49] EUROPEAN COMMISSION REFORM OF EU DATA PROTECTION RULES, *supra* note 24.
[50] *See* Brexit and Data Protection Report, *supra* note 21, at 3.
[51] Allen & Overy LLP, THE EU GENERAL DATA PROTECTION REGULATION (2016) at 3.
[52] *Id.*

forgotten)" requires data controllers to remove content when that consent is withdrawn.[53] The right to be forgotten is enshrined in Article 17. These obligations did not exist uniformly, and certainly not consistently, in the previous state-centric regimes. Lastly, the GDPR establishes the new European Data Protection Board, a new legal entity that will replace the previous Article 29 Working Party in order to "ensure smooth and effective cooperation and consistency between national data protection regulators within the EU," and advising the European Commission on the adequacy of data protection laws.[54]

The Directive is aimed at regulating the security of individuals with regard to transfers of their personal data by government authorities for the purposes of the "prevention, investigation, detection or prosecution of criminal offenses or the execution of criminal penalties, including the safeguarding against and the prevention of threats to public security."[55] The Directive simultaneously enables the cooperation of law enforcement authorities across borders while preventing threats to the security of public information.[56] Another directive, the network and information security (NIS) directive, passed on May 17, 2016, also proposes to increase cooperation among EU member states in order to further cybersecurity efforts.[57] This, along with other cybersecurity legislation, will impact data privacy and will likely be incorporated into any agreement or alignment between the United Kingdom and the EU.[58]

The UK Government has committed to complying with the GDPR, at least in the period between the Brexit referendum and the UK's exit from the EU.[59] The ICO will have to ensure that the requirements of the

---

[53] Daphne Keller, *The Final Draft of Europe's "Right to Be Forgotten Law,"* THE CENTER FOR INTERNET AND SOCIETY STANFORD UNIVERSITY (Dec. 27, 2015), https://cyberlaw.stanford.edu/blog/2015/12/final-draft-europes-right-be-forgotten-law.

[54] Andrew Kimble & Peter Given, *Brexit, the "great repeal bill" and data protection law*, LEXOLOGY (Jan. 9, 2017) http://www.lexology.com/library/detail.aspx?g=a33cff97-0f03-4601-b51d-41fea88944d0.

[55] Council Directive 2016/690, 2016 O.J. (L 119) (EC) at ¶ 11.

[56] *Id.*

[57] European Commission Statement/14/68, Great News For Cybersecurity in the EU, the EP Successfully Votes Through the Network & Information Security (NIS) Directive (Mar. 13, 2014).

[58] *See generally* European Council Press Release IP/251/16, EU-wide Cybersecurity Rules Adopted by the Council, (May 17, 2016), http://www.consilium.europa.eu/en/press/press-releases/2016/05/17-wide-cybersecurity-rule-adopted/. For more information, *see* EU DIGITAL SINGLE MARKET https://ec.europa.eu/digital-single-market/en/cybersecurity (last visited Jan. 16, 2016).

[59] Elizabeth Denham, UK Information Commissioner, Speech: Transparency, Trust and Progressive Data Protection (Sept. 29, 2016), https://ico.org.uk/about-the-ico/news-and-events/news-and-blogs/2016/09/transparency-trust-and-progressive-data-

GDPR and the Directive are complied with in the interregnum period.[60] That duty includes shepherding businesses through the process of GDPR compliance and foreshadowing the requirements that may come with the UK's eventual exit.[61]

IV. BREXIT'S IMPACT ON DATA SECURITY REGULATION: THE UK'S OPTIONS

The UK Government has said that it plans to "make sure that [it] achieve[s] a coherent data protection regime and that data flows with the EU are not interrupted after [the UK] leave[s]."[62] The United Kingdom and the EU are unlikely to have finished Brexit negotiations by May 2018, the date of implementation for the GDPR and the Directive.[63] Therefore, the GDPR will necessarily apply to companies from the date of implementation until the official exit of the United Kingdom from the European Union and the United Kingdom has confirmed its intention to comply with the GDPR before that date.[64]

It is the period after Brexit that is a veritable data protection minefield for the United Kingdom. The United Kingdom has not been transparent about any specific policy intentions beyond intending to ensure uninterrupted data flows after Brexit. The ICO has indicated a likelihood that the United Kingdom will adjust domestic legislation to align with GDPR requirements.[65] But, as of the submission of this Paper, neither the UK nor the EU negotiator have expressed official negotiating positions on this topic. Given the dearth of information, this Paper proceeds to detail the United Kingdom's options for future data relations with the European Union: (1) distinguishing itself from the EU through disparate policy; (2) maintaining the GDPR through membership in the EEA; (3) obtaining an adequacy judgment from the European Commission; or (4) negotiating a bespoke agreement similar to the EU-U.S. Privacy Shield.

---

protection/ [hereinafter Denham Speech]; *see also* Dr. Philip Trillmich, *UK to Implement GDPR Regardless of Brexit* , CEO (Jan. 6, 2017) http://www.thecsuite.co.uk/ceo/information-technology-ceo/uk-to-implement-gdpr-regardless-of-brexit/.

[60] *See* Brexit and Data Protection Report, *supra* note 21, at 10.
[61] *Id.*
[62] *Id.* at 3.
[63] *Id.* at 10.
[64] *Id.* at 3.
[65] *Id.* at 10.

A. OPTION 1: DISTINGUISHING ITSELF FROM THE EU THROUGH DISPARATE POLICY

If the United Kingdom is unwilling or unable to adopt sufficiently protective policies similar to the GDPR it may, as a strategic choice, decide to adopt more liberal data security policies such that its businesses and law enforcement capabilities are at a distinct advantage in the global market. In other words, the United Kingdom would position itself as a more attractive market for other countries and corporations that are unwilling to take on the additional transaction costs imposed by heavy EU regulation.

This scenario is the least likely, and perhaps least beneficial, choice of those listed in this paper given the intimate ties between UK and EU businesses. While the EU is more commercially reliant on US tech companies, if there is disruption to UK data flows to the EU, British economic interests will be severely harmed.[66] In 2015, the United Kingdom exported £223 billion, or 43.7%, of its total exports in goods and services to the EU.[67] Especially reliant on data transfers, trade in services with the EU accounted for nearly £100 billion of UK exports in 2015, and UK imports in services fell just below that mark.[68] These numbers are by no means dispositive. In fact, estimates of trade volumes and projected GDP fall everywhere along the spectrum,[69] but the scenario suggested here would result in a dramatically decreased volume of data transfers between the UK and the EU—a risk the UK is unlikely to take.

As Elizabeth Denham, ICO Commissioner, said in her first speech concerning the GDPR and Brexit, "The fact is, no matter what the future legal relationship between the UK and Europe, personal information will need to flow. It is fundamental to the digital economy. In a global economy we need consistency of law and standards—the GDPR is a strong law, and once we are out of Europe, we will still need to be deemed adequate or essentially equivalent."[70] Anthony Walker, deputy CEO of techUK, an organization representing the technology industry in the UK, echoed that sentiment: "The UK's service-based economy

---

[66] Emily Taylor, *'Brexit' Could Put Data Sharing in Jeopardy*, CHATHAM HOUSE: THE ROYAL INSTITUTE OF INTERNATIONAL AFFAIRS (Mar. 10, 2016), https://www.chathamhouse.org/expert/comment/brexit-could-put-data-sharing-jeopardy#.

[67] United Kingdom Parliament: Economic Policy and Statistics Section, In brief: UK-EU Economic Relations, 2016, Commons 06091, at 5 [hereinafter UK-EU Economic Relations Report].

[68] *Id.* at 6.

[69] *See generally id.*

[70] Denham Speech, *supra* note 57.

means that the transfer of data across borders is fundamental, affecting industries from automotives…to financial services."[71]

Assuming that a full departure from the EU's standards is unlikely given the economic necessity of data flows, the models below present options for continued cooperation with the EU.

B. OPTION 2: MAINTAINING THE GDPR THROUGH MEMBERSHIP IN THE EEA

If the United Kingdom remains a member of the European Economic Area (EEA) but leaves the EU, it may be able to remain party to the GDPR without any bespoke data transfer agreement.[72] Established by the 1992 EEA Agreement, the EEA is a group that enables the non-EU countries of Iceland, Liechtenstein and Norway to partake in the EU single market.[73] While the EEA countries enjoy the four freedoms, the EEA agreement does not address the EU common agriculture and fisheries policy, customs union, the common trade policy, the common foreign and security policy, justice and home affairs, taxation and the economic and monetary union.[74]

The EEA is in the process of adopting the GDPR.[75] At least one analysis claims that the United Kingdom would be required to retain the DPA if it stays in the EEA.[76]

There are, however, several economic and political factors that render this outcome unlikely. While most of those factors are beyond the scope of this paper, the probability of this outcome merits brief discussion. The likelihood that the UK will remain in the EEA, and thus remain under the purview of the GDPR, is diminished by (1) the EU's four freedoms enshrined in the EEA Agreement[77] and (2) Theresa May's

---

[71] Justina Crabtree, *Data flows post-Brexit: The next big headache for business?*, CNBC (July 7, 2016), http://www.cnbc.com/2016/07/07/data-flows-post-brexit-the-next-big-headache-for-business.html.

[72] Brexit and Data Transfers to the UK, PIERSTONE (June 2016), https://pierstone.com/brexit-and-data-transfers-to-the-uk/.

[73] Countries in the EU and EEA, UNITED KINGDOM GOVERNMENT (Feb. 23, 2017), https://www.gov.uk/eu-eea; *see also* EUROPEAN FREE TRADE ASSOCIATION: THE BASIC FEATURES OF THE EEA AGREEMENT, http://www.efta.int/eea/eea-agreement/eea-basic-features (last visited Feb. 24, 2017).

[74] THE BASIC FEATURES OF THE EEA AGREEMENT, *supra* note 73.

[75] Brexit and Data Transfers to the UK, *supra* note 72.

[76] *Alert Memorandum: Some reflections on: Brexit and the U.K. Data Protection Regime*, CLEARY GOTTLIEB (Aug. 15, 2016) at 2 [hereinafter Cleary Report].

[77] EUROPEAN FREE TRADE ASSOCIATION: EEA AGREEMENT, http://www.efta.int/eea/eea-agreement (last visited Jan. 16, 2016).

reported intention to announce a "hard Brexit" on Tuesday, January 16, 2017. First, the vote to leave the EU was, in some respects, motivated by the dislike of the EU-mandated freedom of movement. Remaining bound to the four freedoms is antithetical to the current UK negotiating position. Second, as of the date of the submission of this Paper, it is reported that Theresa May will address ambassadors and high commissioners on Tuesday, January 16, 2017, announcing plans for a "hard" Brexit, characterized by a withdrawal from the single market and the European customs union.[78] If made, this announcement will cement the UK's intention to exit the EEA.

C. OPTION 3: OBTAINING AN ADEQUACY JUDGMENT FROM THE EUROPEAN COMMISSION

Considering the low likelihood that the UK remains in the EEA, the next option would be for the UK to obtain an adequacy judgment from the European Commission (EC). The Great Repeal Bill, a bill proposed by Theresa May's Government to remove the European Communities Act of 1972 and thus unwind EU legislation from UK domestic law, will immediately remove any domestic implementation of the GDPR and other data security regulations. Upon the moment of repeal and the official exit from the EU, the United Kingdom becomes a third party state with the option to implement laws that are disparate from EU policy.

Should the United Kingdom want to maintain data flows between the EU and UK businesses and law enforcement, the United Kingdom will want to obtain an "adequacy decision" from the EC. Under the GDPR, Articles 44 and 45, cross-border data transfers to a third country may take place without further approvals or safeguards if that country or territory receives an "adequacy decision" from the EC.[79]

The process of obtaining an adequacy decision from the European Commission requires that the commission employ the "comitology procedure"[80]: first, the Commission puts forward a proposal regarding the adequacy of a nation's data protection policy; then, the Article 29 Working Party issues an opinion on that proposal; next, the Article 31

---

[78] James Masters, *Brexit: Theresa May to Unveil Plan for 'Global Britain,'* CNN (Jan. 16, 2017), http://www.cnn.com/2017/01/15/europe/brexit-uk-theresa-may/.

[79] Commission Regulation 9565/15, 2015 Art. 44, 45; *see also* Brexit and Data Protection Report, *supra* note 21, at 6.

[80] Comitology encompasses a set of procedures through which Member States might control the implementation of EU law. *See* COMITOLOGY IN BRIEF, EUROPEAN COMMISSION, http://ec.europa.eu/transparency/regcomitology/index.cfm?do=implementing.home (last visited Feb. 12, 2017).

Committee[81] delivers an opinion on behalf of a "qualified majority" of Member States; and last, the College of Commissioners adopts the decision.[82] In its determination of adequacy, the EC may consider the following factors present in the subject nation's data protection regime: "the rule of law… legal protections for human rights and fundamental freedoms; access to transferred data by public authorities; existence and effective functioning of [Data Protection Authorities]; and international commitments and other obligations in relation to the protection of personal data."[83] Thus far, the European Commission has determined that Andorra, Argentina, Canada, the Faroe Islands, Guernsey, Israel, the Isle of Man, Jersey, New Zealand, Switzerland and Uruguay provide adequate levels of protection to qualify for this exception.[84] Once deemed "adequate," a country may receive personal data from EU nations and the three European Economic Area nations of Norway, Liechtenstein and Iceland, without any further safeguards or approvals.[85]

As the ICO's Denham has indicated, "the aim [of a data protection regime in the UK] is a progressive regulatory regime that stands up to scrutiny, that doesn't leave the UK open to having rocks thrown at it by other regimes. And that has consistency and adequacy with the Europe [sic]."[86] In order for the United Kingdom to be deemed "adequate" the European Commission must determine that it offers an "equivalent level of data protection."[87] If the UK is deemed adequate, it is additionally likely that the EU will insist that the UK establish an agreement with the United States equivalent to the EU-US Privacy Shield such that

[81] The Article 31 Committee, established under the authority of Article 31, Directive 95/46/EC, is made of representatives from Member States who are in place to approve of policies or decisions when the Directive requires. *See* https://secure.edps.europa.eu/EDPSWEB/edps/site/mySite/pid/71 (last visited Feb. 12, 2017).

[82] *Id.*

[83] Detlv Gabel & Tim Hickman, *Chapter 13: Cross-Border Data Transfers Unlocking the EU General Data Protection Regulation*, WHITE & CASE (Jul. 22, 2016), http://www.whitecase.com/publications/article/chapter-13-cross-border-data-transfers-unlocking-eu-general-data-protection (summarizing the General Data Protection Regulation).

[84] COMMISSION DECISIONS ON THE ADEQUACY OF THE PROTECTION OF PERSONAL DATA IN THIRD COUNTRIES, EUROPEAN COMMISSION, http://ec.europa.eu/justice/data-protection/international-transfers/adequacy/index_en.htm (last visited Feb. 12, 2017).

[85] *Id.*

[86] Denham Speech, *supra* note 57.

[87] *See* Brexit and Data Protection Report, *supra* note 21, at 11.

companies may not circumvent the EU-US Privacy Shield by transferring data to the US via the UK[88]

There is reason to think that the EC will find that the United Kingdom does not provide an adequate level of protection for EU subjects whose data may be transferred.[89] First, after the CJEU's 2015 decision in *Schrems*, detailed above, it is clear that the EC is likely to consider a regime that allows mass surveillance and data retention to be inadequate.[90] Daniel Zeichner, a Member of Parliament, commented on December 12, 2016 echoing common sentiments about the IPA,

> [the UK] would be a third country and could be required to come to what is termed an 'adequacy decision' with the EU to allow data to flow freely between the United Kingdom and EU member states and to enable trade with the single market on equal terms…A number of commentators fear that the recent Investigatory Powers Act means that the Commission may take some convincing. The risk is that such negotiations could take years to resolve, leaving protections for UK citizens in the meantime weak, as well as hugely disadvantaging the crucial tech sector, one of [the UK's] great success stories…[91]

If the UK seeks and obtains an adequacy decision, the adequacy of its data protection regime will be under review at least every four years under the GDPR.[92] As was mentioned above, the CJEU has already rendered the British Data Protection and Investigatory Powers Act of 2014 (DRIPA) unjustified, exceeding what is necessary in a democratic society. If the CJEU determines any other domestic UK laws to be similarly expansive and unjustified, the EC may repeal, amend, or suspend an adequacy decision if it determines, in turn, that the jurisdiction in question has not continued to provide an adequate level of data protection in accordance with the GDPR and any policy or legal developments.[93] This policy makes maintenance of the adequacy judgment, and the stability of business expectations as a result, a moving target. In order to inject some stability or predictability into data relations between the EU and the UK, the UK may benefit from negotiating

---

[88] Cleary Report, *supra* note 76, at 6.
[89] *See* Brexit and Data Protection Report, *supra* note 21, at 11.
[90] See generally Case C-362/14, Maximillian Schrems v. Data Protection Commissioner, 2015 ECLI:EU:C:2015:627; *see also* Cleary Report, *supra* note 76, at 4-5.
[91] *See* Brexit and Data Protection Report, *supra* note 21, at 11; *see also* Cleary Report, *supra* note 76, at 5.
[92] Gabel & Hickman, *supra* note 83.
[93] *Id.*

involvement in the process of data policy reform. Given the efficiency of adequacy judgments, this is an attractive option. In order to be deemed adequate, the United Kingdom will likely have to commit to reform its domestic policies to meet EU standards.

D. OPTION 4: NEGOTIATING A BESPOKE AGREEMENT

If the UK decides against modifying domestic law in order to achieve an adequacy judgment, the last option available is to negotiate a separate data sharing agreement similar to the EU-US Privacy Shield. The EU-US Privacy Shield Framework is a mechanism providing companies in both regions comply with the data protection requirements of the European Union and Switzerland when data is transferred to the United States.[94] Failing an adequacy decision, the UK government is left with the option of designing and negotiating a bespoke agreement, either as a part of a larger trade agreement or free-standing, that would facilitate data sharing and imbue UK companies with the responsibility to comply with EU data standards. This agreement will have to comply with standards likely to be upheld by the EC as indicated in *Schrems*.[95]

That said, an agreement setting out separate standards from domestic regulation will require United Kingdom businesses comply with two separate frameworks.[96] Furthermore, while a bespoke arrangement appears to be the most flexible option, the time it takes to negotiate an agreement such as this may impose too long a period of uncertainty for UK industry. Safe Harbor, the initial US-EU agreement, took around five years to negotiate.[97] Its successor, the EU-US Privacy

---

[94] PRIVACY SHIELD FRAMEWORK, https://www.privacyshield.gov/welcome (last visited Jan. 16, 2016).

[95] Compliance with these standards under a bespoke agreement will require that companies shoulder strong obligations to protect the personal data of EU citizens and that local agencies, such as the United States Department of Commerce and the Federal Trade Commission, monitor and enforce these protections. The EU described Privacy Shield as an arrangement that "includes commitments by the U.S. that possibilities under U.S. law for public authorities to access personal data transferred under the new arrangement will be subject to clear conditions, limitations and oversight, preventing generalised access." This also included a complaint process routed through an ombudsperson. European Commission Press Release No 16/216, EU Commission and United States agree on new framework for transatlantic data flows: EU-US Privacy Shield (Oct. 6, 2016).

[96] Cleary Report, *supra* note 76, at 6.

[97] MARIN A. WEISS & KRISTIN ARCHICK, CONG. RESEARCH SERV., R44257, U.S.-EU Data Privacy: From Safe Harbor to Privacy Shield 5 (2016) [hereinafter CRS US-EU Data Privacy Report].

Shield Framework, took a little over two years to negotiate.[98] An adequacy judgment may be a more efficient option, although the amount of time it will take to modify domestic law is also a variable. The long-term benefit of a tailored agreement could prove more valuable than the short-term advantage of quick certainty.

Ultimately, the two most plausible solutions are to obtain an adequacy decision or to negotiate a separate data security agreement. There remains uncertainty about the net impact of the extraterritoriality of the GDPR. Should the CJEU aggressively adjudicate instances in which non-EU companies are held accountable to GDPR standards for EU data subjects, the UK may be strong-armed into aggregate corporate compliance. Thus, a government-level solution may prove more efficient for commerce.

This paper predicts and recommends, that the United Kingdom seek an adequacy decision from the European Commission after adjustments to domestic legislation. The adequacy decision will be more efficient and, in many ways, more flexible than a bespoke agreement. First, adequacy decisions are reviewable and domestic legislation is likely more easily amended than an international treaty. Second, the benefits of commercial certainty during the next few years will help, in part, stabilize an otherwise tumultuous economic period for the United Kingdom. Pursuing this option will not preclude the UK and the EU from beginning negotiations for a bespoke agreement in the future. The UK and the EU only benefit from making clear to businesses and law enforcement agencies the rules to which they must adhere before the impact of the larger Brexit hits in full force in 2019. To this end, the United Kingdom should also seek a mechanism through which it stays involved or at least adequately notified of data security policy changes within the EU. This could take many forms and it may be one of many tasks accomplished by a larger cooperation mechanism devised for post-Brexit relations.

V. CONSEQUENCES OF BREXIT FOR INDUSTRY AND SECURITY

Before concluding this analysis, the general consequences of Brexit on industry and security merit some mention. If the UK withdraws from the EU and fails to achieve an adequacy judgment or negotiate an agreement, UK companies will have to turn to other means of guaranteeing continued business. Some of these mechanisms might include: model contract clauses designed by the European Commission to ensure that the data of EU nationals transferred to non-adequate countries is protected; internal corporate rules based on EU data

---

[98] *Id.* at 8-10.

standards that will assist in inter-company data transfers; obtaining explicit consent, in a way compliant with GDPR standards, from the individuals whose data will be transferred; taking advantage of any certification programs developed by the European Data Protection Board; or taking advantage of self-regulatory industry codes of conduct.[99]

Furthermore, even with an adequacy judgment but without membership or incorporation into the GDPR, UK businesses will not have access to the single supervisory body, the European Data Protection Board, established to help regulate the GDPR.[100] In order to resolve disputes or to raise complaints, UK businesses will have to approach each member state's supervisory authority separately.[101] In addition, UK businesses may face parallel investigations launched by UK authorities and EU authorities; and to the extent that UK and EU standards differ, UK businesses will have to fully comply with two disparate data regulatory regimes.[102]

Lastly, the GDPR requires data controllers who are located outside of the EU to hire representatives in the EU.[103] The representative must be located in the EU member state where the data subjects are located.[104]

As the consequences articulated above suggest, the burden on UK businesses to address this change, both through negotiation and accessing administrative entities, will be large.

The National Security implications of the Directive are less frequently discussed in the public domain. Prior to the Brexit vote, the former heads of MI6 and MI5, Sir John Sawers and Jonathan Evans, commented that "the reason [the UK] would be less safe is that [the UK] would be unable to take part in decisions that frame that sharing of data, which is crucial to counter-terrorism work."[105]

Finally, a re-tooling of the UK-EU relationship may also require renegotiation of agreements with third-parties, especially the United States. The UK should consider negotiating its own equivalents to EU-

---

[99] Kenneth Dort, *Post-Brexit Data Security Considerations*, BLOOMBERG LAW: PRIVACY & DATA SECURITY (Dec. 14, 2016), https://www.bna.com/postbrexit-data-security-n73014448544/.

[100] Cleary Report, *supra* note 76, at 5.

[101] *Id.*

[102] *Id.*

[103] *Id.; see also* THE EU GENERAL DATA PROTECTION REGULATION, *supra* note 51, at 3.

[104] Cleary Report, *supra* note 76, at 5.

[105] Kim Sengupta, *What does Brexit mean for Trident intelligence and national security?*, INDEPENDENT (July 3, 2016), http://www.independent.co.uk/news/uk/home-news/brexit-trident-nato-eu-what-it-means-mi5-mi6-national-security-terrorism-a7116706.html.

US agreements, namely Privacy Shield and the law enforcement equivalent found in the EU-US "Umbrella Agreement," which similarly aims to facilitate law enforcement interaction while also protecting personal data. [106] A corollary agreement, or agreements, to maintain its relationship with the United States may be preferable if not required.[107] In fact, if UK domestic policy skews toward less restrictive data security rules, the EU may insist on a special agreement safeguarding the circumvention of Privacy Shield and Umbrella Agreement through transfers to the United States via the United Kingdom. The fact that the UK will remain a member of the international intelligence collaboration group, "Five Eyes," composed of Australia, Canada, New Zealand, United Kingdom, and the United States may temper the need for dramatic relationship changes between the United States and the United Kingdom. [108] Other agreements include the Passenger Name Record Agreement and the Terrorist Finance Tracking Program. While it is beyond the scope of this paper to explore each of these agreements in detail, even this short list of required reevaluations should suggest that the process of aligning UK and the EU data privacy regulations will be a complex one, involving a number of second and third order consequences, regardless of the efficiency gained in the adequacy decision model.

CONCLUSION

The importance of achieving some level of certainty about the future of data relations between the United Kingdom and European Union is only outweighed by the necessity, for businesses and for individual rights, of establishing the right kind of relationship after Brexit. As this paper has demonstrated, the path to the best answer is obscured by options and potential negotiation preferences. With no clear positions yet articulated by either the UK or EU negotiators, this paper attempts to catalogue the various options and recommend the most preferable by building off of the current framework and extrapolating articulated priorities and past agreements. Ultimately, this paper asserts that the United Kingdom will likely, and likely should, seek an adequacy decision

---

[106] *See EU, US sign 'Umbrella Agreement' on data protection*, EURACTIVE.COM (Jun. 2, 2016), https://www.euractiv.com/section/digital/news/eu-us-sign-umbrella-agreement-on-data-protection/.

[107] There are significant questions about U.S. national security raised by the shift in data security norms between the EU and the UK While those are beyond the scope of this paper, they are incredibly important and merit further research.

[108] Margaret Warner, *An Exclusive Club; The 5 Countries That Don't Spy on Each Other*, PBS (Oct. 25, 2013), http://www.pbs.org/newshour/rundown/an-exclusive-club-the-five-countries-that-dont-spy-on-each-other/.

from the European Commission and look for further incorporation in EU data privacy policy decisions moving forward. That said, if Brexit has taught us anything, there is no way to predict the tides of negotiation in such volatile domestic and international political climates. With Brexit negotiations beginning only two months from the drafting of this paper, and with recent rumors about the May government's "hard" Brexit intentions, we can anticipate a better understanding of the UK's negotiating positions shortly. Until then, the best that legal scholars can do is to aggregate what exists of the law in order to better inform those molding our legal future.

CHAPTER 17: BREXIT AND LEGITIMATE EXPECTATIONS: A CASE FOR FOREIGN INVESTORS?

AYMAR CLARET DE FLEURIEU

INTRODUCTION

At last. Winter is coming (to an end) and the end of March with it. Article 50 of the Treaty on the European Union[1] will be invoked on 29 March and Brexit will officially start. After months of speculation and interrogations, Prime Minister Theresa May confirmed in her long-awaited speech that Her Majesty's Government will seek a "hard Brexit": leaving the Single Market and the Customs Union, and securing a bespoke agreement for a new partnership with the European Union.[2] The subsequent White Paper published by the UK Government in early February has clarified its goals and priorities for negotiating with and leaving the EU.[3] This defining issue will have consequences for an incredibly diverse range of areas, from the most important (what will be the UK/EU future trade relationship?) to the most unlikely (will working permit restrictions on the Premier League allow Liverpool FC to finally win a new title?). In between, the world of arbitration will also be impacted and may very well offer new opportunities.

Because of the extensive scope of foreign direct investments in the UK, UK's trade and investment commitments will be shaken by the legal repercussions of Brexit. The UK is the host of more than 45,000 foreign affiliates. Although they represent less than 2% of the total number of firms in the UK, they play a major role in the UK economy. In 2010, they employed at least three million workers, accounting for more than

---

[1] Consolidated version of the Treaty on European Union article 50, 2010 O.J. C 83/01 [hereinafter TEU], http://eur-lex.europa.eu/resource.html?uri=cellar:2bf140bf-a3f8-4ab2-b506-fd71826e6da6.0023.02/DOC_1&format=PDF. The TEU is the amended and consolidated version of the Treaty of Maastricht, effective since November 1, 1993. See also: The Guardian, UK to trigger article 50 on 29 March, but faces delay on start of talks (March 20, 2017), https://www.theguardian.com/politics/2017/mar/20/theresa-may-to-trigger-article-50-on-29-march.

[2] *The government's negotiating objectives for exiting the EU: PM speech* (January 17, 2017), https://www.gov.uk/government/speeches/the-governments-negotiating-objectives-for-exiting-the-eu-pm-speech.

[3] *The United Kingdom's exit from and new partnership with the European Union White Paper* (UK Government, February 2, 2017), https://www.gov.uk/government/publications/the-united-kingdoms-exit-from-and-new-partnership-with-the-european-union-white-paper.

13% of the workforce employed and contributed to at least 36% of the total turnover in the UK.[4] Leaving the Single Market and the Customs Union will invariably frustrate investors' expectations to benefit from the UK membership in the EU. In such context, the challenge lies in the UK's obligation to foreign investors to maintain a stable regulatory framework. International investment law indeed provides that a host State's regulatory framework may give rise to foreign investors' legitimate expectations. As shown by investment tribunals' case law, a subsequent modification of this framework may very well frustrate foreign investors' legitimate expectations and constitute a violation of the fair and equitable treatment standard pursuant to bilateral investment treaties (BITs).

This issue is of particular relevance with regard to the UK's decision to withdraw from the EU. The EU's investment policy is focused on providing investors and investments with market access and legal certainty as well as a stable, predictable, fair and properly regulated environment in which to conduct their business.[5] The UK's 44-year membership in the EU has aimed precisely at offering such legal and business guarantees to UK-based foreign investors. Withdrawing from the EU will require the UK to adopt new trade and investment policies. At the end of the Article 50 two-year negotiation period, the UK will either have found a bespoke agreement with the EU or reverted to World Trade Organization (WTO) rules, which set tariffs on exports to the EU. In that case, every sector would be hit by tariffs, with duties increasing as much as 36% for the food and agricultural industries and 43% for the tobacco industry. Probably no industry though would be impacted as much as the car manufacturing sector, because of its paramount importance in the UK export value. Withdrawing from the EU would result in a 10% tariff imposed on cars exported from the UK to the EU and its free trade network, and would undoubtedly frustrate carmakers' legitimate expectations to export duty-free when they decided to invest in the UK. All in all, the resulting change in the UK's general regulatory framework could be so severe and radical as to constitute a violation of the fair and equitable treatment standard by frustrating foreign investors' legitimate expectations. Put into perspective, this could eventually trigger a chain of claims brought against the UK Government, similar to the

---

[4] *How attractive is the UK for future manufacturing foreign direct investment?*, Government Office for Science (October 2013), p. 5, https://www.gov.uk/government/uploads/system/uploads/attachment_data/file/277171/ep7-foreign-direct-investment-trends-manufacturing.pdf.

[5] See: European Commission, Trade, http://ec.europa.eu/trade/policy/accessing-markets/investment/.

voluminous arbitration saga that followed Argentina's measures to face
the economic crisis in the early 2000s.

This paper assesses whether the UK's decision to leave the EU
Single Market and Customs Union could frustrate foreign investors'
legitimate expectations in violation of the UK's fair and equitable
treatment obligations. We begin with overviews of the doctrine of
legitimate expectations in international investment arbitration (Section I)
and the UK's regulatory framework (Section II). Only then (Section III)
can the scope of the consequences of Brexit over foreign investors'
legitimate expectations be studied, before reaching (Section IV) the
conclusion that does not inevitably provide for a definitive answer.

I. LEGITIMATE   EXPECTATIONS   IN   INTERNATIONAL
INVESTMENT ARBITRATION

Ever since the Treaty of Rome and the creation of a Customs Union
in 1957, the European Union has been attractive to foreign investors.
Free trade amongst its members was one of the founding principles of
the EU, and the integration of 27 countries has made it one of the most
preferred destinations for investment. Today, the EU is the world's
biggest trader accounting for 20% of global imports and exports. The
UK benefited greatly from this integration and became a major recipient
of foreign direct investment: in 2014, the UK had the third highest stock
of inward FDI in the world, just behind the United States and China.[6]
The many advantages provided to investors in the UK through the EU's
trade framework have raised standards of expectations. EU treaties and
UK BITs now offer investors unique protection, both on economic and
legal grounds. In such context, the concept of legitimate expectations
arises to encompass UK's legal obligations to foreign investors. Indeed,
the issue pertaining to (A) the doctrine of legitimate expectations lies in
the delicate balance that needs to be found between (B) the host State's
obligation to maintain a stable regulatory framework and (C) its
sovereign right to regulate.

A. THE DOCTRINE OF LEGITIMATE EXPECTATIONS

The doctrine of legitimate expectations constitutes a subcategory of
the broad "fair and equitable treatment" standard (FET), and is even
viewed by some to constitute an independent ground for a FET claim.[7]

---

6 UK   Trade   and   Investment,   *Inward   Investment   Report   2014/15*,   p.   4.
https://www.gov.uk/government/uploads/system/uploads/attachment_data/file/435
646/UKTI-Inward-Investment-Report-2014-to-2015.pdf.
7 See: *International Thunderbird Gaming Corporation v. United Mexican States*,
NAFTA/UNCITRAL, Award, Separate Opinion of Thomas Wälde (December 2005),

Almost all investment treaties require host States to accord fair and equitable treatment to investors of the other contracting State: it is the treaty standard most frequently invoked before investment tribunals and the one most frequently found to be breached.[8] Fair and equitable treatment is an unclear and imprecise standard of protection. Its elements have been progressively expanded and the scope of the standard gradually developed.[9] International arbitral tribunals have nevertheless identified the protection of investors' legitimate expectations as the "dominant element"[10] and the "most important function"[11] of the FET standard.

Although it has drawn criticism—especially as to its legal basis—the doctrine of legitimate expectations is today firmly rooted in investment arbitration, and has often been upheld by tribunals for more than a decade. As exposed by Michele Potestà, the first tribunal to clearly spell out that FET encompasses protection of investors' expectations was the one in *Tecmed v. Mexico*, which considered that the FET provision in the Spain-Mexico BIT "require[d] the Contracting Parties to provide to international investments treatment that does not affect the basic

---

para. 37: "One can observe over the last years a significant growth in the role and scope of the legitimate expectation principle, from an earlier function as a subsidiary interpretative principle to reinforce a particular interpretative approach chosen, to its current role as a self-standing subcategory and independent basis for a claim under the 'fair and equitable standard.'"

[8] *Redfern and Hunter on International Arbitration* (Sixth Edition), Blackaby, Partasides, et al. (2015), p. 489, para. 8.96. See also: *PSEG Global Inc. v. Republic of Turkey*, ICSID Case No. ARB/02/5, Award (January 19, 2007), para. 238: "The standard of fair and equitable treatment has acquired prominence in investment arbitration as a consequence of the fact that other standards traditionally provided by international law might not in the circumstances of each case be entirely appropriate."

[9] *Enron Corporation Ponderosa Assets, L.P. v. Argentine Republic*, ICSID Case No. ARB/01/03, Award (May 22, 2007), para. 257.

[10] *Saluka Investments BV (The Netherlands) v. Czech Republic*, UNCITRAL, Partial Award (March 17, 2006), para. 302 ; *El Paso Energy International Company v. The Argentine Republic*, ICSID Case No. ARB/03/15, Award (October 31, 2011), para. 348: "There is an overwhelming trend to consider the touchstone of fair and equitable treatment to be found in the legitimate and reasonable expectations of the Parties, which derive from the obligation of good faith." See also: R. Dolzer, C. Schreuer, *Principles of International Investment Law* (Oxford University Press, 2012), 145 ; M. Jacob, S. W. Schill, *Fair and Equitable Treatment: Content, Practice, Method* in International Investment Law, M. Bungenberg, J. Griebel, S. Hobe, A. Reinisch (C.H. Beck, Hart, Nomos, 2015), pp. 700-770, 724 (55).

[11] *Electrabel SA v. Hungary*, ICSID Case No. ARB/07/19, Decision on Jurisdiction, Applicable Law and Liability (November 30, 2012), para. 7.75.

expectations that were taken into account by the foreign investor to make the investment."[12] According to the tribunal:

> [t]he foreign investor expects the host State to act in a consistent manner, free from ambiguity and totally transparently in its relations with the foreign investor, so that it may know beforehand any and all rules and regulations that will govern its investments, as well as the goals of the relevant policies and administrative practices or directives, to be able to plan its investment and comply with such regulations. (…) The foreign investor also expects the host State to act consistently, i.e. without arbitrarily revoking any preexisting decisions or permits issued by the State that were relied upon by the investor to assume its commitments as well as to plan and launch its commercial and business activities.[13]

Similarly, the tribunal in *International Thunderbird v. Mexico* explained that "the concept of 'legitimate expectations' relates to (…) a situation where a Contracting Party's conduct creates reasonable and justifiable expectations on the part of an investor (or investment) to act on reliance on said conduct, such that a failure by the [State] to honour those expectations could cause the investor (or the investment) to suffer damages."[14]

Professor Rudolf Dolzer identifies five elements that determine whether the FET standard will protect the expectations of an investor in a given case: (i) the objective conduct of the host State inducing legitimate expectations on the part of the foreign investor, (ii) reliance on that conduct on the part of the foreign investor, (iii) frustration of the investor's expectation by subsequent conduct of the host State, (iv) unilateralism of conduct of the host State, i.e., absence of meaningful communication and/or consent with investors, and (v) damages for the investor.[15]

In particular, three types of State conduct have been identified to trigger legitimate expectations: contractual arrangements, formal or

---

12 *Técnicas Medioambientales Tecmed, SA v. United Mexican States*, ICSID Case No. ARB(AF)/00/2, Award (May 29, 2003), para. 154. See: M. Potestà, *Legitimate Expectations in Investment Treaty Law: Understanding the Roots and the Limits of a Controversial Concept*, ICSID Review (Spring 2013), 28 (1): 88-122, 99.

13 *Tecmed v. Mexico, supra* n. 12, para. 154 (emphasis added).

14 *International Thunderbird Gaming Corporation v. The United Mexican States*, NAFTA/UNCITRAL, Award (January 26, 2006), para. 147.

15 R. Dolzer, *Fair and Equitable Treatment: Today's Contours*, 12 Santa Clara J. Int'l L. 7 (2014), p. 20.

informal representations, and the general regulatory framework in force in the host State at the time of the investment. The two former refer respectively to commitments undertaken by the host State towards the investor in their establishment of a contractual relationship, and to promises or representations made by the host State on which the investor relied to make his investment. Due to their very own nature, such factual considerations can only be fully asserted in the context of legitimate expectations by adopting a case-by-case approach, which would require investigating each investor individually. With regard to Brexit, this means as many different cases as there would be claims brought by foreign investors against the UK Government. Furthermore, many obstacles could hinder such investigations (e.g., the confidentiality of contractual negotiations, promises and representations made by both parties). This involves too much uncertainty for this legal study. *Au contraire*, the purpose of this article is to rely on the current state of law to provide a possible answer to the question of how a legal claim could be brought by foreign investors against the UK. To this end, the UK's obligation to foreign investors to maintain a stable regulatory framework seems most relevant in the light of its decision to leave the EU. Specific commitments and representations may then be used as supplements to characterize a FET violation by reference to foreign investors' legitimate expectations, but won't be treated in this article.

B. THE OBLIGATION TO MAINTAIN A STABLE REGULATORY FRAMEWORK

Regulatory framework is what Brexit is all about. As long as the UK is an EU Member State, it remains subjected to EU Treaties and law, i.e., an attractive regulatory framework for investors since 1973. However, the perspective of reverting to the WTO rules and tariff framework is preoccupying. Investors are therefore looking with great interest to know whether this new framework will match the expectations they have developed under the current EU state of law.

Investors can indeed claim that they relied on expectations purely based on the regulatory framework in force at the time of their investment, and that these expectations were frustrated as a result of its subsequent alteration by the host State.[16] This argument has enjoyed a certain fortune in the investment treaty context.[17] To grant such claims,

---

[16] *Total v. Argentine Republic*, ICSID Case No. ARB/04/01, Decision on Liability (December 27, 2010), para. 122: "In such instances, investor's expectations are rooted in regulation of a normative and administrative nature that is not specifically addressed to the relevant investor."

[17] Potestà, *supra* n. 12, p. 112.

arbitral tribunals have justified that protection offered to investors under the FET standard includes an obligation for the host State to maintain a stable and predictable investment environment. As held by the *LG&E v. Argentina* tribunal, "[t]he stability of the legal and business framework in the State party is an essential element in the standard of what is fair and equitable treatment. As such, the Tribunal considers this interpretation to be an emerging standard of fair and equitable treatment in international law."[18] Similarly, the tribunal in *Occidental v. Ecuador* also ruled that "there is certainly an obligation not to alter the legal and business environment in which the investment has been made."[19] The rationale of this obligation is to prevent host States from arbitrarily altering their applicable rules, thus frustrating investors' expectations to rely on the regulatory framework in force at the time of their investment, and ultimately damaging the value of their investment. As buttressed by the *Alpha v. Ukraine* tribunal, "the obligation not to upset an investor's legitimate expectations and the obligation to avoid arbitrary government action (…) means, in part, that governments must avoid arbitrarily changing the rules of the game in a manner that undermines the legitimate expectations of (…) an investor".[20]

Pursuant to this line of case law, the treatment of an investor's investment thus revolves around the stability and predictability of the laws of the host State. From here, it is easy to see how this issue may regard Brexit. As will be further developed, the UK is a party to more than a hundred BITs. Resorting to the FET standard in this context thus draws the parallel with Argentina in the early 2000s. This seems all the more relevant since BITs are intended to contribute towards stability: the FET standard, with its focus on legitimate expectations, appropriately reflects the connection between the flow of investments and legal stability.[21] Additionally, the Energy Charter Treaty—the most frequently

---

[18] *LG&E Energy Corporation and ors v. Argentine Republic*, ICSID Case No. ARB/02/01, Decision on Liability (October 3, 2006), para. 125. See also: *Occidental Exploration and Production Company v. The Republic of Ecuador*, LCIA Case No. UN3467, Final Award (July 1, 2004), para. 183; *CMS Gas Transmission Company v. Argentine Republic*, ICSID Case No. ARB/01/08, Award (May 12, 2005), para. 274 ("there can be no doubt (…) that a stable legal and business environment is an essential element of fair and equitable treatment") ; *Enron v. Argentina, supra* n. 9, para. 260 ; *Suez and ors v. The Argentine Republic*, ICSID Case No. ARB/03/19, Decision on Liability (July 30, 2010), para. 226.

[19] *Occidental v. Ecuador, supra* n. 18, para. 191.

[20] *Alpha Projektholding GMBH v. Ukraine*, ICSID Case No. ARB/07/06, Award (November 8, 2010), para. 420.

[21] Dolzer, *supra* n. 15, p. 23.

invoked international investment agreement in 2016[22], to which the UK is a contracting party since 1994 along with 27 of its BIT partners— expressly recognizes an obligation for the host State to provide for legal stability.[23]

However, the necessity to protect investors against any regulatory change is not absolute. The legal stability requirement does not require that the host State's legal system remain "frozen in time."[24] As was emphasized by a second line of cases, the host State's obligation to maintain a stable regulatory framework must be balanced against its inherent sovereign power to regulate.

C. THE HOST STATE'S RIGHT TO REGULATE

International law recognizes the autonomous right of a State to regulate in the interests of domestic public policy.[25] This is precisely where the investor's legitimate expectations face another prime interest: that of the host State. Indeed, what is at stake here is the balance to be established between the investor's interest to operate in a reliable and predictable legal environment and the State's prerogative to regulate domestic matters in the public interest.[26]

While the first line of jurisprudence tended to narrow the host State's ability to modify its regulatory framework, investment tribunals subsequently rejected the notion that such framework should remain unchanged and asserted instead the host State's prerogative to regulate over the investor's right to invoke a stable framework. In *Saluka v. Czech Republic*, the tribunal thus considered that "no investor may reasonably expect that the circumstances prevailing at the time the investment is made remain totally unchanged" and that "[i]n order to determine

---

[22]   UNCTAD,   *ISDS   Navigator   update*   (February   8,   2017): http://investmentpolicyhub.unctad.org/News/Hub/Home/537.
[23] Energy Charter Treaty (ECT), 2080 UNTS 95; 34 ILM 360 (1995), Article 10(1). The ECT was signed on December 17, 1994 and entered into force on April 16, 1998. The UK is a Contracting Party along with 27 of its BITs partners (Albania, Armenia, Azerbaijan, Belarus, Bosnia and Herzegovina, Bulgaria, Croatia, Czech Republic, Estonia, Georgia, Hungary, Kazakhstan, Kyrgyzstan, Latvia, Lithuania, Malta, Moldova, Mongolia, Poland, Romania, Russian Federation, Slovakia, Slovenia, Turkey, Turkmenistan, Ukraine, Uzbekistan).
[24] Redfern and Hunter, *supra* n. 8, para. 8.102.
[25] See: T. J. Grierson-Weiler, I. Laird, *Part II Substantive Issues, Ch.8 Standards of Treatment* in The Oxford Handbook of International Investment Law in Muchlinski, Ortino, Schreuer (Oxford University press, 2015), pp. 200-304, 273.
[26] F. Dupuy, P-M. Dupuy, *What to Expect from Legitimate Expectations? A Critical Appraisal and Look Into the Future of the "Legitimate Expectations" Doctrine* in International Investment Law in Nassib G. Ziadé (ed), Festschrift Ahmed Sadek El-Kosheri (Kluwer Law International 2015), pp. 273-298, 291.

whether frustration of the foreign investor's expectation was justified and reasonable, the host State's legitimate right subsequently to regulate domestic matters in the public interest must be taken into consideration as well."[27] The tribunal in *Parkerings v. Lithuania* additionally stressed that the investor will have a right to protection of its legitimate expectation "provided it exercised due diligence," which it interpreted to require an investor "to anticipate that the circumstances could change, and thus structure its investment in order to adapt it to the potential changes of legal environment."[28] In the context of Article 10(1) of the ECT, the *AES Summit Generation* tribunal also noted that "a legal framework is by definition subject to change" and that a "[host] State has the sovereign right to exercise its powers which include legislative acts."[29] The tribunal in *Saluka* nevertheless added that the host State's conduct in using such power "does not manifestly violate the requirements of consistency, transparency, even-handedness and non-discrimination."[30] This point was particularly emphasized in *Lemire v. Ukraine*, where the tribunal held that the investor could legitimately expect that "the administrative measures [taken by the host State] would not be inequitable, unfair, arbitrary or discriminatory."[31]

A balance must thus be established between investors' and States' interests. As a sovereign nation, the host State has the right to adjust its regulatory framework to reflect changes of time and public interest, but it must do so in a reasonable and equitable manner so as not to affect negatively investors' investments, otherwise compensation will be required from the host State. Put simply, the host State's power to regulate operates within the limits of rights conferred upon the investor.[32] Such balance is difficult to establish and the scope of interests at stake constitutes an even greater and more delicate challenge for tribunals. The general issue of the relationship between legitimate expectations under the FET rule and the host State's right to regulate

---

[27] *Saluka Investments v. Czech Republic, supra* n. 10, para. 305.

[28] *Parkerings-Compagniet AS v. Republic of Lithuania*, ICSID Case No. ARB/05/08, Award (September 11, 2007), para. 333. The tribunal also recalled that "[a]s a matter of fact, any businessman or investor knows that laws will evolve over time" (para. 332).

[29] *AES Summit Generation Limited and AES-Tisza Erömö Kft. v. Republic of Hungary*, ICSID Case No. ARB/07/22, Award (September 23, 2010), para. 9.3.29.

[30] *Saluka Investments v. Czech republic, supra* n. 10, para. 307.

[31] *Joseph Charles Lemire v. Ukraine*, ICSID Case No. ARB/06/18, Decision on Jurisdiction and Liability (January 14, 2010), para. 267. See also: *Parkerings v. Lithuania, supra* n. 28, para. 332: "[w]hat is prohibited however is for a State to act unfairly, unreasonably or inequitably in the exercise of its legislative power."

[32] Dolzer, *supra* n. 15, p. 21.

was nonetheless properly addressed by the tribunal in *ADC v. Hungary*, whose reasoning deserves full quotation:[33]

> The Tribunal cannot accept the Respondent's position that the actions taken by it against the Claimants were merely an exercise of its rights under international law to regulate its domestic economic and legal affairs. It is the Tribunal's understanding of the basic international law principles that while a sovereign State possesses the inherent right to regulate its domestic affairs, the exercise of such right is not unlimited and must have its boundaries. As rightly pointed out by the Claimants, the rule of law, which includes treaty obligations, provides such boundaries. Therefore, when a State enters into a bilateral investment treaty like the one in this case, it becomes bound by it and the investment protection obligations it undertook therein must be honoured rather than be ignored by a later argument of the State's right to regulate.
>
> The related point made by the Respondent that by investing in a host State, the investor assumes the "risk" associated with the State's regulatory regime is equally unacceptable to the Tribunal. It is one thing to say that an investor shall conduct its business in compliance with the host State's domestic laws and regulations. It is quite another to imply that the investor must also be ready to accept whatever the host State decides to do to it. In the present case, had the Claimants ever envisaged the risk of any possible depriving measures, the Tribunal believes that they took that risk with the legitimate and reasonable expectation that they would receive fair treatment and just compensation and not otherwise.[34]

In this context, foreign investors wishing to bring an FET claim against the UK will face a difficult—but not undefeatable—counterargument: that it was the UK's sovereign right to hold a referendum and implement the will of its people by withdrawing from the EU and the Single Market. The will of the sovereign people of the UK, expressed through the democratic means of a referendum, would justify the UK Government's decision to abandon the Single Market and hence change

---

[33] *Ibid.* p. 29.
[34] *ADC Affiliate Ltd. v. The Republic of Hungary*, ICSID Case No. ARB/03/16, Award of the Tribunal (October 2, 2006), paras. 423-424 (emphasis added).

its regulatory framework to the detriment of foreign investors. However, and as will be developed in Section III, a too critical level of alteration may cause extensive damages to investors and weigh the balance in their favour.

In the meantime, legal and binding instruments relied upon to invoke the FET standard must be reviewed. The invocation of legitimate expectations by foreign investors is indeed only relevant where a specific regulatory framework triggered specific expectations and detrimental reliance. As such, it is necessary to turn to the study of the network of the UK's trade treaties that today constitutes its investment regulatory framework.

II. THE UK'S REGULATORY FRAMEWORK

Built over its 44-years membership of the EU, the UK's regulatory framework constitutes the very incentive that attracted foreign investors. The business and legal guarantees it offers, based upon the EU Single Market and Customs Union, provide unique advantages and protections for foreign investments. Their regulation is therefore paramount, and explains why foreign direct investment became an exclusive competence of the EU rather than of States (A). The UK nevertheless retains the right to conclude international investments agreements, which allowed it to develop one of the world's greatest network of BITs (B).

A. EU'S EXCLUSIVE COMPETENCE OVER FOREIGN DIRECT INVESTMENT

As generally understood, foreign direct investment (FDI) consists in making capital available from one country for carrying out an activity in another country, with a view to exercising a form of control, most commonly by either buying a company in the target country or expanding an investment in an existing company in that country.[35] Since the 2009 Treaty of Lisbon, FDI is part of the EU's Commercial Policy (CPP). The EU has exclusive competence over the CPP, i.e., only the EU has the power to act and legislate in this domain—not Member States (unless they are empowered by the EU or they implement EU acts within their own legal system). Pursuant to Article 3(1)(e) TFEU, competence to regulate FDI was therefore conferred onto the EU, and is now embodied in Articles 206 and 207 TFEU.[36] As explained by the UK Government,

---

[35] See: European Commission, Trade, http://ec.europa.eu/trade/policy/accessing-markets/investment/.

[36] Consolidated version of the Treaty on the Functioning of the European Union, 2008 O.J. C 115 [hereinafter TFEU], http://eur-lex.europa.eu/legal-content/EN/TXT/PDF/?uri=CELEX:12012E/TXT&from=EN. The TFEU is the

the expansion of the CCP to cover FDI was intended to address the potentially distorting effect of the web of different Member State investment protection agreements on investment in the Single Market and to offer harmonized standards of protection for foreign investors in the EU.[37] The EU's investment policy is focused on providing EU investors and investments with market access and legal certainty and a stable, predictable, fair and properly regulated environment in which to conduct their business. As such, the EU has started negotiating investment rules in the context of free trade agreements (FTAs) with third countries as well as stand-alone investment agreements, which include investment protection provisions. The EU has signed 71 international investment agreements, the most recent one being the Comprehensive Trade and Economic Agreement signed with Canada on October 30, 2016 and ratified by the European Parliament on February 15, 2017.[38]

Nevertheless, this European comprehensive investment policy has been introduced progressively, so the EU has adopted measures that permit the UK and other Member States to maintain its existing BITs with third countries (i.e., non-EU States) in the meantime. Regulation 1219/2012 was hence adopted to grant legal security to Member States' almost 1200 existing BITs with third countries until they are replaced by EU-wide investment agreements.[39] To this end, the Regulation allows for the "grandfathering"[40] of existing BITs, thus declaring them temporarily valid under EU law: pursuant to its Article 3, "bilateral investment agreements (…) may be maintained in force, or enter in force, in

---

amended and consolidated version of the Treaty of Rome, effective since 1958. Along with the TEU, it is one of the two principal treaties on which the EU is based.

[37] *Review of the Balance of Competences between the United Kingdom and the European Union: Trade and Investment*, February 2014, para. 2.8. https://www.gov.uk/government/uploads/system/uploads/attachment_data/file/279 322/bis 14 591 balance of competences review Trade and investment governmen t response to the call for evidence.pdf.

[38] For a list of the EU's international investment agreements see: http://ec.europa.eu/trade/policy/accessing-markets/investment/. For an overview of the EU's FTA and other trade negotiations, see: http://trade.ec.europa.eu/doclib/docs/2006/december/tradoc 118238.pdf.

[39] Regulation (EU) No 1219/2012 of the European Parliament and of the Council of December 12, 2012 establishing transitional agreements for bilateral investment agreements between Member States and third countries: http://eur-lex.europa.eu/LexUriServ/LexUriServ.do?uri=OJ:L:2012:351:0040:0046:EN:PDF.

[40] A "grandfather clause" is a "[p]rovision in a new law or regulation exempting those already in or part of the existing system which is being regulated": *Black's Law Dictionary* (5th edition, 1979), p. 629.

accordance with the TFEU and this Regulation, until a bilateral investment agreement between the [European] Union and the same third country enters into force." In its preamble, the Regulation also "notably allow[s] Member States to address any incompatibilities between their investment agreement and [EU] law."[41] However, many voices have risen against Regulation 1219/2012, which is considered to be the prime legislative instrument in the European Commission's quest to control Member States' BIT arrangements. Indeed, one effect of the Regulation is that the UK, while it remains a Member State, cannot engage negotiations on investment agreements unless authorized by the Commission (Article 9(1)). Even then, the Commission retains the right to withdraw its authorization if, most notably, the opening of such negotiations would "constitute a serious obstacle to the negotiation or conclusion of bilateral investment agreements with third countries by the [EU]" (Article 9(1)(a)). This means that during the Article 50 two-year period, the UK would be prevented from entering into investment agreement negotiations with those States with which the EU has already negotiated or is currently negotiating an investment agreement (including Canada, China, Japan, and the United States). Further, it has recently been reported that the EU may consider legal action against the UK should the latter proceed with negotiations with third States.[42]

But in the context of Brexit, it is the UK's existing network of investment treaties rather than its obligations to the EU that constitutes the legal ground upon which foreign investors should base their FET claims. Indeed, the UK is party to more than a hundred BITs that form today its investment regulatory framework upon which foreign investors relied to make their investment.

B. *THE UK'S BIT NETWORK*

The UK currently maintains the fourth largest BIT network in the world with 106 BITs signed with foreign States since 1975,[43] 96 of which are in force.[44] 12 BITs are in force between the UK and other EU

---

[41] Regulation 1219/2012, *supra* n. 39, Preamble, para. 12.
[42] M. Burgstaller, A. Zarowna, *Why Brexit May Be Good for UK Investors Abroad*, Kluwer Arbitration Blog (October 24, 2016): http://kluwerarbitrationblog.com/2016/10/24/brexit-may-good-uk-investors-abroad/?_ga=1.130805386.466162870.1480371150.
[43] Germany ranks first (135 BITs), followed by China (129) and Switzerland (114). The UK is also party to 67 Treaties with Investment Provisions (TIPs), including notable multilateral agreements such as the Energy Charter Treaty and the EU-Canada CETA. Source: http://investmentpolicyhub.unctad.org/IIA (last access: March 15, 2017).
[44] BITs signed with Angola (signed on 04/07/2000), Brazil (19/07/1994), Costa Rica (07/09/1982), Ethiopia (19/11/2009), Kuwait (08/10/2009), Libya (23/12/2009),

Member States,[45] all but one (Malta) are former countries from the Eastern Bloc and all of them joined the EU in 2004 or thereafter. These BITs between the UK and other EU Member States are referred to as "intra-EU BITs," in contrast with the remaining 84 BITs in force between the UK and non-EU Member States ("extra-EU BITs"). 12 of these extra-EU BITs have nevertheless been signed with European countries (non-EU Member States),[46] including three of the five candidates to EU accession.[47]

As of 2017, UK's investment treaties have been invoked in 68 known investment arbitration cases involving the UK.[48] The vast majority were brought under a UK BIT, but an increasing number of cases have arisen with respect to the Energy Charter Treaty.[49] Interestingly, the UK was named as the respondent State in only one case.[50] Unlike States such as Argentina or Venezuela—who have appeared in a vast number of investment arbitration cases as the respondent State rather than the investor's home State[51]—this reflects the status of the UK as a developed country. As will be discussed in Section III, such consideration is important to the extent that legitimate expectations created through a State's general regulatory framework are greater in developed countries.

However extensive, this regulatory framework is not immune to the impact of Brexit. The uncertainty generated by the UK's decision to leave the EU has—to a lesser extent than other impacted sectors—spread to investment arbitration. Whilst it is generally believed that London's

---

Qatar (18/09/2009), Vanuatu (22/12/2003), Zambia (27/11/2009) and Zimbabwe (01/03/1995) have not yet entered into force.

[45] Bulgaria, Croatia, Czech Republic, Estonia, Hungary, Latvia, Lithuania, Malta, Poland, Romania, Slovakia and Slovenia.

[46] Albania, Armenia, Azerbaijan, Belarus, Bosnia and Herzegovina, Georgia, Kazakhstan, Moldova, Russia, Serbia and Turkey, Ukraine.

[47] Albania, Serbia and Turkey.

[48]   UNCTAD,   *Investment   Dispute   Settlement   Navigator* http://investmentpolicyhub.unctad.org/ISDS/CountryCases/221?partyRole=1   (last access: March 15, 2017).

[49] *Ibid.*: 55 investment arbitration cases have been brought under UK BITs, 10 under the ECT, and 3 under both a UK BIT and the ECT.

[50] *Ashok Sancheti v. United Kingdom*, UNCITRAL (2006). The claim was raised by a London-based lawyer of Indian nationality pursuant to the India-UK 1994 BIT, out of the increase in the rent price for the investor's lease of a commercial space owned by the city   of   London.   A   summary   of   the   case   is   available   here: https://www.iisd.org/itn/2008/11/28/indian-lawyer-pursues-claim-against-the-united-kingdom-under-the-india-uk-bit/.

[51] UNCTAD, *supra* n. 48: Argentina was named as respondent State in 59 cases and appeared as home State in only 3, and Venezuela was named as respondent State in 41 cases while appearing only once as home State.

position as a leading centre for international arbitration is unlikely to be adversely impacted by Brexit,[52] the same thing may not be true regarding the UK's BIT network and the protection it grants to investors. Possible ramifications of the UK's withdrawal from the EU on intra and extra-EU BITs have been exposed in the recent Special Brexit Issue by the Journal of International Arbitration.[53] Most relevant to this present paper, it addresses the question of the applicability and the status of UK BITs after the UK withdraws from the EU. The conclusion calls for a distinction. With regard to intra-EU BITs, as long as the UK is still an EU Member State, its intra-EU BITs remain in force and investors may seek to rely upon them.[54] However, if and when the UK withdraws from the EU, the UK's intra-EU BITs will necessarily lose their intra-EU character and become extra-EU BITs.[55] On the other hand, under public international law, extra-EU BITs concluded prior to the Lisbon Treaty's entry into force (i.e., December 1, 2009) also remain in force.[56] This is also confirmed by Article 3 of Regulation 1219/2012.[57] However it must be noted that, pursuant to that same Article 3, if the UK and the EU agree to their own BIT (or a FTA with investment provisions), this agreement would ultimately replace the UK's existing BIT network with its current fellow Member States. This is in fact the scope and aim of the agreement that the UK and the EU need to find within the Article 50 two-years period.

A delicate issue may thus arise as to the timing of potential claims brought by investors against the UK. Indeed, claims under intra-EU BITs would need to be brought before the UK officially withdraws from the EU (i.e., the end of the Article 50 two-year period) since, from this

---

[52] See: M. McIlwrath, *An Unamicable Separation: Brexit Consequences for London as a Premier Seat of International Dispute Resolution in Europe*, Journal of International Arbitration (Kluwer Law International 2016), Volume 33 Issue 7, pp. 451-462 ; T. Laurendeau, J. Sharpe, *Brexit: Potential Implications for International Arbitration in London* (Shearman & Sterling LLP, October 18, 2016), http://www.shearman.com/en/newsinsights/publications/2016/10/brexit-implications-international-arbitration.

[53] M. Burgstaller, A. Zarowna, *Possible Ramifications of the UK's EU Referendum on Intra- and Extra-EU BITs*, Journal of International Arbitration (Kluwer Law International 2016), Volume 33 Issue 7, pp. 565-576.

[54] *Ibid.*, p. 568.

[55] *Ibid.*

[56] *Ibid.*, p. 570.

[57] Regulation 1219/2012, *supra* n. 39, Article 3: "Without prejudice to other obligations of the Member States under Union law, bilateral investment agreements notified pursuant to Article 2 of this Regulation may be maintained in force, or enter into force, in accordance with the TFEU and this Regulation, until a bilateral investment agreement between the Union and the same third country enters into force."

moment, investments structured in the UK will necessarily lose their intra-EU character. But, it is probably not before the end of these two years and the—eventual—signing of a UK/EU bespoke agreement that investors will know with certainty what the future investment regulatory framework will be in the UK. Hence, intra-EU BITs claims against the UK may be purely hypothetical. In any event, this would not preclude UK-based investors from bringing claims under extra-EU BITs (which would include former intra-EU BITs that become extra-EU BITs after the withdrawal of the UK from the EU), based in particular on the frustration of their legitimate expectations by the change of regulatory framework. As such, it remains to be seen to what extent the consequences of Brexit on the UK regulatory framework can constitute a violation of the FET standard.

III. BREXIT AND FOREIGN INVESTORS' LEGITIMATE EXPECTATIONS

As the official triggering of Brexit and Article 50 is imminent, foreign investors and stakeholders have shown growing concerns as to the state of uncertainty they are facing. Japanese businesses operating in Europe, for example, have issued a variety of concerns and requests as to the post-Brexit landscape, which Japan has passed on in a strong and alerting message to the UK and the EU.[58] Requests are straightly directed at the UK and the EU for "maintenance of the current tariff rates and customs clearance procedures," "maintenance of the freedom of establishment and the provision of financial services, including the "single passport' system," "maintenance of the freedom of cross-border investment" etc. The 15-page memo warns about "drastic changes in the business environment that could be caused by Brexit" and testifies "to the expectation that the UK and the EU will continue to lead the world in enlarging and promoting a free and open market economy."

The importance of the doctrine of legitimate expectations as an element of the FET standard has clearly been demonstrated. The protection of legitimate expectations is not only a well-established general principle of EU law,[59] but also a concept of general international law that investment arbitration case law has particularly highlighted. The crucial question asked is that of the balance that must be found between, on the one hand, stability and investors' legitimate expectations and, on

---

[58] *Japan's Message to the United Kingdom and the European Union*, http://www.mofa.go.jp/files/000185466.pdf.
[59] See e.g.: CJEU, June 28, 2005, Joined Cases C-189/02 P, C-202/02 P, C-205/02 P to C-208/02 P and C-213/02, *Dansk Rørindustri A/S and others v. Commission*, [2005] ECR I-5425, para. 211.

the other hand, the host State's right to regulate and amend its regulatory framework. That is, in the context of Brexit, the balance between investors' expectations to access the EU single market and not be subjected to tariffs and customs, and the UK's sovereign right to withdraw from the EU and its free trade network. However, there is a difference between merely changing the law and fundamentally altering a country's regulatory framework. As expressed by Roger Alford in a recent conference at the University of Notre Dame's London Global Gateway on the topic of UK trade and Brexit, when the UK is negotiating its withdrawal from the EU they must consider the possibility that if the regulatory framework changes too much, they open themselves to the potential liability for fundamentally altering the regulatory environment so as to violate the FET standard.[60] A host State's right to regulate is indeed not absolute, and must not generate a change so severe and radical so as to constitute a violation of the FET standard by reference to the frustration of investors' legitimate expectations. The issue at stake thus becomes (A) whether the change resulting from leaving the EU constitutes a fundamental alteration of the UK's regulatory framework in violation of the FET standard, and (B) what could be the precise content of foreign investors' legitimate expectations to assert subsequently.

A. A FUNDAMENTAL ALTERATION OF THE UK'S REGULATORY FRAMEWORK?

The investor must take the local law as it stands at the time of making the investment.[61] It is at that moment that the expectations are assessed.[62] The element of stability pertaining to investors' legitimate expectations to rely upon a stable regulatory framework is materialized at this precise moment: the making of the investment. It seems however that stability of the regulatory framework alone is insufficient to protect investors' legitimate expectations. As explained previously, the current trend developed by investment arbitration case law is that investors cannot expect the host State's regulatory framework to remain frozen. Further still, in the words of Michele Potestà, for an investor to legitimately claim damages as a result of the alteration of the general framework, additional guarantees are needed, such as specific

---

[60] R. Alford, *Brexit and Foreign Investors' Legitimate Expectations* (Kluwer Arbitration Blog, December 17, 2016), http://kluwerarbitrationblog.com/2016/12/17/brexit-and-foreign-investors-legitimate-expectations/.

[61] Potestà, *supra* n. 12, p. 111.

[62] *Ibid.*, p. 112.

commitments.[63] Stabilisation clauses constitute a good example of such commitments, and offer higher protection to investors as they reflect a State's commitment to an investor individually.[64] The most difficult question, however, is whether there can be instances where the changes in the regulatory framework are so severe and radical that, even in the absence of a stabilisation clause, a tribunal may nonetheless find a violation of fair and equitable treatment due to frustration of the investor's legitimate expectations.[65] Recent investment tribunals have cautiously advanced such a legal threshold (1) and its reach is therefore difficult to assess with regard to Brexit and its consequences on the UK investment regulatory framework (2).

1. Legal Threshold: The "Total Alteration" of the Host State's Legal Framework

The threshold of the "total alteration of the legal framework" was raised by the *El Paso v. Argentina* tribunal. After adopting the reasoning of *Saluka* with regards to the absence of expectations of absolute legal stability and the host State's right to regulate,[66] the tribunal went on to consider that "[t]here can be no legitimate expectation for anyone that the legal framework will remain unchanged in the face of an extremely severe economic crisis. No reasonable investor can have such an expectation unless very specific commitments have been made towards it or unless the alteration of the legal framework is total."[67] The tribunal was however very cautious in its assertion and did not further detail or explain what could constitute a total alteration of a host State's regulatory framework. It only stated that the measures impugned by the Claimant as a breach of its right to fair and equitable treatment under the Argentina-USA BIT were the measures adopted by the Argentinian Government during the 2000-2002 economic crisis to modify the legal

---

[63] *Ibid.*, p. 114.

[64] According to the definition given by the tribunal in *Total v. Argentina*, "[s]tabilisation clauses are clause, which are inserted in state contracts concluded between foreign investors and host states with the intended effect of freezing a specific host State's legal framework at a certain date, such that the adoption of any changes in the legal regulatory framework of the investment concerned (even by law of general application and without any discriminatory intent by the host State) would be illegal." (*Total v. Argentina*, supra n. 16, para. 101).

[65] Potestà, *supra* n. 12, p. 116.

[66] *El Paso v. Argentina*, *supra* n. 10, para. 372: "[u]nder a FET clause, a foreign investor can expect that the rules will not be changed without justification of an economic, social or other nature. Conversely, it is unthinkable that a State could make a general commitment to all foreign investors never to change its legislation whatever the circumstances, and it would be unreasonable for an investor to rely on such freeze." See also: paras. 365-367 and 371.

[67] *Ibid.*, para. 374 (emphasis added).

framework adopted at the end of the 1990s in the electricity and the hydrocarbon sectors. In trying to ascertain what the Claimant could reasonably have expected when it decided to invest in Argentina and whether there were any commitments on the part of Argentina not to change the basic tenets of the regulatory framework put in place, the tribunal adopted the view that "the legitimate expectations of any investor entering the oil and gas market had to include the real possibility of reasonable changes and amendments in the legal framework, made by the competent authorities within the limits of the powers conferred on them by the law."[68] Adding to that, the tribunal stated it would thus consider "whether any of the measures complained of by (the Claimant) can be considered as adopted outside *the acceptable margin of change* that must be taken into account by any investor and therefore be characterised as unfair and inequitable treatment"[69] and set the defining question of "whether the measures adopted exceeded the normal regulatory powers of the State and violated the legitimate expectations of the Claimant."[70] Ultimately, the tribunal rejected the Claimant's claim that the changes introduced at the end of 2001 and at the beginning of 2002 to cope with the crisis transformed the existing deregulated system into a completely different one, amounting to unfair and inequitable treatment.

Subsequent tribunals have been confronted with extensive changes in host States' regulatory frameworks and elaborated on the test to apply to characterize the "total alteration" threshold. Where the *El Paso v. Argentina* tribunal studied the extent of the change, the tribunal in *Toto v. Lebanon* reasoned about the "drastic or discriminatory effect of the change," [71] while the *Impregilo v. Argentina* tribunal looked for "unreasonable modifications."[72] However, it does not appear that these

---

[68] *Ibid.*, para. 400.

[69] *Ibid.*, para. 402 (emphasis added).

[70] *Ibid.* (emphasis added).

[71] *Toto Costruzioni General S.P.A v. Republic of Lebanon*, ICSID Case No. ARB/07/12, Award (June 7, 2012), para. 244: "[i]n the absence of a stabilisation clause or similar commitment, which were not granted in the present case, changes in the regulatory framework would be considered as breaches of the duty to grant full protection and fair and equitable treatment <u>only in case of a drastic or discriminatory change in the essential features of the transaction</u>. Toto failed to establish that Lebanon, I changing taxes and customs duties, brought about such a drastic or discriminatory consequence" (emphasis added).

[72] *Impregilo S.p.A. v. Argentine Republic*, ICSID Case No. ARB/07/17, Award (June 21, 2011), para. 291: "[t]he legitimate expectations of foreign investors cannot be that the State will never modify the legal framework, especially in times of crisis, but certainly <u>investors must be protected from unreasonable modifications of that legal framework</u>" (emphasis added).

latter tests would be relevant with regard to Brexit and its consequences for the UK trade and investment regulatory framework. Indeed, it is most unlikely that the UK Government ends up implementing "discriminatory measures" since abandoning the EU Single Market would, precisely, affect every investor based in the UK, regardless of any origin, sector, scope of activity, etc. Further, the subjectivity in defining the reasonableness of regulatory framework modifications hinders any legal consideration and does not provide for an established and recognized standard. As such, studying the extent of the change of the UK trade and investment regulatory framework by withdrawing from the EU seems more *pertinent* in the light of foreign investors' legitimate expectations.

This conclusion also finds support in the early Argentina cases. Although the *CMS*, *LG&E*, and *Enron* cases adopted the—apparently —obsolete consideration of the stability of the host State's regulatory framework, they all evidenced their findings by characterizing the entire transformation of Argentina's legal and business environment. Referring to the same measures exposed in *El Paso v. Argentina*, the *CMS* tribunal concluded that "[t]he measures that are complained of did in fact entirely transform and alter the legal and business environment under which the investment was made."[73] Similarly, the *LG&E* tribunal was of the opinion that "Argentina went too far by completely dismantling the very legal framework constructed to attract investors."[74] Finally, in *Enron v. Argentina*, the tribunal observed that "[t]he measures in question (...) have beyond any doubt substantially changed the legal and business framework under which the investment was decided and implemented."[75]

In fine, and although the context of the Argentinian economic crisis does not compare to the UK's decision to withdraw from the EU, these decisions usefully contribute to provide answers to the question of whether foreign investors' legitimate expectations could prevail. They identify a threshold of alteration of the UK's investment regulatory framework that, if reached, could very well constitute a violation of the FET standard. Hence, the question that now needs to be addressed is the following: what could be the extent of the consequences of Brexit for the UK's trade and investment regulatory framework?

---

[73] *CMS v. Argentina*, *supra* n.18, para. 275.
[74] *LG&E v. Argentina*, *supra* n. 18, para. 139.
[75] *Enron v. Argentina*, *supra* n. 9, para. 264.

2. Brexit Consequences for the UK Trade and Investment Legal Framework

As of today, and throughout the Article 50 two-year negotiating period, the UK remains a Member State of the EU. It thus remains subject to EU treaties and part of the Customs Union and the internal market they implemented (most commonly referred to as the "Single Market"). The internal market is defined by Article 26(2) TFEU as comprising "an area without internal frontiers in which free movement of goods, persons, services and capital is ensured in accordance with the provisions of the Treaties."[76] The objective of the four freedoms therein defined is to abolish barriers between Member States, such as tariffs on the trade of goods. Most relevant to this paper, the free movement of goods is protected under Articles 28-37 TFEU. These provisions aim to create an open market and competition through the abolition of tariffs, quotas and other barriers between Member States. Indeed, tariffs have been completely removed between Member States and EU Treaties do not allow for any exceptions. Abolition of customs tariffs reduces the costs associated with business and in turn means lower prices. Originally envisaged by the 1957 Treaty of Rome, the Customs Union was completed and entered into force on July 1, 1968. The common customs tariff was introduced to replace national customs duties in trade with the rest of the world and to apply to goods entering from outside the EU. The UK joined the EU five years later, on January 1, 1973, i.e., two years before it signed its first BIT, with Singapore on July 22, 1975.

UK's trade has since exploded, especially with the EU. As reported by a paper for the House of Commons in 2016, the EU is by far the UK's most important trading partner. In 2015, it accounted for 44% of UK goods and services exports (£222 billion) and 53% of UK imports (£291 billion).[77] The UK has also become the world's third recipient of inward foreign direct investments, behind the United States and China,[78] primarily from the EU. In 2014, EU countries accounted for just under half the stock of FDI in the UK (£496 billion out of a total of £1,034 billion, 48%).[79] According to a survey, the UK even attracted more FDI

---

[76] Article 26(2) TFEU, *supra* n. 36.
[77] V. Miller, *Brexit: impact across policy areas*, House of Commons Library, Briefing Paper (August 26, 2016), p. 13, http://researchbriefings.parliament.uk/ResearchBriefing/Summary/CBP-7213.
[78] See: UK Trade and Investment, *supra* n. 6.
[79] ONS Statistical Bulletin, *Foreign Direct Investment Involving UK Companies 2014* (December 3, 2015) http://webarchive.nationalarchives.gov.uk/20160105160709/http://www.ons.gov.uk/ons/rel/fdi/foreign-direct-investment/2014/stb-fdi-2014.html.

projects than any other European country in 2014,[80] from which one may draw the conclusion that the UK greatly benefited from its long-lasting membership of the EU. The abolition of tariffs and the free movement of goods within the EU indeed provided the UK with a great competitive advantage and contributed to the UK's ranking today of being amongst the biggest trading nations in the world. But leaving the EU casts great uncertainties as to the UK's ability to maintain its position.

Within the next two-years of negotiating with the EU, the UK will need to find an agreement on the trade framework and system it wishes to establish for its post-Brexit trade relations. The UK eventually has a choice between different trade models which have been extensively debated since even before the referendum.[81] However, only one can eventually provide trade regulations that could substantially frustrate foreign investors' legitimate expectations: reverting to WTO rules. Indeed, pursuant to Article 50(3) TEU, "[t]he (EU) Treaties shall cease to apply to the (withdrawing) State in question from the date of entry into force of the withdrawal agreement or, failing that, two years after the notification (of the State's intention to withdraw from the EU)." In the case of the UK, failing to find an agreement with the EU would mean reverting to WTO rules, which represent a minimum threshold. The UK would lose its status as an EU member of the WTO and would take up its membership as an individual member of the WTO. However, this could prove devastating for the UK. In the words of the UK Government, "[i]t would be the most definitive break with the EU, offering no preferential access to the Single Market (…). This would cause a major economic shock to the UK, with serious consequences for companies, consumers, jobs and prices. The UK would face immediate and heavy costs to (its) trading relationships, both with the EU and with the wider world. If reciprocal tariffs were introduced on imports from the EU, these goods would become more expensive. (…) Under WTO

---

[80]   EY, *European attractiveness survey 2015*, p. 2, http://www.ey.com/Publication/vwLUAssets/EY-european-attractiveness-survey-2015/SFILE/EY-european-attractiveness-survey-2015.pdf.
[81] For a thorough review of the possible trade models for the UK post-Brexit, see: *Alternatives to membership: possible models for the United Kingdom outside the European Union*, HM Government (March 2016), https://www.gov.uk/government/uploads/system/uploads/attachment_data/file/504661/Alternatives_to_membership_possible_models_for_the_UK_outside_the_EU_Accessible.pdf ; J.-C. Piris, *If the UK votes to leave: The seven alternatives to EU membership*, Centre for European Reform (January 2016), https://www.cer.org.uk/publications/archive/policy-brief/2016/if-uk-votes-leave-seven-alternatives-eu-membership ; H. Hofmeister, *Splendid Isolation or Continued Cooperation? Options for a State After Withdrawal from the EU*, Columbia Journal of European Law (2016), Vol. 21.2, pp. 249-287.

rules neither the UK nor the EU could offer each other better market access than that offered to all other WTO members."[82]

Indeed, under WTO rules, the EU is required to apply a "common external tariff" in line with the "Most Favoured Nation" principle, which means that WTO members must offer the same terms to all 161 other WTO members.[83] Recent research conducted by Civitas shows that were such scenario to occur, UK exporters could face the potential of £5.2 billion in tariffs on goods being sold to the EU.[84] Such estimation results from the fact that around 16% of UK-exports to the EU-27 would face tariffs of more than 7%; of that 16% half of which would be represented by motor cars which would face a tariff of 10%.[85] The car industry is indeed the sector most likely to be impacted by WTO rules, and has constituted one of the most debated topics of concern since the referendum. This is largely due to the fact that the car industry represents the biggest element of the UK export value: in 2015, UK exports of cars to the EU were worth £10.2 billion, which represents more than half of the UK's car exports.[86] In particular, the North-East of England has one of the highest shares of EU exports in the UK's regional economy, with major foreign investment from Japanese car manufacturers.[87] A 10% tariff would imply an additional charge of £1.3 billion.[88] Moreover, if the UK were forced to raise tariffs under WTO rules, components sourced from the EU would become more expensive for UK-based vehicle manufacturers: as over 40% of components purchased by these manufacturers come from the EU, this could place such exporters at a further disadvantage.[89] But the car industry would not suffer from the highest tariffs. Even though they represent a considerably less important source of UK export value, other industries could be hit hard by WTO tariffs. Beyond vehicles, it is the food and agricultural industries whose

---

[82] HM Government, *supra* n. 81, p. 35.

[83] *Ibid.*, p. 37.

[84] J. Protts, *Potential post-Brexit tariffs costs for EU-UK trade* (Civitas, October 2016), http://www.civitas.org.uk/reports_articles/potential-post-brexit-tariff-costs-for-eu-uk-trade/.

[85] *The World Trade Organization: A Safety Net for a Post-Brexit UK Trade Policy?*, UK Trade Policy Observatory, Briefing Paper 1 (July 2016), p. 2, https://www.sussex.ac.uk/webteam/gateway/file.php?name=briefing-paper-1.pdf&site=18.

[86] HM Government, *supra* n. 81, p. 35

[87] *Ibid.* Japanese companies' car manufacturing plants in England and most at risk after UK leaves the EU include Honda (Swinson), Nissan (Sunderland) and Toyota (Burnaston). See: *UK car factories face uncertain future after Brexit*, Financial Times (July 13, 2016), https://www.ft.com/content/27d7b066-447c-11e6-b22f-79eb4891c97d.

[88] Civitas, *supra* n. 84, p. 5.

[89] *Ibid.*

exports would suffer the most from the introduction of tariffs, as they would face an average of 36.1% as dairy tariffs.[90] The tobacco and manufactured tobacco substitutes industry would also be imposed an average tariff of 43.7%,[91] with tariffs as high as 74.9% for smoking tobacco (!).[92] It is thus undeniable that the introduction of tariffs on any goods traded between the UK and the rest of the EU and the world would significantly damage the business of exporters and UK-based foreign investors. But would it be sufficient to constitute a change so severe and radical as to violate the FET standard by reference to the frustration of foreign investors' legitimate expectations?

The lack of clear and unequivocal explanation of the *El Paso* "total alteration of the legal framework" threshold could make one lean toward a positive answer. Still, the exposed early Argentina cases provide interesting insight into the total alteration of the regulatory framework by the dismantlement of the tariffs regime. For example, in concluding that the "measures that are complained of did in fact entirely transform and alter the legal and business environment under which the investment was decided and made," the *CMS* tribunal explained that the attractive tariff regime established by Argentina in the 1990s to attract foreign investors was "no longer present in the regime governing the business operations of the Claimant," after the Government of Argentina had modified it to face the economic crisis.[93] Similarly, the tribunal in *LG&E* found that the guarantees enacted to attract foreign investors were "laid down in the tariff system"[94] and, in recognizing the complete dismantlement by Argentina of the very legal framework constructed to attract investors,[95] concluded that "Argentina acted unfairly and inequitably when it prematurely abandoned (...) tariffs adjustments and essentially froze tariffs."[96] Likewise, the tribunal considered that "the Government's Resolution (...) to discontinue all tariff reviews and to refrain from adjusting tariffs or prices in any way, also breaches the fair and equitable treatment standard."[97] Finally, the *Enron* tribunal observed that the Claimant's legitimate expectations were grounded in "the statutory enshrinement of the tariff regime" laid down by Argentina,[98]

---

[90] HM Government, *supra* n. 81, p. 36.

[91] Civitas, *supra* n. 84, p. 6.

[92] *What the Deals Might Look Like: Trade After Brexit*, Wall Street Journal (June 24, 2016), http://graphics.wsj.com/trade-after-brexit/#world-trade-org 240319000.

[93] *CMS v. Argentina*, *supra* n. 18, para. 275.

[94] *LG&E v. Argentina*, *supra* n. 18, para. 134.

[95] *Ibid.*, para. 139.

[96] *Ibid.*, para. 136.

[97] *Ibid.*, para. 138.

[98] *Enron v. Argentina*, *supra* n. 9, para, 265.

and concluded that Argentina violated the FET standard because a decade later, "the guarantees of the tariff regime that had seduced so many investors, were dismantled."[99] Although these cases, once again, relate to the obsolete assertion of the element of absolute stability by investment tribunals, they establish a clear connection between the dismantlement of a tariff regime by the host State and its subsequent violation of the FET standard by reference to foreign investors' legitimate expectations.

Reverting to WTO rules and enforcing higher tariffs for exports to the EU would clearly fall within the scope of such connection. Still, it does not seem that such a change would clearly reach the threshold established by the *El Paso* tribunal. Although WTO high tariffs could significantly harm the most Brexit-concerned industries (car making, agriculture), these measures could hardly be considered as being adopted "outside the acceptable margin of change" and as "exceeding the normal regulatory powers" of the UK Government. Hence, it seems improbable that reverting to WTO rules and tariffs, *alone*, would be enough to constitute a change so severe and radical as to totally alter the UK's legal and business environment and breach the FET standard by violating investors' legitimate expectations. However, an abstract requirement of good governance cannot serve as the only measuring instrument. Expectations as to the regulatory framework must be assessed *in concreto* with regard to all circumstances.[100] Precisely, it is the contention of this paper that reverting to WTO rules and tariffs, coupled with all the circumstances pertaining to foreign investors' decisions to make investments in the UK, *could* reach the level of a fundamental alteration of the UK's regulatory framework and constitute a violation of the FET standard.

B. CONTENT OF UK-BASED FOREIGN INVESTORS' LEGITIMATE EXPECTATIONS

This section relates to the precise content of investors' expectations with regard to the regulatory framework wherein the investment is made, i.e., the degree of reasonableness of these expectations. Tribunals have observed that the investor's legitimate expectations must relate to the specific characteristics of the investment environment in the host State, which naturally varies from one country to another.[101] Following this line of argument, the tribunal in *El Paso* went on to consider that "fair and

---

[99] *Ibid.*, para. 266.
[100] Potestà, *supra* n. 12, p. 114.
[101] *Ibid.*, p. 119.

equitable treatment is linked to the objective reasonable legitimate expectations of the investors and that these have to be evaluated considering all circumstances." [102] As such, the reasonableness requirement inherent to legitimate expectations allows for, or even mandates, an examination of all circumstances that the investor should have considered when making the investment.[103] Indeed, various sets of circumstances arise from the study of the UK post-Brexit legal investment framework and would be relevant in characterizing foreign investors' legitimate expectations. Altogether, the level of development of the UK (A), the EU context (B) and Article 50 only recent provision (C) could trigger a greater level of expectations for foreign investors.

1.   The Level of Development of the UK

Foremost, taking into account all circumstances pertaining to the investors' investment requires one to consider the specificities of the host State, and in particular, its level of development. Indeed, the level and extent of protection an investor can legitimately expect in a developing or emerging country are not the same as in a highly-developed country like the UK. As noted in *El Paso*, it has been recognized that legitimate expectations might differ between an economy in transition and a more developed one.[104] Most notably, the tribunal in *Generation Ukraine v. Ukraine* pointed out that "[t]he Claimant was attracted to the Ukraine because of the possibility of earning a rate of return on its capital in significant excess to the other investment opportunities in more developed economies. The Claimant thus invested

---

[102] *El Paso v. Argentina, supra* n. 10, para. 364, citing to different tribunals: *Noble Ventures, Inc. v. Romania*, ICSID Case No. ARB/01/11, Award (October 12, 2005), para. 181 ("… the question whether [FET] standards have been violated has to be considered in the light of the circumstances of each case.") ; *Waste Management, Inc. v. The United Mexican States*, ICSID Case No. ARB(AF)/00/3, Award (April 30, 2004), para. 99 ("… the standard is to some extent a flexible one which must be adapted to the circumstances of the case.") ; *Continental Casualty Company v. Argentine Republic*, ICSID Case No. ARB/03/9, Award (September 5, 2008), para. 255 ("… the content of the obligation incumbent upon the host State to treat a foreign investor in a fair and equitable manner […] varies in part depending on the circumstances in which the standard is invoked: the concept of fairness being inherently related to *keeping justice in variable factual contexts*."). See also: *Mondev International Ltd. V. United States of America*, ICSID Case No. ARB(AF)/99/2, Award (October 11, 2002), para. 118 ("A judgement of what is fair and equitable cannot be reached in the abstract; it must depend on the facts of the particular case") ; *Spyridon Roussalis v. Romania*, ICSID Case No. ARB/06/1, Award (December 7, 2011), para. 316 ("The precise scope of the standard is therefore left to the determination of the Tribunal which '*will have to decide whether in all the circumstances the conduct in issue is fair and equitable or unfair and inequitable*'").

[103] Potestà, *supra* n. 12, p. 119.

[104] *El Paso v. Argentina, supra* n. 10, para. 360.

in the Ukraine on notice of both the prospects and the potential pitfalls."[105] Similarly, the *Methanex* tribunal observed that an investor cannot pretend to have legitimate expectations of stability of environmental regulations in a State such as California, where concerns for the protection of the environment and of sustainable development are high.[106]

The standard of reasonableness to which legitimate expectations are being held differs because the risk is not the same for investors. Although earning rates and returns are presumably higher, there is indeed a greater risk for investors to make investment in developing countries or economies in transition. As evidenced with Lithuania[107] and Ukraine[108] following the collapse of the Soviet Union, such context weighs on the extent to which legitimate expectations can be justified with regard to the stability of the investment environment.[109] By accepting the risk of instability and investing in a transitioning or emerging economy, investors reduce their legitimate expectations that the regulatory framework will not be subsequently altered. All in all, this means that legitimate expectations created through the host State's regulatory framework are greater in developed countries like the UK.[110] In the context of Brexit, foreign investors' legitimate expectations would thus presumably be held to a lower standard of reasonableness due to the UK's status as a highly-developed country.

2. The EU Context

The reasonableness of foreign investors' legitimate expectations encompasses various elements and does not only relate to the factual context of the investment. In *Duke Energy v. Ecuador*, the tribunal indeed established that "[t]he assessment of the reasonableness or legitimacy must take into account all circumstances, including not only the facts surrounding the investment, but also the political, socioeconomic, cultural and historical conditions prevailing in the host State."[111] Context is thus a prime factor to consider when seeking to determine the content of investors' legitimate expectations, as was further expanded in *Bayindir*

---

[105] *Generation Ukraine, Inc. v. Ukraine*, ICSID Case No. ARB/00/9, Award (September 16, 2003), para. 20.37.

[106] *Methanex v. United States*, UNCITRAL (NAFTA), Final Award (August 3, 2005), para. 9 of Part IV – Chapter D.

[107] *Parkerings v. Lithuania*, *supra* n. 28, paras. 335-6.

[108] *Generation Ukraine v. Ukraine*, *supra* n. 105.

[109] Potestà, *supra* n. 12, p. 120.

[110] Alford, *supra* n. 60.

[111] *Duke Energy Electroquil Partners & Electroauil S.A. v. Republic of Ecuador*, ICSID Case No. ARB/04/19, Award (August 18, 2008), para. 340.

v. Pakistan (climate affected by a high degree of "political volatility")[112] and *Toto v. Lebanon* ("post-civil war situation in Lebanon"). [113] The context of the EU and its attractive regulatory framework for investment is no exception, and must be assessed in seeking to establish the precise content of what foreign investors could legitimately expect by investing in the UK.

The current UK's investment regulatory framework was forged upon a 44-years membership of the EU and its Customs Union. Since 1973, the UK has improved and allowed its framework to evolve based on the political, historical and economic tenets of the EU. These tenets are today firmly rooted in the UK's regulatory framework and reflect the regime to which foreign investors are being held in their trade relations with the EU and the rest of the world. This has been a paramount and omnipresent objective that the EU has been striving for since its origins. The objective of the 1957 Treaty of Rome was thus the establishment of a Customs Union and this treaty already proposed to create a single market for goods, persons, services and capital across the EEC. The Customs Union entered into force in 1968, one and a half years earlier than planned in the Treaty of Rome. This was the economic context when the UK joined in 1973. The 1986 Single European Act went even further in implementing these objectives and creating deeper integration by announcing the establishment of a Single Market by December 31, 1992 and the intent to remove barriers and increase regulatory harmonization and competitiveness among the European Community's countries.[114] The 1992 Maastricht Treaty definitely embodied the Single Market by integrating European countries within the EU and establishing the pillar structure of the EU. As such, the EU investment regulatory framework as it is known today was implemented in the early 1990s, which coincides with the moment when the number of UK's BITs erupted.

Considering the EU context proves particularly relevant when looking at the chronology of UK's BITs. As shown in the chart below, the number of signatures of BITs between the UK and foreign countries exploded following the 1986 Single European Act.

---

[112] *Bayindir Insaat Turzim Ticaret VE Sanayi A.Ş. v. Islamic Republic of Pakistan*, ICSID Case No. ARB/03/29, Award (August 27, 2009), para. 195.
[113] *Toto v. Lebanon, supra* n. 71, para. 245.
[114] Single European Act, 1987 O.J. L 169/1 [hereinafter SEA], http://www.consilium.europa.eu/uedocs/cmsUpload/SingleEuropeanAct_Crest.pdf.

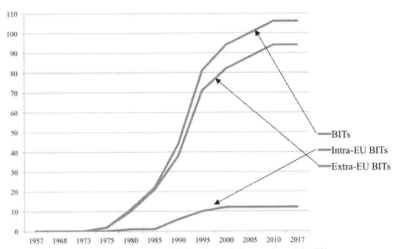

The UK BIT network: evolution through the creation of the EU

27 BITs were signed from 1986 to 1992, more than all signed by the UK
in the previous thirteen years of its EU membership (twenty-two). The
trend became even more exponential after the fall of the Soviet Union:
nine countries signed a BIT with the UK in 1993,[115] twelve in 1994,[116]
eleven in 1995[117] and five more in 1996.[118] All the fifteen former Soviet
Socialists Republics (except Tajikistan)—including the Russian
Federation—had contracted BITs with the UK by 1997. Similarly,
almost all former communist signing countries to the Warsaw Pact and
ex-Yugoslavia countries had contracted BITs with the UK within the
eight years following the fall of the Berlin Wall. Further still, nineteen
BITs were concluded between the UK and (then) extra-EU European
States within the seven years of the Treaty of Maastricht, including ten
future EU members.

One may draw an interesting conclusion from this. Not only was the
EU very attractive in terms of investment opportunities, especially for
communist countries of the Eastern Bloc, but the theory also met in
practice with the explosion of the number of BITs signed by the UK
during the 1990s. As a consequence, since 1990 the inward foreign direct

---

[115] Armenia, Barbados, Honduras, Lithuania, Nepal, Peru, Trinidad, Ukraine and
Uzbekistan.
[116] Albania, Belarus, Brazil, Colombia, Ecuador, Estonia, India, Kyrgyzstan, Latvia,
Pakistan, South Africa and Tanzania.
[117] Bulgaria, Ivory Coast, Cuba, Georgia, Kazakhstan, Laos, Oman, Swaziland,
Turkmenistan, Venezuela and Zimbabwe.
[118] Azerbaijan, Chile, Moldova, Nicaragua and Slovenia.

investment stock in the UK has risen six-fold, from US$204 billion in 1990 to US$1,199 billion by the end of 2011.[119] On the whole, this reflects the high degree of expectations that foreign investors could legitimately rely upon when investing in the EU: the abolition of tariffs, quotas and other barriers between Member States, the establishment of a Single Market for goods, persons, services and capital, and the increased regulatory harmonization and competitiveness were as many promises that foreign investors considered by investing in the UK. Besides, the expectation to benefit from the EU's ever-extending integration was further enhanced by the fact that no Member States ever left the EU, as the possibility of withdrawing was introduced in the Treaties only recently.

3. Article 50 and the Absence of Express Provisions for Withdrawal

That Article 50 TEU has drawn the world's attention since June 23, 2016 is an understatement. The EU Treaties' provision allowing a Member State to withdraw is the core of the Brexit procedure, and its issue has even been debated in front of the UK Supreme Court. Nevertheless, it is only since the Treaty of Lisbon entered into force on December 1, 2009 that EU Treaties have explicitly acknowledged the right of a Member State to leave the EU. Article 50 TEU was adopted from the abandoned 2004 Draft Constitutional Treaty (Article I-59).[120] Thus, until the Treaty of Lisbon, there were no provisions either in the European Treaties or in EU law allowing a Member State to withdraw or secede—either in a negotiated or unilateral manner—from the EU.

Although it was arguable whether or not such an inherent right existed under the Treaties in the absence of an express provision,[121] the common view before the Lisbon Treaty came into force was that the European Community/Union Treaties did not allow for a unilateral or free right to withdraw.[122] Only three territories have left the EU or the

---

[119] Government Office for Science, *supra* n. 4, p. 5.

[120] Draft Treaty Establishing a Constitution for Europe, 2004 O.J. C 310/1 (never ratified) [hereinafter Draft Constitutional Treaty], http://register.consilium.europa.eu/doc/srv?l=EN&f=CV%20724%202003%20REV%201.

[121] For further commentaries and studies on the debate regarding the existence of a right to withdraw from the EU before the Lisbon Treaty, see: A. F. Tatham, *'Don't Mention Divorce at the Wedding, Darling!': EU Accession and Withdrawal after Lisbon* in EU Law after Lisbon (A. Biondi, P. Eeckhout, and S. Ripley, Oxford Scholarship Online, 2012), pp. 128-154 ; C. Hillion, *Accession and Withdrawal in the Law of the European Union* (August 18, 2014 ; available at SSRN: https://papers.ssrn.com/sol3/papers.cfm?abstract_id=2482232).

[122] Tatham, *supra* n. 121, p. 142.

EEC in their 60-year-old history, but none of them was a Member State: Algeria seceded from France after achieving its independence in 1962, Greenland left the EEC in 1985 following a referendum, and French Guadeloupe's Caribbean island of Saint Barthélémy withdrew from the EU in 2012.[123] While Algeria is now an independent state, Greenland and Saint Barthélémy are listed as EU Overseas Countries and Territories (OCT), a status under which the EU Treaties allow some States with close ties with EU Member States, as well as some territories of EU Member States, to stand outside the territorial scope of application of the Treaties, but to hold a special association status with the EU that grants them special rights of access to the internal market.[124]

However, these examples only set a precedent for the fact that *part* of a Member State may leave the EU. Member States did not have the ability to withdraw because legal pillars of the EU construction—the Treaties—never provided so until the Treaty of Lisbon. In the context of Brexit and legitimate expectations, this may be a paramount argument in favour of foreign investors. Since FDIs in the UK exploded during the 1990s, the vast majority of foreign investments were made before 2007 and the signature of the Treaty of Lisbon. This may even be extended to 2004 and the Constitutional Treaty, when the idea of a provision for withdrawal was introduced for the first time. Further still, the UK has signed only five BITs since 2007 (Colombia, who signed a new BIT with the UK in 2010, already had one in force since 1994). Even more, it has been put forward that Article 50 was never meant to be used.[125] In conclusion, the absence of any legal provision for withdrawal and, subsequently, the presumably understood impossibility to leave the EU before 2009 could be considered as a powerful incentive for investments and the guarantee of a stable framework: that of the EU. UK-based foreign investors' legitimate expectations to benefit from the EU Single Market and its abolition of tariffs could thus be assessed following a two-fold basis: the UK's membership of the EU since 1973, and the impossibility—at the time of their investment—to withdraw from the EU and its regulatory framework. Expectations for the

---

[123] See: *Exiting the EU? Algeria, Greenland and Saint Barthélémy experiences* (Nationalia, February 23, 2016), http://www.nationalia.info/new/10722/exiting-the-eu-algeria-greenland-and-saint-barthelemy-experiences ; P. Bowers et al., *Brexit: some legal and constitutional issues and alternatives to EU membership*, House of Commons Library, Briefing Paper (July 28, 2016), p. 9-10.

[124] See: European Commission, International Cooperation and Development, http://ec.europa.eu/europeaid/regions/octs_en.

[125] Former Prime Minister of Italy Giuliano Amato, who says he authored Article 50, says the treaty clause was not actually designed to be used: *Brexit: Article 50 was never actually meant to be used, says its author*, Independent (July 27, 2016).

regulatory framework not to be fundamentally altered—such as by leaving the EU—would be embodied in the Member State status. From this standpoint, UK's membership in the EU would hence constitute the very core and base of foreign investors' legitimate expectations, which, after all, is exactly the type of integration that the EU Founding Fathers were striving for.

IV. CONCLUSION

The impact of Brexit on foreign investors could prove devastating. Its full extent still remains unclear, and will only be asserted once the Article 50 two-years negotiation period renders its verdict. If the UK finds a bespoke trade agreement with the EU, the change to its regulatory framework could be limited. However, in the absence of such agreement, reverting to the WTO regime would trigger the imposition of tariffs on UK's exports to the EU. With tariffs averaging 10% for car manufacturing, 36% for dairy, and 43% for tobacco, the change on some sectors could be so severe and radical as to frustrate foreign investors' legitimate expectations in violation of the UK's fair and equitable treatment obligations.

Legitimate expectations remain a powerful and controversial tool. This concept also offers sufficient flexibility to accommodate both the interests of foreign investors and of host States.[126] This seems to be the trend followed by investment arbitral tribunals in recent years. Where will Brexit and foreign investors' eventual claims stand? Can foreign investors have a claim against the UK Government for frustrating their legitimate expectations? Nothing is sure, and with Brexit, the only certainty is uncertainty. However, a path may have been drawn. By referring to the fundamental alteration of the host State's legal and business framework, investment tribunals have established a threshold that, if reached, constitutes a violation of the FET standard by reference to foreign investors' legitimate expectations. Fact specific considerations dominate the application of the FET standard, and the consequences of Brexit provide a wide range of factors in this regard. The White Paper reiterates the UK Government's intention to pursue a new strategic partnership with the EU, including an ambitious and comprehensive Free Trade Agreement and a new customs agreement.[127] However, the EU has already shown reluctance and negotiations will prove tedious, without any guarantee of an agreement as a result. Withdrawing from the EU Single Market and Customs Union and reverting to WTO tariffs

---

[126] Jacob and Schill, *supra* n. 10, p. 727 (63).
[127] UK Government's White Paper, *supra* n. 4, p. 35.

could, in certain sectors, be considered as tantamount to a fundamental alteration of the UK's regulatory framework. The UK's highly-developed country status generates even greater expectations which, considered along with the EU context and the absence of express provisions regarding withdrawal at the time of the investment, could be elevated to a violation of the FET standard if frustrated. The path is narrow and full of hindrances, but the FET concept is not barred from evolution and still requires further definition in the context of this study.

Overall, the legal study of Brexit raises more questions than it answers. Many other investment-related issues could be raised by the UK's eventual violation of its international obligations: could foreign States terminate their BITs with the UK by invoking a fundamental change of circumstances under Article 62 of the Vienna Convention on the Law of Treaties? Would compensation resulting from the threat of investment claims not constitute state subsidy, thus violating WTO rules? Etc. Issues for the UK are enormous and will require extensive consideration when commencing negotiations with the EU. It may very well be possible that FET claims end up not being sufficiently legally grounded, but it should at least constitute an incentive for the UK Government to negotiate economic and tariff measures that are not to the detriment of foreign investors. The *Enron* tribunal's assessment here finds a resounding but alerting echo: "[w]here there was certainty and stability for investors doubt and ambiguity are the order of the day. The long-term business outlook enabled by the tariff regime, has been transformed on a day-to-day discussion about what comes next."[128] Brace yourselves, Brexit is coming.

---

[128] *Enron v. Argentina, supra* n. 9, para. 266.

CHAPTER 18: A VIOLATION OF THE FAIR AND EQUITABLE TREATMENT STANDARD UNDER BILATERAL INVESTMENT TREATIES AS A RESULT OF BREXIT: THE EXAMPLE OF TATA MOTORS

RAPHAELLE JOHNSTON

I. INTRODUCTION

On June 23, 2016, 51.9% of United Kingdom (UK) voters elected to leave the European Union (EU). This historic referendum represents the biggest shock to the political establishment in Britain and across Europe for decades. The uncertainty of the post-Brexit landscape has since become a source of concern for the numerous businesses concentrated in the UK that operate in Europe.[1] Businesses are having to plan a wide range of outcomes. While negotiations have yet to begin, the EU's position is very clear: there will be no compromise on the Union's four founding principles—freedom of movement of goods, services, people and capital. Prime Minister Theresa May's systematic dismissal of a free movement deal to retain access to the single market suggests the UK is veering towards a 'hard'[2] Brexit.[3] Moreover, if no deal is struck within two years on the exit settlement and any transitional arrangements, the UK will be left with only the World Trade Organization (WTO) rules for support.

Failure to conclude a Free Trade Agreement (FTA) or customs union between the UK and EU would mean the end of the circulation of UK goods into the EU without tariffs. Under WTO rules, UK exports would become subject to the EU's common customs tariffs applicable to all non-EU members of the WTO. Though rates of duty vary significantly,[4] "even seemingly small tariff changes can be significant."[5]

---

[1] *See* Japan's Message to the United Kingdom and the European Union, http://www.mofa.go.jp/files/000185466.pdf (last visited Jan. 15, 2017).

[2] A 'hard' Brexit would essentially result in the UK giving up its access to the EU's single market and would also likely mean a withdrawal from the EU's customs union.

[3] Joe Watts, *Theresa May indicates 'hard Brexit' and dismisses free movement deal to keep single market access*, THE INDEPENDENT (Oct. 2, 2016), http://www.independent.co.uk/news/uk/politics/theresa-may-hard-brexit-soft-article-free-movement-deal-single-market-access-a7341886.html.

[4] Jason French, Jovi Juan & Jason Douglas, *Trade After Brexit*, WALL STREET JOURNAL, (June 24, 2016, 12:19 AM), http://graphics.wsj.com/trade-after-brexit/.

[5] Sarah Gordon, *How a hard Brexit might affect three industries*, THE FINANCIAL TIMES, (Nov 20, 2016), https://www.ft.com/content/92d985c0-acd1-11e6-9cb3-bb8207902122

Where investments were made in order to produce a good in the UK for export duty-free to the rest of the EU, the application of EU-WTO tariffs to UK exports may deprive a considerable part or the entirety of the value of these investments.[6]

In 2015, the EU represented 44% of the UK's total exports.[7] A 'hard' Brexit will therefore impact many industries in the UK. For example, motor vehicle manufacture industry contributed £12 billion to the economy in 2014,[8] with around 50% of car exports going to the EU.[9] In 2015, the total export value to the EU of all motor vehicles constituted over £8 billion.[10] A rise in tariffs from 0% to 10% under a 'WTO scenario' will thus have a substantial impact on competitivity profits. Car manufacturers could mitigate this loss by lobbying the government for some form of compensation, as Nissan appears to have done. [11] However, where a manufacturer fails to come to an agreement with the UK, foreign direct investments (FDI) will be impacted.

FDI in the UK is significant with many foreign investors having chosen to invest in the UK as a base to access the European single market. BITs signed between the UK and investors' home states protect many of these investments. These agreements establish the terms and conditions for FDI and grant investors a certain number of guarantees.[12]

(quoting Pierre Mercier, senior partner at the Boston Consulting Group, who gives the example of a product, whose margin is 5%, affected by a shift of 5% which jeopardizes 100% of profit).

[6] *See* Wojciech Sadowski and Dominika Jedrzejczyk, *Brexit and Investment Treaty Arbitration*, K&L GATES, (Sept. 1, 2016), http://www.klgates.com/brexit-and-investment-treaty-arbitration-09-01-2016/; *See also* Peter Campbell and Kana Inagaki, *UK car factories face uncertain future after Brexit*, THE FINANCIAL TIMES, (July 13, 2016), https://www.ft.com/content/27d7b066-447c-11e6-b22f-79eb4891c97d.

[7] Campbell and Inagaki, *supra* note 6.

[8] Chris Rhodes and Dominic Sear, THE MOTOR INDUSTRY: STATISTICS AND POLICY, (Number 00611) 2015, H.C. at 3 (UK), available at http://researchbriefings.parliament.uk/ResearchBriefing/ Summary/SN00611; *See also* Dominic Webb and Matthew Keep, IN BRIEF: UK-EU ECONOMIC RELATIONS, (Number 06091) 2016, H.C., (UK) available at http://researchbriefings.parliament.uk/ResearchBriefing/Summary/SN06091#fullrepo rt.

[9] Jaguar Land Rover, *Manufacturing in the UK: Busting the Myths*, JAGUAR LAND ROVER, https://apps.warwickshire.gov.uk/api/documents/WCCC-688-153 (last visited Jan. 15, 2016); Rhodes and Sear, *supra* note 8, at 9.

[10] Campbell and Inagaki, *supra* note 6.

[11] Sean Farrell, *Nissan demands Brexit compensation for new UK investment*, THE GUARDIAN, (Sept. 30, 2016, 6:10 AM), https://www.theguardian.com/business/2016/sep/30/nissan-hard-brexit-compensation-new-uk-investment-tariffs.

[12] The UK has currently signed 110 BITs with countries such as India, Indonesia, Russia and Mexico. *See generally Bilateral Investment Treaties* under *United Kingdom*, INVESTMENT POLICY   HUB   –   UNCTAD,

Among these guarantees is the fair and equitable treatment (FET) standard which protects investors from drastic violations of their legitimate expectations, including legal and regulatory change.[13] The UK's withdrawal from the EU may impose liability on the UK under these BITs for breaching investors' expectations that they would have access to the EU market indefinitely.

Any investment requires due diligence and an analysis of potential risks. However, the recent result from the British referendum to leave the EU is a risk few investors had considered. Among the plethora of issues Brexit raises, a fundamental concern for the UK will be its obligations to foreign investors. More specifically, the UK needs to examine whether Brexit might trigger foreign investor claims.

This paper aims to serve as a hypothetical case study to be applied to other foreign investments covered by extra-EU BITs. Using the example of the Indian corporation Tata Motors' investment in English car manufacturer Jaguar-Land Rover (JLR), it will determine whether the UK can be held liable under BITs for an increase in duties as a result of Brexit. Part II will describe the legal basis and the necessary elements to make a claim for violation of the FET standard. Part III will evaluate the success of such a claim, analyzing the strengths and weaknesses of Tata Motors and the UK's likely arguments. Finally, this paper will conclude that though in this particular example Tata Motors is unlikely to obtain compensation, the eventuality that other investors may be successful in suing the UK must be taken into account by the UK in its negotiations with the EU.

II. LEGAL BASIS FOR A CLAIM BY TATA MOTORS AGAINST THE UK: THE 'FAIR AND EQUITABLE TREATMENT' STANDARD UNDER THE INDIA-UK BIT

Before determining whether Tata Motors can obtain compensation, one must establish whether a claim can be brought before an arbitral tribunal under the India-UK BIT. Section A will explore the India-UK BIT standards Tata Motors could rely on to obtain compensation. Section B will examine the elements Tata Motors must demonstrate to show a violation of the FET standard by the UK.

A. A CLAIM UNDER THE INDIA-UK BIT

The UK has concluded BITs with over 100 different countries, both intra- and extra-EU.[14] These agreements are concluded between states in

---

http://investmentpolicyhub.unctad.org/IIA/CountryBits/221 (last visited Feb. 24, 2016) (list of all UK BITs).

[13] The exact definition of FET will be explored later.

[14] *See generally Bilateral Investment Treaties, supra* note 12 (list of all UK BITs).

order to promote and protect their citizens' investments in the other party's territory. They provide five core guarantees,[15] among which is the favorable treatment of foreign investments by the host State. These include the national treatment standard, the most favored nation standard, the FET standard and the full protection and security standard. Where one of these guarantees is violated, investors sometimes have the ability to submit a claim against the host state to international arbitration.[16]

Extra-EU BITs will remain in force following the UK's exit from the EU.[17] Under Regulation 1219/2012, extra-EU BITs concluded prior to the Lisbon Treaty's entry into force remain in force unless replaced by an agreement concluded by the EU.[18] Given that most of the UK's 96 extra-EU BITs[19] were concluded prior to Dec. 1 2009, including the UK-India BIT, they will remain in force whether the UK is in the EU or not.[20]

Given these BITs will remain in force, in the event that UK exports will be subject to the fall back of paying current EU-WTO tariffs, foreign investors such as Tata Motors could potentially argue that this change has violated its rights under the BIT. Given the EU's tariff schedule will apply indifferently to all exports from the UK to Europe, there can be no violation of the national treatment or most favored nation standards. Moreover, a 'WTO scenario' would not physically harm Tata Motors and therefore does not constitute a violation of the full protection and security standard.[21] Consequently, a claim based on the FET standard is worth considering.

---

[15] Office of the United States Trade Representative, *Bilateral Investment Treaties*, TRADE AGREEMENTS, https://ustr.gov/trade-agreements/bilateral-investment-treaties (last visited Jan. 15, 2016).

[16] Agreement between the Government of the United Kingdom of Great Britain and Northern Ireland and the Government of the Republic of India for the Promotion and Protection of investments art. 9(3) & 10, *signed* March 14, 1994, Treaty Series No. 27 (1992), available at http://investmentpolicyhub.unctad.org/Download/TreatyFile/1613, *known as India-UK BIT*.

[17] Markus Burgstaller and Agnieszka Zarowna, *Possible Ramifications of the UK's EU Referendum on Intra- and Extra-EU BIT's*, 33 JOURNAL OF INTERNATIONAL ARBITRATION ISSUE 4/1 569 (2016), available at https://www.kluwerlawonline.com/document.php?id=JOIA2016033.

[18] Regulation (EU) 1219/2012 of the European Parliament and of the Council of 12 Dec. 2012 establishing transitional arrangements for bilateral investment agreements between Member States and third countries (2012) OJ L351/40, 20 Dec. 2012, recital 5 Art.3.

[19] Burgstaller and Zarowna, *supra* note 17, at 565.

[20] *Id.*, at 571.

[21] The traditional definition of full protection and security is physical security. Some arbitral decisions have extended it to include the stability of the legal framework. However this principle is better established under the FET standard.

Under several of its BITs, the UK has made the specific commitment to accord foreign investors in the UK 'fair and equitable treatment' which includes the protection of an investor's legitimate expectations. A recent study noted, "FET remains the most relied upon and successful basis for a treaty claim. In all 13 decisions on the merits rendered in 2008, a claim based on FET was addressed by the tribunal."[22] This particular obligation is included in the UK-India BIT under Article 3(2) which states that "Investments of investors of each Contracting Party shall at all times be accorded fair and equitable treatment ... in the territory of the other Contracting party."[23] A fundamental element of the FET standard is the protection of investors' legitimate expectations. As an Indian investor, Tata Motors could rely on this provision and argue that the application of tariffs on exports to the EU violated its legitimate expectation that it would continue to export duty-free. However, Tata Motors must successfully fulfill the requirements of such a claim.

B. THE ELEMENTS OF A CLAIM BASED ON FET

Given that the burden of proof rests on the investor to prove a violation of the FET standard, the elements of a successful claim must be determined to measure whether Tata Motors can successfully argue a breach of FET.

Arbitral tribunals through case law have generally held that four conditions must exist to successfully claim a breach of FET: (i) an action attributable to the host, (ii) that constitutes a violation of the applicable FET clause under the BIT (iii) which has caused a damage suffered by the investor. Finally, (iv) causality must exist between these three elements.[24]

The exact content of FET is broad. Acts that constitute violations of FET have been found to include lack of transparency,[25] non-discrimination[26] and lack of due process.[27] There is now an

---

[22] UNCTAD, *Latest Developments in Investor–State Dispute Settlement,* IIA MONITOR No. 1, UNCTAD/WEB/DIAE/IA/2009/6/Rev1, 8 (2009) available at http://unctad.org/en/Docs/webdiaeia20096_en.pdf

[23] India-UK BIT, *supra* note 16, art. 3(2).

[24] ALEXANDRA DIEHL, THE CORE STANDARD OF INTERNATIONAL INVESTMENT PROTECTION: FAIR AND EQUITABLE TREATMENT 325 (Julian D.M. Lew QC, INTERNATIONAL ARBITRATION LAW LIBRARY, No. 26, 2012).

[25] Maffezini v. Spain, ICSID Case No. ARB/97/7, Award, (Nov. 13, 2000), 16 ICSID Rev. 248 (2001), available at http://www.italaw.com/sites/default/files/case-documents/ita0481.pdf.

[26] Lauder v Czech Republic, Final Award, (Sept. 3, 2001), available at http://www.italaw.com/sites/default/files/case-documents/ita0451.pdf.

[27] Rudolf Dolzer, *Fair and Equitable Treatment: A Key Standard in Investment Treaties,* 39 THE INTERNATIONAL LAWYER 87, 100 (2005), available at http://www.jstor.org/stable/40707790.

"overwhelming trend" [28] in arbitral case law to the effect that the "dominant element"[29] of FET is legitimate expectations. The *TECMED* case was the first to explicitly define the principle of legitimate expectations as an obligation of States not to affect the basic expectations taken by the foreign investor to make the investment.[30] This award has formed the basis of much of the arbitral jurisprudence on legitimate expectations, having even been adopted as binding precedent for several BITs.[31] Legitimate expectations in investment law are usually described as "the entitlement of an individual to legal protection from harm caused by a public authority resulting from a previous publicly stated position."[32] However, what type of act violates an investor's legitimate expectation has yet to be explicitly defined.

The difficulty with a claim based on legitimate expectations is that their invocation has largely been founded on precedent, which renders measuring the success of a claim based on FET challenging. Indeed, the nature of arbitration also means an arbitral tribunal can completely disregard the decisions of other tribunals if it so chooses. However, tribunals have and do generally take into account precedents established by previous tribunals.[33] The tribunal in *ADF Group* highlighted that the requirement to accord FET does not allow a tribunal to adopt its own idiosyncratic standard but "must be disciplined by being based upon State practice and judicial or arbitral case law or other sources of customary or general international law."[34]

---

[28] El Paso Energy International Company v. Argentina, ICSID Case No. ARB/03/15, Award, ¶ 348 (31 October 2011), available at http://www.italaw.com/sites/default/files/case-documents/ita0270.pdf.

[29] Saluka Investments BV v. The Czech Republic, UNCITRAL-PCA, Partial Award, ¶ 302 (17 March 2006), available at http://www.italaw.com/sites/default/files/case-documents/ita0740.pdf.

[30] Tecnicas Medioambientales TECMED S.A. v. United Mexican States, ICSID Case ARB (AF)/00/2, ¶ 154 (29 May 2003), 43 ILM 133 (2004), available at http://www.italaw.com/sites/default/files/case-documents/ita0854.pdf.

[31] Trevor Zeyl, *Charting the Wrong Course: The Doctrine of Legitimate Expectations in Investment Treaty Law,* 49 ALTA. L. REV. 203, 220 (2011-2012), available at http://heinonline.org/HOL/Page? handle=hein.journals/alblr49&collection=journals&id=207&startid=207&endid=240.

[32] Dumitru Filip, *The role of legitimate expectations in establishing a jurisprudence constante in international investment law,* 5 MANCHESTER REV. L. CRIME & ETHICS 28, 49 (2016), available at http://heinonline.org/HOL/Page?handle=hein.journals/manrvlce5&collection=journ als&id=29&startid=29&endid=58, citing Chester Brown, *The Protection of Legitimate Expectations as a "General Principle of Law": Some Preliminary Thoughts* 6(1) Transnational Dispute Management 2, (2009).

[33] El Paso, *supra* note 28, at ¶ 220.

[34] ADF Group, Inc. v. United States of America, ICSID Case No. ARB (AF)/00/1, Award, ¶ 184 (9 January 2003), 6 ICSID Reports 470, available at

The case law on legitimate expectations is highly focused on factual analysis. It essentially constitutes a list of examples of the type of behavior that breaches the FET standard. Arbitral tribunals through these examples have gradually posed limits and qualifications to the recognition of legitimate expectations, with different types of state conduct having been found to produce legitimate expectations. Arbitral tribunals have found violations of an investor's legitimate expectations in three circumstances: where the host State (i) acts contrary to contractual commitments, (ii) violates unilateral assertions or promises, and (iii) fundamentally changes the legal or regulatory environment in which the investment was made.[35] However, FET clauses are not stabilization clauses.[36] States may still alter the investment environment so long as their behavior does not constitute one of the aforementioned violations.

Given the unprecedented novelty of Brexit, finding parallels in past cases is difficult. However, "[t]he standard of 'fair and equitable treatment' is certainly no less operative than was the standard of 'due process of law,' and it will be for future practice, jurisprudence and commentary to impart specific content to it."[37] Brexit can therefore be part of the FET standard's defining jurisprudence.

III. THE MERITS OF A CLAIM BY TATA MOTORS AGAINST THE UK: CAN TATA MOTORS BE SUCCESSFUL?

As established above, an analysis of arbitral case law shows that for a tribunal to recognize a violation of the FET standard, it will verify that JLR has suffered damage due to the UK violating the India-UK BIT.[38] If the UK fails to work out a trade agreement with the EU this would undeniably cause JLR, and consequently Tata Motors, a significant loss (Section A). As a result, Tata Motors will likely succeed in its claim against the UK if it fulfills the conditions of one of three scenarios in which legitimate expectations arise under the FET standard (Section B).

---

http://www.italaw.com/sites/default/files/case-documents/ita0009.pdf. *See also* Mondev International Ltd. v. United States of America, ICSID Case No. ARB(AF)/99/2, Award, ¶ 192 (11 October 2002), 6 ICSID Reports 192, available at http://www.italaw.com/sites/default/files/case-documents/ita1076.pdf.

[35] Michele Potestà, *Legitimate expectations in investment treaty law: Understanding the roots and the limits of a controversial concept*, 28 ICSID REVIEW 88, 100-119 (2013), available at http://icsidreview.oxfordjournals.org/content/28/1/88.full.pdf+html.

[36] Moshe Hirsh, *Between Fair and Equitable Treatment and Stabilization Clause: Stable Legal Environment and Regulatory Change in International Investment Law*, 12 J. World Investment & Trade 783, 802 (2011).

[37] Prosper Weil, *The State, the Foreign Investor, and International Law: The No Longer Stormy Relationship of a Ménage à Trois*, 15 ICSID Rev.–F.I.L.J. 401, 415 (2000).

[38] DIEHL, *supra* note 24, at 325.

However, the UK is likely to argue the application of the EU-WTO tariff schedule is the result of its sovereign power to regulate which places a great deal of uncertainty on the success of Tata Motors' claim (C).

A. TATA MOTORS' POTENTIAL LOSSES AS A RESULT OF A 'HARD BREXIT'

To succeed in its claim against the UK, Tata Motors must bring factual evidence to justify a claim under the India-UK BIT for a breach of the FET standard. Tata Motors must demonstrate that the UK's decision to leave the EU will cause it to suffer a real damage. The European market is an essential component of many industries in the UK, particularly the automobile industry. Indeed, approximately 45% of UK car exports are to the EU.[39] Currently, the UK exports its cars to the EU with zero levies. However, for non-EU countries, the EU's tariff schedule imposes tariffs 10% ad valorem.[40] If the UK and the EU fail to conclude a trade deal and resort to a 'WTO scenario,' the UK will be treated like all other suppliers and thus pay the long-ago established EU-WTO tariffs.[41]

JLR's increasing exports to the EU currently make up 24% of its profits, while JLR represents 90% of Tata Motors' valuation.[42] If the aforementioned 'WTO scenario' is to materialize, it is estimated JLR would suffer a loss of $1.47 billion in the four years following the application of the EU-WTO tariffs.[43] Though this is only an estimate, it is undeniable Tata Motors will face a loss sufficiently important to justify a claim for compensation. However, it must be noted that the damage

---

[39] *Manufacturing in the UK: Busting the Myths, supra* note 9.

[40] Campbell and Inagaki, *supra* note 6.

[41] For example, a classic Range Rover retails at around £75,000 in the UK. Exporting just one Range Rover would therefore require JLR to pay an extra $7,500 in duties. Moreover, this analysis does not include situations where companies have invested in the UK with the expectation of importing parts or components from Europe to be made into finished goods in the UK for export back to Europe. There very well may be a new UK tariff schedule that is different from the fall-back WTO schedule, assuming the UK and the EU come to an agreement on a new schedule. These businesses will therefore be harmed by the new tariffs on imports the UK chooses to put in place in its tariff schedule, in addition to the application of the EU-WTO tariffs on exports.

[42] Trefis Team, *Tata's Jaguar Land Rover Continues To Accelerate Sales By More Than Its Competitors In 2016*, FORBES, (Sept. 27, 2016, 8:38 AM), http://www.forbes.com/sites/greatspeculations/2016/09/27/tatas-jaguar-land-rover-continues-to-accelerate-sales-by-more-than-its-competitors-in-2016/#7795ab94798e.

[43] Brian Rogerson, *UK auto lessors, German carmakers and Jaguar Land Rover's Tata parent consider the ramifications of Brexit vote*, ASSET FINANCE INTERNATIONAL, (June 27, 2016), http://www.assetfinanceinternational.com/index.php/auto/emea/auto-emea-articles2/13873-uk-auto-lessors-german-carmakers-and-jaguar-land-rover-s-tata-parent-consider-the-ramifications-of-brexit-vote.

suffered by Tata Motors must be qualified and quantifiable.[44] As a result, Tata Motors will have to wait to bring a suit against the UK until it has suffered a demonstrable loss.

B. TATA MOTORS' LEGITIMATE EXPECTATIONS VIOLATED BY THE UK

The central element for a successful claim against the UK for an increase in tariffs is a violation of a standard protected under the India-UK BIT. In this case, Article 3(2) guarantees the FET of all foreign investors.[45] As discussed above, one of the fundamental components of the FET standard has been held to include the respect of an investor's legitimate expectations relied upon when making his investment.

Examining JLR's growth, it is clear that Tata Motors was and is seeking to expand its market share into the EU. Though access to the EU market may not have been the sole reason or even the main reason for purchasing JLR, it undeniably was an important factor. Indeed, "Europe is a key strategic market for [JLR's] business."[46] With JLR's sales in the EU having increased from 19% to 24% in a year,[47] JLR is "absolutely committed to [its] customers in the EU."[48] Tata Motors must therefore demonstrate that its legitimate expectation that it would have continued access to the single market has been violated. In this sense, the "act attributable to the UK" which potentially violates Tata Motors' expectations will be the UK's new regulatory framework, notably the application of WTO-EU tariffs.

To succeed in this claim, Tata Motors must show this expectation was 'legitimate.' Legitimate expectations arise in 3 circumstances: where (i) a State acts contrary to contractual commitments, (ii) a State violates unilateral assertions or promises, and (iii) there is a fundamental change in the legal or regulatory environment.[49]

Given that in the case of JLR and Tata Motors it is unclear whether the UK made any contractual commitments, the focus of this paper will be on the UK's violation of representations (1) and the fundamental change in the British legal and regulatory environment (2).

---

[44] GAMI Investments Inc. v United Mexican States, NAFTA/UNCITRAL, Award, ¶ 83, (Nov. 15, 2004).

[45] India-UK BIT, *supra* note 16, art. 3(2).

[46] Christiaan Heztner, Nick Gibbs and Hans Greimel, *Automakers call for tariff-free trade between UK and EU after Brexit win*, AUTOMOTIVE NEWS (June 24, 2016, 8:20 AM), http://www.autonews.com/article/20160624/COPY01/306249977/automakers-call-for-tariff-free-trade-between-uk-and-eu-after-brexit (citing a JLR spokesperson).

[47] Rogerson, *supra* note 43.

[48] *Jaguar Land Rover Statement to UK Referendum*, TATA MOTORS (June 24, 2016) http://www.tatamotors.com/press/uk-referendum-result/.

[49] Potestà, *supra* note 35, at 100-119.

1. Unilateral promises or representations by the UK

Investors have often claimed violations of their legitimate expectations where a host state allegedly made unilateral promises or representations, on which the investor relied at the time of making its investment, which were then frustrated. Arbitral tribunals have accordingly extended the protection based on the theory of legitimate expectations to these circumstances. [50] Legitimate expectations arise where there are acts "cloaked with the mantle of Government authority and communicated as such to foreign investors who relied on them in making their investments," [51] even though there are no official or contractual commitments.

Several elements could potentially be considered as representations on the part of the British government that the UK's eligibility for access to the EU single market and the application of zero tariffs would remain unchanged. The UK has consistently marketed the UK economy internationally, lauding its strengths as "the best place in Europe from which to succeed in global business," notably focusing on India.[52] The UK's accession to the European Community and EU also constitutes a significant representation that UK companies would be able to export to the EU duty-free. Indeed, with the ratification of the European Communities Act in 1972[53] and later the TFEU in 2007[54] there was little doubt that the UK would remain in the single market. In the case of both the EU and the WTO, the creation of the single market was a very involved, formal process.[55] Furthermore, the UK was a central element in liberalizing trade, notably British policy-makers who were among the first to press for the deepening of free trade within the EU.[56] The UK

---

[50] *Id.*, at 104-105.

[51] Southern Pacific Properties (Middle East) Limited v Arab Republic of Egypt, ICSID Case No ARB/84/3, Award, ¶ 82, (20 May 1992) available at http://www.italaw.com/sites/default/files/case-documents/italaw6314_0.pdf.

[52] UK Trade and Investment, UK Trade & Investment Annual Report and Accounts 2007-2008, 2008, H.C., 9 and 33 (UK) available at https://www.gov.uk/government/uploads/system/uploads/attachment_data/file/248467/0851.pdf; Business and Enterprise Committee, Waking up to India: Developments in UK-India Economic Relations, 2008, H.C. ¶ 8 33 (UK), available at https://www.publications.parliament.uk/pa/cm200708/cmselect/cmberr/209/209.pdf.

[53] Helen Wallace, *The UK: 40 Years of EU Membership*, 8 (4) Journal of Contemporary European Research 531, 532 (2012), available at http://www.jcer.net/index.php/jcer/article/download/539/359.

[54] *See* Bruno Waterfield, *Gordon Brown finally signs EU treaty*, The Telegraph, (Apr. 12, 2008 4:58 PM), http://www.telegraph.co.uk/news/uknews/1572416/Gordon-Brown-finally-signs-EU-treaty.html.

[55] Wallace, *supra* note 53, at 532-536.

[56] *Id,* at 540.

has similarly supported trade liberalization within the GATT and WTO and the role of the EU in pushing for this.[57] These agreements cemented the UK's intention to remain a part of the EU and can be qualified as representations that investors would retain duty-free access to the EU single market.

Arbitral case law shows that the threshold for a State's conduct to constitute the basis of a claim for violation of legitimate expectations is incredibly high. The strongest foundation is when "both formal and official elements are reinforced by government conduct" while the *Continental Casualty* tribunal held that "political statements have the least legal value."[58] Signing the TFEU and the UK's general attitude with regards to the EU and FDI combines both official and informal representations. This can be interpreted as an unambiguous representation that foreign investors would continue to export to the EU duty-free.

However, basing a claim on the UK's general encouragement of FDI, pro-Europe political statements and the signing of the TFEU will be difficult given a State's representations must be unambiguous and individualized if the investor's expectations are to have sufficient weight.[59] 'Individualized' poses a problem in the sense that it is unclear whether the UK made specific guarantees. No official assurances appear to have been directed at Tata Motors. Though statements of a more general nature or general investment-encouraging policies directed towards investors have been invoked as a basis of legitimate expectations, [60] these were usually successful in conjunction with guarantees contained in the regulatory framework.[61] In the case of *PSEG v Turkey* for example, a policy to encourage and welcome investment alone was not held to be a promise made specifically to the investor.[62]

Moreover, representations alone are insufficient. The representation made by the UK must have induced the claimant into investing.[63] The various negotiations and agreements within the EU and WTO are acts on which investors undeniably relied on. Tata Motors will thus have to demonstrate how "Europe is a key strategic market for [JLR's]

---

[57] *Id*, at 536 and 540.

[58] DIEHL, *supra* note 24, at 368.

[59] ROLAND KLÄGER, 'FAIR AND EQUITABLE TREATMENT' IN INTERNATIONAL INVESTMENT LAW 187 (James Crawford & John S. Bell, CAMBRIDGE STUDIES IN INTERNATIONAL AND COMPARATIVE LAW, 2011); *See also* DIEHL, *supra* note 24, at 399 and 402.

[60] Potestà, *supra* note 35, at 107

[61] *Id.*, at 107-108

[62] *Id.*, 107.

[63] Potestà, *supra* note 35, at 104-105

business"[64] and that it chose to invest in a UK car manufacturer as a base from which to develop its share of both the UK and European markets.

Ultimately, though Tata Motors may be able to show it relied on the UK's EU membership, it will have difficulty showing that the UK made unilateral promises that duty-free access to the EU would remain unchanged. Nonetheless, the UK's investment-encouraging policies and pro-Europe stance at the time of Tata Motors' investment will be helpful in a claim based on representations to be found in UK's legal and regulatory framework.

2. A fundamental change in the legal and regulatory environment

Though BITs do not freeze the laws of a particular country, governments still have an obligation to ensure the relative stability of the investment environment. An investor can base his legitimate expectations on representations to be found in the UK's legal and regulatory framework. Consequently, if the host State alters the general legislative and regulatory framework in which the investment was grounded, this can constitute a breach of the FET standard. In the words of the *Total* tribunal, the tribunal must "determine whether the legislation, regulation and provisions invoked by [claimant] constitute a set of promises and commitments [...] whose unilateral modifications entail a breach of the legitimate expectations [...]."[65]

Several arbitral tribunals have held that inherent in respecting an investor's legitimate expectations is the stability and predictability of the legal and business framework.[66] Even in the absence of a stabilization clause or an individualized representation, a tribunal may nonetheless find a violation of the FET by reference to a frustration of the investor's legitimate expectations. However, the factors that justify such a finding vary. For example, the tribunal in *El Paso* held that the change in the legal framework must be "total." [67] Other tribunals have held that modifications will violate the FET standard where they are discriminatory to the investment,[68] where they are so frequent they have a "roller-coaster" effect,[69] where they are unreasonable[70] or where there is negative conduct from the host state.[71] Though in the case of Tata Motors a change in the tariffs applied to UK exports is unlikely to satisfy

---

[64] Heztner, Gibbs and Greimel, *supra* note 46. (citing a JLR spokesperson).
[65] Total v Argentine Republic, ICSID Case No ARB/04/01, Decision on Liability, ¶ 99, (27 December 2010).
[66] KLÄGER, *supra* note 59, at 169.
[67] El Paso, *supra* note 28, at ¶ 374.
[68] Potestà, *supra* note 35,116-117.
[69] *Id.*
[70] *Id.*
[71] Hirsh, *supra* note 36, at 799.

any of these conditions, there is no exact threshold. Given that the effects of Brexit are unparalleled, Tata Motors could argue that the new regulatory framework is so radically and fundamentally different that it constitutes a violation of the FET standard.

In this regard, the *Argentine Gas Sector Cases*[72] offer an interesting example. Like Brexit, these cases emerged from a significant and abrupt change in the investment framework following Argentina's economic crisis. In this series of cases, Argentina had made several promises to foreign investors regarding tariffs as part of its regulatory framework.[73] Following the economic crisis, Argentina passed an emergency law which repudiated these guarantees. [74] Four companies consequently sued Argentina for violating the FET standard, amongst other claims. The tribunals found that the companies had benefitted from "stabilization" guarantees[75] and concluded that where the regulatory framework and guarantees are tailored to attract investors, any significant changes violate the FET standard.[76]

The change following Brexit is unprecedented in economic history. Investors have relied on a legal framework that has existed for over 40 years in the case of the EU and over 20 years in the case of the WTO. There is a significant difference between changing a law and fundamentally altering a country's entire legal and regulatory environment; Brexit falls in the latter category. At the time of Tata Motors' purchase of JLR, the UK exiting the EU was virtually inconceivable. As a result, if foreign investors were able to succeed against Argentina, a parallel could be drawn with the UK's decision to change its regulatory framework completely. As a result, the application of EU-WTO tariffs to UK exports would constitute a violation of the standard of FET.

However, Potestà correctly points out that in the *Argentine Gas Sector Cases*, investors could also invoke licenses. Licenses had been granted by

---

[72] Term coined by José E. Alvarez & Kathryn Khamsi, *The Argentine Crisis and Foreign Investors: A Glimpse into the Heart of the Investment Regime*, YEARBOOK OF INTERNATIONAL INVESTMENT LAW AND POLICY 379, 388-389 (Karl P. Sauvant, 2009) available at http://www.vcc.columbia.edu/pubs/documents/Alvarez-final_000.pdf. (Refers to CMS Transmission Co. v Argentine Republic, ICSID Case No. ARB/01/8, Award (May 12, 2005); LG&E Energy Corp. v Argentine Republic, ICSID Case No. ARB/02/1, Decision on Liability (October 3, 2006); Enron Corp., Ponderosa Assets, L.P. v Argentine Republic, ICSID Case No. ARB/01/3, Award (May 22, 2007); Sempra Energy Int'l v Argentine Republic, ICSID Case No. ARB/02/16, Award (September 28 2007).)
[73] *Id.* Argentina had promised that tariffs would be calculated in US dollars, that tariffs would be reviewed every five years and licenses would not be rescinded or modified without the consent of investors).
[74] *Id.* at 389-390.
[75] *Id,* at 391.
[76] *Id.*

the government by decree, "which, in addition to referring to the guarantees established by legislation, also stated that they could not be modified without the licensee's consent."[77] These cases can therefore be interpreted as being part of the case law on changes in general regulatory framework but also as case law on individualized promises to investors.[78] In the case of Tata Motors there were no specific promises from the UK that applicable tariffs would remain unchanged.

Arbitral tribunals also take into account the specific characteristics of the host state to determine the legitimacy of the investor's expectations regarding the investment framework. Recent cases suggest that the political, socioeconomic, cultural and historical conditions in the host state should be taken into account.[79] Though BITs are not insurance against business risk,[80] investors are more likely to expect regulatory stability in developed countries than in developing countries.[81] As a result, if the host state changes its regulatory framework, an arbitral tribunal is more likely to be lenient with a country like Argentina than the UK. For example, arbitral tribunals have held that ex-communist countries could not be held to have violated the FET standard by changing their legal framework given that they were new democracies and therefore inherently subject to change.[82]

As the UK is a developed country with one of the most stable economies, an arbitral tribunal will expect it to have greater stability. Some will argue that a withdrawal from the EU was always a possibility given that Article 50 of the TFEU constitutes an exit clause.[83] However, it was never intended to be used. [84] It was "a fire extinguisher that should never have to be used. Instead, the fire happened."[85] It was improbable that the UK would exit the EU given its 40-year membership. An investor could therefore legitimately expect that the UK would remain a member state of the EU and, even if the UK's exit from the EU was a possibility, a change in tariffs from 0% to 10% after 20 years was remote.

[77] Potestà, *supra* note 35, at 111-112.

[78] *Id.*, 111-112.

[79] KLÄGER, *supra* note 59, at 186. *See also* Zeyl, *supra* note 31, at 392.

[80] DIEHL, *supra* note 24, at 365.

[81] KLÄGER, *supra* note 59, at 246.

[82] Ursula Kriebaum, *The Relevance of Economic and Political Conditions for Protection under Investment Treaties,* 10 Law & Prac. Int'l Cts. & Tribunals 383, 388 & 390 (2011).

[83] Burgstaller and Zarowna, *supra* note 17, at 574-575.

[84] Christopher Hooton & Jon Stone, *Brexit: Article 50 was never actually meant to be used, says its author,* THE INDEPENDENT (Jul. 26, 2016), http://www.independent.co.uk/news/uk/politics/brexit-eu-referendum-britain-theresa-may-article-50-not-supposed-meant-to-be-used-trigger-giuliano-a7156656.html.

[85] *Id.* (quoting Giuliano Amato, former prime minister of Italy, who later worked with the European Commission and helped draft the European Constitution, which became the Lisbon Treaty).

Where someone could consider the UK would no longer be a part of the EU, it did not necessarily imply it would be subject to the EU's tariff schedule for non-EU members. There is therefore a case to be made that Tata Motors could legitimately expect that such a fundamental change in the regulatory framework would not occur.

Finally, an analysis of an investor's legitimate expectations must also take into account the host State's conduct. Potestà implicitly argues that a breach of the FET standard could be avoided if the host State gives those affected by a regulatory change adequate warning, and, where possible, adopts transitional measures. [86] The adoption of similar safeguards will be a significant element to take into account by the UK when negotiating with the EU.

C. THE CAUSAL LINK BETWEEN TATA MOTORS' FINANCIAL LOSS AND BREXIT

A successful claim for a breach of FET must show: (i) an act attributable to the host State, (ii) that constitutes a violation of the applicable FET standard (iii) which has caused a damage suffered by the investor. Finally, (iv) causality must exist between these three elements. If an investor-state dispute were to arise, Tata Motors must first show a loss. As established, if the aforementioned 'WTO scenario' is to materialize, it is estimated JLR would suffer a loss of $1.47 billion in the four years following the application of the EU-WTO schedule.[87] The UK would however likely argue that there is no causality between such a loss and the UK's decision to withdraw from the EU.[88] It is true that arguing that the referendum or the Great Repeal Bill has directly caused Tata Motors a loss would be incredibly difficult. Indeed, the link between both events is too remote. However, applying WTO-EU tariffs to UK exports is a direct consequence of the UK government's decision to leave the European single market. This is undeniably an act attributable to the UK government that directly impacts Tata Motors. As there is a potential quantifiable loss, a specific act by the UK and a causal link between both, if Tata Motors can establish that the UK's new regulatory framework constitutes a violation of FET all the conditions necessary to bring a claim for a breach of the FET standard will exist.

D. A STATE'S SOVEREIGN RIGHT TO REGULATE AS A COUNTER ARGUMENT

An action by Tata Motors for the violation of the applicable FET clause will fail if the UK successfully counter-argues. If Tata Motors were

---

[86] Potestà, *supra* note 35, at 117.
[87] Rogerson, *supra* note 43.
[88] Burgstaller and Zarowna, *supra* note 17, at 574-575.

to bring a case before an arbitral tribunal, the UK's most probable and most significant argument would be that it was simply exercising its sovereign power to regulate.

Sovereignty constitutes a "meta-principle" of public international law.[89] Though the UK has consented to restrict its sovereignty in matters of investment regulation by concluding BITs,[90] its obligation to maintain a stable framework is counterbalanced by a need for flexible public policy.[91] As established above, an investor cannot expect the framework at the time of his investment to remain completely unchanged. Consequently, a number of tribunals[92] have adopted a balancing test in which the arbitrators weigh the obligations of states against the rights of the investor. States must be allowed "to respond to changing circumstances in the public interest."[93] Brower and Schill note that there is increasing recognition that States "are not required to compensate foreign investors for effects of bona fide, general regulations that further a legitimate purpose in a nondiscriminatory and proportionate way."[94]

The hypothetical application of the EU-WTO tariffs to UK exports will be an indirect result of the UK's referendum to withdraw from the EU. The referendum was an expression of the UK's right to self-determination. Moreover, these additional duties would be the application of a modified international agreement, having failed to conclude a new FTA with the EU. A parallel can be therefore be drawn with the *Pope v Talbot* decision where the tribunal recognized that Canada was permitted to modify its regulatory framework given the new regulations were necessary in order to implement a new international agreement, did not discriminate against foreign investors, tried to mitigate the adverse effects of the change and constituted a reasonable response.[95] The exact circumstances of the new legal order in the UK will vary according to the negotiations, but it will likely be difficult for Tata Motors to argue that the increase in tariffs was unreasonable or discriminatory such that the UK can be held liable.

CONCLUSION

Though a claim for a violation of the FET is at least viable, its success is less certain. The hierarchy of government conduct from which legitimate expectations arise places changes in the legal and regulatory

---

[89] KLÄGER, *supra* note 59, at 154

[90] *Id.*, at 157.

[91] DIEHL, *supra* note 24, at 367.

[92] *Id.*, at 357-376.

[93] Zeyl, *supra* note 31, at 232.

[94] *Id.*, at 233.

[95] KLÄGER, *supra* note 59, at 159-160

framework at the bottom. Indeed, arbitral tribunals are more likely to find a breach where there has been an individualized act directed at the investor than a general change in the law. Without specific assurances to demonstrate the UK intended to remain part of Europe and therefore to retain its current duty-free access to the EU, a tribunal is unlikely to conclude the UK has violated its international obligations under the India-UK BIT. Indeed, the UK has a right to regulate. As stated in *El Paso*, "[t]here can be no legitimate expectation for anyone that the legal framework will remain unchanged [...] unless very specific commitments have been made towards it or unless the alteration of the legal framework is total."[96] Consequently, the success of a claim by Tata Motors will depend largely on whether an arbitral tribunal interprets the ratification of the various EC/EU and WTO agreements and the UK's general trade policy as constituting sufficiently specific promises to consider the UK's new regulatory framework as a violation of the FET standard.

Moreover, there is an increasing concern that the investor-state dispute settlement system permits arbitrators to intrude on fundamental questions of sovereignty or interfere in matters that are fundamentally national concerns.[97] Given the Brexit referendum constitutes a national expression of self-determination, without a contractual or unilateral promise, an arbitral tribunal may be reluctant to side with Tata Motors.

It is however safe to say that there is a real risk that the UK will face suits for violating their obligations under international investment law. Although in this specific case Tata Motors' claim may fail, other investors may be able to show clear contractual or unilateral promises, or even negative conduct by the UK government, such that a violation of the FET standard arises. Given that the amount of FDI in the UK is estimated to be around $1 trillion, when negotiating its withdrawal from the EU, the UK must consider the possibility that if the regulatory framework changes too drastically, it opens itself up to potential liability for violating the FET standard under its BITs.

---

[96] El Paso, *supra* note 28, at ¶ 374.
[97] Alvarez and Khamsi, *supra* note 73, at 383.

CHAPTER 19: ENVISAGING A POST-BREXIT FINANCIAL SERVICES SECTOR UNDER THE GATS FRAMEWORK—A CASE STUDY OF EURO CLEARING

SUSAN YIN[1]

Nearly half of the UK's surplus on trade in services in 2015 derived from export in financial services; thus, preserving backdoor access into the EU single market for the City of London would be key for the UK economy. The average daily turnover in Britain of euro-denominated interest rate swaps totalled $928 billion in April 2013, or 69 percent of the global market. Moreover in 2013, the European Market Infrastructure Regulation (EMIR) came into force pushing OTC derivatives into central clearing, with a result of enlarging the UK's euro-denominated derivatives global market share.[2] Therefore, the City of London is also of systemic significance for the European financial authorities. This paper uses London's euro-denominated derivatives market as the lens through which to study the WTO rules that underlie the regional, minilateral and domestic trade and regulatory rules applying to financial services.

Proceeding from a worst case scenario, the paper envisages a post-Brexit era without a bespoke exit agreement and poses the question: what are the risks posed by the GATS rules and EU's third-country regime which the trade negotiators need to address?

The paper comprises three sections. Section I describes the market structure of the offshore Euro-denominated derivatives market in London; Section II examines EU Regulation of derivatives clearing; Section III considers some future restrictions on the London market; Section IV analyzes the position for London's euro-denominated derivatives market under the GATS regime before drawing some Conclusions.

---

[1] Email: sy453@georgetown.edu. The author would like to thank Professors Jennifer Hillman, Gary Horlick and Chris Brummer for their comments. All limitations are the author's alone.
[2]   https://www.theguardian.com/business/2017/jan/13/eu-negotiator-wants-special-deal-over-access-to-city-post-brexit#img-1.

I. OVERVIEW OF THE OFFSHORE EURO-DENOMINATED DERIVATIVES MARKET IN LONDON

A. MECHANISMS OF INTERNATIONAL DERIVATIVES CLEARING AND SETTLEMENT

A "derivative" can, in general, be defined as a financial product, the cash flow of which is derived from another financial product.[3] This definition encompasses at least three different financial products: futures, options, and swaps.[4] Traditionally, distinctions were drawn between the exchange-traded derivatives which are standardised instruments, and over-the-counter (OTC) derivatives which are bespoke agreements made and settled directly between two parties. However, this distinction has somewhat eroded in the aftermath of the Global Financial Crisis 2007-2010, when the G-20 countries made commitments during the Pittsburgh Summit[5] to require clearing of OTC derivatives similar to that for exchange-traded instruments.

In exchanges trading, the traditional "open outcry" method on a physical trading floor has been replaced by dealers placing orders via an electronic trading system operated by the exchange. With exchange participants able to deal from anywhere in the world, the place of conclusion of an "on-exchange" contract is therefore not where the dealer happens to be situated, but the location of the exchange which provides the trading facilities, and the rules and procedures governing the trading process.[6]

After trades are entered and matched, the process of clearing takes place prior to settlements, in order to manage liquidity and counterparty risk in the financial system. Clearing houses provide for the novation of trades by becoming the central counterparty (CCP) in the trades, i.e. CCP becomes the seller to the buyer and buyer to the seller as per the same terms of the original derivatives contract. Prior to novation, multilateral netting usually takes place, resulting in all participants having a single delivery and payment obligation. In addition, clearing houses may also require clearing members (i.e. those approved financial institutions with the right to novate contracts) to provide capital and collateral as protection against default.[7] Thus clearing houses are able to maintain

---

[3] ALASTAIR HUDSON, THE LAW ON FINANCIAL DERIVATIVES, Section 1-06 (Sweet & Maxwell 5th ed. 2012).

[4] *Ibid.* Section 1-07.

[5] Pittsburg Summit Leaders' Statement (September 2009), para.13.

[6] DERIVATIVES: LAW AND PRACTICE, para. 20.006 (Simon Firth ed. Sweet & Maxwell Dec. 2016).

[7] *Ibid.* para. 10.002.

default funds for covering any shortfalls in the event of insufficient collateral.[8]

B. THE CITY OF LONDON'S EURO-DENOMINATED DERIVATIVES CLEARING

The UK is currently the leading trading hub for the euro-denominated derivatives, accounting for 75% of trades in interest rate derivatives in 2016, and an increase of 4.5% from 2013.[9] This increase of the City's global market share during this period is contemporaneous with the coming into force of the EMIR in 2013, which has contributed to a consistent rise in the volume of OTC derivatives clearing despite a general drop of derivatives trading activity during the same period. There is high market concentration in the City's clearing industry. At the end of 2015 in the UK, the two CCPs LCH.Clearnet Limited and ICE Clear Europe accounted for nearly 94% of the total volume of cleared derivatives transactions reported according to the Bank of International Settlement.[10]

The statistics are indicative of the reasons for the City's dominance in euro-denominated derivatives. Economies of scale are the rationale for the concentration and vertical integration in derivatives (and currencies) trading and central clearing.[11] In addition, the market's preference for English law and courts is also a crucial factor. The standard contracts developed by the International Swaps and Dealers Association (ISDA) have been based on English and New York law. Moreover, decisions by the English courts have been shown to result in reinforcing the market practices as reflected in the ISDA's Master Agreement.[12]

II. EU REGULATION OF DERIVATIVES CLEARING

This section explains the harmonised EU regulatory structure of euro-denominated derivatives clearing.

A. MANDATORY CENTRAL COUNTERPARTIES CLEARING

Prior to the Global Financial Crisis, mandatory clearing of derivatives under EU law had only been applied to exchange-traded

---

[8] *Ibid.* para. 10.008.
[9] Torsten Ehlers and Egemen Eren, *The changing shape of interest rate derivatives markets*, BIS Quarterly Review, (2016).
[10] CPMI, Statistics on payment, clearing and settlement systems in the CPMI countries https://www.bis.org/cpmi/publ/d155.pdf, September 2016, page 419.
[11] *Supra* n. 9.
[12] Joanne Braithwaite, *Standard Form Contracts as Transnational Law: Evidence from the Derivatives Markets*, 75(5) MLR 779 (2012).

instruments. Under the Market in Financial Instruments Regulation,[13] a market operator of a regulated exchange needs to ensure that all transactions entered into in accordance with the operator's market rules are centrally cleared by a CCP. In the aftermath of the Crisis, European Market Infrastructure Regulation (EMIR) was passed to subject certain OTC derivatives transactions to mandatory clearing (hereinafter "ESMA clearing obligation").[14] The types of OTC transactions to be subject to the ESMA clearing obligation (hereinafter "Specified OTC Derivatives") were provided for in two Commission Delegated Regulations promulgated in 2016 which applied to credit and interest rate derivatives.[15]

The Crisis had exhibited the systemic risk emanating from an opaque derivatives trading structure.[16] The EMIR therefore sought to mitigate systemic risk in the global financial market and protect it against market abuse through an extraterritorial application of the mandatory clearing obligation. According to Article 4(1)(a)(iv), the EMIR clearing obligation would apply to the Specified OTC Derivatives contracted between a counterparty established in a third country, and a EU-based financial counterparty[17] or qualifying Non-financial counterparty,[18] so far as the EMIR clearing obligation would have been applicable had the third-country counterparty been established in the EU. Furthermore, under Article 4(1)(a)(v), the EMIR clearing obligation would also apply between two third-country counterparties whose derivatives contract would be subject to the EMIR clearing obligation had they been established in the EU, provided that there is a "direct, substantial and foreseeable effect within the Union." This effect criterion would *à priori* be satisfied if one of the third-country counterparties received a guarantee from an EU financial institution, which amounts to at least EUR 8 billion in liabilities and 5% of OTC derivative exposures on the latter's balance sheet.[19]

---

[13] Formerly the Market in Financial Instruments Regulation is now replaced by Regulation No 600/2014 of 14 May 2014 on markets in financial instruments and amending Regulation (EU) No 648/2012 (MiFID II) (2014) OJ L 173/84, Article 29(1).
[14] Regulation No.648/2012 of 4 July 2012 on OTC Derivatives, Central Counterparties and Trade Repositories ("EMIR") [2012] OJ L201/1 Article 4(1).
[15] Commission Delegated Regulation (EU) 2016/592 of 1 March 2016 ("the Delegated Regulation no.2 on the clearing obligation") OJ L 103 and Commission Delegated Regulation (EU) 2016/1178 of 10 June 2016 ("the Delegated Regulation no.3 on the clearing obligation") OJ L 195.
[16] Steven Schwarcz , *Systemic Risk*, 97 The Geo. L. J. 193 (2008).
[17] A financial counterparty, as defined in Article 2(8) of EMIR, refers to a financial institution or fund that has been authorised under an EU directive.
[18] A non-financial counterparty is defined in Article 2(9) of EMIR as an undertaking established in the EEA, other than a CCP or a financial counterparty.
[19] Commission Delegation Regulation No 285/2014 OJ L 85/1, Article 2(1).

B.   REGULATION OF CENTRAL COUNTERPARTIES

Where the EMIR clearing obligation arises in respect of a derivatives transaction, counterparties must clear their trades through a CCP that is authorised and established within the EU under Article 14, or a recognised third-country CCP under Article 25 of EMIR.[20]

In respect to a CCP established in an EU Member State, EMIR allocates the regulatory power of authorisation and supervision to the Member State of establishment ("home Member state").[21] The authorisation by the home Member State is then effective throughout the EU.[22]

According to Article 25(1) of EMIR, in order for a third-country CCP to provide clearing services to entities which are established in the EU, it needs to be granted recognition from the European Securities and Markets Authority (ESMA).[23] The granting of recognition needs to be based on a finding that the following four criteria are satisfied:[24]

a)   the Commission adopted a decision of "equivalence" in respect of a third country regulatory regime;

b)   the CCP is duly authorised and in compliance according to the relevant third country's laws;

c)   cooperation arrangements are in place between ESMA and the relevant third country's authority; and

d)   the relevant third country's laws provide for equivalent systems for combating anti-money laundering and the financing of terrorism.

At the time of writing, the European Commission has adopted decisions of equivalence in respect of fourteen jurisdictions,[25] and, the ESMA has conferred recognition upon twenty-two CCPs established in nine of these jurisdictions.[26]

---

[20] EMIR Article 4(3).

[21] EMIR Articles 14(1) and 22(1).

[22] EMIR Article 14(2).

[23] ESMA was one of the three European Supervisory Authorities with independent legal personality created by Regulation (EU) ("ESMA Regulation") 1095/2010, OJ L 331/84.

[24] EMIR Article 25(2).

[25] Australia, Brazil, Canada, Hong Kong, India, Japan, Mexico, New Zealand, Republic of Korea, Singapore, South Africa, Switzerland, South Africa, United Arab Emirates (Dubai International Financial Centre), USA. https://www.esma.europa.eu/regulation/post-trading/central-counterparties-ccps.

[26] ESMA, "List of third-country central counterparties recognised to offer services and activities in the Union," December 14, 2016 https://www.esma.europa.eu/sites/default/files/library/third-country_ccps_recognised_under_emir.pdf.

However, it may be observed that Article 25 is silent on whether third country CCPs would also need recognition from ESMA when only providing clearing services to *non-EU* counterparties whose transactions (as above discussed) have "direct, substantial and foreseeable effect" within the EU. Article 4(3) of EMIR requires exclusively that compliance of the ESMA clearing obligation is to be secured via an authorised (Article 14) or recognised (Article 25) CCP. Therefore, in order to clear derivative trades caught by EMIR in practice, a non-EU CCP needs at least to be granted an ESMA recognition, notwithstanding that neither the derivatives counterparties nor the CCP are incorporated in the EU. The exterritorial application of EMIR would have particular relevance post Brexit for UK-based CCPs presently offering clearing services to EU financial institutions.

C. *REGULATION OF CLEARING MEMBERS*

Since CCP membership is generally only available to well-capitalised institutions, most users of financial derivatives would need to establish indirect clearing arrangements via agency arrangements with clearing members. The clearing members of a CCP are firstly subject to clearing house rules. In addition, the activities of clearing and settling of derivatives transactions constitute "provision of investment activities" under MIFID II,[27] rendering a clearing member to be subject to the authorisation of its home Member State (i.e. the firm's place of incorporation).[28] Articles 34 of MiFID II provides for the principles of mutual recognition and home Member State control. The role of the host Member State is preserved by Article 35(8) where the investment firm establishes a branch, but only in respect to matters relating to consumer protection. Unlike the third country CCP recognition regime under EMIR, there is no equivalence regime for third country providers of investment services, which all need to establish a branch in, and thereby be subject to the supervision of, an EU Member State.[29]

D. *APPLICATION OF EU LAW IN THE LONDON DERIVATIVES MARKET*

The two major London-based clearing houses are LCH Limited ("LCH") and ICE Clear Europe Limited ("ICE Clear"). They provide clearing and settlement services for Specified OTC derivatives in a variety of currencies including Euros.[30] LCH and ICE Clear are both

---

[27] Directive 2014/65/EU on Market on Financial Instruments (recast) OJ L 173/349, Article 5(1).

[28] *Id.* Article 6(1).

[29] *Id.* Article 39.

[30] The instruments subject to the EMIR clearing obligation being cleared by ICE Clear and LCH are found in ESMA's "Public Register for the Clearing Obligation under EMIR,"

"recognised Central Counterparties" under the Financial Services and Markets Act 2000 and subject to the regulation of the Bank of England.[31] As a result, LCH and ICE Clear are currently authorised to carry on clearing services throughout the EU under EMIR.[32]

In the event of the UK not being able to secure access to the EU internal market in the aftermath of Brexit, LCH and ICE Clear would no longer be authorised to provide clearing services under EMIR unless they have been conferred recognition by ESMA pursuant to EMIR Article 25(2). However, as will be discussed in the next Section, EU lawmakers might take actions inhibiting the viability of the City of London's euro derivatives clearing market on the grounds of financial stability concerns.

Political and legal uncertainty may be conducive to LCH and ICE Clear moving their London clearing operations to the sister subsidiaries of LCH SA and ICE Clear Netherlands. In addition to relocating clearing and trading activities to other EU countries, the need to move industry-associated services, such as law firms providing English law advice, may also increase the cost of relocation. Moreover, due to the current trend of increasing volumes of US-dollar-denominated derivatives trades, the EU is at the risk of losing more derivatives trading activities to New York. The consequence of market fragmentation could give rise to market opacity and result in regulatory inefficiency. The rest of this paper tries to outline a legal framework from WTO law perspective for the future development of the euro derivatives market, and begins by considering the ways in which EU actions might affect the future of the London clearing business.

III. POTENTIAL EU LAW-RELATED RISKS POST BREXIT

As mentioned in Section I, while derivatives contracts play a key role in risk management, derivatives markets can give rise to financial stability concerns. Since financial stability is thought to be relative to the level of risk tolerance pertaining to the players in a particular market, policy makers are conducive to making decisions which reflect domestic

---

February   8,   2017 https://www.esma.europa.eu/sites/default/files/library/public_register_for_the_cleari ng_obligation_under_emir.pdf. The register is maintained pursuant to Article 6 of EMIR Regulation.

[31] Financial Services and Markets Act 2000 s.285(c), as amended by The Financial Services and Markets Act 2000 (Over the Counter Derivatives, Central Counterparties and Trade Repositories) Regulations 2013 ("OTC Regulations"), s. 3. The OTC Regulations is the statutory instrument implementing the EMIR into the UK.

[32] ESMA, "List of Central Counterparties authorised to offer services and activities in the   Union"   September   19,   2016, https://www.esma.europa.eu/sites/default/files/library/ccps_authorised_under_emir. pdf.

financial stability needs.[33] It is posited that the common interests present among the Eurozone States may differ from the interests of the non-Eurozone Member States, and indeed that of non-EU countries. Therefore, it is conceivable that European policy makers would have concerns about financial stability where an offshore euro-denominated derivatives market has a dominant global market share.[34]

This Section considers a number of possible means by which EU lawmakers could frustrate the development and viability of London's euro-denominated derivatives clearing industry.

A. EQUIVALENCE REGIME UNDER EMIR

It will be recalled that the recognition of a third-country CCP by ESMA must be preceded by a European Commission decision of "equivalence" in respect of the third country's regulatory regime. The ESMA Regulation requires the ESMA to assist the European Commission by drafting regulatory technical standards.[35]

By examining ESMA's technical advice to the Commission, the analytical approach to determining 'equivalence' under the EMIR Regulation comes to light. ESMA adopts an objective-based approach to assessing equivalence. It examines whether the third country's regime, when assessed from a holistic perspective, is capable of meeting the objectives of the EU Regulation, which are, essentially, the promotion of financial stability, the protection of EU entities and investors and the prevention of regulatory arbitrage in respect of CCPs. In its technical advice, the ESMA makes line-by-line factual comparisons between the rules, institutions, and supervisory and enforcement practices of the EU and third country. Where no equivalence is found, the ESMA is likely to consider the consequences entailed by the third country's regime. Moreover, ESMA will take into consideration the IMF's Financial Sector Assessment Programme findings.

Take the situation in the US as an example. In September 2013, ESMA found that the US regulators (the SEC and CFTC) had employed common supervisory practices as those of European authorities, and there are equivalent CCP regulations in most areas, including senior management, governance, and record keeping.[36] On March 15, 2016, the

---

[33] Mads Andenas and Iris Chui, *Financial stability and legal integration in financial regulation*, E. L. Rev 335, 344 (2013).

[34] Christian Noyer, *Brexit means the end of single market access for London There will be no back door into the EU for financial institutions in the City*, FT, March 15th 2017.

[35] ESMA Regulation Article 10(4).

[36] ESMA, *Final report Technical advice on third country regulatory equivalence under EMIR–US*, September   1,   2013,   39   *et*   *seq.* https://www.esma.europa.eu/sites/default/files/library/2015/11/2013-1157 technical advice on third country regulatory equivalence under emir us.pdf.

European Commission adopted an equivalence decision for CCPs in the US.[37]

It will be observed from ESMA's assessment methodology that no consideration was given to the global market share of the domestic CCP industry and the likely systemic implications of such market for the EU. Based on ESMA's EMIR assessments to-date, the UK regime which is already in full compliance with EMIR should be granted equivalence post-Brexit if the UK does not seek to make changes to the existing law. However, such is the size of the London market that systemic risk concerns might cause the EU to consider reforms to equivalence.

> Option 1. Adopting a global market share threshold into all equivalence decisions, whereby market shares above a specified threshold would trigger further assessment criteria relating to prudential standards, supervisory framework and monetary policy requirements (e.g. established central bank swap lines).
> Option 2. Only adopting the additional assessment criteria in respect to the UK due to its prevailing dominance in euro-denominated derivatives clearing.
> Option 3. Repeal the right of recognition under EMIR, and require all CCPs to be authorised in the EU. A European Central Bank (ECB) publication in 2011 favored the authorisation option for large CCPs. However, it was annulled by the EU General Court.

B. EU GENERAL COURT DECISION

The EU General Court decided, on March 4th 2015, in favour of the UK's application to annul the ECB's location policy on CCPs.[38] The implication of this judgement seems to be reinforcing the development of the offshore euro-denominated trading in the City of London.

On July 5th 2011, the ECB published the Eurosystem Oversight Policy Framework ("the Policy Framework"), which describes the role of the Eurosystem in the oversight of "payment, clearing and settlement systems." With the EU treaty not explicitly conferring an oversight function, the ECB purported to have found support for a ECB function to ensure smooth operation of payment systems under Article 127(2) TFEU and Article 3.1 of Protocol No 4 to the FEU Treaty on the Statute of the ESCB and of the ECB (the "Statute"). On the issue of the existence of infrastructures located outside the euro area that participate in the settlement or clearing of euro transactions, the Policy Framework

---

[37] http://europa.eu/rapid/press-release_IP-16-807_en.htm.
[38] Case T-496/11, United Kingdom v European Central Bank.

stated that malfunctioning of these offshore infrastructures may have adverse effects on payment systems located in the euro area, with the euro area having no direct influence on such infrastructures. In relation to CCPs, the Policy Framework contained the following statement on their location: "[t]he location policy is applied to all CCPs that hold on average more than 5% of the aggregated daily net credit exposure of all CCPs for one of the main euro-denominated product categories.... CCPs that exceed these thresholds should be legally incorporated in the euro area with full managerial and operational control and responsibility over all core functions, exercised from within the euro area."

The General Court opined that the ECB's competence under Article 127(2) TFEU does not extend to the clearing of securities, but is limited to cash settlement. The judges suggested that the ECB needs to be more explicitly empowered to oversee clearing houses under legislations made by the co-decision procedure. The ECB's recently published Eurosystem Oversight Policy Framework focuses, instead, on making "arrangements on detailed information exchange" to achieve "close cooperation regarding UK CCPs with significant euro-denominated business." [39]

From the perspective of trade, UK's exiting the internal market could be an impetus for the EU legislators to confer powers on the ECB to implement the "location policy" discussed above. The Financial Times has reported that the EU is developing new legislation to enable territorial restrictions on the clearing of euro-denominated transactions.[40]

IV. EU's GATS COMMITMENTS

When Article 50 of TFEU is triggered by Theresa May's government, the WTO framework would provide the point of departure for the Brexit negotiations. While the UK would need to adopt its own schedules to the WTO agreements after separation from the EU, the UK government has stated an intention to "replicate as far as possible...current [WTO] obligations." [41] Furthermore, the UK will continue to uphold the current EU schedules throughout the duration

---

[39] ECB, *Eurosystem oversight policy framework*, p. 16, Revised version (July 2016) available at https://www.ecb.europa.eu/pub/pdf/other/eurosystemoversightpolicyframework201 607.en.pdf?4cb84eb3183f0bb2c71bc3509af6ffe3.

[40] Alex Barker and Jim Brunsden, *EU prepares rule changes to target City's euro clearing*, Financial times, Dec. 16th 2016.

[41] Statement of Liam Fox, Secretary of State for International Trade and President of the Board of Trade on December 5, 2016. https://www.parliament.uk/business/publications/written-questions-answers-statements/written-statement/Commons/2016-12-05/HCWS316/.

of the Brexit negotiations with the EU.[42] Therefore the discussions below are based on the current EU commitments under the GATS.

A comprehensive understanding of the implications of the GATS obligations is necessary as they provide an international legal framework for trade negotiations between the UK and the EU, and the UK and third countries. In addition, the WTO framework would be the default position in a worst case scenario of failed Brexit negotiations, and thus provide the guide to financial market players and policy makers. This section seeks to map the current GATS commitments of the EU Member States and analyse the implication on the future of London's euro-denominated derivatives market.

A. AN OUTLINE OF THE GATS ARCHITECTURE

The 1994 General Agreement on Trade in Services (GATS) was the outcome of the Uruguay Round of trade negotiations that also produced a new structure of the World Trade Organization (WTO).[43] The GATS applying to trade in services, including financial services,[44] has two interlinking components. The first consists of general agreements (further discussed below), which apply to all WTO members irrespective of any specific commitment. The second component consists of each country's schedules of specific commitments on market access and national treatment, and any member's list of MFN exemptions.

The unconditional most-favored-nation (MFN) treatment and transparency principle are the major "General Obligations and Disciplines" under Part II of GATS. Article II:1 seeking to remove formal and material discrimination, requires members to "accord immediately and unconditionally to services and service suppliers of any other Member treatment no less favourable than that it accords to like services and service suppliers of any other country." The GATS allows a country to schedule exemptions to the MFN obligation in accordance to the rule under the Annex on Article II Exemptions. However, the GATS provides no exemption for the transparency requirement.

National treatment under Article XVII GATS relates to discriminatory measures accorded by a member to the services and/or suppliers of another member, which afford more favourable treatment to the member's own services and/or supplier. For a member who has made commitments to Article XVII in relation to a particular sector or

---

[42] Julian Braithwaite, *Ensuring a smooth transition in the WTO as we leave the EU,* January 27, 2017.   https://blogs.fco.gov.uk/julianbraithwaite/2017/01/23/ensuring-a-smooth-transition-in-the-wto-as-we-leave-the-eu/.

[43] ANDREW GUZMAN ET AL., INTERNATIONAL TRADE LAW, (Wolters Kluwer 2d ed. 2016); MARCUS KLAMERT, SERVICES LIBERALIZATION IN THE EU AND THE WTO (Cambridge University Press, 2015).

[44] Article 1:1 GATS.

mode of supply, it is required to refrain from enacting a non-exhaustive list of prohibited measures.[45] The GATS divides trade in financial services into four "modes of supply":[46]

1. Cross-border supply—the supply of a service from one state to another;
2. Consumption abroad—the consumer of a service being in one state and consuming the service in another state;
3. Establishment—the supply of a service from one state to another through the incorporation of a commercial presence in that state;
4. Presence of natural persons—a service supplier sending individuals from one state to another to supply a service.

Article XVI GATS prohibits six types of restrictions on market access. Distinguishable from NT and MFN obligations, the market access provision regulates quota-like measures which seek to restrict the number of services suppliers, value of transactions, number of operations, number of natural persons, form of legal entity, and share of foreign direct investment. The members' commitments to market access are listed for a particular mode of supply in relation to distinct sectors.

It may be seen that the GATS adopts a positive listing approach to NT and market access commitments, while a negative listing is employed for MFN.

The Annex on Financial Services ("FS Annex") and the Understanding on Commitments in Financial Services (the "Understanding") contain provisions specific to financial services. The FS Annex like the main body of the GATS is applicable to every member.[47] In paragraph 2, members can adopt domestic regulation for prudential reasons, which must not be for avoiding the Member's commitments. Paragraph 3 provides that members may, for prudential reasons, adopt recognition agreements or arrangements whether unilaterally or with other members (without needing to notify under paragraph 4(b) of Article VII GATS). The Understanding provides an alternative approach to scheduling specific commitments for financial services. WTO members which adopted the Understanding are undertaking the commitments relating to market access and NT for all financial services subsectors, unless expressly excluded by a member (i.e. a negative listing approach).

---

[45] KLAMERT, *supra* n. 43, 31.
[46] Article 1:2 GATS.
[47] Panel Report, *Mexico-Telecoms*, WT/DS204/R, April 2, 2004, paragraph 7.4.

B. MAPPING EU'S GATS COMMITMENTS ON CLEARING AND SETTLEMENT

The EU's MFN exemption schedule was entered into in 1994,[48] and has not been updated since. According to the current schedule, there are no operative exemptions in financial services. (Italy was the only country to enter an exemption for the provision of favourable tax treatment to Central, Eastern and South-Eastern Europe, which had expired in 2004.)

The EU and its Member States adopted the Supplement 4 of Schedule of Specific Commitment (the "Schedule") on November, 18th 1999, post the formation of the Eurozone on January, 1st 1999.[49] However, an examination of the Schedule shows that it is still referring to the former national currencies of the Eurozone members and to obsolete EU legislations, e.g., the Investment Services Directive. Under the Schedule, the EU Member States have committed to the Understanding. The limitations on market access and NT that may be relevant to euro-denominated derivatives market are shown in the table below.

EU Member State	Relevant mode of access*	Limitation on access / national treatment (NT)
Italy	3	Access – clearing and settlement services need authorisation of Bank of Italy and CONSOB
Italy	3	NT - Foreign intermediaries cannot carry out investment services through representative offices without seeking authorisation.
Denmark, Spain	3	Access - Financial institutions seeking to trade on a domestic exchange must be incorporated in the country.
Finland	3	Broker on derivatives exchange must be an EEA resident, unless obtains permission from the Ministry of Finance.

*1.Cross-border supply; 2.Consumption abroad; 3.Establishment; 4. Presence of natural persons.

From the above table, the limitations to the NT and market access under GATS relate solely to supply of services by establishment. In

[48] Available on https://www.wto.org/english/tratop e/serv e/serv commitments e.htm.
[49] Available on https://www.wto.org/english/tratop e/serv e/serv commitments e.htm.

relation to clearing and settlement activities, the Schedule contains no relevant limitations on cross-border supply (mode 1) and consumption abroad (mode 2). Therefore the GATS obligations of NT and market access apply to any domestic measures of EU Member States affecting exchanges and clearing houses. In addition, EU's membership in the WTO entails European Commission decisions and the ESMA's technical advice to be "measures" covered within the GATS.[50]

In a post Brexit landscape, the LCH and ICE Clear would be able to supply services to EU Member States via either mode 1 or mode 2, under the full protection of MFT, NT and market access principles. Recall the options considered under Section 3. Adopting the first two options would render the EU in breach of its MFN and market access obligations, unless an exemption could be established. Since Option 2 would only apply to the supply of clearing services from the UK, it would constitute an outright discrimination in breach of the MFN principle. Option 1 seeks to discriminate between suppliers of services on the basis of the global market share of their home country. Therefore, it would also be in breach of the MFN principle. In addition, Option 1 and 2 could also result in restricting the number of services providers in breach of Article XVI. Option 3 is a valid option, but it would entail the repeal of the equivalence regime, which would likely cause market disruption.

Another pertinent question is whether the EU could renegotiate its GATS commitments as a means to address the risks of London's euro derivatives clearing. This option is difficult for two reasons. Firstly, allowing Member States to erect their own barriers under the Schedule is contrary to EU's current uniformity approach to financial market regulation. Secondly, since amending the Schedule would require voting by the WTO membership, it would be a very cumbersome and costly way to address volatile financial risks.

The next section considers how the prudential carve-out may be invoked by the EU.

C. PRUDENTIAL CARVE-OUT

It is necessary that provisions in trade agreements seek to achieve a balance between the goal of liberalisation and other economic policy concerns.[51] Paragraph 2(a) of the FS Annex provides an exemption to

---

[50] GATS Article XXVIII:(a) "measure" means any measure by a Member, whether in the form of a law, regulation, rule, procedure, decision, administrative action, or any other form. Report of the Appellate Body on European Communities – Regime for Importation, Sale and Distribution of Bananas (Banana III), Adopted on November 17, 1997, WT/DS27/AB/R, para 220.

[51] Juan Marchetti, FINANCIAL REGULATION AT THE CROSSROADS: IMPLICATIONS FOR SUPERVISION, INSTITUTIONAL DESIGN AND TRADE, 284 (Kluwer Law International, Panagiotis Delimatsis and Nils Herger ed. 2011).

the GATS obligations in order to preserve members' sovereignty over matters of investor protection, financial market integrity and systemic stability. According to Paragraph 2(a):

> Notwithstanding any other provisions of the Agreement, a Member shall not be prevented from taking measures for prudential reasons, including for the protection of investors, depositors, policy holders or persons to whom a fiduciary duty is owed by a financial service supplier, or to ensure the integrity and stability of the financial system. Where such measures do not conform with the provisions of the Agreement, they shall not be used as a means of avoiding the Member's commitments or obligations under the Agreement.

The scope of the FS Annex covers any measure affecting "the supply of financial services,"[52] which has the same meaning as "supply of service" in the main body of GATS.[53] However, the definition of services does not include services supplied by "governmental authority." [54] In particular, under paragraph 1(b)(i) of the FS Annex, "activities conducted by a central bank or monetary authority or by any other public entity in pursuit of monetary or exchange rate policies" are defined to be within services supplied in the exercise of governmental authority.

According to central banking practice in general, monetary policy power entails the maintaining of price stability,[55] and does not include the supervision of clearing and settlement systems.[56] Therefore, the regulations relating to the clearing and settlement of derivatives trades are the types of measures affecting the supply of financial services within the scope of the FS Annex.

It is contended that the potential application of the prudential carve-out is wide, which could give rise to legal uncertainty and challenge by members under the WTO dispute resolution mechanism. Firstly, one can note that paragraph 2(a) provides for domestic measures promulgated "for prudential reasons," which cover not only rules pertaining to financial prudential regulation, i.e., capital requirement rules, but also any measures the purpose of which would be to promote a prudential public policy. A non-exclusive list of examples of prudential reasons can be

---

[52] Paragraph 1(a) of the FS Annex.
[53] Article XXVIII(b) "supply of a service" includes the production, distribution, marketing, sale and delivery of a service.
[54] Subparagraph 3(b) of Article I GATS.
[55]   See   http://www.bankofengland.co.uk/monetarypolicy/Pages/default.aspx, https://www.ecb.europa.eu/mopo/html/index.en.html.
[56] Article 127(2) TFEU.

found within paragraph 2(a). Secondly, without the "necessity" requirement found in GATS XIV, the prudential carve-out "lacks detailed standard and limitations" on members' discretion.[57] There is a certain degree of scholarly consensus that under general international law principle, a member should invoke the exemption in good faith.[58] This view is commensurate with the wording of the last sentence in paragraph 2(a), that the prudential carve-out must not be used by members as a means of avoiding their GATS obligations.

Finally, it is submitted that since the UK regulatory and supervisory regime is currently fully integrated within the EU regulatory framework, this poses difficulties for the EU to invoke the prudential carve-out. In order to lawfully discriminate service suppliers on the basis of the size of their home market, it must be shown that a highly concentrated offshore derivatives market, while stringently regulated, could still pose a reasonable threat to the EU financial system.

CONCLUSIONS

An analysis of the EU's GATS schedules shows that there are presently no limitations to its Member States' commitments which are of direct relevance to the euro-denominate derivative market. Accordingly, other than invoking an exemption, the EU would have no valid grounds in refusing to recognise the UK's regulatory and supervisory system as equivalent with the EU's EMIR regime. While it is indeed conceivable that a highly concentrated offshore euro-denominated clearing market could pose systemic risk, the UK is home to the world's most sophisticated regulators. The EU therefore would have the task of justifying its idiosyncratic restrictions on the provisions of euro clearing services from the UK using the wide requirements under paragraph 2(a) of the FS annex. As a practical matter, the question is whether the EU would explicitly empower the ECB to regulate the derivatives clearing and settlement, and impose the location policy.

In light of market certainty and stability, it is submitted that the ECB should continue with its current approach of establishing supervisory cooperation with the Bank of England, rather than to try to relocate the

---

[57] Wei Wang, CHINA'S BANKING LAW AND THE NATIONAL TREATMENT OF FOREIGN-FUNDED BANKS 205, (Ashgate 2013).

[58] Juan Marchetti, FINANCIAL REGULATION AT THE CROSSROADS: IMPLICATIONS FOR SUPERVISION, INSTITUTIONAL DESIGN AND TRADE, 284 (Kluwer Law International, Panagiotis Delimatsis and Nils Herger ed. 2011); Alexander Kern, The GATS and Financial services: Liberalisation and Regulation in Global Financial Markets, THE WORLD TRADE ORGANIZATION AND TRADE IN SERVICES 585-590 (Boston : Martinus Nijhoff Publishers, Alexander Kern and Mads Andenas ed. 2008); WTO Secretariat, GUIDE TO THE URUGUAY ROUND AGREEMENTS 176 (Kluwer Law International 1999).

euro market via top-down means. Moreover, it is submitted that mutual recognition initiatives, in accordance with the rights under the FS Annex, need to be explored, as the EU's present equivalence approach is both slow and subject to unilateral withdrawal by the European Commission.

CHAPTER 20: THE EUROPEAN UNION'S WTO RIGHTS AND OBLIGATIONS POST-BREXIT: NEGOTIATION AND ENFORCEMENT

PAVAN KRISHNAMURTHY[1]

On June 23, 2016, the Brexit referendum resulted in a vote to leave the European Union (EU) by a margin of 51.9%.[2] Assuming that the United Kingdom (UK) leaves and there are no negotiated schemes in place—colloquially known as a "hard" Brexit—pursuant to the World Trade Organization (WTO) Agreement,[3] it is likely that the EU will need to enter into negotiations with WTO Member States to renegotiate the terms of its General Agreement on Tariffs and Trade (GATT)[4] and General Agreement on Trade in Services (GATS)[5] schedule of commitments, because changes in the EU composition alter the

[1] Pavan Krishnamurthy is a law clerk in the international trade practice of Sidley Austin LLP in Washington D.C. The opinions expressed in this paper are those only of the author. Pavan Krishnamurthy received his BA from Northwestern University, MSc from the London School of Economics, and will receive his JD from Georgetown Law in Spring 2017. The author would like to thank Jennifer Hillman and Gary Horlick for their thoughtful comments, Andy Shoyer, Jan Yves Remy, Jacqueline Van De Velde, and Carys Golesworthy for their lively discussions, and Francie Berger, Aymar Claret de Fleurieu, and Jin Woo (Jay) Kim for their support.
[2] *See* Steven Erlanger, *Britain Votes to Leave E.U., Cameron Plans to Step Down*, N.Y. TIMES, June 23, 2016, http://www.nytimes.com/2016/06/25/world/europe/britain-brexit-european-union-referendum.html.
[3] *See* WTO Agreement: Marrakesh Agreement Establishing the World Trade Organization, Apr. 15, 1994, THE LEGAL TEXTS: THE RESULTS OF THE URUGUAY ROUND OF MULTILATERAL TRADE NEGOTIATIONS 4 (1999), 1867 U.N.T.S. 154, 33 I.L.M. 1144 (1994) [hereinafter Marrakesh Agreement or WTO Agreement].
[4] *See* GATT 1994:General Agreement on Tariffs and Trade 1994, Apr. 15, 1994, Marrakesh Agreement Establishing the World Trade Organization, Annex 1A, THE LEGAL TEXTS: THE RESULTS OF THE URUGUAY ROUND OF MULTILATERAL TRADE NEGOTIATIONS 17 (1999), 1867 U.N.T.S. 187, 33 I.L.M. 1153 (1994) [hereinafter GATT 1994].
[5] *See* General Agreement on Trade in Services, Apr. 15, 1994, Marrakesh Agreement Establishing the World Trade Organization, Annex 1B, THE LEGAL TEXTS: THE RESULTS OF THE URUGUAY ROUND OF MULTILATERAL TRADE NEGOTIATIONS 284 (1999), 1869 U.N.T.S. 183, 33 I.L.M. 1167 (1994) [hereinafter GATS].

conditions of competition of certain previously negotiated commitments.

WTO disciplines govern the procedure and negotiations necessary to alter commitments in trade in goods and services. Moreover, the WTO may find itself adjudicating whether the changes in EU composition undermines the spirit of the negotiated commitments laid out during the establishment of the WTO and the enlargement of the EU with respect to global trade governance. Much of Brexit scholarship has focused on the risks to which the UK has exposed itself through the Brexit vote; however, the EU remains particularly vulnerable to third-parties who claim the EU is in violation of WTO procedure and substantive obligations. Better understanding of the political and legal repercussions of a hard Brexit with respect to the EU may help temper those on the Continent who wish the UK difficulty in the Brexit process. Negotiations will structure the EU-UK relationship moving forward, and the parties on both sides of the table have a strong incentive to cooperate before they turn, together, to the global trading system.

The remainder of this paper addresses the EU's legal relationship with the WTO (Section I), post-Brexit strategy from the perspective of the EU, UK, and US (Section II), the enforcement mechanisms available should negotiations fail (Section III), and conclusions (Section IV).

I.   CURRENT EU-WTO RELATIONS

The EU is a WTO member in its own right—a privilege of being a founding member of the WTO in January 1995. The EU, for the purposes of the WTO, is currently composed of 28 European States (including the UK) along with the EU itself. Normally, the WTO system has been grounded by the principle of most-favored nations (MFN) (countries cannot normally discriminate between their trading partners) and national treatment (countries cannot normally discriminate between their domestic trade and their like imports). Independently a country cannot transgress these rules, but WTO disciplines do allow for exceptions regarding MFN, particular in the case of a customs union— this is to encourage trade liberalization at the regional level when multilateral negotiations become overly complex and time-intense. For example, the EU is a customs union, which means it is a substitution of a single customs territory (EU) for two or more customs territories (EU-28).[6] Despite providing an exception to the principles of MFN, customs unions "shall not on the whole be higher or more restrictive than the general incidence of the duties and regulations of commerce applicable

---

[6] *See* GATT Art. XXIV(8)(a).

in the constituent territories prior to the formation of such union."[7] If a customs union, *on balance*, reduces barriers to trade it will be generally allowable.

This issue has become particularly important in light of the expansion of the EU and subsequent WTO negotiations by third-countries to accept the new disciplines present in the enlarged EU.[8] The enlargement process was tedious. Hosuk Lee-Makiyama, director of the European Centre for International Political Economy and a former EU trade negotiator indicated that it took up to five years to integrate Bulgaria and Romania into the EU enlargement process solely due to the complexity of their services schedules—that is to say, it took five years without even looking at trade in goods. However each negotiation is unique. For example, when the US and EU were negotiating for compensation due to increased EU tariffs following the 2004 EU enlargement, the United States Trade Representative (USTR) stated:

> On March 22, 2006, the United States and the EC signed a bilateral agreement under GATT rules providing for compensation for breaking of tariff bindings as a result of the EU's May 2004 enlargement. As part of the agreement, the ECUnion opened new country-specific tariff-rate quotas for U.S. exports of boneless ham, poultry, and corn gluten meal. It expanded existing global tariff-rate quotas for food preparations, fructose, pork, rice, barley, wheat, maize, preserved fruits, fruit juices, pasta, chocolate, pet food, beef, poultry, live bovine animals and sheep, and various cheeses and vegetables. It also permanently reduced tariffs on protein concentrates, fish (hake, Alaska Pollack, surimi), chemicals

---

[7] *See* GATT Art. XXIV(5)(a).

[8] For example, in the months following the 2004 EU enlargement, the United States submitted a request seeking consultations with the EU under the auspices of the WTO claiming that customs policy was inconsistently applied after the enlargement process. *See* ICTSD, *WTO Challenges Emerge over EU Expansion*, 8 BRIDGES 33 (2004). However, during that time the EU had also notified that "it would extend a 1 November 2004 retaliation deadline by six months for countries affected by high tariffs resulting from EU enlargement. In order to join the EU, the 10 new members--Cyprus, the Czech Republic, Estonia, Hungary, Latvia, Lithuania, Malta, Poland, Slovakia, and Slovenia-- were required to replace their national tariffs with the EU's common external tariff regime, leading to higher tariffs on certain products." *See id.* Consequently, the US "revealed that it will consider raising tariffs on selected EU imports -- particularly food and agricultural products -- if negotiations fail. In a parallel development, EU officials have reported that talks with the US on a dispute relating to increased rice tariffs are running smoothly." *See id.* This threat was never utilized, because the EU provided compensation pursuant to Article XXVIII(4)(d). *See infra* Section III and accompanying text.

(polyvinyl butyral), aluminum tube, and molybdenum wire. These changes went into effect in July 2006.[9]

It should be noted, however, starting in September 16, 2003, the USTR began soliciting private sector input on enlargement, and by December 2006, the USTR "again entered into negotiations under GATT rules in anticipation of the accession of Romania and Bulgaria to the EU."[10] The process was punctuated, but deals were struck and progress was piecemeal.

Regardless of previous practice, however, the focus must be on the treaty text, GATT Article XXIV(6):

> If, in fulfilling the requirements of subparagraph 5(a), a contracting party proposes to increase any rate of duty inconsistently with the provisions of Article II [schedule of concessions], the procedure set forth in Article XXVII shall apply. In providing compensatory adjustment, due account shall be taken of the compensation already afforded by the reduction brought about in the corresponding duty of the other constituents of the union."[11]

Subparagraph 5(a) states:

> . . . with respect to a customs union, or an interim agreement leading to a formation of a customs union, the duties and other regulations of commerce imposed at the institution of any such union or interim agreement in respect of trade with contracting parties not parties to such union or agreement shall not on the whole be higher or more restrictive than the general incidence of the duties and regulations of commerce applicable in the constituent territories prior to the formation of such union or the adoption of such interim agreement, as the case may be . . . .[12]

GATT Article XXIV(6), consequently, requires that in the event a WTO member state "proposes to increase any rate" negotiations

---

[9] *See* Office of the United States Trade Represenative, *EU Enlargement*, Archive (last accessed February 1, 2017), available at https://ustr.gov/archive/World_Regions/Europe_Middle_East/Europe/EU_Enlargement/Section_Index.html

[10] *See id.*

[11] GATT Art. XXIV(6).

[12] GATT Art. XXIV(5)(a).

pursuant to GATT Article XXVII apply, including the prospect of "compensatory adjustment." Now of course GATT Article XXIV(5)(a) refers to situations involving the *formation* of a customs union, as evidenced by the clause "duties and other regulations of commerce imposed at the institution of any such union," but what about the *modification* of a customs union and the reference in GATT Article XXIV(6) to the preposition "in fulfilling the requirements"—does that imply a running duty?

These questions set the stage for the importance and power of treaty interpretation at the WTO.[13] Despite focuses on UK obligations, currently two theories have emerged regarding Brexit and the WTO. On one hand, purposivist scholars have argued that countries, such as the UK, can unilaterally replace schedules that were multilaterally negotiated, if they are on balance no less trade restrictive.[14] On the other hand, textualist scholars have suggested that the ordinary meaning of WTO law requires negotiations in the event of any formal schedule change and failure to do so may be the basis of WTO dispute settlement and/or compensatory arbitration.[15] Following this debate, this section reviews the WTO disciplines governing the GATT (Part A), GATS (Part B), and tariff rate quotas (TRQs) (Part C) with regards to the EU.

A. GATT

Under the GATT, there is a negotiation and consultation requirement for modification of a member's schedule of concession:

> [A] contracting party . . . may, by negotiation and agreement with
> any contracting party with which such concession was initially
> negotiated and with any other contracting party determined by

---

[13] *See, e.g.*, Joost Pauwelyn & Manfred Elsig, *The Politics of Treaty Interpretation: Variations and Explanations Across International Tribunals*, SSRN, October 3, 2011.

[14] *See, e.g.*, Lorand Bartels, *The UK's Status in the WTO after Brexit*, SSRN, September 22, 2016.

[15] *See, e.g.*, Peter Ungphakorn, *Nothing simple about UK regaining WTO status post-Brexit*, ICTSD, June 27, 2016; Panos Koutrakos, *Brexit and international treaty-making*, EUROPEAN LAW REVIEW (2016) ("Assuming the UK does not enter into a customs union with the EU after its withdrawal, it would no longer be part of the common [tariff] schedules. In this scenario, the UK must submit its own new schedules after the conclusion of an exit agreement with the EU if it is to remain a WTO member. These schedules need to be accepted by all other WTO members in consensus and certified following certain procedures, which might create difficulties."). Ungphakorn correctly emphasizes the legalistic nature of the WTO when compared to the GATT. *See id. See also* J.H.H Weiler, *The Rule of Lawyers and the Ethos of Diplomats: Reflections on the Internal and External Legitimacy of WTO Dispute Settlement*, 13 AM. REV. INT'L ARB. 177 (2002); Pavan S. Krishnamurthy, *Effective enforcement: A legalistic analysis of WTO settlement*, 5 NW. INTERDISC. L. REV. 191 (2012).

the CONTRACTING PARTIES to have a principal supplying interest . . . and subject to consultation with any contracting party determined by the CONTRACTING PARTIES to have a substantial interest in such concession, modify, or withdraw a concession included in the appropriate schedule annexed to this Agreement."[16]

Member states agree to be bound to specific tariff concessions and other commitments such as TRQs in their schedule of concessions.[17] A member state "may, at any time, in special circumstances, authorize a contracting party to enter into negotiations for modification or withdrawal of a concession included in the appropriate Schedule annexed to this Agreement subject to the following procedures and conditions . . . ."[18] Consequently, there will be debate on who gets a say (e.g. "principal supplying interest") and who gets at least a seat (e.g. "substantial interest") at the negotiating table. Moreover, whether or not Brexit constitutes a modification or withdrawal of a concession will turn on interpretation. If a panel or the Appellate Body utilizes purposivist interpretation, it could find that on balance Brexit was neither a modification or withdrawal of the EU's schedule. Alternatively, they could argue—following a textualist interpretation—any change to the conditions of the schedule must be agreed to by the principal supplying interests.

Recall, as well, that a customs union itself "shall not on the whole be higher or more restrictive than the general incidence of the duties and regulations of commerce applicable in the constituent territories prior to the formation of such union."[19] The EU is both a customs union and a member of the WTO; therefore, there are two GATT questions: Has the EU modified or withdrawn a concession as *either* a member *or* a customs union? More legal uncertainty emerges because the EU certified commitments regarding trade in goods are only for the 15 members pre-2004. Subsequent documents are listed as "SECRET" and the 2004, 2007, and 2013 EU enlargement and subsequent WTO negotiations do not appear to be legally enumerated.

B. GATS

Unlike the GATT, there is even clearer language regarding renegotiations of the GATS in case of a "significant modification" of a customs union. GATS Article V(5) states:

---

[16] GATT Art. XXVIII(1).
[17] *See* GATT Art. II.
[18] *See* GATT Art. XXVIII(4).
[19] *See* GATT Art. XXIV(5)(a).

If, in the conclusion, enlargement or any significant modification of any agreement under paragraph 1, a Member intends to withdraw or modify a specific commitment inconsistently with the terms and conditions set out in its Schedule, it shall provide at least 90 days advance notice of such modification or withdrawal and the procedure set forth in paragraphs 2, 3 and 4 of Article XXI shall apply.[20]

The textual-purposivist dialectic maps well with the language of "significant modification"—any way that phrase is interpreted will ultimately privilege some over others. Similar to the GATT, moreover, the EU does not currently have an updated and accepted schedule. Worse so, the service commitments officially only apply to the original members of the EU at the founding of the WTO. Those who joined between 1995 to 2004 have individual commitments, but they have not been integrated into the official EU commitments. Finally, there is no information regarding the status of Bulgaria, Romania, and Croatia—all recent additions to the EU.

C. TARIFF RATE QUOTAS

The TRQ component works together with a specified tariff level to provide the desired degree of import protection. TRQs are committed to in the parties' schedules. "Like the UK, the EU will also have to modify or rectify its TRQs and to negotiate. The UK would want to be part of those talks."[21] Whether these modifications would constitute a rectification as opposed to a modification is again open to interpretation and there are reasonable arguments supporting both contentions, similar to those articulated above. But, take for example, beef:

...[L]ow-duty import quotas for high-quality beef, just two of almost 100 EU quotas. The EU opened these beef quotas after lengthy negotiations with Argentina, Australia, Brazil, Canada, New Zealand, Paraguay, Uruguay, and the US. Extracting UK beef quotas out of the EU's would require negotiations with all of them, plus possibly other suppliers such as Botswana, India, and Namibia, and definitely the EU itself — Ireland, Germany and France have particularly strong beef lobbies. While the exporting countries are pressing for the UK's quota gates to be opened wider, and jostling with each other for paths through the

---

[20] GATS Art. V(5).

[21] Peter Ungphakorn, *Brexit, agriculture, the WTO, and Uncertainty*, TRADEBETABLOG, October 22, 2016.

opening, UK farmers would be pushing in the opposite direction.[22]

Politics aside, the quantitative nature of TRQ will necessitate some form of negotiations—the level of formality of which is, for the aforementioned reasons, uncertain for now.

II. NEGOTIATION AND STRATEGY

Various legal obligations will create a collision course between WTO trading partners post-Brexit. Following the legal framework sketched above, this section reviews the various strategic considerations important to the EU post-Brexit.

Understandably, the EU has an incentive to deter further campaigns of disintegration. With Member States in Southern Europe, e.g., Spain, Italy, and Greece, looking for means to loosen some of the stricter financial and regulatory conditions placed on EU countries, the EU is cognizant of the legal and strategic consequence of a soft-stance. At least from state-leaders in the Continent, there has been talk of "punishing" the UK. This stance is problematic for the reasons described above. The EU, in the process of negotiating must be cognizant of its worst alternatives: a hard Brexit, where the UK-EU relationship is severed without an alternative, means the EU looses privileged access to UK markets. Moreover, as noted above, a hard Brexit for the EU would expose the EU to potential legal liability from third-party states. Therefore the immediate strategic consideration for the EU should be to negotiate a free trade agreement (FTA) with the UK. Yes, the referendum called to leave, but to what extent was never clear. The UK can leave the EU customs union, but still maintain a formalized legal relationship via an FTA. The negotiation of trade agreements fall within the exclusive competence of the EU, which means that individual EU states cannot unilaterally negotiate trade deals with the UK. The EU as a whole will need to identify its key interests and ensure that the negotiations take into account disparate or even divergent interests of EU states.

In addition to ensuring a continued relationship with the UK, the EU could attempt to take steps to mitigate legal challenges that could be mounted against it. Post-Brexit, the EU should submit new schedules pursuant to Article II of the GATT 1994 and Article XX of the GATS—particularly the latter, considering that the EU has been operating without an approved schedule of service commitments.

---

[22] Peter Ungphakorn, *Nothing simple about UK regaining WTO status post-Brexit*, ICTSD, June 27, 2016.

Such modifications will likely be objected to by other WTO members. Because disputes concerning the schedule of commitments are resolved through arbitration, the EU has a further opportunity to mitigate its liability. The EU's unilateral submission of its new schedules should represent an even-handed modification that does not upset the balance of rights between WTO members. Yes, third-party members will argue that the unilateral modification was inappropriate, because it did not take into account the specific needs of that party; however, third-parties will have less evidence of changes in the conditions of competition, if the EU has attempted an even-handed modification and has unilaterally modified its schedule of commitments that is just as favorable to third-parties as they were pre-Brexit.[23]

Finally, dispute settlement proceedings may likely be brought against the EU on the basis that Brexit violated the EU's commitments or that otherwise nullified or impaired the benefits envisioned during negotiations. The EU may be able to further temper third-party positions by expanding the quotas within its TRQs in a pre-emptive manner to, at the very least, reduce the nullification or impairment of expected benefits. Because the EU will have access to the UK's TRQ's (a relationship that was never envisioned when the UK was assumed to be forever part of the EU), other WTO members again will likely dispute such unilateral division and demand a seat at the negotiating table.

III. ENFORCEMENT

If the EU fails to follow the negotiation procedures agreed upon, it may be exposed to a host of legal and political repercussions. As a threshold matter, it should be noted that the WTO Ministerial Conference may, in exceptional circumstances, waive an obligation with the consensus of three-fourths of the members (though in practice unanimous consensus is used). [24] The "exceptional circumstance" requirement has never been specified. It is likely, however, that Brexit could rise to the level of an exceptional circumstance. However, waiver decisions must have a termination date and would therefore only be temporary.[25]

Assuming that a waiver is not granted, the GATT and the GATS outline the necessary negotiation procedure. First, negotiations and agreement are to occur with parties who have a "principal supplying

---

[23] Textualists who emphasize the process, especially in response to preemptive concessions, may still have a strong argument. While the EU in good faith may readjust its schedule—even favorable changes will be met with skepticism, because it was not done according to the official procedure enumerated in the WTO Agreements.
[24] *See* Marrakesh Agreement Art. IX(3).
[25] *See* Marrakesh Agreement Art. IX(4).

interest" in the matter.[26] Pursuant to GATT Article XXVIII(4), a member state seeking to modify its concessions, must reach an agreement with parties who have a substantial interest within the authorized time period. Second, if these initial negotiations are not resolved on their own within the authorized time period, the applicant seeking to modify the concessions will be allowed to, unless the contracting parties "determine that the applicant contracting party has unreasonably failed to offer adequate compensation."[27] Therefore, similar to the EU enlargement process, the EU may need to compensate third-countries affected by Brexit.

Ultimately, if no settlement is reached, the injured party is authorized to modify or withdraw "substantially equivalent concessions initially negotiated with the applicant contracting party."[28] GATT Art. XXVIII(4)(d). Lang places these GATT requirements in the context of UK TRQs and Brexit:

> [T]he EU's scheduled annual quota of frozen bovine meat products is 34,300 tonnes across the entire European market, and this quota is allocated in specific shares to five main exporting countries. If the UK left the EU, this quota would have to be reorganized in a number of ways: the EU quota would have to be changed to reflect the reduced size of its market as well as historical net trade flows between the UK and the rest of Europe; some of the European quota would have to be allocated to the UK; the UK itself would have to impose its own quota and allocate it between different beef exporting nations. Disentangling the UK's from the EU's commitments in this way would count as a modification of both the EU's and the UK's GATT schedules and therefore, according to GATT Article XXVIII, must be done by negotiation and agreement with certain other WTO members. Failing agreement, any modification is subject to reciprocal withdrawal of market access concessions from affected parties. The result of this process is that a potentially large number of other WTO Members would have the ability to significantly impede the process of the UK's exit from the EU—a powerful concern given the current decision-making dynamics within the WTO.[29]

---

[26] See GATT Art. XXVIII(1). Recall as well that those with "substantial interest" must be consulted. See GATT Art. XXVIII(3)(a).

[27] See GATT XXVIII(4)(d).

[28] See id.

[29] Andrew Lang, *The Consequence of Brexit: Some Complications From International Law*, LSE POLICY BRIEF 3 (2014) (arguing both prudential and legal impediments to Brexit).

Similarly under the GATS, the modification of a customs union is governed by specific procedure. Recall, that the GATS states: "[I]n the conclusion, enlargement or any significant modification of any agreement under paragraph 1, a Member intends to withdraw or modify a specific commitment inconsistently . . . its Schedule, it shall provide at least 90 days advance notice of such modification or withdrawal and the procedure set."[30] In terms of the procedure, any WTO Member state which would be affected by such a modification can enter into negotiations with a "view to reaching agreement on any necessary compensatory adjustment" and "shall endeavor to maintain a general level of mutually advantageous commitments" no less favorable than prior to the modification. Should schedule negotiations fail, any affected member may refer the matter to arbitration.[31] As with all negotiations, arbitration is the lurking solution for when parties have reached impasses.

Finally, WTO members might also pursue a non-violation nullification of benefits (NVNB) claim pursuant to Article 26 of the WTO Dispute Settlement Understanding, Article XXIII of the GATT, and Article XXIII of the GATS. A NVNB claim's core requirement is the finding of a nullification or impairment that is contrary to the legitimate expectations of the complainant at the time of the negotiations. Not only are NVNBs rarely to be used, they are limited by the expectations of the complainant at the time negotiations occurred. This means that, at least from the United States perspective, expectations which were established both at the creation of the WTO (with its multiple rounds of negotiations) as well as various moments when negotiations occurred surrounding the WTO implications of EU enlargement. The rationale of the NVNB follows the logic of compensatory adjustment in the cases of enlargement: "In providing compensatory adjustment, due account shall be taken of the compensation already afforded by the reduction brought about in the corresponding duty of the other constituents of the union."[32]

IV. CONCLUSION

While the initial separation of the UK-EU is said to take at least two years through Article 50 of the Treaty of Lisbon, the subsequent negotiations and the refiguring of the global trade system will take decades. As Dr. Markus W. Gehring has suggest: "In other words, if the EU wanted to make life difficult for the UK in trade relations (the Foreign Secretary called it showing the UK a rude gesture), it could.

---

[30] *See* GATS Art. V(5).
[31] *See* GATS Art. XXI(1)(a), (3)(a).
[32] *See* GATT Art. XXIV(6).

Active EU resistance might not make any economic sense but then there have been a couple of political decisions in the EU that were contrary to conventional economic wisdom recently."[33]

How the WTO interprets seemingly simple words such as "modification" or "significant" may greatly privilege one party over the other. As this paper has documented, treaty interpretation can emphasize the object and purpose as well as the ordinary meaning of the text. However in the case of post-Brexit EU trade relations, the EU will need to focus on the object and purpose by showing that it has followed the spirit of the WTO Agreements during the Brexit process and that its trade relations are on balance no less trade restrictive.

As the WTO leaves the neoliberal epoch,[34] it enters its Brexit chapter—marked by a world flirting with economic nationalism. The Brexit process will be complex and multi-faceted, but it may provide an opportunity for the WTO to stabilize Brexit and reemphasize the legitimacy of global trade governance. There is room to fail as well, and soured negotiations in one area can spread. Beyond the UK, and even the EU, ultimately, Brexit will be a key test of the WTO's resilience.

---

[33] *See* Markus W. Gehring, *Brexit and EU-UK trade relations with third state*, EU LAW ANALYSIS, March 6, 2016.

[34] *See, e.g.*, ANDREW LANG, WORLD TRADE LAW AFTER NEOLIBERALISM: REIMAGINING THE GLOBAL ECONOMIC ORDER (2011).

PART IV:

A Roadmap to Legal Aspects of Brexit

CHAPTER 21: A ROADMAP TO LEGAL ASPECTS OF BREXIT

AYMAR CLARET DE FLEURIEU[1]

Table of Contents

---

[1] Aymar Claret de Fleurieu is currently a legal trainee in the Arbitration Group at White & Case LLP (Paris). He holds a Master's degree in Private International Law at the Université Paris II Panthéon-Assas and a Master of Law in Public International Law at the Université de Strasbourg, with whom he won the National Rounds of the Philip C. Jessup International Law Moot Court in 2015. In 2016, he graduated the International Legal Studies LL.M. from the Georgetown Law Center, and subsequently worked as a research assistant to Professor Hillman for her Brexit seminar.

I.   Background

- *Brexit Glossary* (House of Commons Library, December 19, 2016), containing a list of commonly-used terms and acronyms that have needed clarification since the United Kingdom voted in the June 2016 EU referendum.

A.   An overview of Brexit

- *Brexit: impact across policy areas* (House of Commons Library, August 26, 2016), looking at the current situation in a range of policy areas and considering what impact Brexit might have.

- Brexit: The Immediate Legal Consequences (Richard Gordon QC, R. Moffatt, The Constitution Society, May 20, 2016), presenting the thesis that identifying the immediate legal effects of Brexit can neither be avoided nor deferred and that, once identified they need to be planned for well in advance of any exit from the EU. See also:
  - *Legal Aspects of Withdrawal from the EU: A Briefing Note* (P. Eleftheriadis et al., University of Oxford – Legal Research Paper Series, July 14, 2016)
  - *What a British divorce from the EU would look like (Financial Times, June 28, 2016)* [subscription required]

- Brexit: *initial reflections* (A. Menon, J.-P. Salter, Chatham House, November 2016), casting an initial eye over the referendum and its outcome, and the historical relationship between the UK and the EU as well as its evolution until the referendum. On the analysis of origins and events leading to Brexit, see also:
  - *Brexit: A Drama in Six Acts* (P. Craig, European Law Review, August 2016)
  - *How David Cameron lost his battle for Britain* (Financial Times, December 18, 2016) [subscription required]
  - *A Howl of Rage* (The New York Review of Books, August 18, 2016)

- o *Fences: A Brexit Diary* (The New York Review of Books, August 18, 2016)

- European Public Law, Volume 22 (2016), studying a wide range of various legal, constitutional and political issues revolving around Brexit. [subscription required] See also:
  - o *Brexit Supplement* (German Law Journal – Vol. 17, July 1, 2016)

- *Leaving the EU* (House of Commons Library, July 1, 2013), stating – three years before the referendum – that the full impact of a UK withdrawal is impossible to predict, but that from an assessment of the current EU role in a range of policy areas, it is possible to identify issues and estimate some of the impacts of removing the EU role in these areas.

- Responsibility, *Voice and Exit: Britain Alone?* (P. Craig, in A. Biondi and P. Birkinshaw (eds), Britain Alone? The Implications and Consequences of the UK Exit from the EU [2015]), on the concept of "responsibility" and the theme that conceptions of national constitutional responsibility are central to the discourse about voice and exit.

B. EU law

- Legislating *for Brexit: directly applicable EU law* (House of Commons Library, January 12, 2017), explaining what "directly applicable" EU law is (mainly EU Treaty obligations and EU regulations), how it applies in the UK, and how many EU regulations are in force. See also:
  - o *Legislating for Brexit: Statutory Instruments implementing EU law* (House of Commons Library, January 16, 2017)
  - o *Legislating for Brexit: EU external agreements* (House of Commons Library, January 5, 2017)
  - o *Legislating for Brexit: the Great Repeal Bill* (House of Commons Library, February 24, 2017)

- *Rights and obligations of European Union membership* (HM Government, April 14, 2016), setting out the main rights and obligations arising from the UK's membership to the European Union.
  See also:
  o *The European Union explained: How the European Union works* (European Commission, November 2014)

- *The EU and the Legal Sector* (The Law Society, October 2015), aiming to start a discussion about the potential impacts for the UK of remaining in a renegotiated EU or of an EU exit.
  See also:
  o *Untangling Britain from Europe would cause constitutional 'havoc'* (Financial Times, June 20, 2016) [subscription required]

- *Brexit and the EU Court* (House of Commons Library, November 14, 2016), looking – after the High Court ruling – at the questions of revocability of Article 50 notice and referral to the EU Court of Justice.

- *Brexit is not an escape from EU regulation* (London-Brussels One-Way or Return, February 14, 2016), on the reasons for EU regulation, and the question whether Brexit equals escape from it.
  See also:
  o *If EU law is supreme, can Parliament be sovereign?* (M. Elliott, Public Law for Everyone, February 21, 2016)
  o *Brexit, sovereignty and the EU Court of Justice* (London-Brussels One-Way or Return, February 29, 2016)
  o *Referring Brexit to the Court of Justice of the European Union: Why Brexit should be left to the United Kingdom* (O. Garner, European Law Blog, November 14, 2016)
  o *Brexit: can the ECJ get involved?* (S. Peers, EU Law Analysis, November 3, 2016)
  o *The Supreme Court Should Not Refer to the EU Court of Justice on Article 50* (M. Barczentewicz, UK

Constitutional Law Association, November 11, 2016)

II. The Process of Brexiting

- *The process of withdrawing from the European Union* (House of Lords, European Union Committee, May 4, 2016), considering whether Article 50 is the only means of leaving the EU, and whether a decision to withdraw from the EU can be reversed.

- *Brexit: some legal and constitutional issues and alternatives to EU membership* (House of Commons Library, July 28, 2016), considering how the UK will leave the EU, some legal and constitutional issues, and possible alternatives to EU membership.

- *The Constitutional Consequences of Brexit: Whitehall and Westminster* (UCL Constitution Unit, April 21, 2016), focusing on the potential impact of Brexit upon the UK Government and Parliament.

A. *Legal provisions*

1. Article 50 TEU

- *Brexit: how does the Article 50 process work?* (House of Commons Library, January 16, 2017), looking at the process of withdrawing from the EU under Article 50 TEU – the legal mechanism by which the UK will leave the EU.
  See also:
  - *The invoking of Article 50* (House of Lords, Select Committee on the Constitution, September 13, 2016)

- *Brexit and Article 50 TEU: A Constitutional Reading* (P. Eeckhout, E. Frantziou, UCL European Institute, December 22, 2016), arguing that the Article 50 withdrawal process needs to be compliant with EU constitutional law, which has significant implications

for the nature of both the withdrawal process and future EU-UK relations; and suggesting that although the wording of Article 50 is unclear on the question of revocability, the Article 50 clock could technically be stopped.
See also:

- o *Leaving the European Union, the Union way – A legal analysis of Article 50 TEU* (C. Hillion, Swedish Institute for European Policy Studies, August 2016)
- o *Member States' Right to a Decision on Withdrawal from the EU: A Legal Analysis (Article 50(1) TEU)* (B. Kulpa, EU Law Analysis, January 19, 2016)
- o *Brexit, Article 50 and the 'Joys' of a Flexible, Evolving, Un-codified Constitution* (A. Young, UK Constitutional Law Association, July 1, 2016)
- o *'Should I Stay or Should I Go?': A critical Analysis of the Right to Withdraw from the EU* (H. Hofmeister, European Law Journal, Vol. 16, Issue 5, pp. 589-603, September 2010)
- o *Leading EU experts advise that EU Notification of Withdrawal Bill does not disable Parliament's 'constitutional handbrake' on Brexit* (Bindsmans LLP, February 17, 2017)
- o *In the Matter of Article 50 of the Treaty On European Union* (Sir D. Edward et al., February 10, 2017)

- • *How Brexit Will Happen: A Brief Primer on European Union Law and Constitutional Law Questions Raised by Brexit* (H. Hestermeyer, Journal of International Arbitration, October 17, 2016), aiming to explore the prescriptions of EU law with respect to a Member State's leaving the Union and some of its consequences, as well as the procedure to do so under UK constitutional law.
See also:
  - o *What Role for the European Parliament* (D. Harvey, EU Law Analysis, July 14, 2016)

- • *Accession and Withdrawal in the Law of the European Union* (C. Hillion, The Oxford Handbook of European Union Law, 2015), examining the procedures for acceding to and withdrawing from the European Union, and

arguing that, while determined by (Member) states'
decisions, accession and withdrawal are also driven by
EU institutions, and by the canons of the EU legal
order.

- *'Don't Mention Divorce at the Wedding, Darling!': EU
  Accession and Withdrawal from Lisbon* (A. F. Tatham in EU
  Law after Lisbon, A. Bondi, P. Eeckhout, S. Ripley,
  2012), an analysis of both accession and withdrawal that
  considers briefly the historical context of each process
  before continuing to look at the relevant Article of the
  Treaty on European Union, post Lisbon, including the
  criteria and procedure for each issue, as well as
  providing a short commentary on them. [subscription
  required]

- *Triggering Article 50 TEU: A Legal Analysis* (E. Szyszczak,
  E. Lydgate, UK Trade Policy Observatory, October 10,
  2016), focusing in particular on the EU and
  international trade (rather than domestic and
  constitutional) dimensions of withdrawal, in order to
  provide clarity and highlight pitfalls affecting both the
  EU and the UK.

- *Withdrawal from the European Union: A Typology of Effects*
  (P. Nicolaides, Maastricht Journal, 2013), examining
  Article 50 TEU and developing a typology of the
  possible effects of the withdrawal of a Member State
  from the EU.
  On the territories that left the European Communities,
  see:
  - *Exiting the EU? Algeria, Greenland and Saint
    Barthélémy experiences* (Nationalia, February 23, 2016)
  - *Brexit or the art of "doing a Greenland"* (D. Sarmiento,
    Despite Our Differences Blog, July 2016)

- *The Withdrawal Clause of the Lisbon Treaty in the Light of EU
  Citizenship: Between Disintegration and Integration* (C. M.
  Rieder, Fordham International Law Journal, Vol. 37,
  Issue 1, 2013), offering a pragmatic view with regard to

the question as to whether the withdrawal clause of Article 50 should exist at all in the first place.

2. Vienna Convention on the Law of Treaties

- *Withdrawing Provisional Application of Treaties: Has the EU Made a Mistake?* (L. Bartels, Cambridge Journal of International and Comparative Law, Vol. 1, pp. 112-118 [2012]), considering two questions: 1. whether, under Article 25(1) of the VCLT, provisional application must be reciprocal, or whether it can be unilateral; and 2. the conditions under which provisional application may be withdrawn, and whether Article 25(2), which governs withdrawal, is perhaps too strict in certain cases.
  See also:
  o *Brexit v UK in EU (4): Treaties* (C. Crawford, March 28, 2016)
  o *Would Europeans be free to stay in the UK after Brexit?* (The Guardian, June 22, 2016)

B. Negotiation

- *In 'Brexit' Speech, Theresa May Outlines Clean Break for U.K.* (S. Castle, S. Erlanger, New York Times, January 17, 2017), on Prime Minister Theresa May's speech outlining her priorities for the upcoming negotiations to leave the European Union, and confirming that the UK Government will seek a "hard Brexit".
  See also:
  o *The government's negotiating objectives for exiting the EU: PM speech* (Full transcript, Gov.UK, January 17, 2017)
  o *Doing Brexit the hard way* (The Economist, January 21, 2017)
  o *Theresa May's Brexit Speech of 17 January 2017 – Decoding its clarity and ambiguity* (M. Emerson, Centre for European Policy Studies, January 25, 2017)
  o *The process for exiting the European Union and the Government's negotiating objectives* (House of Commons, Exiting the European Union Committee, January 14, 2017)

- *The United Kingdom's exit from and new partnership with the European Union White Paper* (HM Government, February 2, 2017), sketching details of Prime Minister Theresa May's 12-point principles for exiting the European Union and setting out the basis for priorities and the approach to forging a new strategic partnership with the EU.
  See also:
  o *Four principles for the UK's Brexit trade negotiations* (T. Sampson, LSE Centre for Economic Performance, October 2016)
  o *Brexit: Negotiation Phases and Scenarios of a Drama in Three Acts* (V. Kreilinger, L. M. Wolfstädter, S. Becker, Jacques Delors Institut, January 25, 2017)
  o *A well-managed Brexit is a priority for the entire EU* (K. Lannoo, Centre for European Policy Studies, February 3, 2017)

- *Brexit: A tale of two agreements?* (H. Flavier, S. Platon, European Law Blog, August 30, 2016), clarifying the distinction between the two post-Brexit agreements – the withdrawal agreement and the agreement regarding the future relationship between the UK and the EU – and identifying the legal difficulties arising from their articulation.

- *The UK's contribution to the EU budget* (House of Commons Library, February 15, 2017), considering how much the UK contributes to the EU budget and how much it receives back, and discussing potential payments to the EU on or after Brexit.
  See also:
  o *The €60 billion Brexit bill: How to disentangle Britain from the EU budget* (A. Barker, Centre for European Reform, February 6, 2017)
  o *Brexit and the EU budget: Threat of opportunity?* (J. Haas, E. Rubio, Jacques Delors Institut, January 16, 2017)
  o *The Impact of Brexit on the EU Budget: A non-catastrophic event* (J. Núñez Ferrer, D. Rinaldi, Centre for European Policy Studies, September 7, 2016)

- *How to Make a Transitional Brexit Arrangement* (P. Eleftheriadis, Oxford business Law Blog, February 15, 2017), on the important question for the UK economy of transition to the new trade regime after abandoning membership in the single market or of the common customs area.
  See also:
  - *A Brexit Act in 19¾ pages* (Allen & Overy, August 30, 2016)

- *'Stop this DISASTER!' The key European players who want to block EU from punishing Britain* (Express, February 1, 2017), Senior politicians within the Belgian government publishing an extraordinary report calling for Brussels to pursue the continuation of free trade with the UK.
  See also:
  - *Brexit High Level Group submits report to Prime Minister* (Belgian Government, Press release, January 31, 2017)
  - *Report of the Belgian Brexit High Level Group: Towards a Belgian Economic Brexit Strategy* (Belgian Brexit High Level Group, January 2017) (in French)
  - *Federation of Enterprises in Belgium Input to the interim report of the High Level Group on Brexit* (Federation of Enterprises in Belgium, January 20, 2017)

III. Internal UK Law and Brexit

A. The prerogative to implement Article 50

1. High Court proceedings

a. Cases materials

- High Court of Justice (Administrative Court) – *Santos & Miller v. Secretary of State for Exiting the European Union (Full day 1 transcript)*
  - *Report of Proceedings* (R. Craig, UK Constitutional Law Association, October 14, 2016)

- *High* Court of Justice (Administrative Court) – *Santos & Miller v. Secretary of State for Exiting the European Union (Full day 2 transcript)*
  - *Report of Proceedings* (R. Craig, UK Constitutional Law Association, October 20, 2016)

- High Court of Justice (Administrative Court) – *Santos & Miller v. Secretary of State for Exiting the European Union (Full day 3 transcript)*
  - *Report of Proceedings* (R. Craig, UK Constitutional Law Association, October 24, 2016)

b. Judgment

- *Judgment*: R *(Miller) -v- Secretary of State for Exiting the European Union* (November 3, 2016)
  See also:
  - *Critical reflections on the High Court's judgment in R (Miller) v Secretary of State for Exiting the European Union* (M. Elliott, H. J. Hooper, UK Constitutional Law Association, November 7, 2016)

  - *Taking back control* (The Economist, November 6, 2016)

  - *In-Between the Lines of the High Court Brexit Judgment: EU Transnational Rights and their Safeguards* (F. Strumia, EU Law Analysis, November 6, 2016)

  - *The Brexit Case – an alternative view from Andrew Henshaw QC* (Brick Court Chambers, November 10, 2016)
    See also:
    - *The Miller Case – an alternative analysis* (Sir Jeremy Lever KCMG QC, Monckton Chambers, November 16, 2016)
    - *Responding to Miller* (N. Barber, J. King, UK Constitutional Law Association, November 7, 2016)

- *Why the High Court got the law wrong about Brexit* (C. Gardner, Head of Legal, November 4, 2016)

o *Miller and the Art 50 notification: revocability is irrelevant* (London-Brussels One Way or Return, November 14, 2016)
  On the (ir)revocability of Article 50, see also:
  - *The Irrevocability of an Article 50 Notification: Lex Specialis and the Irrelevance of the Purported Customary Right to Unilaterally Revoke* (J. Rylatt, UK Constitutional Law Association Blog, July 27, 2016)
  - *(Un)Crossing the Rubicon: Why the Supreme Court Should Not Refer a Question Regarding the Revocability of Article 50 to the ECJ* (A. Georgopoulos, UK Constitutional Law Association, November 17, 2016)
  - *Miller, Article 50 Revocability and the Question of Control* (F. de Cecco, UK Constitutional Law Association, November 17, 2016)

o *Brexit Live: Article 50 Supreme Court case* (BBC News, December 5-8, 2016)

- *Summary* **Judgment**: *R (Miller) -v- Secretary of State for Exiting the European Union*

2. Supreme Court proceedings

a. Cases materials

- *The Supreme Court: Article 50 'Brexit' Appeal, providing a range of* information and updates on the case *R v. Secretary of State for Exiting the European Union*: case summaries, written arguments ('cases') of the parties and interveners, transcripts, etc.

- *R (on the application of Miller and Dos Santos) v Secretary of State for Exiting the European Union* (Full day 1 transcript)

- o *Report of Proceedings* (R. Craig, UK Constitutional Law Association, December 6, 2016)

- *R (on the application of Miller and Dos Santos) v Secretary of State for Exiting the European Union* (Full day 2 transcript)
  - o *Report of Proceedings* (R. Craig, UK Constitutional Law Association, December 7, 2016)

- *R (on the application of Miller and Dos Santos) v Secretary of State for Exiting the European Union* (Full day 3 transcript)
  - o *Report of Proceedings* (R. Craig, UK Constitutional Law Association, December 12, 2016)

- *R (on the application of Miller and Dos Santos) v Secretary of State for Exiting the European Union* (Full day 4 transcript)
  - o *Report of Proceedings* (R. Craig, UK Constitutional Law Association, December 14, 2016)

b. Judgment

- **Judgment**: *R (on the application of Miller and another) (Respondents) v Secretary of State for Exiting the European Union (Appellant)* (January 24, 2017)
  See also:
  - o *Miller Supreme Court Case Summary* (R. Craig, UK Constitutional Law Association, January 26, 2017)
  - o *Miller: An Index of Report and Commentary* (R. Craig, UK Constitutional Law Association, January 25, 2017)
  - o *"So long (as) and farewell?" The United Kingdom Supreme Court in Miller* (O. Garner, European Law Blog, January 26, 2017)
  - o *Brexit and Parliament: A Second Capitulation or Sovereignty Regained?* (London-Brussels One-Way or Return, January 31, 2017)
  - o *Brexit will require the consent of Parliament — but not of the devolved assemblies* (The Economist, January 28, 2017)

- **Summary Judgment**: *R (Miller) -v- Secretary of State for Exiting the European Union*

B. The devolution issue

1. Overview

- *The Union and devolution* (House of Lords, Select Committee on the Constitution, May 25, 2016), warning that successive UK Governments have taken the Union for granted, without giving proper consideration to the cumulative impact of devolution on the UK as a whole. See also:
  - *Brexit: some legal and constitutional issues and alternatives to EU membership*, pp. 11-18 (House of Commons Library, July 28, 2016)
  - *Devolved External Affairs: The Impact of Brexit* (R. Whitman, Chatham House, February 2017)
  - *Brexit: Devolved Legislature Business* (House of Commons Library, March 13, 2017) [updated every Monday]

- *Brexit: Its Consequence for Devolution and the Union* (R. Hazell, A. Renwick, UCL Constitution Unit, 2016), focusing on the potential impact of Brexit upon Devolution and the Union.
  For a more global and thorough presentation of the devolution in the UK, see:
  - *Devolution and the Future of the Union* (UCL Constitution Unit, April 2015)
  - *Brexit consequentials: why the UK must involve the devolved governments in the process of leaving the EU* (A. Paun, Institute for Government, June 24, 2016)

- *A UK Exit from the EU: the End of the United Kingdom or a New Constitutional Dawn?* (S. Douglas-Scott, Cambridge Journal of International and Comparative Law, March 5, 2015), considering the impact of a UK exit from the EU on the UK devolutionary settlement, as well as considering its effects on Ireland.

- *Four-nation Brexit: How the UK and devolved governments should work together on leaving the EU* (A. Paun, G. Miller, Institute for Government, October 2016), arguing that it is imperative that Scotland, Northern Ireland, Wales and England reach agreement on the UK's Brexit terms and negotiating strategy and outlining potential steps to prevent political spats from escalating into a full-blown constitutional crisis.

2. Scotland

- *Scotland and Brexit: Brave Heart or Timorous Beastie?* (S. Peers, EU Law Analysis, October 13, 2016), examining the legal issues arising from the implicit choice the Scottish government is offering the UK government – negotiate to ensure that Scotland stays in the single market as a distinct part of the UK, or face another independence referendum.
  See also:
  - *The implications of EU withdrawal for the devolution settlement* (A. Page, Scottish Parliament Culture, Tourism, Europe and external Relations Committee, October 4, 2016)
  - *The spectre of Scoxit* (The Economist, October 20, 2016)
  - *Scotland knows what it wants with the EU, while London seems still not to know* (M. Emerson, Centre for European Policy Studies, December 24, 2016)

- *Scotland's choice: Brexit with the UK, independence, or a special deal?* (K. Hughes, Friends of Europe, November 29, 2016), looking at the political and constitutional challenges facing Scotland.
  See also:
  - *Scotland's Place in Europe* (Scottish Government, December 2016)
  - *Scotland's Brexit proposals: stand-off, independence or waiting game* (K. Hughes, Friends of Europe, December 20, 2016), asking whether it is even possible for Scotland to be in the EU's single

market when the rest of the UK is not, and looking at the real goal of the Scottish government's paper.

- *Scotland's Place in Europe: Comments on the Scottish Government's new proposals* (S. Peers, EU Law Analysis, December 20, 2016), revisiting the issue of the impact of Brexit on Scotland in the light of the publication by the Scottish government of its discussion paper 'Scotland's Place in Europe'.
  See also:
  - *Brexit Reflections – How could Scotland remain in the EU?* (M. Keating, Economic & Social Research Council, July 8, 2016)
  - *Brexit and Scotland* (A. Smith, UK Trade Policy Observatory, December 21, 2016)
  - *Scotland's plan to protect its place in European single market* (N. Sturgeon, Financial Times, December 18, 2016) [subscription required]

3. **Northern Ireland**

- *Brexit: UK-Irish relations* (House of Lords, European Union Committee, December 12, 2016), reaching the conclusion that the importance of closer UK-Irish relations and stability in Northern Ireland transcend the referendum result, and are too important to put at risk as collateral damage of the Brexit decision.
  See also:
  - *Northern Ireland and the EU referendum* (House of Commons, Northern Ireland Affairs Committee, May 26, 2016)
  - *The impact of Brexit on Northern Ireland: A first look* (Bruegel, December 22, 2016)
  - *The implications of UK withdrawal for immigration policy and nationality law: Irish aspects* (B. Ryan, Immigration Law Practitioners' Association, May 18, 2016)
  - *The Common Travel Area Between Ireland and the UK* (Migration Policy in Ireland Blog, June 5, 2012)
  - House of Commons, Northern Ireland Affairs Committee

- *Brexit: A Special Status for Northern Ireland* (A. Gilmore, The Institute of International and European Affairs, October 26, 2016), examining what the UK Government's veering towards a 'hard' Brexit might mean for the Northern Irish border, and discussing some possible solutions.

- *After the referendum: establishing the best outcome for Northern Ireland* (EU Debate NI, August 2016), providing a structured and detailed account of the June 23rd referendum results mean, what to expect, and what does Brexit mean for Northern Ireland.
  See also:
  o *Report on Visa Systems* (British-Irish Parliamentary Assembly, Committee B [European Affairs], 2016)

IV. The Impact on International Trade

- *The UK Trade Landscape After Brexit* (E. Lydgate, J. Rollo, R. Wilkinson, UK Trade Policy Observatory, September 2016), discussing the challenges for the UK as it attempts to redefine and renegotiate its post-Brexit foreign trading relationships.

- *UK trade policy and Brexit* (Global Counsel, July 27, 2016), highlighting the fundamental change to the way that the UK makes and implements trade policy as one among the many implications of a UK exit from the EU.

- *Negotiating Britain's new trade policy* (J. Rollo, A. Winters, VoxEU, August 9, 2016), suggesting some strategies for the UK government in reconstituting its trade policy, and emphasizing the need for simplicity, cooperation, and maintaining the goodwill of trading partners.

- *UK Trade Options beyond 2019: First Report of Session 2016-17* (House of Commons International Trade Committee, March 7, 2017), identifying central issues on UK international trade after Brexit - the UK's relationship with the World Trade Organization (WTO), the proposed free-trade agreement (FTA) between the UK and the EU, and the implications of the UK trading with the EU under WTO rules only.

A. The UK-EU trade relationship

1. Trade with the EU

a. Overview

- *Brexit: the options for trade* (House of Lords, European Union Committee, December 13, 2016), considering the principal possible frameworks for trade after the Article 50 two-year period, namely joining the European Economic Area (EEA), a custom union with the EU, a Free Trade Agreement (FTA) or trade based on World Trade Organization (WTO) rules. See also:
  - o *Brexit: trade aspects* (House of Commons Library, January 30, 2017)

- *Life after Brexit: What are the UK's options outside the European Union?* (S. Dhingra, T. Sampson, LSE Centre for Economic Performance, February 2016), describing alternative post-Brexit futures for UK-EU relations and summarizing the economic and political consequences of each option. See also:
  - o *The trade consequences of Brexit: how I see the situation* (R. Abbott, European Centre for International Political Economy, December 2016)

- *Brexit: future trade between the UK and EU in goods* (UK Parliament, EU External Affairs Sub-Committee, 2016), investigating on the implications of Brexit for the UK's trade in goods with the EU, and taking evidence from key sectors in order to determine the implications of the different levels of market access the UK might negotiate with the EU. See also:
  - o *Could leaving the EU make British chocolate taste bad?* (BBC News, June 12, 2016)

- *Splendid Isolation or Continued Cooperation? Options for a State after Withdrawal from the EU* (H. Hofmeister, Columbia Journal of European Law, Vol. 21.2, pp. 249-287), answering to the question whether UK's links with the continent will automatically be severed upon withdrawal or if there is a possibility for continued cooperation.

b. Possible trade models

- *Alternatives to membership: possible models for the United Kingdom outside the European Union* (HM Government, March 2016), looking at the potential models for the UK's relationship with the EU if there were to be a vote to leave – specifically Norway, Switzerland, Canada and Turkey.

- *If the UK votes to leave: The seven alternatives to EU membership* (J.-C. Piris, Centre for European Reform, January 2016), sketching out the various legal options that the UK could follow after a decision to quit the EU in order to maintain access to some or all of the EU's market.

- *The Norwegian Way: A case study for Britain's future relationship with the EU* (J. Lindsell, Civitas, February 2015), holding that the Norwegian EFTA-EEA arrangement, while not ideal, is far more effective in addressing businesses' Brexit concerns than it has previously been given credit for.
  On the Norwegian model, see also:
  o *Norwegian model for the UK: oh really?* (A. Lazowski, UK in a Changing Europe, March 30, 2016)
  o *Norway's deal with the EU still holds lessons for Britain* (The Economist, February 2, 2017)

- *Brexit: 5 things the UK can learn from the Swiss experience* – a perspective from CMS Switzerland (CMS, October 14, 2016), clarifying the scope and scale of the Swiss experience: a bilateral agreement with the EU.

- *RoOs and Rules: Why the EEA Is Not the Same as Membership of the Single Market* (P. Holmes, UK Trade Policy Observatory, October 5, 2016), summarizing two issues that a post-Brexit UK would face if it rejoined the European Economic Area (EEA): the concept of the EEA+EU as a 'regulatory union', and the Rules of Origin (RoOs).
  See also:
    o *The case for the EEA option: Evolution, not revolution* (Adam Smith Institute, 2016)
    o *Brexit: will the UK remain in the EEA despite leaving the EU? (S. James, Clifford Chance, December 1, 2016)*
    o *Could the UK stay in the single market after leaving the EU? The planned case on Article 127 EEA (S. Peers, EU Law Analysis, November 30, 2016)*

- *In a nutshell: Brexit and the UK's trading relations with the EU* (P. Ungphakorn, Trade β Blog, September 29, 2016), providing a summary of the four main options facing the UK for its trade relationship with the EU after Brexit and a clarification of their respective implications.

2. Tariffs

- *Brexit: Trading a new path* (Hogan Lovells, December 5, 2016), exploring what might lie ahead for both the UK and the rest of the EU as relationships and agreements are negotiated.

- *Potential post-Brexit tariff costs for EU-UK trade* (J. Potts, Civitas, October 2016), aiming to determine the potential tariff implications for both UK and EU exporters in the event a free trade deal has not been reached by the time the UK exits the EU.
  See also:
    o *Mitigating the impact of tariffs on UK-EU Trade* (W. Norton, Civitas, January 2017)

- *The Hilton beef quota: a taste of what post-Brexit UK faces in the WTO* (P. Ungphakorn, Trade β Blog, August 10, 2016), elaborating on the "tariff-rate quotas", one of the most difficult challenges facing the UK as it re-establishes its WTO membership.
  See also:
  - *Oranges: a litmus test of UK post-Brexit tariff negotiations* (P. Ungphakorn, Trade β Blog, September 10, 2016)
  - *This EU tariff takes the biscuit* (P. Ungphakorn, Trade β Blog, August 18, 2016)
  - *A special deal for the car industry: how could it work?* (P. Holmes, UK Trade Policy Observatory)

- *What the Deals Might Look Like: Trade After Brexit* (The Wall Street Journal, June 24, 2016), providing an interactive graph detailing what trade and tariffs would look like under the different post-Brexit models.

3. Non-tariff issues (passporting etc.)

- *Post-Brexit trade may hinge on non-tariff barriers* (Financial Times, December 18, 2016), reminding that regulations and standards will be the difficult part of negotiations between the UK and the EU. [subscription required]
  See also:
  - *Brexit Brief: Non-tariff barriers* (Institute for Government, 2017)
  - *EU 'worried English Champagne will flood into continent after Brexit'*, (The Telegraph, February 15, 2017)

- *The curious absence of services trade* (I. Borchert, UK Trade Policy Observatory, December 14, 2016), on the importance that Brexit discussions do not ignore services trade, a key component of the UK's trading environment.
  See also:
  - *Services trade in the UK: What is at stake?* (I. Borchert, UK Trade Policy Observatory, November 2016)

B. The UK's international trade agreements (including but not limited to FTAs)

- *Brexit and EU-UK trade relations with third states* (M. Gehring, EU Law Analysis, March 6, 2016), cautioning that the UK's membership in the WTO and all other mixed trade agreements could be in jeopardy if the UK exited without a successful transitional agreement with the EU.

- *Negotiating the UK's Post-Brexit Trade Arrangements* (P. Holmes, J. Rollo, A. Winters, National Institute Economic Review, November 2016), considering the agenda for UK trade negotiations over the post-Brexit period.
  See also:
  - *Where should Britain strike its first post-Brexit trade deals?* (The Economist, February 4, 2017)

- *Brexit – Trade and Treaties* (J. Gladstone, Clifford Chance, November 25, 2016), analysing what free trade agreements encompass, what the WTO is and how it works; and what third-state agreements might involve.

1. With Europe

- *UK-EU Trade Relations Post Brexit: Too Many Red Lines?* (M. Gasiorek, P. Holmes, J. Rollo, UK Trade Policy Observatory, November 2016), focusing on the UK's future trading relations with the EU itself.
  See also:
  - *Brexit and mixity – the implications for a UK free trade agreement with the EU* (Brick Court Chambers, December 22, 2016)
  - *Europe is growing in importance as a UK trade partner* (Prospect, November 16, 2016)
  - *Can the UK take over existing EU trade agreements?* (BBC News Business, October 7, 2016)

2. With FTA partners

- *The UK's Future Trade Relationships* (C. Bates, Clifford Chance, October 24, 2016), arguing that to recreate something akin to the UK's current global network of preferential trade agreements, the UK will need to negotiate Free Trade Agreements (FTAs) with its other key trading partners.
  See also:
  - *The EU's future trade policy starts to take shape: the Opinion on the EU/Singapore FTA* (S. Peers, EU Law Analysis, December 21, 2016)
  - *What might legal case over EU-Singapore trade deal mean for Brexit?* (A. Shankar, Open Europe, December 20, 2016)

- *Starting Over on Tariffs: Post-Brexit Trade Agreement Partners for the United Kingdom* (C. Bown, Peterson Institute for International Economics, July 12, 2016), examining specific questions facing UK trade negotiators on the importance of import tariffs in FTA negotiations.

- *The Canada-Europe Trade Agreement: Opportunities and Risks for the United Kingdom* (Dentons, November 4, 2016), providing an analysis of the impact of Brexit on the CETA, authored by The Right Honourable Stephen Harper, P.C., Canada's former Prime Minister (2006-2015).
  See also:
  - *Life after Brexit: What happens to Canada's trade deal with Europe?* (CBC News, June 24, 2016)
  - *Ceta failure will undermine basis of EU trade policy* (Financial Times, October 25, 2016) [subscription required]
  - *CETA, Trump and Brexit: An Opportunity for Ireland and Canada* (The Canadian Lawyer, November 28, 2016)

3. With all other partners

- *Will TTIP survive Brexit?* (Bruegel, July 27, 2016), addressing the concerns that the UK's decision to leave the EU may jeopardise future TTIP negotiations.

See also:

- o *The Transatlantic Trade and Investment Partnership* (House of Commons Library, December 4, 2015)
- o *Brexit Clouds TTIP Negotiations But May Not Scupper Deal* (M. Schneider-Petsinger, Chatham House, July 11, 2016)
- o *For a US Trade Deal, UK Should Secure Its Spot in TTIP After Brexit* (M. Schneider-Petsinger, Chatham House, August 25, 2016)

- *Japan's Message to the United Kingdom* (September 2016), offering a detailed analysis of the areas of Brexit-related concern to the thousands of Japanese companies in the UK, and those aspects of the current business environment that these companies want to preserve in the forthcoming negotiations.
  See also:
  - o *Japan Lays Out a Guide to Brexit* (Sir David Warren, Chatham House, September 6, 2016)
  - o *Brexit revives stalled Japan-EU trade deal* (Politico, September 27, 2016)
  - o *A hard Brexit is the last thing Japan wants* (K. Lannoo, Centre for European Policy Studies, December 7, 2016)
  - o *Japanese banks warn of leaving London without Brexit clarity* (Financial Times, December 16, 2016) [subscription required]

- *The EU, Brexit and India – Adapting to changing landscapes* (Friends of Europe, December 5, 2016), reporting on the growing necessity for both the UK and the EU to see India as one of their key partners.
  See also:
  - o *Will India dash UK trade deal hopes?* (BBC, November 5, 2016)
  - o *May's India trip shows the ultimate failure of the Brexit project* (Politics, November 7, 2016)
  - o *May's trade ambitions hit Indian immigration impasse* (Politico, November 8, 2016)

- *China and Brexit: what's in it for us?* (F. Godement, A. Stanzel, European Council on Foreign Relations,

September 9, 2016), suggesting that most of the losses from Brexit will hit the EU or the UK, or both, while China will get most of the gains. See also:

- o *UK-China agreement on trade in services is no substitute for a UK-EU deal* (Bruegel, December 6, 2016)
- o *British government's vaunted China export deals don't add up* (FMT News, February 7, 2017)

• *Brexit and Asia: What impact has the UK's vote to leave the EU had on the APAC region?* (D. Cook, Berwin Leighton Paisner, February 2, 2017), exploring the political impact that Brexit has on the UK's reputation among ASEAN countries and the economic impacts of Brexit on the wider APAC region, both in terms of trade relations and investment into the UK.

• *Discussion Note: Brexit: Its Implications and Potential for the Commonwealth* (The Commonwealth Secretariat, September 20, 2016), examining the various channels through which countries in the Commonwealth could be affected by Brexit and suggesting that there are varied implications for Commonwealth countries, which differ by region and by transmission mechanism. See also:

- o *Trade Hot Topics: Trade Implications of Brexit for Commonwealth Developing Countries* (C. Stevens, J. Kennan, The Commonwealth, August 18, 2016)
- o *Commonwealth Trade Policy Briefing: Brexit and Commonwealth Trade* (The Commonwealth, November 2016)
- o *Trade Hot Topics: Post-Brexit UK-ACP Trading Arrangements: Some Reflections* (M. Razzaque, B. Vickers, November 4, 2016)

C. The role of the WTO

• *The World Trade Organization: A Safety Net for a post-Brexit UK Trade Policy?* (UK Trade Policy Observatory, July 1, 2016), exploring the nature WTO commitments and how they might impact the UK from the date of its exit from the EU.

- o *The "WTO option" for Brexit is far from straightforward* (The Economist, January 7, 2016)
- o *Brexit and the WTO option: Key questions about a looming challenge* (Financial Times, June 12, 2016) [subscription required]

- *Nothing simple about UK regaining WTO status post-Brexit* (P. Ungphakorn, ICTSD, June 27, 2016), warning about the complexity the UK would face to operate as an ordinary WTO member after it leaves the EU. See also:
  - o *Why the UK is already under WTO rules and why that matters for Brexit* (P. Ungphakorn, Trade β Blog, February 8, 2017)
  - o *Second bite – how simple is the UK-WTO relationship post-Brexit?* (P. Ungphakorn, Trade β Blog, August 20, 2016)
  - o *The Hilton beef quota: a taste of what post-Brexit UK faces in the WTO* (P. Ungphakorn, Trade β Blog, August 10, 2016)
  - o *Can EU law really dictates World Trade Organization rules?* (P. Ungphakorn, Trade β Blog, December 1, 2016)

- *The UK's Status in the WTO after Brexit* (L. Bartels, September 20, 2016), addressing the identification of the UK's right to access to EU tariff rate quotas and arguing – contrary to the governing assumption – that, based on WTO law, GATT 1947 practice, and the rules of state succession, the position of the UK within the WTO will not change after it leaves the EU. See also:
  - o *Understanding the UK's position in the WTO after Brexit (Part I – The UK's status and its schedules)* (L. Bartels, ICTSD, September 26, 2016)
  - o *Understanding the UK's position in the WTO after Brexit (Part II – The consequences)* (L. Bartels, ICTSD, September 26, 2016)
  - o *State Succession to International Intergovernmental Organizations under the International Public Law* (N. M.

Vladoiu, International Journal of Law and Jurisprudence, Vol. I, Issue 1, January-June 2015, pp. 13-21)

- *Making Room for Britain at the World Trade Organization* (The Wall Street Journal, February 6, 2017), describing two potential conflicting views of the UK and 163 other WTO Members regarding how the UK should rearrange its WTO tariff schedule after Brexit. See also:
  - ○ *WTO rules means UK-EU divorce and new trade arrangement are not fully separable* (V. Scarpetta, Open Europe, November 2, 2016)
  - ○ *'No deal' Brexit would mean £6bn in extra costs for UK exporters* (The Guardian, February 20, 2017)
  - ○ *Brexit, agriculture, the WTO, and uncertainty* (P. Ungphakorn, Trade β Blog, December 1, 2016)
  - ○ *UK Brexit and WTO farm support limits* (L. Brink, CAP Reform Blog, July 13, 2016)

D. The economics of Brexit

- *Brexit Beckons: Thinking ahead by leading economists* (R. Baldwin, VoxEU, August 1, 2016), aiming to provide a means of moving forward for both the UK and the EU by discussing some key consensus topics (trade agreements; ex ante costs to the UK; labour markets; globalization etc.). See also:
  - ○ *Brexit Is a Bad Trade* (C. Bown, Peterson Institute for International Economics, June 3, 2016)
  - ○ *Brexit: An Impossibly Complex Task for the UK's New Trade Negotiators?* (C. Bown, Peterson Institute for International Economics, September 7, 2016)
  - ○ *Is the UK's role in the European supply chain at risk?* (Bruegel, December 20, 2016)
  - ○ *Brexit and the regions: a lighter shade* (A. Winters, UK Trade Policy Observatory)

- *The Economic Impact of Brexit-induced Reductions in Migration* (J. Portes, G. Forte, National Institute of Economic and

Social Research, December 7, 2016), analyzing the impact of Brexit on migration flows to the UK in both the short and long term, and providing plausible, empirically-based estimates of the likely impacts on growth, employment and wages.

V. Immigration & Free Movement of Persons

- *Brexit: UK-EU movement of people* (House of Lords, European Union Committee, March 6, 2017), examining possible arrangements for migration of EU citizens to the UK after the UK has ceased to be a member of the EU, with a view to identifying the main choices available to the Government and their likely implications – including for UK citizens wishing to move to the EU in future.
  See also:
  o *Brexit: what impact on those currently exercising free movements rights?* (House of Commons Library, January 19, 2017)

- *What free movement means to Europe and why it matters for Britain* (C. Mortera-Martinez, C. Odendahl, Center for European Reform, January 2017), analyzing the historical and political impact of free movement in the EU, examining the possible outcome of the negotiations with the UK on the issue, and also suggesting future EU policies on the matter.
  See also:
  o *Immigration, Free Movement and the EU Referendum* (J. Portes, National Institute Economic Review, May 2016)
  o *Labour mobility after Brexit* (Bruegel, December 2, 2016)
  o *Brexit and immigration: Raising the drawbridge* (The Economist, August 25, 2016)

- *Beyond Free Movement? Six Possible Futures for the UK's EU Migration Policy* (Institute for Public Policy Research, July 2016), identifying and exploring the six main options on free movement that the UK government could pursue.

- *Policy Primer: The UK, EU Citizenship and Free Movement of Persons* (The Migration Observatory, May 1, 2014), detailing movement and residence in all Member States for EU citizens as a defining feature of EU citizenship.

- *Brexit and UK immigration and asylum policy: a reading list* (House of Commons Library, August 2, 2016), collating commentaries on the implications of the EU referendum vote for future UK immigration and asylum policy.

VI. Acquired Rights Issues

- *Brexit: acquired rights* (House of Lords, European Union Committee, December 14, 2016), analyzing what will happen to the EU rights upon which EU citizens and UK nationals rely when the UK leaves the EU, and recommending that if certain EU rights are to be safeguarded on the UK's withdrawal from the EU, they should be safeguarded in the withdrawal agreement itself.

- *What Happens to 'Acquired Rights' in the Event of a Brexit?* (S. Douglas-Scott, UK Constitutional Law Association, May 16, 2016), aiming to clarify the determination of the acquired rights of UK citizens living in other EU Member States and equally of EU citizens living in the UK.

A. EU citizens in the UK and future UK policy on immigrants from the EU

- *What would happen to EU nationals living or planning to visit or live in the UK after a UK exit from the EU?* (H. Wray, EU Law Analysis, July 17, 2014), reflecting on what life would be after Brexit for the 2.3 million EU citizens already living in the UK and for those who might wish to come in the future.
  See also:

- o *Brexit and the illusion of immigration control* (London-Brussels One-Way or Return, January 16, 2016)
- o *Could EU citizens living in the UK claim 'acquired rights' if there is a full Brexit?* (Tim Eicke QC, LexisPSL, March 11, 2016)

B. UK citizens post-Brexit access to the EU

- *What happens to British expatriates if the UK leaves the EU?* (S. Peers, EU Law Analysis, May 9, 2014), discussing what would happen to the nearly 2.5 million UK citizens living in other EU Member States, and presenting different scenarios following the UK's withdrawal.
  See also:
  - o *Goodbye, cruel world: visas for holidays after Brexit?* (S. Peers, EU Law Analysis, April 26, 2016)

C. Acquired rights into the future

- *EU Citizenship and Withdrawals from the Union: How Inevitable Is the Radical Downgrading of Rights?* (D. Kochenov, LSE 'Europe in Question', June 2016), reviewing the possible impact that the law and practice of EU citizenship can have on the conduct of Brexit negotiations.

- *Bargaining Chips No More: The Status of EU and UK citizens after Brexit* (S. Peers, EU Law Analysis, December 11, 2016), inquiring on what should happen regarding EU citizens in the UK as well as to UK citizens in the EU, and discussing the idea of 'associate citizenship'.
  See also:
  - o *Brexit: Could UK get 'associate EU citizenship'* (BBC, November 17, 2016)

- *European Citizenship after Brexit* (P. Mindus [draft], September 29, 2016), investigating European citizenship after Brexit, and the impact of Brexit on the content and the concept of EU citizenship.

VII. Impact on Human Rights

- *The human rights implications of Brexit* (House of Commons, House of Lords, Joint Committee on Human Rights, December 19, 2016), considering the impact of Brexit on EU and UK nationals and the extent to which individual rights currently protected in EU law are likely to be protected under the ECHR.
  See also:
  - *Brexit: UK can't deport millions of EU nationals, report warns* (The Guardian, December 19, 2016)
  - *Brexit and the Future of Human Rights Law in the UK* (S. Peers, EU Law Analysis, December 15, 2016)
  - *Brexit: What It Means for Human Rights* (Freshfields Bruckhaus Deringer, July 6, 2016)
  - *Workers' rights from Europe: the impact of Brexit* (Michael Ford QC, TUC, March 10, 2016)

- *The implications of Brexit for fundamental rights protection in the UK* (J. Murkens, S. Trotter, LSE European Institute, March 2016), discussing the state and fate of fundamental rights under EU law and the EU Charter of Fundamental Rights, the ECHR and the Human Rights Act 1998, and domestic rights protection – in the light of the debate as to the UK's continuing membership of the EU.
  See also:
  - *The Real Record of the EU Charter of Fundamental Rights* (P. Eeckhout, UK Constitutional Law Association, May 6, 2016)
  - *The Application of the EU Charter of Fundamental Rights in the UK: a state of confusion* (House of Commons, European Scrutiny Committee, April 2, 2014)

- *The UK, the EU and a British Bill of Rights* (House of Lords, European Union Committee, May 9, 2016), assessing the UK Government that a British Bill of Rights is necessary and considering its likely impact on different legal areas.
  For more information on the British Bill of Rights, see also:

- o *Brexit and a British Bill of Rights: four scenarios for human rights* (UK in a Changing Europe, May 2016)
- o *Misunderstanding Brexit – Scrapping The Human Rights Act For A British Bill Of Rights* (Forbes, August 23, 2016)

- *Theresa May's case for withdrawing from the ECHR: Politically astute, legally dubious, constitutionally naïve* (M. Elliott, Public Law for Everyone, April 26, 2016), engaging with Prime Minister May's intention to maintain the UK in the EU while withdrawing from the ECHR.

VIII. Effect on Environment, Energy, and Climate Change

- *Brexit: environment and climate change* (House of Lords, European Union Committee, February 14, 2017), shedding light on the likely impact of Brexit on UK environment and climate change policy, and highlighting what action will need to be taken to manage the issues that arise.
  See also:
  - o *The energy revolution and future challenges for UK energy and climate change policy* (House of Commons, Energy and Climate Change Committee, October 15, 2016)

A. Effect of Brexit on UK environmental protection

- *Brexit – the Implications for UK Environmental Policy and Regulation* (Institute for European Environmental Policy, March 2016), exploring the options that might be pursued outside the EU and the potential impact on environment and climate policy.
  See also:
  - o *The potential policy and environmental consequences for the UK of a departure from the European Union* (Institute for European Environmental Policy, March 2016)
  - o *Review of the Balance of Competences between the United Kingdom and the European Union: Environment and Climate Change* (HM Government, February 2014)

- *The EU Referendum and the UK Environment: the Future Under a 'Hard' or 'Soft' Brexit* (C. Bruns, A. Jordan, V. Gravey, UK in a Changing Europe, 2016), reviewing various questions associated with the effect of Brexit on UK environment policies, systems of decision making and environmental quality.

- *Brexit: What next for UK fisheries?* (House of Commons Library, July 27, 2016), on the possible implications of Brexit for fisheries and the high level of uncertainty bearing on this issue.
  See also:
  o *The effect of Brexit on agriculture and fisheries in South West England* (House of Commons Library, October 14, 2016)

B. Energy

- *UK Unplugged? The Impacts of Brexit on Energy and Climate Policy* (Chatham House, May 26, 2016), addressing the likely impacts on the longer-term cost, sustainability and security of the UK's energy sector, as well as the wider regulatory and investment effects.

- *Brexit and energy: cost, security and climate policy implications* (UCL European Institute, May 2016), analysing the implications of Brexit for the UK's energy sector and remarking that leaving the EU would greatly reduce the UK's influence in shaping European energy and climate change policy.
  See also:
  o *The impact of Brexit on the UK Energy Market* (Addleshaw Goddard LLP, October 21, 2016)

- *Brexit Versus Euratom: What the "No" Vote Could Mean for UK Membership in the European Nuclear Peace Treaty* (M. Bruneau, A. L. Hamilton, McDermott Will & Emery, July 19, 2016), considering what the effect that Brexit could have on the UK's membership to the European Atomic Energy Community (Euratom).
  See also:

- o The UK Brexits Euratom: Legal Framework and Future Developments (S. Peers, EU Law Analysis, January 30, 2017)
- o *Brexit goes nuclear: The consequences of leaving Euratom* (Bruegel, February 21, 2017)

C. Climate change

- *Brexit and climate policy: Political choices will determine the future of EU-UK cooperation* (M. Elkerbout, Centre for European Policy Studies, July 15, 2016), looking at the possible implications of Brexit at various levels: at the level of the United Nations, the EU level and the implications for the UK.

- *Brexit: Why a vote to leave the EU is bad news for the climate* (Climate Home, June 20, 2016), reporting leaving the EU would hit low carbon investment and the UK's influence at international negotiations.

- *Brexit and climate change* (J. Curry, Climate Etc., June 25, 2016), offering some speculations on Brexit and climate change.

IX. Impact on Banking and Financial Services

- *Brexit and financial services* (House of Commons Library, August 1, 2016), bringing together responses from financial organisations about the impact of the vote to leave the EU due to the substantial degree of inter-linkage between the 'City' and the EU economies. See also:
  - o *Brexit: financial services* (House of Lords, European Union Committee, December 15, 2016)

- *Brexit: the United-Kingdom and EU financial services* (European Parliament, Briefing, December 9, 2016), describing the prominent role of the UK in the single market for financial services, and highlighting which

activities rely today on passporting for their daily business with the other 27 Member States.
See also:

- o *Making the best of Brexit for the EU27 financial system* (Bruegel Policy Brief, February 8, 2017)
- o *EU Financial Market Access after Brexit* (K. Lannoo, Centre for European Policy Studies, September 29, 2016)
- o *What will happen to the Capital Markets Union After Brexit?* (P. Ständer, Jacques Delors Institut, December 19, 2016)
- o *European Union, Financial regulation, Banking Union, Capital Markets Union and the UK* (L. Quaglia, Policy Network, Sheffield Political Economy Research Institute, January 2017)

- • *The impact of Brexit on the City and the British economic model* (Policy Network, July 18, 2016), focusing on two aspects of the impact of Brexit on the City: the tensions between the City and democratic politics, and the challenges for the future of the City posed by the vote for Britain to leave the EU.
  See also:
  - o *The City Will Decline – and We Will Be the Poorer for It* (N. Véron, Peterson Institute for International Economics, August 18, 2016)
  - o *Brexit and the City: From Big Bang to Brexit* (The Economist, October 27, 2016)
  - o *Stealing London's financial crown would bring both benefits and responsibilities* (Bruegel, November 17, 2016)
  - o *An equivalence deal on Brexit may be the best the City can get* (Financial Times, December 11, 2016) [subscription required]
  - o *What do EU capital markets look like post-Brexit?* (New Financial, September 2016)

- • *Brexit and the industry* (TheCityUK, September 2016), containing information on the new UK Government and changes in Government machinery, as well as an overview of the UK's economic position since the referendum.

- *The impact of the UK's exit from the EU on the UK-based financial services sector* (Oliver Wyman, October 2016), analyzing Brexit's potential impact on the UK-based financial services sector.
  See also:
  - *How to ensure UK and the European financial services continue to thrive after Brexit* (S. Booth, Open Europe, October 17, 2016)
  - *Banks could move assets out of UK by 2017 if 'EU passport' is lost* (The Guardian, October 17, 2016)
  - *The impact of Brexit on the UK-based service sector* (TheCityUK, December 20, 2016)

- *The "EU Brexit" implication on a single banking license and other aspects of financial markets regulation in the UK* (N. Mugarura, International Journal of Law and Management, 2016), providing a review of the implication of Brexit on financial markets regulations in the EU and UK.

- *Policy Uncertainty and International Financial Markets: The Case of Brexit* (A. belke, I. Dubova, T. Osowski, Centre for European Policy Studies, November 2016), assessing the impact of the uncertainty caused by Brexit on both the UK and international markets, and showing that Brexit-induced policy uncertainty will continue to cause instability in key financial markets and has the potential to damage the real economy in both the UK and other European countries, even in the medium run.

X. Other Issues

A. Business

- *A practitioner's guide to Brexit* (TheCityUK, March 9, 2016), addressing the practical questions businesses need to be aware of in the event of a Brexit, and considering the UK's post-Brexit trading arrangements with other countries and three current alternatives to the UK's EU membership from the perspective of the financial and related professional services industry.

1. Impact on UK-based companies

- *A Quick Brexit or a Delayed Departure? Here's Where It Gets Tricky for Businesses* (C. Bown, Peterson Institute for International Economics, July 7, 2016), advocating that, in the case of Brexit, a combination of trade and regulatory policy uncertainty means potential setbacks for companies in the UK.
  See also:
  - *Fears EU Brexit delays will spur bank exodus to Eurozone* (Financial Times, December 18, 2016) [subscription required]
  - *Brexit: Product Regulation and Safety – Further Musings on the Possible Effects on Importers of Goods into the European Union* (Jones Day, December 16, 2016)

- *The Death of British Business* (The New York Review of Books, October 18, 2016), reporting the damage that Brexit has and will continue to inflict on the UK economy, that has become overwhelmingly dependent on foreign enterprise and foreign capital.
  See also:
  - *Brexit and business: British companies may find it harder than expected to unravel the EU's red tape* (The Economist, December 15, 2016)

- *Brexit: employment law* (House of Commons Library, November 10, 2016), discussing the interaction between UK and EU employment law, the potential consequences of Brexit and the Government's position on the issue.
  See also:
  - *Workers' rights from Europe: the impact of Brexit* (Michael Ford QC, advice to the TUC, April 7, 2016)

2. Impact on US businesses

- *How Brexit is expected to impact US industries* (Grant Thornton, 2016), focusing at the important issues that

are likely to affect U.S. companies, as well as at impacts on specific industries.
See also:

- o *Brexit implications for US Businesses* (D. Gent, Bird & Bird, July 19, 2016)
- o *How Will the Exit of the United Kingdom from the European Union Affect U.S. Corporations Doing Business in the UK?* (Vedder Price, June 23, 2016)
- o *Brexit Big Winner? It Could Be New York City* (Foreign Policy, October 18, 2016)

- *The Future of UK-EU Relations: Priorities of the U.S. Business Community* (U.S. Chamber of Commerce, October 18, 2016), elaborating on the concerns of U.S.-headquartered companies investing in the UK.

- *Populist Political Wave in the UK and in the U.S.* (P. Welfens, American Institute for Contemporary German Studies, December 12, 2016), elaborating on Brexit and President Trump's economic policy.
  See also:
  - o *President Trump and Brexit* (A. Winters, UK Trade Policy Observatory, November 9, 2016)

3. Competition law

- *Consequences of Brexit for competition law and policy* (J. Vickers, Oxford review of Economic Policy / British Academy Conference on 'The Economic Consequences of Brexit, December 7, 2016), discussing what would happen to the UK competition policy if the UK leaves the EEA regarding mergers and markets on the one hand, and antitrust on the other hand.
  See also:
  - o *Brexit and EU Competition Policy* (R. Wilsh, Journal of European Competition Law & Practice, May 9, 2016) [subscription required]
  - o *UK Competition Policy and Brexit – Time for a Reset* (O. Bretz, Competition Policy International, July 2016)
  - o *Gaining or losing the competitive edge? Implications for competition law enforcement* (Allen & Overy, March 2016)

- o *Brexit and Competition Law: What to Expect* (J. Ratliff, C. O'Daly, Wilmer Hale, September 15, 2016)

- *Competition law damages actions in England for violation of Articles 101 and 102 after Brexit: Part 1* (Daniel Jowell QC, Brick Court Chambers, September 23, 2016), on whether it will still be possible, if there is a "hard Brexit", to bring actions before the UK courts seeking damages for breaches of Articles 101 and 102 TFEU. See also:
  - o *Competition law damages actions in England for violation of Articles 101 and 102 after Brexit: Part 2* (Daniel Jowell QC, Brick Court Chambers, September 26, 2016)
  - o *Competition law damages actions in England for violation of Articles 101 and 102 after Brexit: Part 3* (Daniel Jowell QC, Brick Court Chambers, September 26, 2016)

- *UK Competition Policy Post-Brexit: In the Public Interest?* (B. Lyons, D. Reader, A. Stephen, Centre for Competition Policy, November 4, 2016), providing an analysis of the UK's future competition policy following its withdrawal from the EU, and focusing on whether the UK should make greater use of public interest tests, or allow antitrust rules to diverge from those of the EU. See also:
  - o *Brexit, Here We Come (or Go)* (Antitrust Law Blog, June 24, 2016)
  - o *What will cartel enforcement look like post-Brexit?* (M. O'Kane, N. Querée, Kluwer Competition Law Blog, June 27, 2016)

B. Arbitration and Litigation

- *Consequences of "Brexit" on International Dispute Resolution: Special Issue of Journal of International Arbitration* (Kluwer Arbitration Blog, October 21, 2016), addressing the impact of Brexit on international dispute resolution and providing references to studies on various related issues. [subscription required]

See also:

- o *Towards the Uncertainties of a hard Brexit: An Opportunity for International Arbitration* (G. Croisant, Kluwer Arbitration Blog, January 27, 2017)
- o *Brexit—the future of state-to-state, investor-state and domestic dispute resolution* (A. Cannon et al., Herbert Smith Freehills LLP, March 2, 2017)

- • *Why Brexit is Not Bad News For UK-Based Arbitration and Litigation* (Dechert LLP, December 15, 2016), contrasting the general uncertainties of Brexit with the clearer picture and more positive outlook of its impact on UK-based arbitration and litigation.
  See also:
  - o *Brexit: Potential Implications for International Arbitration in London* (T. Laurendeau, J. Sharpe, Shearman & Sterling LLP, October 18, 2016)
  - o *Why Brexit May Be Good for UK Investors Abroad* (M. Burgstaller, A. Zarowna, Kluwer Arbitration Blog, October 24, 2016)

C. Privacy & data protection

- • *Brexit and data protection* (House of Commons Library, December 15, 2016), discussing the current reform of EU data protection law, the interaction with UK law, and the potential consequences of Brexit in this area.
  See also:
  - o *Data regulation: Britain faces data privacy confusion after Brexit* (Financial Times, July 6, 2016) [subscription required]
  - o *Post-Brexit Data Security Considerations* (K. K. Dort, Bloomberg Law: Privacy & Data Security, December 14, 2016)
  - o *Transparency, trust and progressive data protection* (E. Denham, UK Information Commissioner, Speech, September 29, 2016)
  - o *Data retention and national law: the ECJ ruling in Joined Cases C-203/15 and C-698/15 Tele2 and Watson (Grand Chamber)* (L. Woods, EU Law Analysis, December 21, 2016)

- o *Implications of the EU's Data Retention Ruling* (Lawfare Blog, December 22, 2016)

- *The EU General Data Protection Ruling* (Allen & Overy, 2016), on the new data protection framework provided by the General Data Protection Regulation (GDPR) and will apply starting May 25, 2018.
  See also:
  - o *Chapter 13: Cross-Border Data Transfers – Unlocking the EU General Data Protection Regulation* (White & Case, July 22, 2016)
  - o *U.S.-EU Data Privacy: From Safe Harbor to Privacy Shield* (M. Weiss, K. Archick, Congressional Research Service, May 19, 2016)
  - o *EU General Data Protection Regulation, Frequently Asked Questions* (EUGDPR.org)

D. Universities & Students

- *The determinants of international demand for UK higher education* (Final Report for the Higher Education Policy Institute and Kaplan International Pathways, January 2017), showing that UK universities could lose students while gaining financially from Brexit, but any new restrictions on international students could cost the UK economy an additional £2 billion a year.
  See also:
  - o *Funding support for EU students* (UK Government, Department for Education, Press release, October 11, 2016)
  - o *Higher Education and Research Bill* (House of Commons, November 21, 2016)

- *The impact of Brexit on UK tertiary education and R&D* (Bruegel, February 14, 2017), looking at the impact of Brexit on UK's education and research and development sector in terms of students and staff, as well as funding.
  On the impact of Brexit on paediatric research, see also:
  - o *The challenge of Brexit for paediatric research* (M. Turner, S. Collen, NHS Confederation, February 15, 2017)

- *What Does Brexit Mean for Students* (TopUniversities, December 19, 2016), exposing implications of Brexit on various students-related issues students (funding, visa, etc.).
  - *Universities and Brexit: A first-class mess* (The Economist, July 21, 2016)
  - *Oxbridge set for Brexit boost from student fees* (Financial Times, January 12, 2017) [subscription required]
  - *Brexit fears may see 15% of UK university staff leave, group warns* (The Guardian, September 25, 2016)
  - *Oxford academics warning of Brexit 'disaster'* (BBC News, January 11, 2007)

E. State aids

- *Brexit: UK funding from the EU* (House of Commons Library, December 29, 2016), looking at the funding received by the UK from EU institutions and considering the implications of Brexit on the EU as a source of funding for regional development, agriculture support, research and innovation and other areas.

- *Brexit: Implications for State Aid/Control of Subsidies* (Wilmer Hale, November 22, 2016), explaining key differences between EU State aid rules and the WTO anti-subsidy regime – in the light of the UK's choice to leave the EU.

- *Together forever? How State aid law will affect the UK even after Brexit* (F. Schöning, Kluwer Competition Law Blog, July 2, 2016), asking whether the end of EU membership also bring to an end the application of State aid provisions.
  See also:
  - *Brexit and state aid* (J. Branton, Local Government Lawyer, June 16, 2016)
  - *George Osborne: Brexit government likely to keep controversial state aid rules* (New Statesman, November 3, 2016)

- *The Impact of Possible Migration Scenarios After 'Brexit' on the State Pension System* (National Institute of Economic and Social Research, June 2, 2016), exploring the impacts of changes in migration flows – in particular, those resulting from possible migration policy changes after Brexit – on the finances of the UK state pension system.
  On the impact of Brexit on pensions, see also:
  - o *Brexit and state pensions* (House of Commons Library, February 7, 2017)
  - o *The Brexit bill: uncertainties in the estimate of EU pension and sickness insurance liabilities* (Bruegel, February 17, 2017)

F. Ireland

- *Brexit: UK-Irish relations* (House of Lords, European Union Committee, December 12, 2016), reaching the conclusion that the importance of closer UK-Irish relations and stability in Northern Ireland transcend the referendum result, and are too important to put at risk as collateral damage of the Brexit decision.

- *Getting Ireland Brexit ready* (Republic of Ireland, Department of Finance, October 2016), providing an overview of how Brexit may impact on the Irish economy as well as the policy responses to Brexit that have been introduce in the Irish Budget 2017 to enable exposed sectors of Ireland's economy to remain competitive, and to protect the public finances. See also:
  - o *Business Critical Changes to Irish-UK Trade Rules: How Should Irish Agri-Food Producers Plan for Brexit?* (McCann Fitzgerald, September 22, 2016)
  - o *Hard Brexit: What Would It Mean For Irish Agri-Food Producers?* (McCann Fitzgerald, December 6, 2016)
  - o *Irish preparations for border checks bring home the reality of Brexit* (New Statesman, February 12, 2017)

G. Gibraltar

- *Brexit: Gibraltar* (House of Lords, European Union Committee, March 1, 2017), seeking to highlight the key challenges posed by Brexit to Gibraltar, including its service-based economy, its land border with Spain, and for Gibraltar's future relationship with the EU.
  See also:
  - *Rocked by Brexit vote, Gibraltar lays plan for new kind of EU relationship* (The Guardian, October 22, 2016)
  - *Brexit: Gibraltar – EU Committee launches short inquiry* (House of Lords, EU Select Committee, December 8, 2016)
  - *Gibraltar puts a brave face on Brexit* (Financial Times, February 1, 2017) [subscription required]

- *Brexit Advisory Newsletter 1* (Isolas, September 2016) and *Brexit Advisory Newsletter 2* (Isolas, November 2016), detailing the potential implications that Brexit could have in areas likely to most affect Gibraltar.
  See also:
  - *Spain, Gibraltar and Brexit: Rock out* (The Economist, July 13, 2016)
  - *Democracy, Sovereignty, Brexit and Gibraltar* (J. Trinidad, July 6, 2016)
  - *Brexit or no Brexit – Gibraltar can be your solution* (Isolas, October 12, 2016)
  - *Funds in Gibraltar Post-Brexit* (Isolas, July 2016)

XI. The Future of the EU

- *The exit option: How contagious could Brexit be?* (Global Counsel, August 1, 2016), focusing on political actors in the EU who will take inspiration from the UK's choice to leave and assessing the prospect of others following the UK towards the exit door.
  See also:
  - *Brexit: The Consequences for the EU's Political System* (O. Patel, C. Reh, UCL Constitution Unit, 2016)
  - *The impact of Brexit on the EU* (C. Grant, Centre for European Reform, June 24, 2016)
  - *Brexit: the impact on the UK and the EU* (Global Counsel, June 2015)

- ○ *Which Europe Now?* (The New York review of Books, August 18, 2016)
- ○ *Brexit: The Consequences for Other EU Member States* (O. Patel, A. Renwick, UCL Constitution Unit, 2016)

- • *EU economic governance after Brexit* (L. Quaglia, W. Schelkle, Policy Network, November 29 2016), providing insights on how fragmented political and economic interests, both internationally and intranationally, have been shaping EU economic policy making in the wake of the global financial crisis, the Eurozone crisis and the UK's referendum on EU membership.
  See also:
  - ○ *Britain's special status in Europe* (A. Duff, Policy Network, March 3, 2016)
  - ○ *Brexit and the Distribution of Power in the Council of the EU* (W. Kirsch, Centre for European Policy Studies, November 25, 2016)

- • *Brexit: the Economic and Political Impact of a Possible Withdrawal of Great Britain's from the European Union* (S. Moagar-Poladian et al., Global Economic Observer, 2015), arguing that Great Britain's withdrawal from the European Union would not only change the internal political climate, but it could have important political repercussions within the EU and also on its relations with other European Community's countries, as well as stimulates the other EU Member States to re-evaluate the terms and conditions of their membership.
  See also:
  - ○ *The (Uncertain) Impact of Brexit on the United Kingdom's Membership in the European Economic Area* (U. Schroeter, H. Nemeczek, European Business Law Review, 2016) [subscription required]
  - ○ *Impact of Brexit on the EU budget* (A. Matthews, CAP reform, September 10, 2016)
  - ○ *After the UK's EU referendum: redefining relations between the "two Europes"* (T. Chopin, J.-F. Jamet, Fondation Robert Schuman, July 5, 2016)

- *Brexit and Europe's Future – A Game Theoretical Approach* (M. Diermeier, H. Goecke, M. Hüther, Cologne Institute for Economic Research, December 2016), examining the questions of how UK-EU relations should be conducted and what long and short-term advantages can be obtained.

  See also:

  o *After Brexit* (A. Duff, Policy Network, October 2016)

  o *The Elements of a New EU-UK Relationship*, (J. T. Lang, Institute of International and European Affairs, July 12, 2016)

- *Brexit and Beyond: How the United Kingdom Might Leave the European Union* (UK in a Changing Europe, 2016), providing of what might transpire from the modalities of triggering Article 50 and how, given the nature of British and European politics, the structure of the British state, and the legal frameworks within which both sides must operate.

- *EU external action and Brexit: Relaunch and reconnect* (N. Koenig, Jacques Delors Institut – Berlin, December 1, 2016), analysing the consequences of Brexit in the fields of diplomacy, development and crisis management, and showing that both sides are likely to lose in terms of global influence and power.

- *The UK and EU Foreign, Security and Defence Policy After Brexit: Integrated, Associated or Detached?* (R. Whitman, National Institute Economic Review, November 2016), assessing how the future EU-UK foreign and security policy relationship might be organized post-Brexit.

XII. Conclusion

- *Brexit Brief Issue: March 2017* (A. Gilmore, The Institute of International and European Affairs, March 6, 2017), covering developments in the on-going debate in the United Kingdom – and between the UK and the other EU Member States – on the UK's negotiations over its membership of the Union. [updated every month by the IIEA]

- *The United Kingdom's exit from and new partnership with the European Union White Paper* (HM Government, February 2, 2017), outlining details of Prime Minister Theresa May's 12-point principles for exiting the European Union and setting out the basis for priorities and the approach to forging a new strategic partnership with the EU.
See also:
  - *As Bad as it Gets: the White Paper on Brexit* (S. Peers, EU Law Analysis, February 3, 2017)

- *The process of Brexit: what comes next?* (A. Renwick, UCL European Institute, January 2017), setting out the process through which the United Kingdom will pursue its withdrawal from the European Union, after Theresa May set out her objectives in her 17 January speech and the government reiterated these in a White Paper on 2 February, and asking whether the government will be able to secure these goals, how it will seek to do so, and what might hold it back.

Institute of International Economic Law—
Georgetown Law

600 New Jersey Avenue, NW
Washington, DC 20001
www.iiel.org
Email: lawiiel@georgetown.edu

The Institute of International Economic Law is the focal point for the study of international economic law at Georgetown University.

It is also one of the leading centers for international economic law and policy in the world.

Originally focused on trade, the Institute now boasts leading capabilities and international renown in a range of areas including investment and financial regulation, tax, business and monetary law. The Institute actively approaches these fields as interrelated and at times overlapping policy spheres that impact how law is devised, practiced and enforced.

The IIEL's reputation in trade, financial regulation, arbitration, tax and transnational business stems directly from the scholarly work and real world contributions of our faculty. More than any other institute in the field, the IIEL's instructors are leading scholars and thinkers who routinely participate in the highest level policy discussions on each of the core fields of international economic law. Their writings are in law reviews, think tank policy pieces, op-eds and Congressional testimony consistently, and help shape national and international economic affairs. In the classroom, students gain an insider and cutting edge look into international economic rulemaking.

Alongside IIEL's instructors and administrators are nearly a dozen additional visiting researchers, adjunct and visiting professors who teach international economic law courses for our students.

IIEL Faculty & Professional Staff

Chris Brummer—IIEL Faculty Director; International Financial Regulation and Monetary Affairs,
and International Trade
Lilian Faulhaber—International Law, Taxation
Michael Gadbaw—International Trade and International Business
Anna Gelpern—International Financial Regulation; Sovereign Debt and International Monetary Affairs
Itai Grinberg—International Tax, International Tax Policy, Tax Reform
Daniel Heath—International Monetary Affairs and International Trade
Jennifer Hillman—International Trade, WTO, and International Business Transactions
Joost Pauwelyn—International Trade, International Investment, and Public International Law
David Stewart—International Business, Public International Law and National Security
Robert Thompson—Business Organizations and Securities Regulation
Anne Marie Whitesell—International Arbitration, Dispute Resolution, and International Negotiations
Christine Washington—Director, Programs & External Affairs
Jacquelyn Williams—Program Associate

Printed in Great Britain
by Amazon